Media Relations in Sport

Titles in the Sport Management Library

Media Relations in Sport

— THIRD EDITION —

Brad Schultz, PhD
University of Mississippi

Philip H. Caskey, MA
West Virginia University

Craig Esherick, JD
George Mason University

Fitness Information Technology
A Division of the International Center
for Performance Excellence
West Virginia University
262 Coliseum, WVU-CPASS
PO Box 6116
Morgantown, WV 26506-6116

Library of Congress Card Catalog Number: 2010924682

ISBN: 978-1-935412-14-4
Cover Design: Bellerophon Productions
Cover Photo: Courtesy of George Mason Athletics/John Aronson
Typesetter: Bellerophon Productions
Production Editor: Matt Brann
Copyeditor: Matt Brann
Proofreader: Maria denBoer
Indexer: Maria denBoer
Printed by Sheridan Books, Inc.

10 9 8 7 6 5 4 3 2

Fitness Information Technology
A Division of the International Center for Performance Excellence
West Virginia University
262 Coliseum, WVU-CPASS
PO Box 6116
Morgantown, WV 26506-6116
800.477.4348 (toll free)
304.293.6888 (phone)
304.293.6658 (fax)
Email: fitcustomerservice@mail.wvu.edu
Website: www.fitinfotech.com

Contents

Foreword

Despite the myriad developments that have changed the landscape of media relations in sport, there has been nothing but an increase in the demand for *more*: more events, more athletes, more media outlets, more analysts, more analysis, more specialty coverage, more technical innovations, graphics and video, more data, more insider connections, more cross-branding, more components of an audience demanding more input and interaction.

Today's grandparents grew up listening to baseball games on the radio, watching a featured game (often just one game!) each week in college and professional football and learning about the personal side of teams and athletes through newspaper columns and features. Their sports "fix" came from scanning the agate columns for stats and scores, reading full-length magazine features, and tuning in for a substantial chunk of the nightly local TV newscast.

Contrast that, just a few decades later, with 24-hour coverage of not only sporting events, but practices, training sessions, press conferences, player drafts, recruiting—pushing athletes and sporting events into a non-stop maelstrom of celebrity-driven entertainment.

Since the 1980s, the advent of all-sports national and regional cable television channels; the ability to access national and local newspapers via the Internet; the wide-ranging scope and dialogue of sports talk radio; and the proliferation of speciality media covering a single sport or team have given immeasurable opportunities for the posting of sports-related content.

These unlimited options extend the life and scope of news items. Where media relations directors once prioritized according to news cycles, print deadlines, and "hits" on the six o'clock news, now public relations staffs find themselves responding to items with more immediacy and from a much wider range of sources in order to provide timely updates on topics and stories around the clock. Social media, in-house reporting, and citizen journalists in the blogosphere supply not just more opportunities to share the message, but also a much broader expanse of origination for the patchwork of opinion, fact, and conjecture that make up the diverse coverage of athletics in the 21st century.

A philosophical change in the coverage angles has certainly taken place. Where sports were once primarily feel-good, upbeat stories of epic battles and heroes in the making, now, the mainstream problems of legal issues, family dramas, and financial affairs are as much a part of the sports report as the tabloids.

Of course, driving and accelerating many of these developments have been the extensive innovations in technology, enhancing how we collect, produce, and distribute news. Emerging technologies have made it easier to find information, to voice an opinion, to connect with other fans, and to "participate" in sporting events without the need to buy

a ticket. Ideas and inquiries that spread through the web quickly become items of interest to the media and public; conversely, the archival abilities of the Internet mean that
no story is ever totally lost or forgotten. The scene is kaleidoscopic, with images emerging with such speed and variety that no one can predict future patterns.

It's easy to chronicle the changes in the sports media industry—yet it's more important to keep in the forefront what hasn't changed.

The goal is still telling the story of teams and individuals as they compete and strive
for accomplishment.

Reporting this story—and maintaining the audience's wish and willingness to become involved in its journey and outcome—is the objective at the heart of media relations in all aspects of athletics.

Sports are the ultimate "reality" shows and their ever-evolving narratives fascinate us.
Finding ways to attract an audience and tell those stories with description, facts, com-
petence, and flair is the ultimate aim of sports media relations.

— Shelly Poe

Director of Football Communications, The Ohio State University

College Sports Information Directors of America (CoSIDA) 2006 Hall of Fame inductee

Preface

In today's environment of 24-hour news, instant access to information, and interactive consumers, it is very easy for a single story or event to spread like wildfire across the media landscape. Stories that a few years ago might have merited a couple of paragraphs in the next day's newspaper are now extensively covered by a growing number of sports media professionals and amateurs. Such a change has significant consequences for the process of sport communication.

Consider a hypothetical story that has unfortunately become all too common in today's world of big-time college athletics: the star player for the local college team is arrested on charges of drug possession. Now consider all the different people involved in the sport communication process and their roles in the unfolding story:

- *The sports information director at the school.* He (or she) is now suddenly besieged with requests for information from the media, alumni, and fans. In full crisis mode a number of decisions have to be made—how much information should be made available and who should be allowed to talk? How should it be released and in what form? How can the demands of the media be balanced with the wishes of the school administration? All of these decisions have to be made as quickly as possible.

- *The local media.* Television stations, newspapers, radio stations, and now Internet sites all want as much information as possible as quickly as possible. The competition between these different media, and growing interest among audiences, has created an insatiable demand for sports content. As a result, the news cycle has become so fast that sometimes the story will appear online even before some people at the school know about it. The media must find content related to the story to get to audiences as soon as possible. This could include digging through various Internet and blog sites for more information, especially those sites run by rabid fans. The media must also figure out how to distribute their content over a variety of integrated media platforms, such as print, broadcast, and the Internet.

- *The player and his/her family.* Depending on the circumstances of the arrest, the player and/or his/her family may want to control the information released to the public—what might be called "damage control." Most often, this is done by limiting the information released, but today damage control can also be proactive through the Internet, blogging, Twitter, or a variety of other technologies. The player's family might post a message to a social networking site such as Facebook or to a personal web page in hopes of lessening critical public reaction. In this way, the athlete can speak directly to sports audiences without having to go through the mainstream media.

- *The coach or athletic administrator.* This person has a difficult balancing act, trying to protect the interests of the player, his/her family, and the school, but at the same time needing to work with the media to release information. Certainly a coach would not want to give out too much information, especially if it is damaging. But at the same time, too much stonewalling only increases media frustration and creates a poisonous atmosphere of distrust. The coach, in conjunction with the SID, will also have to work with local police, the school president, and a variety of other factions.
- *Sports audiences and consumers.* They make the ultimate decision about how and where to access sports information related to this story. Where do they go first? Perhaps to the Internet, accessible through their computers or maybe even their cell phones. If no information is available there, the local television or radio station might have something. And don't forget that in today's media environment, the audience can create as well as receive sports information. It may be that some audience members have inside knowledge about the situation that they can distribute through Internet blogs, message boards, websites, or Twitter accounts.

Our hypothetical story reveals the complex nature of today's sports media relations. In the old days the process was fairly simple—the school (or other authorities) released the information, the media distributed it, and audiences consumed it. Today, the process is much more complicated because the various participants in the process—athlete, school, family, media, coaches, and audience—are all interconnected. It is the aim of this third edition of *Media Relations in Sport* to unravel some of this complexity and help students gain a better understanding of these often confusing interconnections.

While the second edition of this widely adopted textbook became a valuable asset to the sport management field, we believe that this third edition provides a much needed update. For one thing, the media landscape is continually evolving, and some changes have been especially pronounced since the last edition. Newspapers, which for so long were the bedrock of the sports media industry, have fallen on very difficult times and there are very real questions about their economic viability. Technology has shifted much of the sports media focus away from the traditional print media and into new online areas like blogs, podcasts, and Twitter. The third edition goes much deeper into these areas and others that are shaping the future of media relations in sport.

This volume also recognizes that these are fundamental and historic changes. The model of sport media communication was fairly static for more than 100 years, but has seemingly changed overnight. Of course, the changes did not take place so quickly, but the last 30 years have seen a dramatic shift in how sports media communication takes place, particularly as it relates to the creation and distribution of sports content. The changes seem to be related to an interplay of technology, economics, and culture, and this edition rightly focuses on the importance of these factors and how they intersect. At the same time, the consequences of these areas are also addressed in-depth. For example, much more attention is given to the increasing globalization of sport media, which is described at length in Chapter 11.

While this third edition rightly goes into emerging areas of the field and examines sport media relations from a global perspective, it also retains the focus of the first two editions, specifically on the basics and principles of sport media that remain its foundations. Any student interested in a career related to sports media has to know certain essentials—how to interview, how to effectively create and distribute content, and how to deal with communication problems that will invariably arise. All of these subjects and more are extensively addressed, as are more specialized topics such as those dealing with law, ethics, and new technologies.

The emphasis of these topics is not so much related to a theoretical understanding of the sports media, but rather a practical one. The book is written with the idea that sports media communication does not exist as only something to be discussed in the abstract. Rather, there are fundamental skills, approaches, and procedures that relate directly to the success of communication. The authors all have "how to" knowledge gained through many years of working in various areas of the sports media relations industry and they want to pass that knowledge on to the next generation of practitioners.

In fact, what makes this third edition of *Media Relations in Sport* so unique is that the backgrounds and experiences of the three authors cover every angle of sport media relations, which should give readers a complete understanding of the subject matter from every possible perspective. Brad Schultz, PhD, is an associate professor at the University of Mississippi, where he teaches courses on sports journalism, broadcast management, and mass communication. An author of three books and editor of the *Journal of Sports Media*, Schultz also gained 15 years of experience in local television sports. Philip H. Caskey is an associate sports information director at West Virginia University, where he has worked for nine years. In addition to his practical experience, Caskey, who has a master's degree in sport management, is an adjunct instructor at WVU, teaching undergraduate and graduate courses in sport media relations. Craig Esherick, JD, is an assistant professor at George Mason University, where he teaches courses on sport management and sport law. A few of the "hands on" experiences on his résumé include being a college basketball TV analyst, a contributing writer to AOL Sports, and the head men's basketball coach at Georgetown University. Esherick provides a coach's viewpoint as it relates to specific topics addressed in this book by writing "Coach's Corner" sections that appear throughout the chapters.

Getting back to the hypothetical scenario about the college star arrested on charges of drug possession, what is the "best" way for everyone involved in the sport communication process to handle the breaking story? There is no one particular answer to that question simply because each incident provides its own unique set of circumstances and challenges. But this book should provide students will a solid blueprint that will enable them to approach those challenges with skill and confidence.

Acknowledgments

I would like to thank the staff in the International Center for Performance Excellence at West Virginia University, and especially editor Matthew Brann, for the excellent work in getting this edition published.

—BS

When approached by Fitness Information Technology to co-author this book, I was extremely honored and grateful. Having never ventured down this road before, this project was certainly a learning experience.

I'd first like to thank Shelly Poe for taking a chance on me in 1999 to be one of her graduate assistants in the WVU Sports Communications Office. This profession has been very rewarding and I thank her for giving me that opportunity as a wet-behind-the-ears graduate assistant more than a decade ago. I'm thankful that I got to learn from one of the industry's best and most-respected SIDs. I also would like to thank all my colleagues in the Sports Communications office for their insight and camaraderie.

I'd like to thank the students of my previous and future classes for having an active interest in sport communication.

I can't forget the many thanks that need to go to my parents, Larry and Joan, my sisters Laura and Caitlin, my brother-in-law Mark, and my niece and nephew, Lydia and Silas, for their continued love and support. A very special thanks goes to Ms. Jessica Ewing for being a supportive, caring, and wonderful girlfriend when the book's writing doldrums reared their wary heads. And I have numerous friends, too many to name, that I thank for their never-ending support.

Lastly, I'd like to acknowledge the fine work of the authors of the first two editions of this textbook—Allan Hall, Patrick Moynahan, William Nichols, and Janis Taylor—for giving us a foundation from which to proceed. Some of their hard work and efforts are still present in this third edition.

—PC

I would like to thank Dave Wiggins, the Director of Recreation Health and Tourism at George Mason University, and Bob Baker, the head of sport management at George Mason, for their many helpful thoughts as I worked on this book. The students at George Mason continue to be an inspiration and my thanks to them as well.

Matt Brann, our editor at Fitness Information Technology, was very patient with this basketball coach and I want to thank him as well.

My wife, Theo, and my two sons, Nicko and Zachary, also were as patient as my editor during the research, writing, and editing of this book. I continue to be in their debt.

—CS

1

Introduction to Media Relations in Sport

The late Texas "Tex" Schramm (1920–2003) earned his football reputation as the general manager who helped build the Dallas Cowboys into "America's Team" during the 1960s and '70s. But he started in football in 1947 as director of publicity for the Los Angeles Rams. During that time Schramm said he practically had to beg local newspapers to cover the team. "Papers didn't staff our training camp," he said. "I wrote stories for the papers and the papers would put some other writer's by-line on the story. Not only that, I wrote the headline and helped ship the copy to the composing room" ("Tint of," 1994). Schramm later made the somewhat infamous comment about free agency in the National Football League (NFL), saying it would never happen because "you guys (the players) are cattle, and we're (owners) the ranchers. And ranchers can always get more cattle" (Farmer & Johnson, 2008).

Times have certainly changed.

Most certainly for the NFL, whose players now have a measure of free agency. But for our purposes, the changes in sports media have been just as great. Certainly the days of the NFL having to beg for media attention have long since passed; the media have helped turn the league into perhaps the most dominant and iconic sports organization in American history. And Schramm's comment about cattle and ranchers may have been aimed at NFL players and owners, but it has an important corollary for sports media.

The sports media used to be the ranchers—controlling production and distribution of content; deciding the what, when, and where of audience consumption. But that system, just like Schramm's vision of free agency, is long gone. In its place has risen a new model fueled by new technology and defined by interactivity, audience fragmentation and empowerment, and instantaneous access. The evolution marks an important transition for what we call media relations in sport. Sports media have evolved from a fairly closed, one-way communication system based on distribution of content to mass audiences (see Figure 1.1) to a much more open and interactive system aimed at interconnected niche audiences who can now also create and distribute their own content (see Figure 1.2).

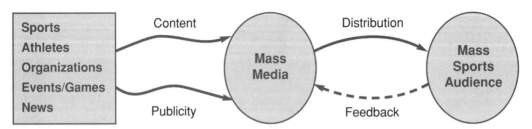

Figure 1.1. Historic model of sports-media-audience communication, 1850s–1980s.

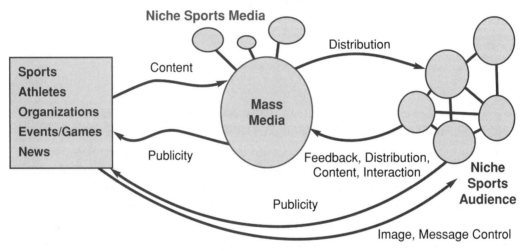

Figure 1.2. Modern model of sports-media-audience communication, 1990s–present.

THE EVOLUTION OF THE SPORTS COMMUNICATION MODEL

To fully understand the change requires a closer look at how we define media relations in sport. As the phrase would suggest, there are three key components—media, sport, and communication (relations). All of these parts of the sports communication process have evolved drastically over the years.

The Old Model (1850s–1980s)

There is no precise time to date the emergence of mass media coverage of sports in the US. According to Enriquez (2002), one of the earliest known sports stories was a description of a prize fight that appeared in a Boston newspaper in 1733. Media coverage of sports was fairly sporadic until the middle of the 19th century. Sowell (2008) argues that the birth of national sports coverage began in 1849 when the telegraph was first used to help cover a championship boxing match, and partly for that reason we'll use 1850 as the starting point for the model. By that time the forces that helped create the mass audiences needed for mediated sports coverage—industrialization, urbanization, and the growth of education—were already under way.

The media during this time were characterized by the traditional mass media that still exist today: first newspapers and magazines, followed by radio and then television.

These outlets had exclusive access to the athletes, games, events, and news related to sport. They would take this content and distribute to large mass audiences through their distinct media. In return, the athletes and events received the important publicity they needed for economic growth and survival. Even as far back as 1950, long-time baseball manager Connie Mack (1950) observed, "How did baseball develop from the sandlots to the huge stadiums? From a few hundred spectators to the millions in attendance today? My answer is: through the gigantic force of publicity. The professional sporting world was created and is being kept alive by the services extended the press."

That publicity made both sports and the media unbelievably rich. As the media helped the sports become more popular, the rights to distribute the content became more valuable, and the fees sports and leagues charged to distribute their product skyrocketed. For example, in 1960 CBS paid $394,000 for the rights to televise the Summer Olympic Games in Rome. In 2012, the same rights will cost NBC $1.18 billion (Martzke, 2003). In 1962, the NFL sold the rights to televise its games to CBS for $4.65 million. The league's current contract is worth $17.6 billion, paid over eight years by CBS, FOX, NBC, and ESPN (Andreff & Staudohar, 2000). Television rights fees for the NFL have increased 10,000% since 1970, which reflects the tremendous audience interest in NFL programming. The 30 seconds of commercial time in the Super Bowl that cost $239,000 in 1967 goes for around $2.5 million today (Hiestand, 2004).

TV rights fees afford networks such as CBS great control of the distribution of content for events such as the NCAA men's basketball tournament. (Courtesy of George Mason Athletics/John Aronson)

All that money coming in drastically increased the economic power and prestige of sports organizations and athletes. While the effect of free agency cannot be discounted, it has been primarily the infusion of media dollars that have enriched athletes beyond anyone's wildest dreams. In 1969 the average Major League Baseball salary was $24,909. By 1990 the figure had risen to $578,000 and in 2006 it was $2,699,292 (Brown, 2008). In 2007, golfer Tiger Woods became the first athlete to surpass $100 million in income for a single season. His combination of salary, winnings, and endorsement money totaled nearly $112 million (Freedman, 2007).

For its investment, the media had almost total control in shaping the presentation and image of the content providers. While the number of media outlets was still fairly small, the publicity generated by the media was typically positive. Sports reporters could develop relationships with athletes and coaches that often developed into friendships. As a result, reporters would be reluctant to publish material that would damage the athlete's reputation. There is a story, possibly apocryphal, of reporters covering Babe Ruth during the baseball star's height of popularity in the 1920s. While the team was riding the train between cities Ruth ran through one of the cars stark naked. Right behind Ruth was a similarly naked woman chasing him with a knife. One reporter who witnessed the scene turned to another and said, "It's a good thing we didn't see that; otherwise we'd have to report on it" (Braine, 1985).

This symbiotic relationship worked well for sports and media, but in many ways limited the enjoyment of the audience. The media completely controlled the content in terms of its amount, scheduling, and distribution. McCombs and Shaw (1972) called this the *agenda-setting* function of the media—their ability to exert a significant influence on public perception through the control, filtering, and shaping of media content. For example, the three New York City baseball clubs banned live radio broadcasts of their games for five years in the 1930s because they were concerned the broadcasts were hurt attendance. More recently, television networks have scheduled event times to maximize potential profit, even if it inconveniences a large portion of the viewing audience. World Series games, even those on weekends, have shifted from daytime to much later at night, in some cases not ending until after midnight in the Eastern time zone. Bear Bryant, the legendary former football coach at Alabama once commented, "You folks (the networks) are paying us a lot of money to put this game on television. If you want us to start at two in the morning, then that's when we'll tee it up" (Patton, 1984).

Technology was also a limiting factor for sports audiences for several reasons. The distribution of sports content has depended on technology such as radio and television airwaves, and broadcast receivers. During the primitive stages of development for these technologies the quality of sports content often suffered. Recalling the early days of sports on radio in the 1920s, pioneer sportscaster Harold Arlin remembers, "Sometimes the transmitter worked and sometimes it didn't. Sometimes the crowd noise would drown us out and sometimes it wouldn't. And quite frankly, we didn't know what the reaction would be; if we'd be talking in a total vacuum or whether somebody would hear us" (Smith, 1987). Television went through similar growing pains. Long-time football

Table 1.1. The Growth of Television Technology

To commemorate the 61st anniversary of the first televised baseball game, Fox broadcast the Cubs-Dodgers game on August 26, 2000, to highlight the advances in television sports technology. Fox broadcast the first few innings as they would have looked to viewers in different television eras. Thus, the game started off in black and white with only two cameras, and ended with modern technology.

Era	Video innovations	Audio innovations	Graphic innovations
1939	2 cameras; no zoom or replays possible	1 microphone for announcer	No graphics
1944	3 cameras; no zoom or replays possible	1 microphone for announcer	No graphics
1953	4 cameras; no zoom or replays possible	Microphone for crowd noise added	One monochrome line of graphics
1957	5 cameras; one added in centerfield	2 microphones; analyst added	Two lines of graphics possible
1961	5 cameras; limited zoom and replay	2 microphones	Two lines of graphics possible
1969	5 cameras; color now standard	2 microphones; improved audio	Electronic graphics introduced
1974	7 cameras; split-screen and chromakey used	Audio still mono	Electronic graphics
1985	8 cameras; super slo-mo introduced	Mono	Computer-generated graphics with multiple colors
2000	10 cameras; digital technology	Stereo surround; Wireless mics	Computer-generated

Source: *Fox Sports*. Chicago Cubs vs. Los Angeles Dodgers, August 26, 2000.

director Harry Coyle remembers that "the equipment always kept breaking down. There were always hot smoldering irons laying around for repairs. You could recognize a television guy by the burn marks all over his clothes from those irons" (Halberstam, 1989).

The technology obviously improved, but remember that during this time sports content providers had total control over distribution. The only place to get the content was from the established mass media, which determined all facets of distribution, including how much, when, and where. Even as sports started to become extremely popular on television in the 1950s there was a limit on how much content could be provided by the three major networks at the time. And into the early 1980s television networks offered no more than one or two games per week, no matter if it was professional football, baseball, basketball, hockey, or college sports. In a broadcast sense, audiences were typically restricted to getting games or information for a few hours on the weekends, which provided great depth, but not much frequency. Fans had the opposite problem with print outlets like newspapers. The information came out daily, but generally not in great depth.

Looking back at Figure 1.1 you see a solid black line going from the mass media to mass sports audiences, which represents the power and control these media had in the distribution of sports content. The fainter dashed line going back from audiences to the media represents a limited amount of feedback and participation. In almost every sense of the word, sports audiences during this time were *passive*. They were participants in the communication process only to the extent that they watched, read, or listened to the content distributed by the mass media. Otherwise, sports audiences had very little input other than the occasional letter to the editor in the newspaper or an appearance on sports talk radio, and sports radio was very limited. The format didn't appear until the 1970s and sports talk truly didn't catch on until the late 1980s when WFAN in New York became the first all-sports talk radio station in the country (Eisenstock, 2001). Thus, not only could audiences not really talk with the content providers, but they also had a hard time connecting with each other. In many respects, sports audiences were isolated and powerless.

As a result, sports content providers did not look at the audience as comprised of distinct individual units, but rather as a homogenous whole. They were a *mass* audience defined by sheer size. For print outlets it meant circulation and for broadcasters it meant ratings, but in both cases the bigger the better. Content providers wanted those big audiences so they could get more advertising dollars. Even today, the economic system is still largely based on this simple principle; it just worked better in the old days because technology limited the amount of sports programming and content providers had relatively captive audiences.

Mass also meant captive. Audiences tended to congregate around the same type of content simply because they didn't really have anyplace else to go; because of limits in technology there wasn't much in the way of choice in programming. Events like Major League Baseball's "Game of the Week," and the NFL's "Monday Night Football" became extremely popular in part because they had no real sports competition. When you consider the *most-watched* programs of all-time, the top five are all recent Super Bowls (see Chapter 3). That's no surprise, because more people are watching television today than ever before. But when you look at the *highest-rated* programs in terms of percentage of the audience watching, most of the shows on the list are from the 1980s or earlier. The last episode of M*A*S*H, which aired in 1983, had an audience of more than 77% of all people watching television that night. By contrast, today's top-rated shows get a share percentage of 20–25% ("Nielsen television," 2009).

Let's take a closer look at how a sports event would have been covered under this old model (Figure 1.3). Consider the example of tennis star Billie Jean King's announcement on May 1, 1981, that she was gay. King had long been considered one of the top female tennis players in the world, and her 1973 "Battle of the Sexes" match with Bobby Riggs garnered enormous media attention. However, her private life had never been

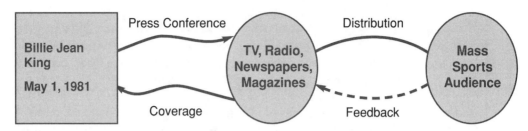

Figure 1.3. Coverage of a sports story in historic communication model.

mentioned in the media and her sexual orientation probably would have remained secret if not for a lawsuit filed by her longtime partner Maryilan Barnett. (Barnett sought half of King's income for the years they were together in the 1970s. A judge later dismissed the suit).

When the lawsuit became public, King decided to hold a press conference and explain her situation. "I felt very violated," she later said. "I felt blackmailed. And yet I wanted to tell the truth. I argued with my publicist and my lawyer for two days so I could do that press conference. They didn't want me to do it, but I was insistent. I did the right thing" (LaRosa, 2009). The media gave huge coverage to the announcement, with major stories appearing in *Newsweek*, *People*, the *New York Times*, *Chicago Tribune*, *Sports Illustrated*, and a host of other magazines and newspapers. Television and radio also gave extensive coverage to the announcement on the day of the press conference and in succeeding days. But it's important to remember that the media acted reactively, not proactively. Only after King's announcement did the media cover the story, even though some media members may have suspected the truth before then. Audiences were completely in the dark about King's lifestyle until her press conference, and once the announcement filtered through the news cycle the media moved on to other stories.

The King story is just one example of how sports content moved through the historic communication model. The mass media exercised their agenda setting and gate keeping functions by deciding how much importance to attach to the story, how much time/space to give to it, how often to let the story continue beyond the original date, and how to distribute the story to audiences. On May 1, 1981, sports audiences most likely heard about the story on radio or television, which were the most immediate media at the time. The story might have rated a minute or so in local and national news programs later that evening, but no channels dedicated solely to sports yet existed. For more in-depth information sports fans would have to wait until the following day for coverage in the morning newspapers. Fan interaction and feedback was still limited to writing letters to sports editors or calling sports radio programs.

The King incident is a good illustration of the importance of owning distribution during this time period. The sports content was valuable, but it didn't mean anything unless it could get to audiences. Perhaps no one understood this better than media mogul Ted Turner, who bought the Atlanta Braves in 1976. Turner already owned the distribution outlet, WTBS in Atlanta, but needed programming to attract audiences. With the Braves providing almost year-long content Turner turned WTBS into one of

Table 1.2. Media Owned Sports Franchises, 2000–2010		
In 2000 several media companies owned sports franchises, but as the model evolved sports franchises began looking for new ways of delivering their content. Many teams created their own distribution networks, including the New York Yankees, who in 2001 started the YES network to showcase their games and other related programming. Other teams followed suit and by 2010 only Cablevision and Comcast-Spectacor retained their franchise holdings.		
Team(s)	**2000 Owners**	**2010 Owners**
Anaheim Angels (MLB)	Disney	Arturo Moreno
Anaheim Mighty Ducks (NHL)	Disney	Samueli family
Atlanta Braves	Time-Warner	Liberty Media
Atlanta Hawks (NBA) Atlanta Thrashers (NHL)	Time-Warner	Atlanta Spirit consortium
Chicago Cubs (MLB)	Tribune Corp.	Ricketts family
Los Angeles Dodgers (MLB)	News Corp.	Frank McCourt
New York Knicks (NBA) New York Rangers (NHL)	Cablevision	Cablevision
Philadelphia Flyers (NHL) Philadelphia 76ers (NBA)	Comcast-Spectacor	Comcast-Spectacor

the country's first "superstations" distributed to national audiences through cable outlets. Other media companies followed suit, such as Chicago's Tribune Company which bought the Cubs in 1981 as programming for its television, radio, and newspaper outlets.

By 2000, media ownership of a professional sports team had become extremely popular (see Table 1.2), although this would not last long. By the first year of the millennium the old communication model was well on its way out, as was the emphasis on ownership of distribution. In its place rose a new model, built on startling new technologies that made the consumer, and more importantly content, king.

The New Model (1990s–Present)

Through the 1970s the sports distribution system remained much as it had since the advent of television—radio and the three major television networks distributed the majority of live sports programming, while delayed coverage of those events was handled by television, radio, newspapers, and magazines. These mass media had a monopoly in terms of agenda setting and gate keeping; they decided all facets of distribution, including the *what*, *when*, and *how*.

The first cracks in this system began showing in the 1970s through the rise of pay cable television. Home Box Office (HBO) began programming in 1972 relying first on a network of microwave relays then ultimately satellites. It was satellite technology that in 1975 allowed HBO to show its subscribers a live transmission of the heavyweight boxing match between Muhammad Ali and Joe Frazier from Manila; the broadcast networks had to wait for taped copies of the bout before they could show the fight ("Wired, zapped," 2009).

Thus, it was the growth of technology that signaled a new era in sports content distribution, especially live satellite transmission. Other important advances included the development of fiber optic cables, which could carry 65,000 times more information than conventional copper wires, and home video recording. In 1977, RCA introduced a VHS version of the video cassette recorder, which soon came to dominate the market ("Wired, zapped, 2009). In the following years breakthroughs in technology would introduce into American homes the personal computer, Internet communication, home satellite reception, and digital transmission.

These new technologies had two immediate impacts for sports communication—they weakened the power of the traditional mass media and they empowered the sports audiences as never before. The "Thrilla in Manila" between Ali and Frazier showed that the networks no longer had exclusive control over sports content, and that control continued to fragment in succeeding years with the growth of new regional and specialized content providers. When ABC still owned exclusive rights to televise almost all college football games the NCAA limited teams to six appearances over two years. Some of the big-time programs filed a lawsuit and in 1984 the U.S. Supreme Court ruled that such a plan violated anti-trust laws (Hiestand, 2004b). Today, there are literally dozens of national and regional networks that televise college football, increasing the viewing options for the sports audience (see Table 1.3).

The growth of college football on television is just one example of how the audience has much more choice in consumption. In addition to the television offerings, fans could also listen to the games through several Internet and satellite radio services. In some cases, games not available on television could be viewed via live streaming on the Internet. And it's not just college football. During a typical week, nearly 645 hours of sports-related content is available across a multitude of broadcast and cable outlets (Brown & Bryant, 2006).

These multiple consumption options caused the sports audience to fragment into smaller niche audiences. Where once there was one mass audience that received the same content from a single provider, technology had created literally hundreds of audiences based on content interest. Under the old model, someone might be labeled as a "college football fan" and get one football game a week on national television. That same person might read about the sport in the local paper and subscribe to a general interest magazine like *Sports Illustrated*.

Today, that same fan could more precisely be called a "Big South Conference football fan" or "Virginia Military Institute football fan" because there is specialized content devoted to those niche topics. He/she might visit or subscribe to specialized Internet sites or magazines that focus on Big South football. This same person might look at the col-

Table 1.3. A Typical Television Week in College Football, 2009

Below is the schedule of televised college football games for the week of November 16–21, 2009. The demand for the games led networks to program beyond Saturday, and football on weeknights has become a staple on ESPN. ESPN GamePlan games were available for purchase on pay-per-view outlets.

Date/Time (EST)	Game	Network
Wednesday, November 18, 6 p.m.	Buffalo at Miami, OH	ESPNU
Wednesday, November 18, 8 p.m.	Central Michigan at Ball State	ESPN2
Thursday, November 19, 6:30 p.m.	Tennessee St. at Eastern Illinois	ESPNU
Thursday, November 19, 7 p.m.	Nicholls St. at SE Louisiana	SLCTV
Thursday, November 19, 7:30 p.m.	Colorado at Oklahoma State	ESPN
Friday, November 20, 5:30 p.m.	Akron at Bowling Green	ESPNU
Friday, November 20, 9:30 p.m.	Boise State at Utah State	ESPN2
Friday, November 20, 7 p.m.	Eastern Michigan at Toledo	ESPN
Saturday, November 21, Noon	Duke at Miami	ESPNU
Saturday, November 21, Noon	Harvard at Yale	Versus
Saturday, November 21, Noon	Louisville at South Florida	SNY/MASN
Saturday, November 21, Noon	Maine at New Hampshire	CSNE
Saturday, November 21, Noon	Maryland at Florida State	ESPN GamePlan
Saturday, November 21, Noon	Minnesota at Iowa	ESPN
Saturday, November 21, Noon	North Carolina at Boston College	ESPN2
Saturday, November 21, Noon	Ohio State at Michigan	ABC
Saturday, November 21, Noon	Mississippi State at Arkansas	SEC Network
Saturday, November 21, Noon	Tenn-Chattanooga at Alabama	SEC Network
Saturday, November 21, Noon	Memphis at Houston	CSS
Saturday, November 21, Noon	William & Mary at Richmond	TCN
Saturday, November 21, Noon	Youngstown St. at N. Dakota St.	North Dakota NBC*
Saturday, November 21, 12:30 p.m.	FIU at Florida	ESPN GamePlan
Saturday, November 21, 12:30 p.m.	Lafayette at Lehigh	ESPN GamePlan
Saturday, November 21, 12:30 p.m.	Oklahoma at Texas Tech	Fox Sports Net
Saturday, November 21, 1 p.m.	Albany at Wagner	FCS Atlantic
Saturday, November 21, 2 p.m.	TCU at Wyoming	MTN
Saturday, November 21, 2 p.m.	Montana at Montana State	KPAX/Montana*
Saturday, November 21, 2 p.m.	Tulane at Central Florida	BHSN
Saturday, November 21, 2:30 p.m.	Bethune-Cookman at Florida A&M	ESPN Classic
Saturday, November 21, 2:30 p.m.	Connecticut at Notre Dame	NBC

Table 1.3. — *Continued*

Below is the schedule of televised college football games for the week of November 16–21, 2009. The demand for the games led networks to program beyond Saturday, and football on weeknights has become a staple on ESPN. ESPN GamePlan games were available for purchase on pay-per-view outlets.

Date/Time (EST)	Game	Network
Saturday, November 21, 3 p.m.	Wofford at Furma	Sports South
Saturday, November 21, 3:30 p.m.	Air Force at BYU	CBSC
Saturday, November 21, 3:30 p.m.	Delaware at Villanova	CSNE
Saturday, November 21, 3:30 p.m.	LSU at Ole Miss	CBS
Saturday, November 21, 3:30 p.m.	N.C. State at Virginia Tech	ESPNU
Saturday, November 21, 3:30 p.m.	Penn State at Michigan State	ABC/ESPN
Saturday, November 21, 3:30 p.m.	Purdue at Indiana	Big Ten Network
Saturday, November 21, 3:30 p.m.	UAB at East Carolina	MASN/GamePlan
Saturday, November 21, 3:30 p.m.	Virginia at Clemson	ABC/ESPN
Saturday, November 21, 3:30 p.m.	Wisconsin at Northwestern	Big Ten Network
Saturday, November 21, 3:30 p.m.	Rutgers at Syracuse	ESPN360
Saturday, November 21, 4 p.m.	Arizona State at UCLA	Fox Sports Net
Saturday, November 21, 4 p.m.	San Diego State at Utah	Versus
Saturday, November 21, 4 p.m.	Army at North Texas	KTXA*
Saturday, November 21, 4:15 p.m.	Florida Atlantic at Troy	ESPN GamePlan
Saturday, November 21, 4:30 p.m.	Arkansas St. at Middle Tennessee	ESPN GamePlan
Saturday, November 21, 5 p.m.	UC-Davis at Sacramento State	CSCA
Saturday, November 21, 6 p.m.	Colorado State at New Mexico	MTN
Saturday, November 21, 6 p.m.	Eastern Washington at N. Arizona	NAU-TV*
Saturday, November 21, 7 p.m.	Vanderbilt at Tennessee	ESPNU
Saturday, November 21, 7:30 p.m.	Tulsa at Southern Miss	CBSC
Saturday, November 21, 7:45 p.m.	Kansas State at Nebraska	ESPN
Saturday, November 21, 7:45 p.m.	Kentucky at Georgia	ESPN2
Saturday, November 21, 8 p.m.	Kansas at Texas	ABC (Regional)
Saturday, November 21, 8 p.m.	Oregon at Arizona	ABC (Regional)
Saturday, November 21, 9:30 p.m.	California at Stanford	Versus
Saturday, November 21, 10:30 p.m.	Nevada at New Mexico State	ESPN GamePlan

*game available only to a local audience

Source: Various

A glance at any newsstand will reveal some of the many magazine options for niche sports audiences. (Courtesy of Brad Schultz)

lege football television schedule for November 1, 2008, and decide not to watch any of the games, but instead take advantage of the three Big South games streamed live on the Internet through the conference's subscription "Edge" service, including VMI against Charleston Southern.

As the technology improved, the options for sports consumption increased dramatically, including delivery of establishing programming, more channels, and creation of new programming for niche audiences.

It's important to remember that the demand for sports content did not suddenly appear overnight. People didn't wake up one day and decide they wanted to see two dozen college football games on Saturday instead of one. The demand has always been there; it's just recently that technology has been able to meet that demand through such developments as digital transmission, home satellite reception, and Internet streaming.

A good example is how the media are using broadband to increase delivery of sports content. ESPN's broadband efforts, called ESPN3 (formerly ESPN360), included 3,000 live events. The network says distribution has grown 41%, while both unique viewers and total minutes were up nearly 400% (Miller, 2008). CBS Sports has also done well by streaming the NCAA basketball tournament. In 2008, consumers streamed nearly five million hours of "March Madness on Demand" video and audio through CBSSports.com, up 81% from the previous year. Ad revenue hit $4 million in 2006, $10 million in 2007, and a record $23 million in 2008 (Lemire, 2009). "There is tremendous growth in live streaming sports," said Jason Kint, senior vice president and general manager of CB-SSports.com. "It is not cannibalizing television audiences, but providing dynamic opportunity across platforms" (Miller, 2008).

Such technological developments have increased the number of new channels, which is nowhere more evident that in the explosive growth of ESPN. The Entertainment and Sports Programming Network began operations in 1979 as a small outfit broadcasting sports through cable television. In its early years the network didn't have the money or audience to attract big sporting events, so instead it programmed such things as college lacrosse, soccer, and Australian Rules football. But the company took a giant leap forward in 1984 after its purchase by ABC, then again in 1995 when it was acquired by Disney. Today, ESPN is arguably the dominant creator and distributor of sports content on the planet (see Table 1.4).

ESPN's ventures into event management show how new content and programming are being created to reach the many niche audiences of sports fans. Under the old model,

Table 1.4. The State of ESPN, 2009	
What started in a small Connecticut studio in 1979 now reaches almost every corner of the globe.	
ESPN Outlet	**Offerings**
Television	ESPN on ABC; 7 domestic cable networks; regional, syndicated, pay subscription packages, 30 international networks
Radio	ESPN Radio; ESPN Deportes Radio, syndicated radio in 13 international countries
Online	ESPN.com; ESPNDeportes.com; ESPNRadio.com; ESPNSoccer net.com; EXPN.com
Print Publishing	*ESPN the Magazine, ESPN Deportes Magazine, Bassmater Magazine, BASS Times, Fishing Tackle & Retailer,* ESPN Books
Emerging Technologies	ESPN On Demand, ESPN360, ESPN HD, ESPN2 HD, Interactive TV
Wireless	Mobile ESPN
Consumer Products	CDs, DVDs, ESPN Video Games, ESPN Golf Schools, ESPN Racing Schools, ESPN The Truck, ESPN-branded trading cards
Event Management	X Games, Winter X Games, International X Games, ESPN Outdoors & BASS, ESPYs, Bowl Games, Jimmy V Men's and Women's Basketball Classics
Source: ESPN Corporate Fact Sheet, 2009. (http://sports.espn.go.com/espn/news/story?page=corporatefactsheet)	

the mass media typically covered the same sports—a lot of football, basketball, and baseball, with a little bit of boxing, hockey, and horse racing thrown in. These were the sports that appealed to the predominantly white, male, 24–54 year old group of sports fans that consumed most mediated sports.

But in 1993, ESPN decided to devote some of its resources to "action sports" like skateboarding, snowboarding, and mountain biking that appeal to younger viewers. The idea eventually became the X Games, an international gathering of the top extreme sports athletes from around the world. By 2009, the winter and summer X Games were carried on three ESPN networks and aired in 75 countries ("This history," 2007). Primarily because of ESPN, extreme sports went from almost complete obscurity to international recognition. Athletes like Tony Hawk and Shaun White became household names, and earned millions from clothing, video game, and sporting equipment deals. Several of the extreme events are now contested in the Olympic Games.

Again, the audiences and athletes for these events did not suddenly sprout up overnight. Under the old model they lived in the fringes because there weren't enough of them to create a mass audience that would attract advertisers or networks. This was especially true given the limited channel space at the time. But now that the channel capacity has increased dramatically there are all kinds of opportunities for athletes and events that were previously ignored. And it's not just the niche sports that are benefitting. Technology has also increased the availability of the so-called traditional sports—football, basketball, and baseball—through pay-per-view and subscription services. Almost every major professional sport now offers a service that allows interested fans to purchase and watch additional games. One of the most popular is the NFL's Sunday Ticket, an exclusive service to DirecTV, which has around 2 million subscribers (Umstead, 2008). For $250 fans can get television access to every NFL game played on every Sunday of the regular season. Radio fans can purchase a similar package through satellite provider Sirius XM.

So when we speak of greater audience empowerment we can understand it partially in terms of better technology and more content offerings. The other part of that empowerment is that audiences have become actual participants in the mediated sport communication process, and not just in the limited sense of providing feedback to the established media outlets. Not only are audience members much more connected to each other, they are now starting to challenge the mainstream media in terms of creating and distributing their own content.

The Internet has revolutionized this process because it's relatively easy, inexpensive, and has worldwide distribution. Sports fans immediately developed an attraction to the Internet because of the ease in retrieving and accessing almost unlimited information on favorite players, teams, and organizations. In just a single month in 2007 Yahoo!Sports brought in more than 24.5 million unique visitors. During that same time period, ESPN.com had 24.1 million and NFL.com totaled 18.0 million unique visitors (Woodson, 2006).

But the Internet goes far beyond data storage and retrieval in that it allows average fans to create and distribute their own content. As a result, many of the same people who used to passively watch sports on TV or read about it in the newspaper are now writing about it themselves in a blog or directly posting their own video reports to a website. In northern Virginia, teenager Marc James started a blog as a personal home-page offering sports news. It now has grown into a sports commentary content site with more than 120,000 postings and a staff of about 40 people who publish original sports columns three days a week. "I think blogs are the wave of the future because they give a voice to the ordinary fan that has an intelligent opinion, but in the past didn't have the medium to voice it," James said. "People want to hear less of what the so-called experts have to say and more of what the sports geek down the street thinks" (Bruscas, 2004).

One area where this kind of coverage has mushroomed is high school sports. The lo-cal high school team might get a few column inches in the newspaper or a few minutes on the local television news, but that has been far exceeded by specialty websites. The leading high school site MaxPreps, which primarily focuses on recruiting news, received about 1.5 million visits per month in 2007. Even smaller outfits, like DigitalSports—which uses a combination of former journalists, fans, and parents to report on high school sports—has about 250,000 visitors per month (Goldfarb, 2007). An even more interesting project is GrandStadium.TV, which is creating live sports content produced entirely by high school journalism students. GrandStadium has become so successful that it is now partnering with state high school athletic associations and at least four lo-cal television stations in three states ("Site, stations," 2009).

Such efforts also show how the sports media are becoming "hyper local." Hyper lo-calism simply means more attention is being paid to local athletes and teams by content providers. Television stations and newspapers are using their time and space to focus more on local sports and engage audiences in local conversations. Not only has the technology allowed them to do this, but national content providers like ESPN have es-sentially captured the national sports market. And now, even ESPN is going local. In 2009 and early 2010, it created local web content in several cities, such as Dallas, Boston, New York, and Chicago. Thus, audiences who visit espn.com/dallas get coverage of the Cowboys, Stars, Mavericks, Rangers, and a host of area colleges. The content is split be-tween ESPN staffers (who voice over SportsCenter updates targeted to the specific mar-ket) and local writers and bloggers who cover the local market on a daily basis.

The mainstream media obviously see such attempts as a direct threat. In fact, ESPN Dallas poached several staffers who were working as reporters with the *Dallas Morning News*. The local media are feeling pressure from several directions—large content providers like ESPN, small content providers like GrandStadium, and now even indi-vidual fans. In 1996, University of Alabama fan Rodney Orr started *Tider Insider*, a web version of his newsletter on Alabama football. Since Orr can devote all his attention to Tide football he often scoops the local media covering the team, such as his reporting on the alleged sordid activities of former coach Mike Price. Orr's reports were eventually picked up in the mainstream media and Price lost his job. *Tider Insider* regularly gets millions of hits per month, and now includes a 30-minute weekly television show that appears on cable, DirectTV, and the Dish Network in Alabama ("Meet Rodney," 2008).

Tider Insider is just one of hundreds of websites run by fans with a passion for a par-ticular team or sport, and newspaper and television sports reporters now scour these sites to make sure they don't miss out on anything. In some cases these sites become essential tools for the traditional media. For example, on February 23, 2009, *Austin* (TX) *American-Statesman* sports reporter Alan Trubow announced on his "Bevo Beat" blog that, "Gerry Hamilton of burntorangebeat.com just called to let us know the Longhorns picked up their 12th (football) commitment of the season, Lufkin safety Carrington Byndom. Hamilton said he expects the Longhorns to take two or three cornerbacks in the class. Head on over to burntorangebeat.com to find out more about Byndom" (Trubow, 2009).

These websites also reflect how interconnected the community of fans are in this new model. *The American-Statesman* is one of hundreds of newspapers and television outlets that use their Internet sites for live audience chats (see Table 1.5). Although chats can be on any number of topics, all of them are designed to create more audience interest and involvement. Chats take place at hundreds of different media outlets every day across the country.

As of 2009, the *Dallas Morning News* offered 12 sports blogs, five different audience forums, and two different chat formats. Given the popularity of the Cowboys in Dallas, the newspaper's Cowboys blog is one of its most popular, often receiving hundreds of audience comments to posted information, even in the offseason.

Fans do not have to go through the major media outlets to talk to each other. A variety of message board and fan outlets exist in cyberspace—some run by professional media companies, others by fans who just want a place to talk about their favorite team. A fan of the Ohio State Buckeyes, for example, can belong to any number of interactive message boards, including buckeyeplanet.com, ohiostaterivals.com, buckeyesports.com, buckeyegrove.com, buckeyes247.com, and bucknuts.com to name but a few. The list does not include the specialized Ohio State message boards attached to media outlets like CBS Sportsline or the *Columbus Dispatch* newspaper.

All of these blogs, message boards, and chat rooms have done more than just given fans a way to talk back; they have created their own distinct social communities of sports fans. Visit any sports message board and observe how certain fans represent themselves (usually with pseudonyms), and the pattern of communication between fans that have developed a relationship. Haag (1996) and Tremblay and Tremblay (2001) noticed this with sports talk radio. Sports talk and these developments on the Internet are simply technological extensions of the local sports bar. Instead of gathering at the local watering hole to talk about the game or a favorite player, fans are now gathering around their laptops and cell phones to connect with other fans. That the traditional sports media are no longer required in this process is perhaps the most significant development of the new sports communication model.

These older media are also finding themselves replaced in another way. Historically, newspapers, radio, television, and magazines have been the dominant (and in some cases only) provider of content to sports audiences. But in the new model technology is making it possible for the content providers, including athletes, organizations, and coaches, to communicate directly with fans. When University of Washington football coach Steve Sarkisian hired a new wide receivers coach in 2009 he announced the move

Table 1.5. Typical Internet Audience Chat

The following is part of an Internet chat that took place in the *New York Daily News* on February 24, 2009. Reporter Michael Obernauer covers the NHL Rangers, who had just fired coach Tom Renney and replaced him with John Tortorella (general manager Glen Sather and Rangers owner Jim Dolan are also mentioned in the chat).

1:31	*[Comment From Jonathan]* What the mood after Torts' practice this morning?
1:34	I am at practice today, sitting in a media work room that is never this full, so you know something big went down. The on-ice session was about as upbeat as you could hope for, I suppose, some interesting skating drills led by Jim Schoenfeld (follow the leader?) and then some work with the lines. The players seem a little bit of two minds—on one hand, their tails are between their legs a bit because a good guy lost his job over their recent slide. At the same time they're trying to be excited about this change, and calling this a fresh start—"We're zero and zero," were Chris Drury's words.
1:37	*[Comment From Bill R]* At what point will Dolan finally realize this team needs a change at the top as much as a new coach and players?
1:37	*[Comment From Chris Sec 341]* What will it take to get Sather fired? A lawsuit?
1:40	I guess I have to admit, Jim Dolan doesn't confide in me much. That may not surprise you. I can't say what the criteria are for the Garden to decide Sather has had enough—I guess you could say that missing the playoffs this season, a real possibility, would cause some serious assessment at the top levels.
1:40	*[Comment From Anthony]* Was Tortorella Sather's first choice?
1:42	Yes. He said others were in consideration (he wouldn't elaborate), but Torts was the guy they had targeted from the start, and once that was the case, it was a slam dunk the other way—this is a job Tortorella has wanted for years and years, ever since he was an assistant here, and working at TSN he was dying to get back into coaching.
1:43	*[Comment From Lou]* Does Sather know what he got himself into? Does he realize that when Redden, Kalinin and Rozy play terrible that Torts will bench them, completely undermining Sather's decision to sign and/or re-sign each player? Torts is the first coach hired by Slats that has a mouth!
1:45	I'm guessing Sather does know what he got himself into. In making this change, he wanted to bring in a personality with more fire into the room, and when that means showing certain players a seat in the press box, then that's what will happen. I wouldn't expect Tortorella to come in and start throwing chairs around on the first day, but he'll take action where he sees fit. And you're right, it's a new character under Sather and a departure from his usual tack of bringing in guys he knows and has experience with.

Source: *The Blueshirts Blog*. Retrieved February 24, 2009, from http://www.nydailynews.com/blogs/rangers /2009/02/live-chat-tort-reform.html

Professional and collegiate athletes have begun to embrace new methods of com-munication that have forced sport communication professionals to adjust how they gather and report news. (Courtesy of WVU Sports Communications)

not through the traditional media, but on Twitter, a form of short text messaging available to anyone connected to the service (Yannity, 2009). In March 2009, Major League Baseball pitcher Curt Schilling announced his retirement on his blog site and within a day had more than 800 comments. Avoiding the mainstream media allows content providers to connect with audiences directly, unfiltered and unedited. Said *Miami Herald* sports columnist Dan LeBatard, "We're fast approaching the day when they (athletes) don't need the media at all. They can just create their own connection to the fan without our help. It's publicity on their own terms" ("Pardon the," 2009).

A younger generation of coaches and athletes seems to have embraced these new methods of communication. "We're hitting (Twitter) hard," said Chris Bosh of the NBA's Toronto Raptors, who like many athletes also has a personal website. "You can put up what you're doing. Or if you have a question, you'd be surprised how much people know. You can be, like, 'I need directions to this spot. People will tell you'" (Feschuk, 2009). As of February 2010, Bosh had Twitter connections with more than 89,000 fans following his tweets, which sounds like a lot but is dwarfed by fellow NBA star Shaquille O'Neal' who had more than 2.8 million followers. Shaq got involved because some imposter was using Twitter ("tweeting") in his name. "Somebody out there was trying to use my language and trying to speak for me," said O'Neal. "Rather than have that happen, I thought I'd do it myself." O'Neal added: "It's a fun thing. It's a way for fans to connect" (Beck, 2008). The NBA even sponsors an annual Technology Summit where players can learn about Twitter and other new communication gadgets.

As we did with the Billie Jean King story in the old model, let's take a look at a specific example of how a story might be covered in the new model (see Figure 1.4). For our example we'll use one of the biggest stories of 2009—the discovery that baseball superstar Alex Rodriguez of the New York Yankees had taken performance enhancing drugs. On the night of Friday, February 6, 2009, *Sports Illustrated* broke the story on its website, announcing the details and saying that its reporters would have much more information when the print version of the magazine came out the following Monday. Under the old model details of the story might have waited until Monday, but *SI* used its website to generate advance publicity and potentially increase magazine sales. A short time after the story appeared on SI, other major sports websites, including ESPN, Fox Sports, and CBS Sportsline, picked up and repeated the information. Not long after that the story was under full discussion in chat rooms and message boards all across the web. Within minutes, it had reached virtually every corner of the globe.

The following day, television, newspaper, and other outlets gave the story extensive coverage. The writers who broke the story for *SI* gave several interviews, including a lengthy discussion with Bob Costas on MLB Network. The story also appeared in non-sports outlets such as Fox News and CNN, and remained in the main news cycle for several days. When the new issue of *Sports Illustrated* came out on Monday, February 9, the story was prominently featured and Alex Rodriguez appeared on the cover. That same day, Rodriguez decided to explain his side of the issue in an interview with ESPN. (Rodriguez did not cooperate with the *Sports Illustrated* story other than to answer the reporter's request for a comment with "talk to the union.") Although ESPN rightly claimed the interview was "exclusive," portions of it eventually circulated across the Internet, including on YouTube.

The story remained in the news cycle for several more days, thanks in part to Rodriguez's status as a baseball superstar, but also because it kept circulating through all the

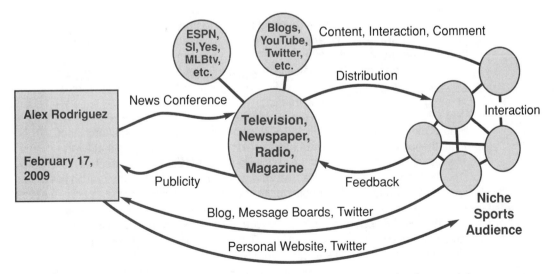

Figure 1.4. Coverage of a sports story in modern communication model.

various media. It picked up new life on February 17 when Rodriguez reported to the Yankees' spring training complex in Tampa. Rodriguez used the occasion to hold a news conference and more completely explain his position. His belief was that the issue would be a continuing distraction throughout spring training unless he did not address it fully.

The February 17 news conference is an excellent example of how an event is covered and the information distributed in the new sports model. Obviously, the event was covered by the national and New York sports media, including newspapers, television stations, and magazines. The event was blogged live by several outlets, including *USA Today*, the *New York Daily News*, and the *New York Times*. Interestingly, the *Times* reporter who blogged the event wasn't even in Tampa; Alan Schwarz admitted to his readers that he was in New York watching a live transmission of the news conference.

The *Times'* blog also showed how important the Internet has become in today's sports reporting (see Table 1.6). The underlined sections of the blog represent hyperlinks, which allow readers to jump to another website for more information (whether or not they come back is another issue). The reporting style is also much more conversational and relaxed, suggesting more of a two-way conversation with readers than the one-way reports under the old model. Within an hour the blog had 351 responses from readers in all parts of the country. The *Times'* website also included two videos that allowed viewers to hear Rodriguez in his own words.

Table 1.6. Covering A-Rod	
The way the *New York Times* covered the Alex Rodriguez news conference on February 17, 2009, is a good example of how sports media works in the new communications model. The following is a brief segment of the live blog of the news conference by *Times* reporter Alan Schwarz (underlined phrases are hyperlinked stories and other material). The *Times* also had video segments featuring some of Rodriguez's comments.	
2:20 p.m.	For the second time since it was reported that he tested positive for steroids in 2003, Alex Rodriguez will answer reporters' questions about his use of performance-enhancing drugs. But instead of a one-on-one with Peter Gammons, the Yankees' third baseman will face the full phalanx of New York media and baseball beat writers Tuesday at 1:30 p.m. ET under a tent down the third-base line at Steinbrenner Field in Tampa.
2:22 p.m.	A friend of mine, Lyle Spatz from the Society of American Baseball Research, just sent me the following e-mail: "Evidently steroids is one of those topics that everyone has an opinion on, no matter their background or familiarity with baseball history. I only hope Cal Ripken doesn't get implicated. (Not that I have any reason to believe he will be). I think that would be the last straw for many people."
2:34 p.m.	A reporter asked Rodriguez whether his 2001–3 seasons should be wiped out of the record books. Rodriguez replied, "That's not for me to decide," but he would have been entitled to say, that's totally impossible."
Source: http://bats.blogs.nytimes.com/2009/02/17/as-it-happens-watching-a-rod/?hp	

The event generated heavy interest among sports fans, some of whom decided to offer their own take on Rodriguez. The website *Sox & Dawgs* is run by some New England sports fans who focus on the Red Sox, Patriots, and University of Connecticut. The site redistributed the video feed of the news conference (from the Yankees' own YES Network), and allowed other fans to submit comments. Dozens of other fans sites did the same thing, but interestingly Alex Rodriguez did not use his own personal website to explain himself. The "unofficial" sites created by fans of Rodriguez were also silent on the matter. In addition to same-day coverage, the news conference was extensively covered in the succeeding days through newspaper, television, radio, and magazines.

A CHALLENGING MODEL

Coverage of the Alex Rodriguez story is a good illustration of the importance of content in the new sports communication model. In today's technological environment content is king; the demand for it continues to increase, the ability to store and distribute it constantly improves, and anyone can create it. If ownership of distribution was the key to the old model, then content is what drives the new model. That creates several challenges for sports communicators as we head into the second decade of the new millennium. Specifically:

- **How will technology continue to impact sports communication?** Blogging, tweeting, podcasting . . . the list of new communication technologies continues to grow. It's difficult to predict what the next breakthrough in technology will be, but we can say two things with some degree of certainty: 1) communication technologies will continue to get faster, smaller, and more powerful and 2) they will continue to empower sports audiences in the communication process. Without a doubt, sports audiences will have greater power in terms of mediated consumption; there will be more to watch, read, and listen to than ever before. But their ability to take part in the communication process should also drastically increase. We already live in a time in which athletes and fans can communicate directly, quickly, and unedited; the balance of power in the original communication model has started to tilt drastically in the direction of the audience and will only continue to do so.

- **What does this mean for the traditional mass media?** Dan LeBatard's statement that athletes "won't need the media anymore" is probably premature, but there is a sense that the role of television, newspapers, radio, and magazines are evolving. Their traditional role—that of the communications bridge between athletes and audiences—has already begun to crumble. Fans can already communicate directly to athletes through websites, Twitter, and the like, and that relationship is only going to grow. There will always be a role for the traditional media as mass distributor as long as they control the rights to live events like the Super Bowl. But these media need to rethink their position and how they fit into the evolving sports communication process.

In many cases, the evolution has already started and many traditional media outlets are streamlining and eliminating some outdated areas of their operations. Several local television stations, for example, have made drastic changes to the sports segments that appear in their newscasts. KVVU-TV in Las Vegas is among the stations that dropped sports entirely from local news, at least on weekdays. "The sportscast is not what the viewers come to us for," said news director Adam Bradshaw. "Research has been telling us that for years. The economics of broadcasting dictate we put our resources in places where we're going to get ratings" (Bornfeld, 2009). Increasingly, these resources include more interactive strategies that allow for more audience participation. More and more television stations and newspapers are offering ways for audience members to contribute content, such as with blogs, message boards, and home video.

- **What does this mean for athletes, events, and organizations?** As a positive benefit, the changes taking place give athletes much greater control in shaping their own image. We've already noted how several athletes have their own websites, blogs, and Twitter accounts. These allow the athlete to bypass the mainstream media, which can filter, edit, or reshape the message. As one example from 2008, NBA player Jamal Crawford responded to a story in the *New York Post* from writer Marc Berman that he had criticized a teammate: "You've been around me four years, have I EVER did anything like throw a teammate under the bus? He says 'No,' so then I said, 'So why would I do it now? Why, when we're trying to build team chemistry, do something like that?' He couldn't really answer me, so I said, 'Well, now I'm going to have to write about you on my blog'" (Edwards, 2008).

On the negative side, athletes have to be much more careful about what they say and how they act in private. Now that fans have the ability to create and distribute their own content, the athlete runs the risk of winding up on YouTube every time he/she leaves the house. In September of 2008, a fan with a cell phone captured NBA player Josh Howard making disparaging (and profane) comments about the National Anthem at a charity event. The video was posted to YouTube and created a public furor, which forced Howard to issue an apology through his own blog site. Even so, his public image still suffered.

SUMMARY

Primarily because of technology, a new model of sports communication has evolved. The old model (Figure 1.1) was based on a one-way system in which the traditional mass media (newspaper, radio, television, and magazines) dominated the creation and distribution of sports content. Communication was one-way from medium to audience members, who had a passive, reactive role in the process. But starting in the 1970s, technological developments such as satellite transmission, the Internet, and digital communication helped create a new model (Figure 1.2). These technological advances have taken power away from the traditional media and transferred it to sports audiences.

Such audiences now have much more choice in terms of mediated consumption, and they have a greater ability to take part in the communication process. Audiences are now able to create and distribute their own sports content.

This shift has important consequences for all parts of the sports communication equation—the media, the athletes, and audiences. The media must rethink their position relative to audiences and adapt to changing times. Many of the more traditional media have begun using technology to encourage audience interactivity and participation. Athletes can now bypass the media and communicate directly with audiences, but that also has a down side. Audiences can create and distribute their own content, including things that may damage the image of athletes or organizations. It is believed that power will continue to shift away from the mass media and toward the sports audience as the technology continues to develop.

DISCUSSION QUESTIONS

1. Does technology seem to be the driving force in modern day sports communication? Why or why not? What other factors play a key role in how sports communication continues to evolve?

2. Critics argue that today's sports reporting is obsessed with scandal and celebrity. Do you agree? What role does that suggest culture plays in the sports communication process? If Babe Ruth were playing today would he be treated differently in the sports media than he was in the 1920s? If so, in what way?

3. How does economics figure into the sports communication process? Given that media outlets are businesses that need to make profit, how does that influence communication between them and audiences? Between them and athletes?

4. Dan LeBatard commented that eventually athletes might not need the traditional mass media (television, radio, newspapers, and magazines). Would you agree? Why or why not? How might these media evolve in the future?

SUGGESTED EXERCISES

1. Consider a recent sports story or issue that received a lot of media attention. Detail how this story was/would have been covered under the two models of sports communication.

2. We can do the same kind of analysis for individual media such as *Sports Illustrated*, which has created a vault of every issue it has ever published. Using the *SI* Vault website (http://vault.sportsillustrated.cnn.com/), analyze how the sports communication process has evolved at *SI* over the years. How is the magazine communicating differently with audiences? Is it possible to determine when this evolution started taking place?

3. Along with *Sports Illustrated*, *The Sporting News* is another good example of how today's sports media integrate their content through the web, print, radio, television, and other outlets. Specifically, detail how *TSN* is using these various media

to distribute content and communicate with audiences. What kind of strategy seems to be involved? Does it seem like *TSN* is trying to reach two (or more) different audiences?

4. In addition to "how" sports audiences are behaving more interactively (creating and distributing content, posting comments to message boards, blogs, etc.), media scholars are also interested in "what" they are saying. Pick a particular blog, message board, or fan site and analyze it for a period of time. What is the content? What are these fans trying to say? What is the tone of the conversation? What does it possibly mean for the sports communication process?

2

The Print Media

We talked at length in Chapter 1 about how sports communication has evolved from a one-way process dominated by the traditional mass media into a two-way process where audiences have increasing power. To continue the evolution metaphor there are many in the media industry who believe the print media—newspapers and magazines—are like the dinosaurs on their way to extinction. But others say that in true "survival of the fittest" fashion the print media will evolve to continue as relevant entities within sports media.

A BRIEF HISTORY

It's hard to believe that newspapers and magazines once dominated the sports media landscape much like the feared Brontosaurus or Tyrannosaurus Rex. Back when print was the only source of sports news, periodicals like *The Sporting News* were essential to fans. The first issue of *TSN* came out on March 17, 1886, at a cost of five cents per issue or $2.50 for the entire year. Alfred Spink was the founder and publisher, but was having trouble until his brother Charles pitched in. "The paper was having a hard row to hoe and made little headway until he took hold of its business management," said Alfred. "From that day it prospered" ("History of," 2009). *TSN* became so popular that it eventually became known as the "Bible of Baseball."

Although competitors popped up now and then, *TSN* dominated the sports magazine industry until the arrival of *Sports Illustrated* in 1954. *SI* also had trouble getting its early footing, but soon it found the right combination of writing, color pictures, and coverage to attract large audiences. By 2009, the magazine boasted a circulation of three million for each weekly issue, and a total weekly readership of 23 million, helped in no small part by its popular swimsuit issue ("Sports Illustrated," 2009). *SI* successfully branched out into other media areas, including *Sports Illustrated KIDS*, cnnsi.com, and *Sports Illustrated Almanac* annuals. Another magazine that focused on writing and color photography, *Sport* magazine, actually predated *SI* by eight years, but ceased publication in 2000 because of financial problems.

Extensive newspaper coverage of sports began in the late 1800s, due in large part to the newspaper wars taking place in New York. Under the leadership of Joseph Pulitzer,

Grantland Rice and the Four Horseman

Grantland Rice was among the many colorful newspaper reporters who worked during the 1920s. Their writing style was flowery, evocative, and effusive, and it helped make heroes of athletes such as Babe Ruth and Red Grange. Below is a small portion of Rice's account of the Notre Dame-Army football game from 1924. Not only did this article create the legend of Notre Dame's Four Horseman, it helped elevate the small Indiana school to iconic status in college football.

Outlined against a blue-gray October sky, the Four Horsemen rode again. In dramatic lore they are known as Famine, Pestilence, Destruction and Death. These are only aliases. Their real names are Stuhldreher, Miller, Crowley and Layden. They formed the crest of the South Bend cyclone before which another fighting Army football team was swept over the precipice at the Polo Grounds yesterday afternoon as 55,000 spectators peered down on the bewildering panorama spread on the green plain below.

A cyclone can't be snared. It may be surrounded, but somewhere it breaks through to keep on going. When the cyclone starts from South Bend, where the candle lights still gleam through the Indiana sycamores, those in the way must take to storm cellars at top speed.

Yesterday the cyclone struck again as Notre Dame beat the Army, 13 to 7, with a set of backfield stars that ripped and crashed through a strong Army defense with more speed and power than the warring cadets could meet.

Notre Dame won its ninth game in twelve Army starts through the driving power of one of the greatest backfields that ever churned up the turf of any gridiron in any football age. Brilliant backfields may come and go, but in Stuhldreher, Miller, Crowley and Layden, covered by a fast and charging line, Notre Dame can take its place in front of the field.

Source: *New York Herald-Tribune*, October 19, 24.

the *New York World* became one of the first newspapers to create a distinct sports department. To keep up, the *New York Times* began running sports photographs in a special Sunday picture section, and in 1895 the *New York Journal* became the first newspaper in the US to print a section entirely devoted to sports (Wanta, 2006).

Newspaper coverage flourished in the early 20th century and focused mainly on baseball. Reporters played a major role in exposing the Black Sox betting scandal in 1919, and in elevating Babe Ruth to iconic status in the 1920s. Sportswriters of the 1920s created other heroes as well, including Bobby Jones, Red Grange, and Jack Dempsey. In many cases, the sportswriters themselves reached a level of celebrity status; men such as Ring Lardner, Dan Daniel, and Grantland Rice (see sidebar). With radio still in its relative infancy, audiences were almost completely dependent on these writers to learn more about their favorite teams and athletes.

Even as radio and television came onto the scene, print sports reporting did not lose any of its importance. While TV and radio could carry the games live, it was newspapers and magazines that provided the depth, even if fans had to wait several hours to get the information. During the heyday of the Dodgers, Giants, and Yankees in the 1950s, there were nearly a dozen New York papers covering the teams on a daily basis.

"Every night at nine we would stand in front of the candy store waiting for the *Daily News* truck to come up," said Brooklyn native and baseball author Donald

Honig. "It was like the docking of a luxury liner. Why was this such an important event? Because the details of the Dodger game were in there. We already knew every pitch that was thrown. We listened to the game on the radio. We discussed it for three hours. Now we were going to read about it." (Golenbock, 1984, p. 260).

It was also during the 1950s that sports reporting began to take on a harder edge and leave behind the fawning heroism of previous generations. A combination of cultural and industry forces (primarily competition from television and radio) forced reporters out of their chummy relationships with athletes. One of the leaders of the movement was Dick Young of the *New York Daily News*, who would antagonize players by analyzing, explaining, and describing their weaknesses in great detail. According to modern sportswriter Michael Shapiro, "It's hard to imagine today's (sports audiences) being satisfied with the sort of sportswriting of the era before 1950, before Dick Young made his way from the comfort of the press box down to the clubhouse, shoved his mug in a ballplayer's face and asked, 'What were you doing trying to steal third with two men out?'" (Shapiro, 2000, p. 50).

But as the as the old sports communication model began to give way to the new (see Chapter 1 for more details), print reporting began to lose a bit of its luster. A major shift occurred in 1980 when ESPN began broadcasting 24 hours a day, seven days a week. Other cable networks and channels soon followed suit, and sports

The Death of *Sport* and *The National*

Sport was always thought of as a competitor of *Sports Illustrated*, but it came out only once a month as opposed to *SI*'s weekly publication. Maybe that's why *Sport* seemed to emphasize reflective, in-depth reporting while *SI* stuck more with news. Both magazines focused on quality reporting, vivid color photography, and mass sports appeal, but as the times changed *Sport* found itself the odd man out. Citing declining advertising revenues, its publisher called it quits in 2000. At the time of its passing, former editor Roger Director said, "*Sport* lurched around searching for the right demographic niche these last years. But there was really only one reader, and he was doing a bit of lurching around, too. He's the one wondering how in so many pages there can be nothing he wants to read" ("Scorecard," 2000).

In 1990, *The National* debuted as the first national sports daily in the country. With a strong stable of writers headed by editor Frank Deford, the paper had high hopes, but it never got above 250,000 circulation. While Deford blamed the paper's demise on distribution problems, others suggested that "those buying the paper were not regular newspaper readers hungry for more sports statistics, but young men who were rabid fans and spent much of their leisure time watching sports on television" (Jones, 1991).

The disappearance of *Sport* and *The National* continued the transition from the mass appeal sports magazine to the niche publication targeting specific audiences of sports fans. *Sports Illustrated* and *The Sporting News* are the strongest mass appeal magazines, but they have also reached out to niche audiences.

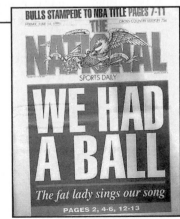

fans no longer had to wait for the newspaper to get the details they wanted. In part because of more choices and options, the mass sports audience began to fragment into
smaller niche audiences, which might have hastened the death of *Sport* magazine and
the ill-fated *National Sports Daily* (see sidebar). Although *Sports Illustrated* remained
strong, the magazine was not infallible; it tried and failed with niche offerings such as
Sports Illustrated Women (launched in 2000, ceased publication in 2002) and *Sports Illustrated on Campus* (launched in 2003, ceased publication in 2005, although a web version remains).

Print readership was further eroded in the mid-1990s with the rise of the Internet,
which provided fans with an instantaneous, and almost limitless, storehouse of sports
information. It also allowed audiences to communicate more directly with sportswriters, and in many cases create and distribute their own content through such practices as
blogging. Blogging and the Internet both seemed to grow almost exponentially in the
early 2000s. By 2008, blogs in the US reached more than 77 million unique visitors
with a total Internet audience of 189 million. In just one week, bloggers made 1.5 million posts; 7.4 million in four months ("State of", 2008).

As sports audiences started to turn their attention to the Internet so did advertisers.
Print outlets began to find themselves in serious financial difficulty, which was further
compounded by the serious economic downturn of the late 2000s. While the *New York
Times* fell $1 billion in debt and the Tribune Company filed for bankruptcy, several
other newspaper groups faced shutdown and liquidation (Hirschorn, 2009). Among the
casualties were the *Cincinnati Post*, the *Seattle Post-Intelligencer* and Denver's *Rocky
Mountain News*, which in 2009 published its final edition less than two weeks from its
150th birthday.

While there is no shortage of media experts who think newspapers and magazines
will follow dinosaurs into the graveyard of history, there are also many who think the
print media are simply going through a natural evolution. Former *USA Today* editor
Ken Paulson noted, "Journalism works; there is nothing wrong with the product. There
is just a disconnect between what we deliver and what people are willing to pay for that
delivery. That's bad for newspapers, but it's a little early to write an obituary. The newspaper business is in better shape than it looks" (Smillie, 2009).

An obvious strategy has been to turn to the web to reach new audiences. Even as the
New York Times announced the layoffs of 100 reporters in 2008, executive editor Bill
Keller said the newspaper understands that "what we sell is journalism," and he promised "fresh investments . . . to expand our web journalism . . . (and) advancing a digital
strategy" ("Transcript of," 2008). In some cases the online investment has been as-
tounding, such as with the *Christian Science Monitor*, which in 2009 became the first
national circulation newspaper to completely replace its print edition with an online
version (Cook, 2008).

Sports media have also jumped into the digital world with both feet. From the very
biggest, like *Sports Illustrated*, down to the smallest weekly paper covering the local high
school, almost all newspapers now have some sort of Internet presence. It could include
reporter blogs, video posts of local games, or simply an online version of the print edi-

tion. In 2008, *The Sporting News* debuted what it called the nation's only daily digital sports newspaper. The free edition was delivered by a link sent to subscribers via e-mail. More than 75,000 initial subscribers signed up for what was called "the first step in a reinvention of a title continuously published for 120 years; perhaps the ultimate test of how to take part in the transition to online beyond a website" (Kramer, 2008). At the same time, *TSN* decided to move from a weekly sports magazine to a revamped bi-weekly with larger pages, better paper, and less emphasis on news.

Again, many would regard this as a natural evolutionary move for the print media. When radio and television arrived on the scene newspaper sportswriters had to adjust.

> "In the era of television and radio," said veteran baseball writer Roger Kahn, "you don't say, 'The Dodgers beat the Giants, 6 to 2,' you say, 'Yesterday, in the Dodgers' 6-2 win over the Giants, the most interesting thing that happened was . . .' That's the best definition of what a morning story of a ballgame ought to be. (Dick Young) worked that out by himself, and that was the New Journalism." (Golen-bock, 1984, p. 317)

In a similar way, print reporters have had to adjust to the Internet, blogging, and audience interactivity, and in many ways their job has changed dramatically.

RELATING WITH CONTENT PROVIDERS

"Content providers" is just another way to say athletes, coaches, and sports organizations. They are the ones who play and coach the games, organize the competition, and make the news that sports audiences want to know about. Reporters need access to these people in order to generate content for their readers; the content providers need the reporters for promotion and publicity.

When the athlete is playing well and the team is winning, access is easy. Players are always willing to tell reporters how they hit the game-winning home run or scored 30 points in the championship basketball game. The fans are happy because the local team is winning, and the reporters have no trouble filling their pages with feel-good stories and interviews. But just as obviously, access becomes extremely difficult when the athlete is playing poorly, the team is losing, or there is a scandal involved. The fans get angry because they don't want to hear bad news about the local team. This is especially true of highly involved fans that have an emotional investment in their favorite team or player (Wann, 2006), and there can be a tremendous backlash against reporters who write critically of the local team. When the *Lexington* (KY) *Herald-Leader* published accounts of illegal payments to players of the University of Kentucky basketball team in 1986, the paper received hundreds of angry phone calls and letters, a bomb threat to its building, shots fired through the press room windows, and 400 subscription cancellations. Even though the newspaper eventually won the Pulitzer Prize for its reporting, a poll revealed that fully half of its readers believed it should not have published the stories (Green, 1991).

Such criticism can also come directly from the content providers themselves. Former NFL coach Jim Mora (ironically, now a television football analyst) spent much of a

Sports reporters have become more critical in their coverage of the athletes, coaches, and teams that they cover. (Courtesy of WVU Photographic Services)

memorable press conference answering criticism by telling the media, "You don't know (what you're talking about). You just don't know." At another press conference, former Purdue football coach Jim Colletto told a reporter he didn't know "his butt from a hot rock." Long time sportswriter Bill Plaschke (2000) noted that former Dodgers outfielder Raul Mondesi once threatened to beat him up after a critical column.

The increase in the amount of sports media, the speed at which material gets to the public, and the demand for more content to satisfy audiences suggests that the critical reporting will continue. There may have been a time in which reporters and athletes could develop trusting relationships; former baseball sportswriter and author Roger Kahn covered the Dodgers during the 1950s and admits to making friends with the players (Gietschier, 1994). But for the most part the relationship today is wary at best, adversarial at worst. "We're everywhere," said Bill Plaschke (2000, p. 44). "We surround them as they are preparing for a game; we barely give them room to dress afterwards; and we're not looking to make friends, but front pages." Added former Major League Baseball pitcher David Cone, "We feel like targets. A lot of times [the media are] looking for a reason to get on you. Negativity sells" (Schultz, 2005, p. 25).

Content providers try to control such negativity through various means, including news releases (see Chapter 6), media guides (Chapter 7), and news conferences (Chapter 8). They can also limit the time and place of access, which is particularly common on the high school and college level. The schools justify this by saying that the student-athletes are not paid and need to be protected from constant media scrutiny. School administrators, athletic officials, or sports information department staffers (Chapter 4) serve as filters through which the media must go to get access to players and coaches. There are similar positions within professional sports organizations, but at the pro level access is more often determined by the individual athlete. For the most part, if an athlete doesn't want to talk, he/she doesn't talk. Several athletes, including stars like Barry Bonds, became well-known for their refusal to grant media access at particular times.

Interestingly, new technology may be helping reporters reestablish better relations with content providers. We discussed in Chapter 1 how athletes are highly engaged in communications technologies like Twitter and blogging. Reporters are now using these technologies to maintain better relationships with athletes by developing more frequent communication (see sidebar).

The print reporter's job is to not only work within the access rules established by the content provider,

---

"R U able to talk?"

Text messaging has become increasingly more important for print reporters, not only for keeping up with athletes and coaches, but in their actual stories. Below are some examples of how text messaging is affecting the way reporters do their jobs.

"I'm ready to prove u wrong again, Mr. King. Can't wait." (King, 2008)

> May 2, 2008, text message from New England safety Rodney Harrison to *Sports Illustrated* reporter Peter King, who had suggested in print that injuries might have derailed Harrison's career.

And now he's not speaking publicly. I sent him a text message Monday afternoon and asked him to call me so we could discuss his arrest and his denial that he was drunk or belligerent to the arresting officers. He returned a one-word reply: "Tomorrow." (Golden, 2008)

> May 6, 2008, story by Cedric Golden in the *Austin (TX) American-Statesman*. Golden was trying to get more details from former Chicago Bears running back Cedric Benson on the latter's arrest for drunken boating.

"I'm retiring; is that still news?" ("Report," 2007)

> July 4, 2007, text message from NHL star Jeremy Roenick to a reporter at the *Philadelphia Inquirer*. The story was immediately posted on the paper's website.

Then, just when we thought all the bad Pacers-related news was done for the day, I get a text message from the Pacers informing me that Danny Granger is out 10–21 days with a partial tendon tear. ("Feb. 19,", 2009)

> From "Sixty Feet, Six Inches," a sports blog covering Indiana sports.

"I don't know what's gonna happen, but if they want me, I will be an Eagle tomorrow" ("T.J.," 2009).

> February 2009 text message reportedly sent from wide receiver T.J. Houshmandzadeh to 905 ESPN Radio in Philadelphia. Houshmandzadeh signed with the Seahawks the following week.

"Totally false" ("Suns deny," 2009)

> February 13, 2009, text message from Phoenix Suns general manager Steve Kerr regarding rumors that the team would fire head coach Terry Porter; sent to a producer on the "Doug and Wolf Show," Sports 620 AM radio in Phoenix. The Suns fired Porter three days later.

but also to find access in other ways when necessary. We've already learned how players, coaches, and fans can get upset when the media report bad news. When that happens, the content providers typically go into "lock down," either refusing to talk to
anyone or limiting communication to carefully crafted statements. Former sports broadcaster and now college educator Charlie Lambert observed, "Journalists who cover top-
level sport are facing a real challenge. Teams and organizations are so powerful and so
wealthy that they want to control everything that is said or written about them"
("Spoiled sports," 2008).

Access can be virtually impossible during crisis situations and reporters must find a
way to get beyond the official information and find what they need. In 2004, the *Denver Post* wanted to uncover the story behind allegations of gang rape and other miscon-
duct on the University of Colorado football team. Chris Dempsey of the *Denver Post* always had a pretty good relationship with CU Athletic Director Dick Tharp, but that
changed as the scandal heated up. One morning, Dempsey stood in the parking lot
waiting to talk to Tharp as he arrived for work. "I'm asking him questions. He's saying,
'Chris, I'm not going to answer that. I can't answer that.' I followed him into the general office area of the athletic department and he slammed the door on me." Even after
the scandal settled down, Dempsey waited two months for an interview with Tharp. He
was told, 'Chris, it's tough for me to do an interview with the *Post*. You guys were calling for my head" (Potter, 2006).

Reporters Lance Williams and Mark Fainaru-Wada ran into similar stonewalling
when they started looking into the BALCO steroids scandal, which took more than
two years of investigative work. The only way they could report the story was to promise anonymity to the one source who would talk. Williams and Fainaru-Wada defied a
U.S. District Court judge by refusing to identify their source, but were spared jail time
when the source voluntarily came forward (former attorney Troy Ellerman pleaded
guilty Feb. 14, 2007, to leaking the information, lying to prosecutors, obstructing justice, and disobeying a court order not to disclose grand jury information). "Sometimes,
the press' watchdog role requires the judicious use of confidential sources," Fainaru-
Wada said in his statement to the court. "Some stories simply cannot—and would
not—be told without people providing information under the promise of anonymity.
If those stories cannot be told because reporters fear being jailed or whistle-blowers fear
being exposed, the public interest will be irrevocably compromised" ("Fainaru-Wada's
statement," 2006).

Fainaru-Wada and Williams won a Pulitzer Prize for their reporting, in part because
of their tenacity, patience, and persistence in working around official sources. "Throughout the BALCO affair, critics have questioned the motives of our reporting, suggesting
that it has been little more than a witch hunt or an effort to profit off the big names
who have been drawn into the scandal," said Fainaru-Wada. "For us, however, BALCO
has always been an earnest and sincere effort to present the truth" ("Fainaru-Wada's
statement," 2006). Getting to that truth, with or without the help of content providers,
is still the cornerstone of good sports writing.

RELATING WITH AUDIENCES

The primary relationship between the print outlet and audiences remains unchanged in that the outlet provides audiences with content. But several other things *have* changed, including how much content is provided, the nature of the content, and how that content is provided to audiences. New technologies are the driving force behind these changes and they have allowed audiences to take a much greater role in the communication process.

In some ways, the type of content provided by print outlets is not much different than it was 50 or even 100 years ago. The sports event is still the major attraction for audiences and reporters spend a great deal of time previewing, analyzing, critiquing, and rehashing live game action. Some reporters specialize in commentary, analysis, or opinion, while others, like Mark Fainaru-Wada and Lance Williams, focus on investigative work. Another type of sportswriting is the feature story, a longer form of writing that centers on the emotional aspects of a particular story. Many sportswriters are beat reporters, which means they cover the same story or team over a long period of time. This not only helps them stay on top of potential stories, but also develop a better relationship with athletes and coaches. "That's 90 percent of sports reporting," said longtime sportswriter Bill Plaschke (2000, p. 44), "standing around batting cages and end zones and practice courts, just talking. The best sports reporters are the people who are the best at hanging out."

This is not a textbook on sportswriting and there is no need to go into great detail on the process (if you are interested in the basics of sports reporting see Schultz, 2005). However, it is important to note that in terms of creating content, the role of the sportswriter has changed in recent years. Under the old model of sport communication a reporter might cover a particular game then file a story for the next day's newspaper. Thus, the reporter had at least a few hours to gather quotes, process information, and write the story. The reporter might even have time to create an additional sidebar story—a supplemental story related to the game.

Today, the reporter has a lot more work to do and less time to do it. There is still the main game story that will run in the next day's newspaper, but most reporters must now also write for their Internet audiences. This could include posting several short updates throughout the game, or in some cases running an ongoing game blog. In fact, reporters blogging during games has become something of a controversial topic (see sidebar).

The laptop or portable computer has become almost mandatory for the modern sports reporter, and the ability to write and transmit stories directly from the game allows reporters to work faster and keep up with rapidly shrinking deadlines. Computers can also be used to transmit video and audio, and the print reporter could tape game action or interviews using a small camera. This material would then be posted on the newspaper's website as soon as possible after the game. Thus, the reporter might be required to write a story (or two) for both the Internet and print editions of the paper, maintain a blog, take digital photographs, and shoot video/audio for posting on the web. The outlet might also want two different versions of the story—one for the web

Blogged Down

In June 2007, Brian Bennett, a reporter for the *Louisville Courier-Journal*, was ejected from an NCAA tournament baseball game for blogging the event live for the newspaper's website. An NCAA official told Bennett that blogging a championship event was not permitted; Bennett was told to leave and had his credential revoked. According to the NCAA, blogging constituted a "live representation of the game" and was thus prohibited until the game had ended (Bozich, 2007). When the newspaper threatened a lawsuit on First Amendment grounds the NCAA decided to revise its policy. In December 2007, the NCAA instituted special live blogging rules for anyone credentialed to cover NCAA events. The rules vary by sport, but they prohibit "real-time" (continuous) blogging and limit how many times someone can blog during the course of a game. Interestingly, the rules apply only to credentialed reporters, which means a fan could buy a ticket, sit in the stands and blog with no restrictions (for more details see "NCAA Blogging Policy" at http://www.ncaa.org/wps/ncaa?ContentID=638).

The NFL also has restrictions on live blogging and limits media outlets to 90 seconds per day of audio and/or video of interviews, press conferences, and team practices that may be posted on a website. The NFL blogging policy states, "While a game is in progress, any forms or accounts of the game must be sufficiently time-delayed and limited in amount (e.g., score updates with detail given only in quarterly game updates, fewer than 10 photographs during the game) so that the Accredited Organization's game coverage cannot be used as a substitute for, or otherwise approximate, authorized play-by-play accounts" (Reisinger, 2009)

Regarding the use of video on websites, the NBA, MLB, and NHL have no restrictions.

and the other for the next day's newspaper. It all adds up to a lot more work, and usually for not much more pay.

As just one example, on March 10, 2009, *New York Post* writer Bart Hubbuch posted in his blog, "Here is video I shot today of (Mets manager) Jerry Manuel's reaction to the sudden release of reliever Duaner Sanchez. As you can tell, Manuel doesn't seem entirely pleased by GM Omar Minaya's move" (Hubbach, 2009). The blog then led to an embedded four-minute video interview with Manuel. On the day the video appeared Hubbuch wrote the main story of Manuel's reaction for the print and web editions of the paper. He also posted eight entries to the *Post* Mets blog; the first at 9 a.m. and the last at 5 p.m. All of the posts allowed readers to add their own comments and opinions, and one included a blog poll asking if Pedro Martinez should return to the team.

The "Covering the Story: Old and New Models" sidebar and Figure 2.1 details how print outlets are using technology to stretch their coverage resources, which is especially important in an era when newspapers face an uncertain economic future. If one reporter can do all these different things it adds to the outlet's content at minimal cost. According to one newspaper journalist, "I bet 95 percent of [those journalists] who have been forced to blog don't get paid an extra penny for doing it. That means we've added an extra story per day . . . with no raise at all" (Schultz & Sheffer, 2007, p. 71). Dan Conover (2006), director of new media development for the Charleston (SC) *Post and Courier*, writes, "Media companies of late have been far more interested in adding new publications and products [without adding staff] than they've been in improving quality. Squeeze your staff and production capabilities harder and get growth out of new products."

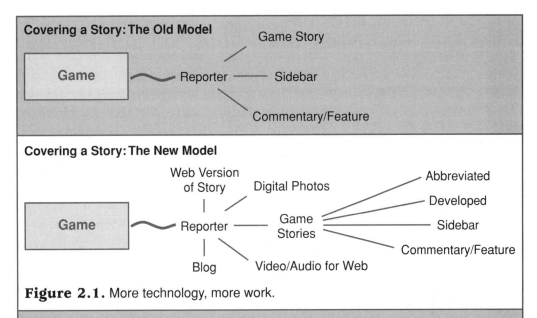

Figure 2.1. More technology, more work.

Covering the Story: Old and New Models

As noted previously, responsibilities of the print sports reporter have increased drastically in the new model of sport communication. Reporting in the new model is quite different (see "One Game, Three Stories" sidebar). The reporter might be asked to blog during the game. The outlet's website requires an *abbreviated game story*, which runs immediately after the game, usually within the first hour. At that point, audiences typically want a sports version of the traditional journalism "five Ws"—who, what, where, when, and why. This would be a bare-bones version of the story; one that had all the important details, but not any interviews or other information that would provide depth. These types of stories usually get posted quickly to the Internet and may appear in the printed version of the newspaper if the game ran late and there was not time to write a more developed story.

When the reporter has had time to get quotes and find more detail he/she posts a *developed game story*. The developed game story is an extension of the abbreviated story, and should give the audience a sense of not just what happened, but how it happened and why. This can be done by focusing on strategy, analysis, key plays in the game, and the like. It's also important to try to add some emotion and feeling to the story, which can be done effectively with good quotes from players and coaches. Finally, the reporter should try to put the game into some type of perspective or context. Why was this game important? What does it mean? Is there anything from the game that will have a long-term impact on the players, coaches,

or team? The developed game story is essentially what will run in the next day's newspaper.

The *sidebar feature* is a supplemental story that accompanies the main game story. Sidebars aren't written for every game, usually only the most important game that would warrant sending an extra reporter. Typically, one reporter would write the game story and another would handle the sidebar, although it's not unheard of for one reporter to do both, especially at newspapers with a smaller staff. A sidebar can be on any number of issues related to the game, such as player profiles or fan interest. In some cases, these side issues are important enough to become the focus of the main story and push details of the game to the background. Consider someone who played for a particular team for several years before leaving for that team's main rival. When the player returns to face his former team, it will likely become the most important theme of the game coverage. What happens in the game itself becomes secondary, unless the play is especially outstanding or unusual.

In addition to all this the reporter may have to gather video and audio material to post to the website, including digital photos. Larger outlets might assign a photographer for this job, but smaller newspapers often do not have the resources to send an extra person to the game. The equipment has developed to the point where decent quality audio and video can be captured with small, digital cameras, and the modern print reporter should know the basics of electronic news gathering.

One Game, Three Stories

Today's print reporter may have to write a variety of stories to cover the same game. The abbreviated game story goes to the website right after the game. The developed game story also goes to the website and is essentially the story that will run in the next day's paper. The sidebar feature is a story related to the main action that might interest different types of readers; it also goes both on the web and in the newspaper. There might also be a commentary story written by the paper's columnist (or even the same reporter for a smaller newspaper). And don't forget any video, audio, or pictures that need posting to the website!

Consider a fictional basketball game between Fresno Tech and Pacific Coast. A reporter covering the game might have to write three stories for the web, with two versions appearing in the next day's newspaper:

Abbreviated Game Story (runs immediately after the game on the web)

FRESNO, Calif.—Johnson Jones scored 28 points as Fresno Tech held off Pacific Coast 78-76 Thursday night. Last place Fresno (12-17 overall, 3-10 conference) needed a missed 3-pointer at the buzzer by Luke Stollen to seal the victory. Fresno also got 17 points from Zach Littler, while Jones added 13 rebounds. Pacific (16-11, 8-5) had its three-game winning streak snapped and lost for the first time in nine tries against Fresno.

Developed Game Story (later version that replaces the abbreviated story; it usually also appears in the newspaper)

FRESNO, Calif.—Johnson Jones scored 28 points and pulled down 13 rebounds, but it was one play on the defensive end that may have made the biggest difference.

With just seconds to play Thursday night and Fresno Tech leading Pacific Coast by two, the Beachcombers had one last chance to pull out the win. Conference three-point leader Luke Stollen streaked down the wing and appeared to get free for a potential game-winner, but Jones came flying in to disrupt the shot and preserve the Aggies' 78-76 win.

Continued on next page

Blogging has especially become an important part of the reporter's job because it reflects the growing interactivity of sports media. Nardi, Schiano, Gumbrecht, and Swartz (2004) define a web blog or blog as a web-based form of communication that includes frequent updates and a series of archived entries made in reverse chronological order. It also allows for dialogue and interaction between the blogger (in this case the reporter) and the audience member. Audiences can post comments and sometimes engage in real-time conversations with sports reporters. Blogging has become extremely popular among fans, teams, and players, and many of them have started their own blogs. Athletes and teams find it a good way to present their message to fans, and fans like it because they have a much more active role in the process.

One group that may not be thrilled about the growing presence of blogs is sportswriters. As noted, outlets typically do not pay their reporters extra money for blogging and often times reporters are unsure about what exactly to put in a blog. Because it is by nature personal and subjective, blogging raises issues about journalistic integrity and ethics. In addition, reporters are by nature reluctant to change engrained work habits. For all of these reasons and more, blogging has not been universally embraced by sports journalists. Consider this comment on blogging from a newspaper reporter:

"Without a doubt that was the play of the game," Aggies coach Brian Barton said. "If Johnson doesn't get there his 28 points probably go for nothing."

"I've really worked hard on the defensive end," said Jones, who is second in the California Conference in scoring. "People want to talk about my shooting, but I can play defense, too. I saw Stollen get free on a pick, so I left my man and got over in time to help out."

Led by Jones' 13 first-half points the Aggies zoomed out to a 41-29 lead at the break. Stollen helped fuel Pacific's comeback in the second half, at one point hitting three straight 3-pointers to finish with 21 points. A Stollen jumper with 12 seconds left cut the lead to two, then the Beachcombers forced a turnover to set up the dramatic finish. Stollen fired his final shot from the deep corner with two seconds left, but Jones got just enough to preserve the win.

Fresno players rushed the court as the buzzer sounded to celebrate their first win over Pacific in nine tries. The Aggies are still in last place, but improved to 12-17 overall and 3-10 in the conference. Pacific saw its three-game winning streak snapped and dropped to 16-11 and 8-5. "It's been a tough year and we've had some bad breaks," said Barton, "but a win like this helps remind you why you keep playing."

The Aggies travel to Pomona on Saturday, while the Beachcombers return home to face Stockton State.

Sidebar Feature Story (often done by a different reporter, but sometimes written by a game reporter)

FRESNO, Calif.—As the clock ran down to less than five seconds left and Luke Stollen got set to fire one of his trademark 3-pointers, Aggie assistant coach Kevin LaSalle held his breath. "I thought about closing my eyes, too," he said, "but then I saw a streak of blue flash by."

That streak was Johnson Jones, who seemingly came from nowhere to disrupt Stollen's shot and seal the Aggies' 78-76 win over Pacific. "I don't think I exhaled until well after the buzzer sounded," the 62-year-old LaSalle laughed. "I must have been holding my breath five or six seconds, which is pretty good for an old guy."

There hasn't been much to laugh about for Fresno Tech this season. Even with the win the Aggies are still in last place in the California Conference and have won only 12 games. But as the game ended Thursday night LaSalle ran onto the court to hug Jones, the player he calls his "special project."

"Johnson didn't know anything about defense when he first got here," said LaSalle, "so Coach Barton turned him over to me. I told him I would find some way to get this kid to defend."

LaSalle's methods have included special workouts before and after practice, often at six in the morning. Many times, Jones never picked up a basketball the entire time.

"I knew he could shoot," said LaSalle. "The point was to get him to play without the ball. That means footwork, conditioning and position."

"Man, it was boring sometimes," admitted Jones about the morning sessions. "Running steps, jump roping, backpedaling. But I believed in what he was doing and it's paying off. Coach LaSalle has made me a much better defender."

Jones still has his problems on the defensive end. He'll occasionally lose his man in transition or get lost trying to fight his way through a screen. But the effort seems to be there, and Thursday night it paid off in a big way.

"First time I got my name in the headlines for something other than scoring," said Jones trying to hide a big grin.

And if his defense continues to improve the smiles may return again to the entire Aggie program.

One View of Modern Sports Journalism

The following is a story by David Schexnaydre Jr. (2008) that ran in the NOLA Sports Report on February 26, 2008. It is an excellent example of how modern sports journalists are using the emerging tools of communication—blogs, message boards, text messaging—to create a new style of "micro journalism." Notice also how the reporting is much more personal and subjective.

Asante. Samuel. Holy. Crap. That was my initial reaction last night when I read the rumor that the Saints have agreed in principle to terms with Asante Samuel. My next thought was to hurriedly check SaintsReport to see if it was on there yet. When I got to the forum I saw the thread entitled, "Samuel to Saints a Done Deal." It had been viewed 17 times, commented on 16 times, and 98 people were currently viewing it. A few seconds later it was over 170 people viewing. A few minutes later, 200 people viewing. I had never seen that many people viewing one thread at the same time. This could mean only one thing. We were officially in "Where Were You When?" territory.

Now, obviously I realize that it is just a rumor. I'm fully aware of this. Nothing is set in stone until he signs on the dotted line and holds up his black and gold jersey with his number on it. However, I don't know if you can tell from my writing or not, but I tend to get really excited about things. And I don't mean excited like I simply sit in my computer chair and victoriously pump a fist. I mean excited like I completely overreact and start to have the decision making process of a 12-year-old. An immature, candy loaded, hyper 12-year-old. This being said, I'm sure you can imagine how I reacted to the news. In case you can't, I kept track of it all for you . . .

9:40—I read the rumor at ProFootballTalk .com. They've had their share of hits and misses in the past, but I think they're actually pretty accurate. I've been a reader since 2004 and check the site probably 4 to 5 times a day. It all just paid off . . .

9:41—I check SaintsReport.com. The forum is already out of control. I leave a post in the thread just so I can one day tell my grandchildren about it.

9:43—I send out a mass text message on my phone. The message: ProFootballTalk is reporting that Asante Samuel to Saints is a done deal. Number of Recepients: 132.

9:45—I remind myself that it is just a rumor. I look at my phone, which is still in the process of sending out all those messages, and realize that I will wind up looking like a total idiot if they don't sign him. Then I realize that all of the people who I just texted already know me, therefore probably already know I'm a total idiot. I'm glad I don't have to worry about that anymore.

9:47—I begin to think about what the contract must be like. Probably something like 90 million for 9 years with 23 million or so guaranteed. Then I think about how I'm going to have to listen to idiots bring up the 90 million every time someone completes a pass on him. I think about the game where somebody catches a touchdown or two against him and some idiot starts with "This is what we paid 90 million for?!" Then I think about all the people who don't understand football contracts and walk around saying things like, "I can't believe they gave someone 90 million dollars just to play sports! What is this world coming to? Do you know how many homeless people we could help with that money?" Yeah, but homeless people don't play solid man to man defense or cause turnovers. Duh.

You know, as if he really is going to get every cent of the whole value of the contract. Like Mickey Loomis and Tom Benson walk up to Asante Samuel with a metallic briefcase, punch a code in, and it opens to reveal 90 million dollars in cash. They simply hand it over to him and say, "Here you go!" and that's it. However, the 10 million a year part makes me a little nervous, then I think, "Screw it, it's not my money!" and I'm happy again.

9:49—I start to think about how this will impact our defense. It will be great to have a bonafide shutdown corner. However, won't this just make the opponent throw at Jason David even more? Hmm . . .

Continued on next page

I also think about Mike McKenzie. Just think if he comes back at full strength. The thought of having McKenzie and Samuel at the corners with Jason David as a Nickel back makes me really happy. But that's only if McKenzie comes back healthy. However, I also realize that if McKenzie doesn't tear his ACL, then we probably never sign Samuel to begin with. It's funny how things work out.

9:51—I remind myself that it is just a rumor. Then I start to think of things that could go wrong. What if another team finds out the parameters of our "agreement" and decides they can beat it? What if it turns out that everything about the rumor is totally false to begin with? Then I imagine this scenario . . .

Everything is worked out and everyone is together for Asante to put his name on the contract and make it official. Mickey Loomis happens to glance down at his shirt and notice the Saints logo on it right before Samuel signs the contract and thinks to himself, "Wait a minute . . . I work for the Saints . . . we're about to make a huge free agent signing . . . we don't normally do this . . . we normally just sign middle of pack free agents that don't even have large roles on their old team . . . What Am I Doing? What Is Going On!" Then he screams "NOOOOOOO!!!!" while he grabs the contract out of Samuel's hands and rips it to shreds until he is totally out of breath and sweating profusely. Charles Grant laughs in the background and gets up to leave as he struggles to keep all the hundred dollar bills from falling out of his pockets. A woman asks him, "What'd you do to get all that money?" and Charles replies, "Um, nothing really . . ."

9:53—I wonder what jersey number Asante will wear. I hope it's a good cornerback number like something in the low 20's and not a horrible cornerback number like something in the high 40's. He wore 22 in New England and if Fred Thomas is not back I'm sure that's what he will wear here. Even if ole' Freddy T is back I'm sure Asante will buy the number from him. Afterall, it's not like money is going to be an issue . . .

9:58—I start to daydream. I picture the Saints on defense in a close game. 3rd and about 6 in the 4th quarter and we need a stop. The opponent . . . oh screw being ambiguous . . . let's use this scenario.

We're down by 4 in Tampa Bay late in the year. The winner clinches the division. It's 3rd and 6 and Tampa needs a first down or two in order to run out the clock and preserve victory. Jeff Garcia takes a three step drop and fires into the flat to a wide open Joey Galloway who is just past the first down marker. Right before the ball gets into his hands Asante Samuel blazes through, picks it off, tip toes the sideline, and takes it 65 yards to the house. Ball game. Jim Henderson is going nuts, Saints fans are celebrating a division title, and I'm so pumped up that I punch myself in the face. Repeatedly. Everyone immediately gets on the Internet to start reserving hotel rooms in New Orleans for the first playoff game. If just reading this paragraph doesn't get you fired up, you're not a Saints fan.

10:01—I re-read the previous paragraph. I drink a Heineken to celebrate.

10:05—I realize I can write about this whole thing on my blog. Finally, something to write about. Have you seen how much I've been struggling lately? The last two things I wrote were my ideas that I had kept for when things got slow . . . and I used them both in a span of a few days. If this rumor wouldn't have surfaced you were about 3 or 4 days away from an entry on something like the history of chairs or the Dewey Decimal System.

10:07—I remind myself it's just a rumor . . . it's just a rumor . . . it's just a rumor . . . it's just a rumor . . . it's just a rumor . . . it's just a rumor . . . . . . Then I look at my phone and the 74 incoming text messages, and the nearly completed blog I've written and I think, "Wow. I really overreacted to this. I surely hope it's not just a rumor. Not only for the Saints' sake, but for my sake as well . . ."

Oh well, I guess this is what being a fan is all about. Overreacting and celebrating. Well, here's to both . . . (Finishes Heineken).

Source: Schexnaydre, D. (2008, February 26). Asante Samuel . . . holy crap. *NOLA Sports Report.* Retrieved from http://blog.nola.com/nolasports/2008 /02/asante_samuelholy_crap.html

It's the worst kind of insidious, stupid-creep to have ever infected our profession. Blogging blurs the lines between journalism and pajama-wearing nitwits sitting in their mothers' basements firing off bile-filled opinions. Newspaper editors and managers sit around at meetings and wonder why their circulation is falling and they have themselves to blame for lowering all of us into the foul-smelling muck of the blogworld. (Schultz & Sheffer, 2007, p. 71)

Not all reporters are as reluctant to get involved. A growing number of sports journalists, mostly young and technologically savvy, have used blogs, podcasts, and a host of other new technologies to reach fragmenting audiences. The modern sports reporter realizes that the audience has much more control and choice in terms of accessing content, and while these audiences may or may not be "pajama-wearing nitwits," they cannot be ignored. Good media relations means creating good relationships with audiences by any means necessary (see sidebar).

ANOTHER VIEW OF MODERN SPORTS JOURNALISM

Q&A with Wright Thompson

Wright Thompson is a senior writer for ESPN.com and *ESPN The Magazine*. Prior to joining ESPN, he covered college football for the *New Orleans Times—Picayune* and was a projects reporter for *The Kansas City Star*. He lives with his wife, Sonia, in Oxford, Mississippi, where he spends half the fall Saturdays in Vaught-Hemingway Stadium.

Q: What is the key to creating and maintaining good relations with athletes/coaches/players? Is getting access a problem for you?

A: Access is always a problem and it seems to get worse every year. I suppose the only way to assure access would be to never say anything bad, but obviously that doesn't work. You have to realize that they aren't your friends. Reporters, and especially beat reporters, can develop a level of trust to the point where when you write something critical the athlete may not like it, but he understands why you did it. Part of the code also says that when you write something bad you have to show up the next day and allow the athlete you criticized to confront you.

Q: How involved are you with your readers in terms of their feedback and interaction?

A: I'm incredibly involved. I read all the e-mails and they go straight to my Blackberry. After a really big story I can get 4,000 e-mails. It helps me relate with readers and I have gotten some good story ideas. But I don't let people second guess my story process and I don't try to guess what America wants to read. Also, you have to realize that the people motivated to respond are often angry and don't represent the views of the majority.

Q: Have these new communication technologies affected the way you write or report?

A: Any means of communication is a reporting tool. Text messaging is great because if I'm in constant communication with someone I can confirm a story and its details without calling that person 600 times. The blog is simply a highly evolved printing press; another delivery mechanism. It hasn't changed the way I write, but some journal-

Wright Thompson

ists feel like they need to change their tone for a blog. They think they need to become funny, pithy, or entertaining. And that's part of the problem. If they can write funny and entertaining they should write funny and entertaining all the time. If your newspaper voice is boring that's a huge problem.

Q: How do you feel about today's print reporters getting more involved with shooting audio and video for a website?

A: I think it's a disaster. Reporters already don't have time to write relevant stories, partly because the guys who run these media outlets look at the writing simply as content. Then when readers get less interested, instead of looking at the problem as reporters not having enough time, they see it as simply needing more content. They don't get it.

Q: You seem to suggest that there is a big problem. Talk more about that.

A: Sports journalism today is based on giving everyone a side to talk, but that's not journalism, it's only transcription. Not everybody deserves a side. Also, we have to remember that anybody who wants to know the basic information about the game probably already knows it because they saw the game on TV. That's why the game story is dead. Instead, we have to give people something in the next day's newspaper they couldn't get watching the game the night before. Give them the inside story, the internal drama, the relationships that help them get a better understanding of what happened. People will read that. On the other hand, if you tell people everything they need to know in the second paragraph, there's no reason to keep reading the story. It's not so much a matter of time, but interesting writing. The idea that people don't have time to read is wrong; people won't spend time to read something boring.

Q: What do you think print sports writing will look like in 10 years? Will it be substantially different?

A: A lot of what you see going on in journalism schools around the country regarding convergence is just a knee-jerk reaction. They're panicking and that's only making things worse. People need to understand the fundamentals, and then they can learn the small stuff. Sports reporting has to be built on the fundamentals of asking questions, digging for information, and getting to the truth. No matter what the delivery system, those fundamentals don't change—ever.

SUMMARY

The print media dominated sports coverage through the 1950s. Periodicals such as *The Sporting News* and *Sports Illustrated*, along with daily coverage in thousands of local newspapers, helped make the print media essential for sports fans and audiences. However, the growth of electronic media, specifically television and now the Internet, has seriously damaged many print media outlets. Many of them are losing money; others have cut budgets or simply shut down. Faced with these challenges, many of the print sports media are turning to new technologies. Newspapers and magazines are getting more involved in online formats and working harder to become more interactive and audience-friendly.

New technologies such as blogs, web pages, and Twitter also bring a new set of issues to the print media in terms of access to players and coaches. While players and coaches can now use these technologies to get their messages out unfiltered, in some ways it's now easier for the print media to contact and interview sports newsmakers. Access becomes extremely difficult during scandals and other crisis situations, and the print sports reporter must find other sources to help tell the story.

Technology is also changing the way the games get reported. Laptops, blogs, Twitter feeds, and text messaging make a print reporter's job easier, but also more varied and time-consuming. Instead of producing just one print story for the magazine or newspaper, today's reporter often has to include video, an additional story for the website, and both an in-game and post-game blog. In addition, the reporter might have to respond to fan comments posted about the story. Thus, the print sports reporter of today is becoming more multimedia oriented.

DISCUSSION QUESTIONS

1. At the beginning of this chapter it was suggested that, like the dinosaurs, the print sports media might be headed for extinction. What is your opinion on that? What are the advantages and disadvantages of a print outlet moving completely online (like the *Christian Science Monitor*)? If the print media are to survive how will they do it? What might they look like in 10 years?

2. Wright Thompson said he sometimes gets 4,000 reader e-mails after a big story. If you were the reporter what would you do with all that response? Would you try to

answer some or just delete them all? Would you even read them all? How involved should reporters be with audiences in terms of feedback and interaction?

3. Some print reporters having to shoot video, audio, and digital pictures for use on the web. Is this a good idea? Does the modern print reporter need these types of multimedia skills or should someone else be responsible? Why or why not? In the future is there going to be such a thing as a "print reporter" who is different from a "broadcast reporter?"

4. To follow up on the previous question, should journalism schools now be training students to be "only" print reporters and/or broadcast reporters, or should they be teaching these multimedia reporting styles? If you were going to teach someone how to be a sports reporter what would be important for that person to know?

SUGGESTED EXERCISES

1. Make arrangements to go with a newspaper reporter to a local game (for a high school game it shouldn't be much of a problem getting permission and you might even get to help out some). Observe how the reporter goes about covering the game. How many stories does he/she need to write? How much time do they have? Do they also have to take pictures or shoot video? If the reporter has a few years of experience you can also ask how this process has changed over the years.

2. Wright Thompson made the point that some reporters write their blogs differently than their newspaper stories. Select a newspaper sportswriter who writes for both a blog and the print version of the paper and compare the writing styles. Do they seem to be different? Should they be? Which version seems to be more interesting and why? What does this mean in terms of communicating with readers?

3. After a big game go to a print outlet's website. Over the course of a few hours see if you can identify the abbreviated story, developed story, and possible sidebar story related to the game. How do these stories differ in terms of style, length, tone, approach, etc.? You might also try to look at two different events on two different levels. For example, how the local newspaper covered a big game compared to *Sports Illustrated*.

4. As a hypothetical example, say the coach of the local high school football team has been suspended by the school for an unspecified violation of school policy. Develop a strategy for getting the access you need to report on the story. How would you try to work through official sources? Unofficial sources?

3

The Broadcast Media

For many years the broadcast media have been the golden geese of sports communication. Radio and television, followed by cable and satellite, dominated the creation and distribution of content, and became the main channels of communication between sport providers and audiences. As a result, they also became exceedingly rich. But as with other media, times are changing for broadcast outlets. They may not be in the same dire straits as newspapers and magazines, but there is no doubt that the broadcast media are going through a period of transition and looking for ways to remain dominant in the new media age.

Before we get further into our discussion we need to clarify some definitions. Satellite and cable outlets are important in the conversation, but they are in essence just different delivery methods. The Internet has also impacted television and radio, but it is technically more of a hybrid medium between print and broadcast. (Further discussions of the Internet and its impact can be found in Chapter 13). So when we speak of the broadcast media we are talking primarily about radio and television. In terms of sport communication, both started as dominant national media before eventually transitioning into a more local emphasis.

RADIO

Radio and television went through similar evolutionary phases related to sport communication, especially in their early years. The first radio sports broadcast took place on July 2, 1921, and involved a heavyweight boxing match arranged by RCA founder David Sarnoff as a way to promote radio. Later that same year, the World Series went on radio for the first time and again, Sarnoff played a leading role. Recognizing that the new medium needed programming, Sarnoff made baseball one of the cornerstones of the industry. "We had to have baseball in order to sell enough sets to go on to other programming," he later wrote (as cited in Schultz, 2005, p. 173). By the end of the 1920s, Cubs owner William Wrigley had his team's games on *five* different stations and reportedly said, "The more outlets the better; we'll tie up the entire city" (Hilmes, 1997).

Live sports programming helped radio become a rich and powerful mass medium through the 1930s and '40s. Network links carried the events to every corner of America, which provided advertisers with the mass audiences they needed to make radio extremely profitable. By 1935 CBS, NBC, and Mutual were all broadcasting baseball on a national basis. In 1937, rights to broadcast the World Series on radio were worth $100,000; in 1949, Gillette signed a seven-year, $1 million deal to become the exclusive radio sponsor of the World Series and All-Star games ("*Broadcasting*," 1949).

But that was the high-water mark for network radio sports. By the 1950s television had successfully shown that it had the technology to broadcast live sports and could attract enough audience to interest advertisers. (Ironically, a demonstration of television's viability was provided by Gillette, whose sponsorship of a televised boxing match in 1946 reached 100,000 viewers in just four cities). By 1958, television had far surpassed radio in terms of advertising revenue (see Table 3.1).

To survive, radio turned to local sports and the talk format. While networks still carry some big events (like the Super Bowl and World Series) the main attraction of radio today is its localism. For the most part, radio is the only place local audiences can get live game broadcasts of area high schools, and the radio broadcast is still a powerful force in many communities. However, even this is starting to change. ESPN and Fox Network have started offering television coverage of high school games and athletes on a limited basis, and improvements in technology are now allowing small cable companies and local television channels to produce and broadcast high school games on their own.

Westwood One is the major network carrier of live sports programming and its events include the Super Bowl, other NFL games, and several NCAA sports. But in a sense, satellite radio has replaced over-the-air networks in terms of carrying major sporting events. The merged XM-Sirius satellite radio company gives listeners access to NFL, MLB, NBA, NHL, and NCAA games, along with several sports talk shows. Of course, the major difference is that satellite listeners must pay a subscription fee to access the service (see Table 3.2).

Table 3.1. Advertising Money Spent for Television and Radio in Millions of Dollars, 1949–1956

Year	Radio	Television
1949	571	58
1950	605	171
1951	606	332
1952	624	454
1953	611	606
1954	559	809
1955	545	1,035
1956	567	1,225

Source: Robert J. Coen, McCann-Erickson, Inc. (as cited in Sterling, 1984).

Table 3.2. The Growing World of Satellite Sports Radio

The merger of satellite radio companies XM and Sirius in 2008 created a sports radio powerhouse. The following list is a sampling of the offerings available via satellite in March 2009. In the fall, the list would include live broadcasts of NFL games.

Offering	Description	Channel Number
Sports XM Scoreboard	Schedules, scores and updates	95
Calendrier Sportif	Schedules, scores, updated (French)	97
Best of Sirius Sports Play-by-Play	Play-by-play of various games	102–114
Best of NFL Radio	24/7 NFL Talk	124
Best of Sirius NASCAR	24/7 NASCAR	128
ESPN Radio	Sports Talk	140
ESPN Xtra	Sports News	141
Fox Sports Radio	Sports Talk	142
Sirius XM Sports Nation	College Sports Talk	143
Mad Dog Radio	Chris Russo Talk	144
IndyCar Series Racing	IndyCar Series Racing	145
PGA Tour Network	Golf Talk	146
XM Deportivo	Spanish Sports Talk	147
MLB Play-by-Play (Spanish)	Spanish MLB game action	174
MLB Home Plate	24/7 MLB coverage	175
MLB Play-by-Play	MLB game action	176–189
Sports live game action	Atlantic Coast Conference	190–192
Sports live game action	Pac-10 Conference	193–195
Sports live game action	Big 10 Conference	196–198
Sports live game action	SEC	199–201
Sports live game action	Big East Conference	203
NHL Home Ice	NHL Talk	204
NHL live game action	Play-by-Play	205–209
Sports live game action	Big XII Conference	231
NBA live game action	NBA Play-by-Play	232–236
Various live game action	Play-by-Play	237–246

Source: XM Channel Lineup, March 10, 2009. Retrieved from http://www.xmradio.com/onxm/full-channel-listing.xmc

Table 3.2 also shows how modern sports radio caters to fragmented audiences. It's not just the delivery system that has changed; the audience has changed from one of mass interests to more specialized niche audiences based on type of sport, preference of format (play-by-play or talk), and language.

The other major force in modern sports radio is the talk format. The format itself is extremely simple and inexpensive: a host (or more than one) talks about the sports issues of the day and encourages listeners to call in to share their opinions. Sometimes people call in to vent their frustrations, comment on a certain topic, or just make sure their voice is being heard. Radio was the original interactive broadcast sports medium and sports talk is still an important way for stations to maintain loyal audiences. "I think the biggest thing to remember about local sports talk radio, is that local is what works," says veteran sports talk show host Mike Gastineau of KJR-AM in Seattle. "I can go on this afternoon and talk ad nauseum about what is going on nationally, but I've got to somehow relate it to the people here in Seattle. That's a key, finding the local angle that will provoke calls" ("Sports talk," 1999).

Radio coverage of live events is now also available via the Internet and satellite radio.
(Courtesy of Dale Sparks/*The Dominion Post*)

ESPN, Fox Sports Radio, and Sporting News Radio (SNR) have become the dominant providers of national talk radio. In 2009, SNR had 425 station affiliates reaching 13 million listeners in North America and the Caribbean ("Sporting News," 2009); ESPN and Fox had similarly large networks. As with much of radio, many of these talk shows have moved on to the Internet (via live streaming) or to satellite. Mike Francesa and Chris Russo dominated the tough New York sports talk market for nearly 20 years on WFAN, but in 2008 Russo left for his own show on XM-Sirius.

As with newspapers, the growth of new technologies has led some media analysts to predict the demise of local radio. In a sports sense, many of the functions of sports radio (including the talk format and live play-by-play) are now available to audiences on the Internet or on satellite. Even the mainstay of local radio—coverage of local teams and athletes—is being threatened by the ability of audiences to use technologies and provide the content themselves. Thus, local sports radio is very much at a crossroads and its future remains unclear.

TELEVISION

National Level

Fans may be able to call into their local radio station and talk sports for hours. They may also be able to see live streaming of sports on the Internet or take part in the web's many live sports chats or blogs. The newspaper also comes to the front door every day with detailed sports stories, features, and pictures. But none of these media have dominated the sports communication process like television. Television is still the unquestioned and unchallenged leader in terms of delivering sports content to audiences, both big and small. "Sports makes compelling TV and provides great storytelling for producers in the non-scripted side of the business," said Bob Horowitz, president of Juma Entertainment, which produces sports content. "When you have authentic, real competition like the Olympics, it can result in unbelievable numbers. Best of all, sports is TiVo-proof—you can't DVR sports" (Pursell, 2008).

The first telecast of a Major League Baseball game occurred on August 26, 1939, but featured only two cameras. Reception was fairly poor, but hardly anyone seemed to notice—only about 400 sets existed in New York to pick up the signal. The *New York Times* noted, "Television set owners as far away as 50 miles viewed the action" between the Reds and Dodgers from Brooklyn ("Ebbetts Field," 2001). Other sports programming suffered similar handicaps. Pro football also televised its first game in 1939, which consisted mostly of fuzzy camera shots of the player with the ball. Cameramen were frequently faked out, and on several occasions announcers had to invent intricate lateral passes to explain why the home viewer could not see the ball. Coverage slowly improved, but even by 1948 in a broadcast of the college football game between Oklahoma and Texas on WBAP-TV, the bands that performed at halftime had to stay in between the 35-yard lines so as to remain in range of primitive cameras.

Initially, the cost of a television set was too much for the average American family and most sports were watched at the local tavern. Boxing and wrestling predominated during this early period, not only because they appealed to the blue-collar tavern crowd, but because the action could fit neatly onto the television screen and be covered with only one or two cameras. By the mid-1950s television technology had improved, the cost of the sets had come down, and television quickly made its way from the tavern to the home. Sports played a major role in the growth of television, particularly the NFL Championship game of 1958, in which the Baltimore Colts beat the New York Giants in overtime. "I still think the biggest game we ever had was the Colts' win over the Giants," said former NFL Commissioner Pete Rozelle. "I think that was the first game that got television coverage across America. It reached fans who had never seen pro football before" ("Tint of," 1994).

Television sports exploded throughout the 1960s, as the three major television networks—ABC, CBS, and NBC—dramatically increased their production and distribution of live sports content. The networks jockeyed with each other for exclusive broadcast rights for popular events such as the Olympics, NFL, MLB, and the NBA (CBS was the first network to broadcast the Olympics in the US, but the rights eventually passed to ABC and now NBC). The competition dramatically increased the amount of sports on television and the rights fees to broadcast those events (see Table 3.3). Network competition helped increase the value of television rights fees, but the Sports Broadcasting Act of 1961 (SBA) also played a vital role. Up until that time teams were required by anti-trust law to individually negotiate their own television rights deals. The Act removed the anti-trust restriction and allowed leagues to negotiate as a whole on behalf of their member teams (and distribute the money equally in a revenue-sharing plan). The NFL was the driving force behind passage of the SBA and today has one of the richest rights-fees packages among all sports leagues. The average yearly NFL rights of $3.7 billion is more than the yearly average of the television rights of the NBA, MLB, NASCAR, NHL, PGA, NCAA basketball, and Summer Olympics *combined*.

Table 3.3. NFL Rights Fees

Total Value of Rights Deal	Network(s)^	Years	Runs Through
$11 billion	CBS and Fox	6	2011
$4 billion	DirecTV[#]	4	2014
$1.1 billion	ABC/ESPN*	8	2013
$600 million	NBC[@]	6	2011

^ Does not include the eight regular-season games carried annually on the NFL Network, which is owned by the NFL and does not pay rights fees

Sunday Ticket subscription package

* Monday Night Football package (ESPN spends $2.2 billion per year for all sports rights fees)

@ Sunday Night Football package

Sources: Gorman, 2009; King, 2009; Consoli, 2005; Stewart, 2004

Televised sports content was controlled by ABC, CBS, and NBC until more competition came along in the 1970s. Ted Turner's WTBS began distributing Atlanta Braves games through national cable, and suddenly the networks began to lose their power. More content providers emerged, and in the late 1980s media mogul Rupert Murdoch attempted to create a fourth national network. One of the keys to the eventual success of the Fox Broadcasting Company was its acquisition of NFL television rights in 1993. Fox outbid CBS for the rights to televise National Conference games, spending $1.6 billion for four years. "Having NFL football really made us a network," Murdoch said (Sandomir, 1997); in 1998 CBS got back in the game with an eight-year, $4 billion deal to televise American Conference games (Stewart, 1998).

Today, there are more content providers than ever before and more people watching. The worldwide viewership for the Summer Olympics continues to grow—3.6 billion for Sydney in 2000, 3.9 billion for Athens in 2004, and 4.7 billion for Beijing in 2008 (Bialik, 2008; Bryant & Holt, 2006). The numbers for the World Cup soccer tournament are even more staggering. The 2006 event was showcased over 73,000 hours and 376 channels, reaching a cumulative audience of more than 26 billion ("2006 FIFA," 2007). "The only thing that seems not to be dropping off these days is sports viewership," says Lee Berke, a sports media consultant. "You have increasing competition for a finite set of properties and that is going to squeeze margins" (Gorman, 2009).

The Olympics, World Cup, and Super Bowl can still draw enormous audiences (see Table 3.4), but while these megaevents continue to see their viewing audiences increase,

Rank	Show	Date	Total number of viewers (in millions)^
Table 3.4. The Most Watched Programs in U.S. Television History			
1	Super Bowl XLIV New Orleans—Indianapolis	2-7-2010	106.5
2	Super Bowl XLIII Pittsburgh—Arizona	2-1-2009	98.7
3	Super Bowl XLII New York—New England	2-3-2008	97.5
4	Super Bowl XLI Indianapolis—Chicago	2-4-2007	93.2
5	Super Bowl XL Pittsburgh—Seattle	2-5-2006	90.7

^ Average viewership is a measure of how many people watch over a certain period of time. Super Bowl XLIV eclipsed the previous record of 105.97 million viewers set in 1983 by the final episode of M∗A∗S∗H.

Source: Nielsen Media.

they are the exceptions. Ratings for most individual events continue to decrease due to an increase in competition—in a multi-channel media universe there are too many other competing programs that draw away interest. So while there may be more people watching, for the most part the viewers have splintered into smaller, niche audiences, which has several consequences for content providers. In addition, the content providers haven't done themselves any favors by scheduling night games that often don't end until the majority of viewers have gone to bed. "Ratings are smaller than ever, and the sports world is the exaggerated tip of it," said advertising media officer Peter Gardiner (Sandomir, 2003).

Today's sporting events need compelling storylines and interesting personalities to get people to watch (such as with swimmer Michael Phelps in the 2008 Summer Olympics). Unfortunately, the World Series hasn't had either in recent years, and in 2008 its ratings were the worst in history (see Table 3.5). But it's important to remember that the other sports have all suffered similarly, including the NCAA basketball tournament, the NBA Finals, and even NASCAR, which saw double-digit ratings declines for the first part of 2009 (Humphrey, 2009). As a result of declining ratings, content providers have a much more difficult time making money from advertising. The audiences are smaller and advertisers have a difficult time recouping their investment, which means they spend less. In the 2000s, NBC dropped both its NBA and MLB packages in part because they were costing the network $400 million per year. NBC Sports president Ken Schanzer said at the time, "At the end of the day, our company is going to be hundreds and hundreds of millions of dollars better off for having done this and our competition hundreds and hundreds of millions worse" ("Lights out," 2001). Even though NBC decided to get back into the NFL, the network is losing money on its $600 million contract; ESPN and ABC will lose around $350 million on their current $1.1 billion NFL contract (Consoli, 2005).

Table 3.5. Down, Down, Down			
Year	World Series teams	Rating*	Share#
1968	Detroit—St. Louis	22.8	57
1978	New York—Los Angeles	32.8	56
1988	Los Angeles—Oakland	23.9	39
1998	New York—San Diego	14.1	24
2008	Philadelphia—Tampa	8.4	14
* Rating refers to the percentage of all television sets watching			
# Share refers to the percentage of sets turned on and watching at that time			
Source: World Series ratings (2008)			

Table 3.6. Niche Sports Networks, 2009

Sports leagues still receive big money from broadcast networks for the rights to show live events, but there is additional revenue available through cable and satellite outlets. Not only do most professional leagues have subscription/pay-per-view offerings, but they have also created specific channels to showcase their sports to cable and satellite audiences, primarily through live programming, historical content, and studio shows. Channels have also been created by individual teams (such as the New York Yankees with YES Network and the New York Mets with SportsNet New York), college conferences (the Big Ten Network), and now even individual schools. In 2008, the University of Texas announced plans to create a 24/7 Longhorn Sports Network, the first for college sports on television (Lowry, 2008).

An important issue is whether these channels appear on "basic" cable/satellite service (such as MLB Network and the Big Ten Network) or whether they appear on a "premium" tier that requires the customer to pay an additional fee for access (such as Tennis Channel, NBA TV, and NHL Network). Those channels appearing on basic tiers have more subscribers but don't receive the additional subscription revenue. The NFL Network and Comcast Cable wrangled over this issue for three years, a fight that started when Comcast moved the network from a tier that had 8 million subscribers to a tier that cost an additional $8 per month and had only 2 million subscribers. The NFL sued Comcast, but the two sides finally came to terms in 2009, signing a 10-year contract that puts the NFL Network on a Comcast package that reaches 10 million subscribers ("NFL, Comcast," 2009).

Network or Channel	Debut	Owned by	Subscribers (in millions of homes)*
Golf Channel	1995	Comcast Cable	81
SPEED Channel	1996	News Corp. (Fox)	78
MLB Network	2009	MLB (67%) and various cable/ satellite companies (33%)	50[#]
NFL Network	2003	NFL	42[+]
Big Ten Network	2007	Big Ten Conference (51%) and Fox networks (49%)	30–35
Tennis Channel	2003	Independent	25
NBA TV	1999	NBA, but leased to Turner Sports	15
NHL Network	2007	NHL/Comcast	12.2[^]

* as of 2009

The January 2009 debut of MLB TV into 50 million homes was the largest launch for a cable channel in U.S. television history

+ Does not reflect new subscribers under the 2009 Comcast agreement

^ Does not reflect the audience for the Canadian version of NHL Network, which has been on the air since 2001

Sources: Various

In response, content providers have turned to alternative revenue sources, including cable and satellite outlets. ABC picked up NBC's NBA contract in 2002, but the league also cut a six-year deal with cable channels ESPN and TNT. The move put several of the league's marquee events, including the All-Star game, on cable-only outlets. The NBA, NFL, MLB, and NHL also created their own channels that are available only to cable or satellite subscribers (see Table 3.6). The leagues make money through advertising and fees paid by cable and satellite companies to carry the programming. There is also additional money available through the Internet and specifically live streaming of events. CBS has had tremendous success with its "March Madness on Demand" streaming of NCAA Tournament basketball (see Chapter 1). In 2008, the NFL began an experiment to stream Sunday Night Football games live online. "The NFL's most important constituency has been the television networks, but the world is moving online," said Bobby Tulsiani, an analyst at market research firm JupiterResearch. "They haven't wanted people to watch games online because that could mess up their television deals. . . . This is going to get interesting as they move forward" (James, 2008).

Each of the niche sports channels listed in Table 3.6 also has an Internet site. That means the content provider is making money through broadcast network rights fees, advertising (for broadcast, cable/satellite, and Internet), and carriage fees from cable/satellite distributors that carry the channel (e.g., the Big Ten Network makes between 70 and 80 cents per subscriber, while the NBA makes 38 cents per subscriber for NBA TV; because DirecTV has a stake in the MLB Network there are no carriage fees charged) ("Comcast," 2008). Add in money for subscription/pay-per-view packages like NFL's "Sunday Ticket" and you can see how content providers are taking advantage of new media technologies.

The creation of these channels and Internet sites not only means more money, it means that teams, leagues, and even individual athletes can more directly control the flow of information in the sport communication process. It could also suggest significant consequences for the traditional broadcast outlets—television and radio—which now find themselves in uncharted territory. In a sports sense, the main function of national television and radio outlets is the distribution of popular content to audiences. That will change when one of two things happen: 1) the content becomes too expensive to distribute or 2) technology makes it possible to distribute the content in a different, better way.

It has already been noted how expensive broadcast rights fees have become and how many networks are losing money on their deals. Yet, the system still works because there is no other efficient way for content to reach large audiences. As technology continues to develop it may be that some more efficient system will emerge, as we're starting to see with Internet streaming, niche channels, and pay-per-view. If some new system emerges the role of the national broadcast sports media will change drastically.

Local Level

While the national broadcast sports media go through a time of great uncertainty, the situation is even more drastic for local television broadcasters. The same forces affecting the national media are also at work on the local level, but local broadcasters do not have the same revenue opportunities. In addition, the national media are also taking over many of the functions of the local broadcasters. Thus, there is a serious concern that local sports television may not survive, at least in its present form.

When we speak about sports television at the local level we're talking about two main functions—live production of local sports and regularly scheduled broadcasts of sports within the local newscast. Both functions are in danger; national media and even audience members are starting to take over production and distribution of local sports content, while economic conditions have seriously threatened the role of sports within the local newscast.

In Chapter 2 we talked in some detail about the distressing financial picture for the print media and the situation is somewhat similar for local broadcasters. In 2008, television newsrooms across the country lost about 360 positions and 2009 was not much better. "2009 (was) a tough year," said Bob Papper of Hofstra University and author of the TV news staffing survey. "However, many stations have little room to do any more cutting unless they cut newscasts. That's hard to envision given more than 40 percent of local station revenue is derived from local news. At some point, cut backs become suicide" ("TV newsrooms," 2008).

Rather than suicide, many stations are restructuring, streamlining, and combining operations. In 2009, stations in Syracuse, New York and Peoria, Illinois, announced plans to stop producing local news. Stations WTVH in Syracuse and WHOI in Peoria had both broadcast locally since the 1950s, but fell victim to rising costs, a poor economy, and low ratings. The stations merged with competitors in their own markets at a cost of about 70 jobs ("TV news," 2009). The moves reflected the troubled times for the broadcast industry; Young Broadcasting filed for bankruptcy in February 2009, while station groups Nexstar, Gray, Allbritton, Barrington, Newport, and Ion Media were all in serious financial trouble (Colman, 2009).

Such conditions have endangered the position of sports within local television newscasts. Almost from the very beginning, local television news usually included sports and weather. In 1961, for example, WKMG started the first full-time news department in Orlando and the newscast included a sports report by Frank Vaught ("The history of," 2003). But in the past decade or so, television managers and consultants have started to rethink how a sports segment fits into a local newscast. For one thing, research shows that the average local news viewer does not care that much for sports. A survey by the Radio and Television News Directors Foundation indicated that only 31% of viewers said they were "very interested" in the sports segment, while 32% said they were "somewhat interested" ("Journalism and ethics," 1998). But 72% expressed an interest in the weather. "Sports is extremely polarizing," said television news consultant Brent Magid. "The majority can either take it or leave it, or despise it" (Greppi, 2002).

Around 2000, many stations started taking new approaches to their sports segments. In some cases, that meant reducing the amount of time allotted for sports. Depending on the day of the week (weekends get more sports time), sports segments have traditionally received anywhere from three to five minutes of the local newscast. Now that

Economic hardships have forced some local TV stations to alter the way in which they provide coverage of sports on nightly newscasts. (Courtesy of George Mason Athletics/ John Aronson)

number has dropped to as little as a minute. In 2002, KDKA in Pittsburgh reduced its time commitment to only three and a half minutes of sports for its three hours of news. Other approaches included making sports more viewer-friendly and appealing to different demographic groups. On the national level, almost all research (Gantz & Wenner, 1991; Perse, 1992) suggests that men have a much greater interest in television sports and watch more of it. By making the local sports presentation more appealing to the casual fan, stations hoped to increase viewership, ratings, and revenue. "What we're trying to do now is treat sports more as news," said former KDKA news director Al Blinke. "We want to do the stuff that transcends sports" (Finder, 2002).

The most drastic approach of all has been to simply pull the plug on local sports and remove it from the newscast. Dozens of stations across the country have gone down this road, including stations in such large markets as Tampa, Las Vegas, and Norfolk, Virginia. "Whether it's medical or education or crime or government or Michael Vick, all news has to earn its way into the newscast," said Shane Moreland, news director at WTKR in Norfolk in 2007 when the station dropped sports from its nightly newscasts. "There's no longer going to be a segment where you just give someone three minutes. Time is too valuable to give it to somebody and say, 'Whatever you can come up with, put it in there'" (Holtzclaw, 2007). When WTSP in Tampa dropped sports from both of its early evening newscasts in 2000, then-news director Jim Church noted, "Telling a story when nobody's listening is not a good use of air time" (Deggans, 2000).

Those stations that have maintained a local sports presence continue to search for ways to make the sports content more relevant to audiences. First and foremost, this means emphasizing local athletes, teams, and organizations. Before the days of ESPN and the Internet, local sports broadcasters used to include many national highlights and scores. But all of that information is now easily accessible and audiences that tune into local sportscasts have probably already seen it. Thus, the emphasis today for local sportscasts is *localism.* "I haven't broken it down to say sports is running the audience off," said Ron Comings of KLAS in Las Vegas, "but some local sportscasters haven't adapted to the change in the media environment and turned enough attention to local sports, which won't be seen anywhere else" (Bornfeld, 2009).

Beyond localism, stations are also looking at ways to connect more closely to audiences. This is especially important in an age where the sports consumer has multiple viewing choices and can take more of an active role in the communication process. Local television is reaching out to these audiences through blogging, twittering, and other interactive strategies that give the consumer a more direct stake in how sports content is created and distributed (see "Local Sports and New Technologies" sidebar).

LOCAL SPORTS AND NEW TECHNOLOGIES

Q&A with C.J. Hoyt

C.J. Hoyt

One station that is trying to make sports more relevant to its local audience is WFIE in Evansville, Indiana (http://www.14wfie.com/). News director C.J. Hoyt discusses how the station is emphasizing new technologies in this process. Hoyt has also served as the news director at KLFY in Lafayette, Louisiana, and has worked in TV newsrooms in Knoxville, Tennessee; Greenville, South Carolina; and Lincoln, Nebraska. Hoyt graduated in 1998 from the S.I. Newhouse School of Public Communications at Syracuse University.

Q: What emphasis are you (organizationally) putting on new technologies like Twitter, blogging, and the like related to communicating with audiences? Why?

A: More than ever, we are living in a get-it-now society. Our viewers are no longer interested in waiting until 6 p.m. to get the news of the day. It's why news websites have become so popular and one reason why traditional mediums like newspapers are failing. New technologies like Twitter, blogging, and Facebook are an extension of what we're already doing online. Plus, these methods give us the added advantage of connecting with viewers on a personal level. That builds loyalty and can often generate great story leads. Stations that ignore these tools are going to be left behind.

Q: Do you feel like this changes the nature of news or news reporting? Are your reporters doing things differently in terms of the way they gather, edit, and create the news?

A: So far, it hasn't changed the nature of news or news reporting in any major way. Twitter has been around for years, but the media just now seems to be catching on. It's the latest, greatest trend and the value of these tools still isn't known. What the tools are doing is giving us an additional way to get feedback and communicate directly with viewers. In the short time we've been using Twitter we've developed sources for stories and also broken news on Twitter before we break it anywhere else. While not earth-shattering changes, it shows the potential for these tools.

Q: With this type of micro journalism are we losing the "mass" of mass communication? Is that a good thing or a bad thing?

A: I suppose we're losing the "mass" of mass communication, but I certainly wouldn't say that's a bad thing. Too many journalists hold the belief that journalism should be left to the "professionals" as though working for a newspaper or a television station makes us better able to talk about what's happening in the world around us. That's just not the case. Today, anyone with a smart phone has every tool needed to tell a story. Video, sound, pictures, words . . . all at their fingertips. And the more people out there telling stories, the more likely we are to get a complete picture of the story.

Q: Do you feel like the need to connect to audiences is more pronounced for sports because of the attachment fans have to their teams and players?

A: That's probably the case. I'm a huge sports fan myself and I'm constantly staying in touch with my favorite teams through blogs and websites. Living as far from home (Pennsylvania) as I am could make it hard to keep up. Now I have satellite radio and live web broadcasts. The same is true for a local sports department. High school football and basketball are huge. And using things like Twitter give us a chance to connect with all of those fans in real time.

Q: Do you have any specific examples as to how you feel this has helped your sports coverage?

A: I don't think we've used it as much in our sports coverage as we could. As part of our efforts to make our high school coverage more interactive, we're going to want our viewers to become part of our coverage. We'll want them to shoot their own video and pictures and send them to us. We'll want them to use Twitter to get us score updates during basketball or football games. We could conceivably use the power of tools like Twitter and YouTube to deploy dozens of sports reporters to every high school basketball and football game in the Tri-State.

Q: How have your sports reporters and anchors reacted to the direction your station is taking?

A: The sports department, and the station as a whole, has been very receptive to these new initiatives. We all understand that the journalism business is changing and if you don't change with it, you'll be lost. From weather, to news, to sports, we're constantly seeking new ways to reach out and connect with our audience. We want them to be a part of the process. Thankfully, this newsroom understands that.

Q: Does this seem to be the future of broadcast news, at least in the short term? Where do you see this going in 10 years?

A: That's the toughest question. Twitter wouldn't be the first fad to come and go. That doesn't mean, however, that these trends should be ignored. What technology is doing is changing the way we all work. Ten years ago, you had a reporter and a photographer working together on a story before editing it together on massive tape decks. Now, traditional reporter crews are becoming outnumbered by "video journalists," a reporter with a light, digital camera and a computer for editing. The age of digital video means anyone with a camera and a computer can become a reporter. That's the future of journalism—taking advantage of the citizen journalist. Twitter, Facebook, YouTube, and the next big thing will all continue to bridge the gap between the "professional" journalist and the "amateur." In 10 years, we may not be able to tell the difference anymore.

— o — o —

The second great challenge for local sports content providers is event production, either live or on tape delay. Even with today's newer, smaller equipment, producing a televised event is not an easy job. For example, a typical Super Bowl production now includes about 25 pedestal cameras, six hand-held cameras, two remote control cameras, and another camera on the blimp. The production list also includes around 75 monitors, 30 video tape recorders (VTRs), 60 microphones, 20 miles of cable, 35 production trucks, and a crew of more than 300 (Schultz, 2005). Obviously, local productions don't use all that equipment, but they still require more equipment and more manpower than what

Productions of high school sports by local TV stations may be effected by alternative production and distribution avenues made available through the growth of the Internet. (Courtesy of Stock.xchng)

goes into a studio show. Even a relatively small production like the local high school football game will require two cameras, a switcher, microphones, cables, and perhaps some sort of microwave or satellite relay. Necessary personnel would include at least two camera operators, a director, producer, audio person, graphics person, engineer, and the play-by-play or color analyst (see Table 3.7).

The production of local high school and college games by WTLW in Lima, Ohio, has been extremely popular over the years, primarily because it showcases teams and

Table 3.7. Local Game Production

Television stations all across the country produce and air games involving local schools. WTLW in Lima, Ohio, has one of the most ambitious production schedules of any station, producing and airing more than 30 basketball, volleyball, and wrestling events to its audience in northwest Ohio. What makes the schedule even more remarkable is that WTLW is a small religious station in the 185th market and has a production staff of less than a dozen people. As an independent station, WTLW has the schedule flexibility to air these games that a local network affiliate that is obligated to carry network programming may not have. Some games were shown live and others on tape delay.

Date	Event	Date	Event
3/11/2009	Liberty Benton vs. Coldwater	1/24/2009	New Knoxville at Shawnee
3/11/2009	Spencerville vs. Ottawa—Glandorf	1/23/2009	Delphos Jefferson vs. Spencerville
3/10/2009	Delphos Jefferson vs. Pandora—Gilboa	1/17/2009	Mt. Vernon vs. UNOH ~ Men's
3/10/2009	Delphos St. Johns vs. Kalida	1/17/2009	Mt. Vernon vs. UNOH ~ Women's
3/7/2009	Crestview vs. Delphos St. Johns	1/10/2009	Elida at Liberty Benton
3/6/2009	Celina vs. Bath	1/9/2009	Ottawa—Glandorf vs. Kenton
3/6/2009	Elida vs. Shawnee	1/3/2009	Shawnee vs. Bluffton
3/3/2009	LCC vs. Marion Local	12/27/2008	Ada vs. New Knoxville
3/3/2009	Parkway vs. Spencerville	12/20/2008	Allen County Wrestling Tournament
2/27/2009	Shawnee vs. Ottawa—Glandorf	12/13/2008	Ada vs. Pandora—Gilboa
2/21/2009	Allen County Wrestling Sectionals	12/12/2008	Marion Local vs. Ottoville
2/20/2009	Ft. Recovery vs. Delphos St. Johns	12/6/2008	Van Wert vs. Lincolnview
2/13/2009	St. Henry vs. Coldwater	12/6/2008	Wayne Trace vs. Crestview
2/8/2009	Liberty Benton at Pandora—Gilboa	12/5/2008	Bath vs. LCC
2/7/2009	Columbus Grove at Continental	12/5/2008	Elida vs. Shawnee
2/3/2009	Ohio Dominican vs. UNOH	11/29/2008	Ottoville vs. Van Wert—Girls
1/31/2009	LCC at Lima Sr.	11/29/2008	Wayne Trace vs. Crestview—Girls
1/30/2009	Kenton vs. Celina	9/18/2008	UNOH vs. Mt. Vernon Volleyball

Source: WTLW-TV (http://www.wtlw.com)

athletes that normally wouldn't get televised exposure anywhere else. But as we've already noted in Chapter 1, new technologies are allowing sports audiences to create and distribute their own programming, which threatens the traditional content providers. An example is a company called Prep Sports Online, which solicits content from member high schools in exchange for website construction, maintenance, and funding. As of 2009, PSO had 121 schools across the country streaming video and images on the web ("PSO schools," 2009). Of the scores of Internet sites dedicated to high school athletics, MaxPreps may be the biggest. It uses a staff of 500 photographers and 40 sports videographers to distribute articles, photographs, video, and rankings. MaxPreps has 10 million pages of content and claims more than 2.5 million visitors each month ("About MaxPreps," 2009). Sites and companies like these present a strong challenge to local broadcast outlets in that they provide direct competition for audiences.

All of this is part of a growing online trend of sports production and distribution, especially for younger viewers. While younger audiences consistently turn away from traditional nightly newscasts on local television, they are turning to participatory formats like YouTube, Current, and CNN's I-Report. Online consumption of video material rose 66% between 2007 and 2008, and YouTube owned a third of the 10 billion online video views in February 2008. That compared to CNN.com's 133 million views or 1.3% (Nakashima, 2008). As just one example of how sports content can catch fire online, consider the now infamous rant by Oklahoma State football coach Mike Gundy in September 2007 ("I'm a man," Gundy shouted at a reporter at a post-game news conference. "I'm 40!"). As of 2010, at least five different versions of the rant had appeared on YouTube with a total of more than 1.6 million combined hits. "Somebody told me I ended up sixth overall on YouTube in total hits (that) year," Gundy said. "That's pretty good" (George, 2008).

Papper (2006) reported that not only are younger audiences increasingly turning to online news sources, but regardless of age, more than 40% of the public has an interest in creating its own newscast and more than 60% want more interaction with television news. "Are our younger audiences drifting away from the television as the centerpiece of their experience? Absolutely," said British Broadcast Corporation platform executive Troy (only one name). "If we don't respond to the need to make ourselves relevant and accessible in new and convenient ways, we risk losing our relevance" (Nakashima, 2008). Local television outlets have certainly taken notice. The CBS affiliate WNEM in Flint, Michigan, recently increased its amount of online offerings, resulting in 1.5 million unique visitors. At the same time, WRAL-TV in Raleigh, North Carolina, quadrupled its online offerings, which led to a 40% growth in site traffic and 2 million unique visitors (Barnes & Steele, 2008).

The Fan Media Network (www.fanmedianetwork.com) is a good example of how the sports media may be shifting to these new online platforms. Fan Media Network began in 2008 as "an independent news & entertainment media company that gives sports fans tools to cover their sports teams" ("CTO for," 2007). The site actively solicits content related to college and professional sports, although for copyright reasons the material has to be related to fan activity and not network video. Contributors are told that they can "watch fan video reports from other cities, get discovered, or help discover new talent [and] change the way sports media is generated and consumed" ("Sports reporters," 2008). CEO and founder Kirk Berridge said the company had nearly 500 regular contributors as of 2009.

In terms of live event production it seems unlikely that the average sports consumer would be able to produce something that would be able to seriously compete for either large audiences or advertising dollars. But such an analysis misses the point entirely. The people shooting these events and posting them online to YouTube, Fan Media Network, Prep Sports Online, or some other outlet aren't necessarily interested in making money; research (Schultz & Sheffer, 2009) has shown that these "citizen journalists" are far more interested in making themselves heard and sharing their work with others. The technology already exists for them to create very specific sports programming that could potentially reach an audience of millions, but may interest only a few hundred, such as a local high school game. But if those few hundred watch on YouTube rather than the local television channel that could spell trouble for the established media.

The answer may be some sort of partnership between the broadcast media and motivated fans, especially if local stations can get audience members to contribute the material to the station website instead of somewhere else. This would be an arrangement similar to the freelancer or stringer arrangement that newspapers have successfully used for a long time; the person contributing the content would get a nominal fee and the station would have more content (although typically at lower quality) for its local audiences. Because of the cost savings benefits it's not out of the question that one day a station could depend entirely on citizen sports journalists for all of its content. That may seem a bit far-fetched, but in the new media environment all the old rules are slowly being rewritten.

SUMMARY

In terms of media relations and the sport communication process, what do all these changes mean for the broadcast media?

- **Although still dominant, the role of the broadcast sports media is changing.** From their traditional role as one-way content provider and distributor, television and radio must now become more interactive and consumer-friendly, especially if they hope to attract newer, younger audiences. These are not your grandfather's media anymore. He may have grown up listening to the game on the radio or more likely watching it on television, but today's younger audiences have found newer ways to experience mediated sports. Simply producing and distributing the content in hopes that large audiences will watch doesn't always work in today's media environment. The older media must accommodate and incorporate these newer media as a means of attracting new audiences and involving them in the communication process.
- **The broadcast sports media must change because technology is changing the way people communicate.** Media theorist Marshall McLuhan believed in a tech-

nological determinism in which each new media technology fundamentally changed cultural practices. According to McLuhan (as cited in Griffin, 1997), "Family life, the workplace, schools, health care, friendship, religious worship, recreation, politics—nothing remains untouched by communication technology." Are blogging and Twitter merely fads or do they hold the potential to fundamentally alter our cultural practices? In some cases, overuse may be an issue. During the height of the Twitter craze *Sports Illustrated's* Cory McCartney (2009) noted, "Everyone is tweeting . . . but just because some coaches are showing how hip they are by opening a Twitter account doesn't mean *every coach* should be living life 140 characters at a time. West Virginia's Bill Stewart set the hip factor back decades with this tweet: 'Driving at 4:15 a.m., I was listening to *Little Deuce Coupe* by the Beach Boys. Talk about getting pumped up early in the morning.' Thanks, Twitter. Now coaches have officially entered the TMI Age." Even so, 15 years ago very few people had cell phones; now they are virtually an indispensible communications tool that shapes how we work, play, and live. If blogging and twittering don't catch on, history tells us something better eventually will.

- **New technologies are making it more difficult for the broadcast media to control information in the communication process.** The Internet, blogging, twittering, message boards, fan forums, and the like have drastically reduced the gatekeeping and agenda-setting functions of the media (see Chapter 1). Fans can communicate with the media, with each other, and even directly with athletes. In 2009, NBA player Charlie Villanueva was reprimanded by the Milwaukee Bucks for posting a message to his Twitter feed via cell phone during *halftime* of a game. "The halftime twitt actually motivated me," he later posted. "That's why I did it, plus of course to keep you guys in the loop of some live action" ("Skiles to," 2009). A younger generation of consumers and athletes are embracing these technologies, which must be taken into account by today's broadcast media.

- **The future of broadcast sports may be through citizen participation.** With a few exceptions, sports ratings are down, stations are losing money, and broadcast corporations are facing bankruptcy. The economic realities of today's competitive media environment may shift more of the burden of content production and distribution to the consumer. This is not to say that the Super Bowl will one day wind up as a home video distributed on YouTube, but it's a common practice for businesses to shift costs to consumers (think of the self-checkout lines at the grocery store, for example—you're doing their work for them at no cost). It makes economic sense for outlets to let audiences shoot and contribute sports content— the audiences are usually highly motivated, they have the technology to do it, and it costs them virtually nothing other than the time they put in. The quality may suffer a bit, but that certainly hasn't stopped YouTube from becoming a multibillion dollar media empire. Today's broadcast media are learning the YouTube lesson—letting the audience take part in the process works on multiple levels, most especially economically.

DISCUSSION QUESTIONS

1. One of the main issues in broadcast sports media today is the growth of subscription and/or pay-per-view programming. If a mega event like the Super Bowl could be sold on a pay-per-view basis for around $75 do you think audiences would go for it? What would be the advantages and disadvantages of such an idea? Will we eventually see a time in which *all* sports programming is pay-per-view? What would that mean for the future of sports advertising?

2. It is very easy today for anyone to take a hand-held (or smaller) video camera, go shoot highlights of the local high school game, and post the material online. Do you see this kind of "citizen sports journalism" as the future of the sports media? Why or why not?

3. You are the general manager of a local radio or television station. Discuss some ways in which you can make your sports content more relevant to local audiences. As you think through your options be sure to consider the economic, cultural, and technological issues that might affect your ultimate decisions.

4. NBA player Charlie Villanueva twitters his fans during halftime of a game; other players have their own blogs and websites. How do these types of things change the dynamic of media relations between athletes and fans? Between fans and the media? Media and athletes?

5. Do you agree with McLuhan's vision of technological determinism? How would it apply to our discussions of sport media and communication?

SUGGESTED EXERCISES

1. Record a live sports event either from radio or television. As you review the game make a note of how the content provider is trying to

   - include audience members in the communication process,
   - incorporate new media technologies such as blogging or twittering,
   - address economic concerns (which don't necessarily have to be through advertising), and
   - reach out to new audiences such as casual fans.

2. Use the same approach as with #1, but do it for the sports segment of the local television newscast.

3. Pick a particular athlete and analyze the content of his/her blog site or webpage. What is the nature of the material? What is the athlete trying to do with the communication? Why?

4. You can also analyze the sports content on citizen journalism sites like Fan Media Network (http://www.fanmedianetwork.com). Do you think sites like FMN could eventually replace the traditional sports media? How would you assess the content posted by average sports fans on the FMN site in terms of its quality and interest/relevance for sports fans?

4

Sports Information Specialists

Amy Ufnowski's typical day is anything but typical. The fifth-year Marquette associate media relations director thrives off expecting the unexpected and, depending on the season, sport, and time of year, she's busier than most in a profession that is anything but a traditional 9 a.m. to 5 p.m. job.

"There isn't a typical day in this profession," Ufnowski said. "Every single day is different. The day goes by so quickly because it's a constant output of work."

But don't think that bothers her in the least. She thrives on being one step ahead of the athletes, coaches, and media as she tirelessly works to promote the Golden Eagles in any way she can.

"Expecting the unexpected in season is sometimes the most exciting part of the job," Ufnowski said. "You can't forecast on a day-to-day basis what is going to happen because it's out of your hands. Game days are great. You can be the worst team in the league and have a huge upset and vice versa. I love the atmosphere around games. It's unpredictable and that's what makes the job worth while because something great has happened to a team or a player."

On any given day in season, Ufnowski will be writing press releases, working on game notes, pitching stories to the media about her student-athletes, working with her coaches, and generally working to promote Marquette in any way she can. Out of season, there's still work to be done, but on a much less hectic schedule.

So why does she work in a field few have heard about but many would love to be in; one in which you must be willing to sacrifice personal and social time to get the job done?

"It's the thrill of pitching stories and having that pitch be accomplished by an outside entity," Ufnowski said. "I think what we do is like sales. You're selling your team and great human interest stories. I like to get those out there and have our players put out in the best light possible. If I'm obnoxious or not, with the media, it still all comes down to building relationship with local, regional, and national media and pitching those stories and getting the most positive information out about Marquette athletics."

The sports Ufnowski has overseen in her job throughout her career seem endless: wrestling, men's and women's basketball, tennis, volleyball, women's soccer, lacrosse, swimming and diving, and men's hockey. And her career has taken her from the U.S.

Olympic training center in Colorado Springs, Colorado, to the University of Denver, and now to Marquette, in Milwaukee, Wisconsin.

With a bachelor's degree in exercise and sport sciences, with an emphasis in sport management, and a minor in business administration, Ufnowski is now working towards a master's degree from Marquette.

"I don't know if this is my career for the next 30 years of my life," she admits. "But I wanted to see how far I could get within college athletics."

Now that you have read a first-hand account of what it's like to be involved in sports media relations, and have a grasp of the different entities that make up part of the sports mass media by reading Chapters 1–3, let's delve more deeply into the world of the sports information specialist.

WHAT'S IN A NAME?

They go by many different names: sports information directors (SIDs), sports media relations practitioners, sports information specialists, or simply a sports team's or organization's public relations (PR) person. Despite the different names or acronyms, it's what they do on a daily, weekly, monthly, and yearly basis that bring notoriety, prominence, recognition, and a continual, and hopefully, positive brand name to a sport organization, an athletic department, a specific team and its coach, and most importantly to the athletes and student-athletes that are the backbone and foundation of the organization.

At the collegiate level, a group of sports information specialists created an organization in 1957 called the College Sports Information Directors of America (CoSIDA) in an attempt to bring some uniformity and standards to the profession.

> "Previously, sports information directors, as a group, were a part of the American College Public Relations Association but most SIDs at those ACPRA meetings felt that a separate organization was needed. There were 102 members at the original meetings; since that time, CoSIDA has grown to over 2,400 members in the United States and Canada. The association is designed to help the SID at all levels. It is the desire of the members to have the profession take its rightful place on the decision-making levels of college athletics. Everything done is geared to this objective." (CoSIDA.com)

CoSIDA is an important organization that represents the best interests of SIDs at all levels of college athletics. A national convention is held yearly and all members are encouraged to attend to discuss growing trends and new topics that affect the industry. CoSIDA also has a code of ethics that it asks all of its members to abide by. (See the CoSIDA Code of Ethics.)

Confidentiality is directly related to ethics. In the fast-paced world that is sport communications, especially at the collegiate level, the SID will be privy to information that is confidential with regard to a student-athlete's health and private matters (information that is protected under the Student Privacy Act), information that is not for the public or media's consumption (time-sensitive material), and behind-the-scenes or inside information. In collegiate athletics, academic records, personal and family matters, and in-

CoSIDA CODE OF ETHICS

In order for the Sports Information Director to serve his/her institution and the College Sports Information Directors of America most effectively, he/she should observe these basic tenets:

- Always be mindful of the fact that he/she represents an institution of higher learning and that exemplary conduct is of paramount importance.

- Intercollegiate athletics is an integral part of the total university program, not the dominating force. Promote them accordingly and not at the expense of other areas.

- Policies of the institution, its governing board, administration, and athletic hierarchy must be acknowledged and supported whether or not the Sports Information Director agrees with them.

- A challenge of controversial policies should be resolved within the appeals framework of the institution. No public forum should be encouraged or developed. Internal problems, such as disagreement over policy, should not be "leaked" or in any other way exploited.

- Loyalty to the athletic administrator, his/her aides, and the coaching staff is imperative. No confidence should ever be violated, regardless of how apparent or insignificant it might appear. Above all, avoid criticism of staff members. Administrators and coaches should be encouraged to answer questions from the media honestly and accurately. In the event they choose to avoid a sensitive question or area for any reason, it is incumbent upon the Sports Information Director to honor the "no comment" by refraining from any subsequent "briefing" session with the media, particularly in an informal atmosphere where misuse of the intonation could be most damaging to all concerned.

- Respect for athletes and their values should be encouraged. The confidence of an athlete must not be violated, particularly as it pertains to information regarding academic, disciplinary, and health information. To release this type of information without the athlete's permission is a violation of the Family Privacy Act of 1974. Also it is highly unethical to falsify weights, heights, and other personal data.

- Relations with the media must be established and maintained at a high professional level. Fairness in the distribution of information is paramount, regardless of the size or importance of the publications or stations. Student media must be accorded the same privileges and rights of the commercial or non-campus media.

- Operation of all facilities in which members of the media may be in attendance should be professional in all aspects. Cheerleading in the pressbox, for example, is gross and undesirable. Other distractions, such as extraneous descriptive and unrelated announcements should be discouraged.

- Criticism of officials is totally unethical, either before, during, or after a contest.

- It is essential that the Sports Information Director be cognizant and observant of all institutional, conference, and national governing body regulations as they pertain to his/her functions within the framework of his/her institution.

- It is incumbent upon a Sports Information Director to take immediate and appropriate action when he/she has knowledge of a fellow/sister Information Director who has violated the CoSIDA Code of Ethics, institutional, conference, or national regulations.

- Participation in organized gambling activities is discouraged.

- Endorsement of products or commodities which reflect a conflict with regular duties is not in the best interests of the institution or the profession.

- Lack of cooperation by members of CoSIDA in not responding promptly and accurately to requests is deemed irresponsible, hence unethical.

juries are some items that should be kept confidential unless the student-athlete specifically allows release of such information. At the professional level, sports information
specialists should adhere to their organization's policy regarding the release of injuries
and other such sensitive information. It is of the utmost importance that the SID is
honest and trustworthy with the confidential information, respecting the athlete and
the organization.

A career or profession as an SID can be extremely gratifying because you have the
opportunity to work with some of the finest athletes in the world and some of the most
brilliant minds in the coaching profession. At the collegiate level especially, SIDs have
the opportunity to make a positive impact in the molding of young people, namely
their student-athletes. Know that no two days are alike and be prepared to expect the
unexpected. After all, it is the world of public relations and dilemmas rarely arise at a
moment of our own choosing (dealing with public relations dilemmas is detailed in
Chapter 10). And there are certainly days when the SID will look down at the clock and
wonder where the time went.

"Like many sports careers, there are few 'typical days' for SIDs, who may spend a
morning editing a future media guide, an afternoon welcoming media for a team day,
and an evening tracking statistics in the press box during a game. If you're a sports
junkie who enjoys the idea of working closely with a team, coaches, and athletic department as well as the media that cover the teams, sports information positions could
prove rewarding" (Angst, n.d.).

Being a part of a winning program with continual, annual success creates new avenues
for being creative in promoting your team or organization. The SID builds myriad types
of skills such as time management, communication, teamwork, and multi-tasking capac-
ities regardless of a team's success. Conversely, losing teaches humility and character. Try
covering a team that perpetually loses and it will certainly teach the SID ways to bring
about creative public relations practices and skills while attempting to remain positive;
there are always silver linings to everything. And because SIDs interact with so many
people driven by a competitive nature, conflict is sure to arise during losing times, thus
helping to build effective problem-solving skills.

So what exactly is the sports information profession and what does the SID do? Simply put, a sport organization's SID is usually the first contact a media member, a fan, an
opposing team, or even an alumnus has with that sport organization. They are the liaisons between those respective entities and the sport organizations. They work very
closely with the coaches as a member of their support staff. And it's imperative to leave
the most positive lasting impression possible with whomever they come across because
ultimately the bottom line of the job is to create a memorable and lasting positive image of their sport organization.

SIDs are like puppeteers, pulling the public relation's strings from the behind-the-
scenes background, allowing the flow of positive information to reach media that cover a
team and its coaches and athletes, without gathering their own fanfare. Whatever the
mode or mean that achieves the utmost coverage is the path one must choose in order

One of the many duties of a sports information specialist is ensuring that press conferences and interviews are successfully orchestrated. (Courtesy of George Mason Athletics/ John Aronson)

to be the most successful and creative SID. Sometimes it's a thankless job and very seldom will the SID be congratulated for actually doing the job at hand and doing it well. The trick to knowing great work has been done is seeing one's coaches and particularly student-athletes receiving the recognition they deserve through whatever medium it may occur, be it a feature story in a local paper, a taped interview that runs on the nightly news, or a regional or national award bestowed on an athlete based on your nomination of that respective athlete. Or recognition of a job well done may come from a media member using a note, story idea, or just having a positive influence from dealing with the SID. Also know that very few people remember or acknowledge a job well done, but a mistake has a lasting impression and will most definitely be brought to one's attention.

An easy way to recognize what an SID does is to compare it to that of being a doctor on call, but instead of his/her office being a hospital or an operating table, the place of work is an athletic facility or playing field. Breaking news never sleeps and whether it be positive or negative, proactive or reactive, messages and assistances need to be delivered to the media and the general public in a timely, organized fashion. Hence, SIDs are always ready to spring into action at a moment's notice, which is why they can most often be found in the office, especially when their athletic teams are in season. It's not out of the ordinary for a sports information specialist to work 60–70 hours in a week while in season. Think about it. The profession ultimately revolves around the team's sporting event. And when, typically, are those events? They're not at 2 p.m. on a Tuesday afternoon (unless it's a mid-week baseball game). They're in the evenings. And they are during the weekends, when contests are scheduled at many different times, ranging anywhere from mid-morning to late in the evening. So it's easy to see why the work week for an SID can sometimes span all seven days of the week and easily double the working hours of a "normal" profession.

ESSENTIAL SKILLS

So what is required of being an SID? "There are three simple rules to follow to be well on your way to being successful: 1) communicate well; 2) get along well with others; 3) be a leader" (Shutt, 1998, p. 5).

Again, communication is the backbone of the industry. Working well with co-workers, coaches, athletes, and media is of the utmost importance because you can't do your job on your own and being a team player will make life much easier for you. And there's a great cliché that comes from the military: "Lead, follow, or get out of the way." That phrase couldn't be truer in this profession. Grab the proverbial bull by the horns, step forward, and assume the responsibility bestowed with open arms. Get the job done, but don't hesitate to delegate to one's subordinates to help with the completion of one's tasks.

In addition to the three key components listed above, what follows is a look at some of the more specific skills required of an SID.

Effective Writing Skills

The skill set required to be an SID is extensive and the backbone of it all starts with successful, creative, and excellent writing skills using The Associated Press (AP) style. If you're not a good writer, then sports public relations may not be for you. That said, if you're not already a great writer, you can acquire those skills via practice and patience. But know that a professional cannot succeed without a thorough understanding of the parts of speech, sentence structure, grammar, spelling, punctuation, and theme development, etc.

The ability to understand and use proper grammar and AP style while writing on deadline is arguably the most important aspect of an SID's job. The SID's writing will be seen and viewed by many in both news story and news release form and it will be in many different types of work such as news releases, news stories, game notes, media guide text, feature story writing, internal organization communication, speech writing for the coaches and student-athletes, and various other forms of writing.

NEWS RELEASES

The lifeline and arguably the most important job an SID will have is writing news releases. A news release, which is very similar to a news story written by the print or broadcast media, represents *hard news* and utilizes the inverted pyramid comprising the 5Ws and the H (who, what, where, when, why, and how). When a sporting event has concluded, the SID will write a news release and distribute it to the media for those that weren't there in attendance. The story is also usually placed on the athletic department or sporting organization's website.

How to write news releases will be discussed in detail in Chapter 6.

GAME NOTES

A conglomeration of quick points, story lines, statistics, trends, historical information and records, updated profile information, etc., is compiled on a game-by-game basis by the SID and used by the media to assist with game stories and an SID's own news releases.

Game Notes

Game Information

DATE: Saturday, April 3, 2010
LOCATION: Lucas Oil Stadium (71,300) in Indianapolis, Ind.
TIPOFF: 8:47 p.m.
SERIES: Duke leads 17-7
TV: CBS (Jim Nantz and Clark Kellogg)
RADIO: MSN (45 affiliates) Tony Caridi, Jay Jacobs and Kyle Wiggs
OFFICIALS: Announced on game day No. 3/3 Duke

No. 3/3
Duke Blue Devils
(33-5)

No. 6/5
West Virginia
Mountaineers
(31-6)

2010 NCAA Championship Final Four

- No. 2-seed WVU earned an automatic bid to the NCAA tournament by winning the BIG EAST Conference championship.
- WVU's No. 2 seed is the school's highest since earning a No. 5 seed in the 1982 NCAA tournament.
- The Mountaineers, winners of the East Region, are making their second NCAA Final Four appearance. The other was in 1959, when WVU, led by Jerry West, defeated Louisville in the Final Four before falling to California, 71-70, in the finals.
- Bob Huggins is making his second Final Four appearance. His 1992 Cincinnati team fell to Michigan, 76-72, in the Final Four.
- Joe Mazzulla, making his first start of the season against Kentucky, was named Most Outstanding Player of the East Region. Da'Sean Butler and Kevin Jones were named to the East Region all-Tournament team.
- West Virginia is making its 23rd appearance in the NCAA championship, dating back to 1955.

MEDIA GUIDE TEXT

Regardless of the sport he/she is responsible for overseeing, the SID is the chief executor of a media guide, which includes writing and editing the entire body of its text. While creating a media guide will be discussed in detail in Chapter 7, know that the media guide is arguably the first-ever glimpse into a program or a sport organization. In it will be rosters, schedules, bios of players, coaches' bios, historical information and records, last season's statistics, and myriad other informational items fully promoting the sport from both a recruiting and media coverage standpoint.

FEATURE WRITING

Very similar to writing news releases, feature writing uses the *soft news* angle to tell a story about athletes, coaches, or administrators. The SID usually writes features for the department's game-day programs, the department or organization's website, and smaller media outlets that may utilize a feature story that focuses on a hometown athlete or coach.

Keen Visual Skills

This skill set is almost just as important as having effective writing skills. An SID needs these skills for understanding basic layout, design, and presentation of media guides, game notes, and other various pamphlets, brochures, etc. that will emanate from his or her office. An SID will also need great visual ability when it pertains to the department or organization's website to know what will be visually appealing.

Strong Speaking and Interviewing Skills

Not only does an SID work with the general public, always presenting the best foot forward for the organization with great customer service skills, but he/she will also need excellent speaking skills for opening press conferences, pitching and selling story ideas to the media that cover the athletes and teams, and doing the same with the administration. There will also be times when SIDs will act as an interviewer with coaches and athletes when writing news releases and feature stories and need quotes to enhance the information that they are providing.

Effective Problem-Solving Skills

As is fully dissected in Chapter 10, there are certainly going to be times of public relations dilemmas. Some of the most trying times while being an SID involve crisis management in the most un-likeliest of times. Therefore, a good SID will be able to think on his or her feet in high-pressure situations in an attempt to deflect as much as possible any negative publicity for the athletes, coaches, program, department, and organization.

Good Interpersonal Skills

You can't do this job by yourself. It requires organization and teamwork. In many cases, SIDs have subordinates and delegation is key to being an effective leader. Good leadership starts at the top and trickles down through the ranks. Know that no SID's job can be done on one's own, so being a true team player is also vital to his or her own success. Outside of the organization, an SID must foster a professional and amicable relationship with members of the media.

RESPONSIBILITIES OF AN SID

Now that an SID's necessary skills needed has been delved into, what are the areas where those skills are put to use?

Game Management/Game-Day Media Operations

Depending on the sport and the amount of media coverage it receives, game days and the days that lead up to them may be hectic. And once the game is over there's no rest for the weary. An SID will turn right back around and repeat the same process all over again in preparation for the next upcoming event. The game itself is the premier showcase for the job and it will be a full culmination of all the hard work and positive endeavors leading up to and following the event.

Interviews

When a member of the media wants to speak to a coach, an athletic department employee, or a student-athlete, that media member will contact the sports information director to set up an interview. Traditionally, the unwritten rule of the business is to expect 24 hours to process the interview request. At the collegiate level an SID is dealing with many different schedules such as classes, study hall, practice, and strength and conditioning, so it can take time to fulfill the request based on a student-athlete's hectic schedule.

Of course, there will be interview opportunities pre- and post-game day. Postgame simply entails a press conference with the coach and requested players. Pre-game usually consists of interviews a few days prior to a game that will ensure proper coverage prior to the contest.

It also falls on the SID to not just assist with the setup of the interviews and seeing them come to fruition, it is also a key responsibility to "coach up" the athletes prior to the interview itself. An SID deals with all types of athletes—some that love the limelight, others who view the interview as a chore or task, and those that avoid the media at all costs simply because of shyness. It is the duty of the SID to assist in any way possible, which could include sitting in on the interview with the shy athlete or acting as a mediator if an interview could turn precarious. It's not out of the realm of responsibilities for an SID to limit questions for an athlete that can only give a few minutes of their time.

At certain schools or sport organizations, handbooks are created and given to the athletes as it pertains to dealing with the media and how to always represent the organization in the best manner. The handbooks (such as the NFL player's handbook) are used as a tool or reference for athletes to consult in how to work with the media. For an example of such a handbook, see the end of this chapter for a portion of West Virginia University's Media Relations handbook that is given to all student-athletes each year.

Working with Athletes and Coaches

One of the most appealing truths of working as a collegiate sports information director is the daily interaction with student-athletes. The SID is ultimately in the business of shaping and molding a portion of a young person's future. The SID will get to know them, their strengths and weaknesses, as it pertains to interviews and public appearances. And by working with them, the SID will work closely with coaches when it comes to nominating student-athletes for national awards such as All-America status, Academic All-America status, and all-conference accolades.

Articulate and punctual student-athletes will often times be requested multiple times during a week or month for interview requests (depending on the sport), so it's imperative that the SID work to alleviate the media pressures imposed on those athlete by creating a workable schedule to fulfill those requests. Study hall, strength and conditioning, practice, and classes have their time-consuming

It is essential that a sports information director have a good working relationship with his/her coach in order to help promote the program. (Courtesy of WVU Sports Communications)

MITCHELL LAYTON PHOTOGRAPHY

Coach's CORNER

by Craig Esherick

The relationship between a coach and his/her sports information director is an important one. The SID has the ability to provide the press with valuable background information when the coach makes decisions that might seem unpopular or ill-advised at the time. Coaching strategy is different for each coach, and coaches should inform SIDs about their coaching philosophy. A good SID is like a good assistant coach. Coaches should spend time with their SIDs talking about their sport, how they coach, and what strategies they prefer; that all enable the SID to form an accurate picture of the coach as a professional. That picture of the coach will be what the press sees when they talk to the SID.

Sports information specialists should also be encouraged by coaches to sit in on practices and film sessions. The SID should meet the coach's family and also spend time with assistant coaches. He/she should be comfortable around all of the players. Remember that the SID will be a trusted advisor for these players when they are dealing with the media. Postgame interviews with the press are done during the emotional highs and lows of a season. A trusting relationship between the player and the SID will enable the SID to help manage these emotions, which will help to create a positive image for the player, coach, team, and school or organization.

The coach experiences some of the same emotions that players feel during, before, and after contests. The coach also has the added pressure of the job insecurity associated with the coaching profession. A good working relationship between the coach and SID will benefit the coach during these emotional times. A smart SID can sense when a coach is on edge after an emotionally charged game. A few quick thoughts about how to handle the impending questions can help refocus the coach to the task of discussing the game rather than focusing on any frustrations of the game.

An SID that knows the coach he/she is working with can also sense during interviews when a well-timed interruption can prevent the coach from saying something that under normal conditions the coach would not have said.

The SID and the coach will discuss how to handle press conferences, how the press should contact the coach, what will be the policy for locker room interviews, and other procedural issues relating to media access to members of the team. These conversations will help the interaction between a coach and sports information specialist grow into a productive and professional relationship. A good SID will not be afraid to offer advice the coach may not want to hear. This is also why it is important for an SID to build the relationship of trust with his/her coach. It is a long season. No coach is perfect—and an SID may have to remind the coach of that from time to time.

rigors. The effective SID will be able to juggle the student-athlete's hectic schedule with interviews desired by the media.

Working with coaches has the same principles as working with athletes. The SID is ultimately helping promote the team or school and working closely with the coach is a necessity. In season, an SID will be in constant daily contact with the coach, fulfilling interview requests, getting quotes for his/her own personal use (i.e. news releases) and working for the betterment of the athletes. The effective SID will create a working interview schedule for the coach, especially in season, when the coach's time is in high demand. Out of season, an SID will still be in touch with the coach, depending on the sport and the coach's schedule, on a daily or weekly.

Working with the Media

The effective sports information director cultivates an open and honest relationship with members of the press and the community. The relationship is based on trust and mutual respect. The SID understands the push for details on a big story among competitive media and forgives the overzealous reporter who becomes a bit too pushy on occasion. The journalist recognizes the administrative constraints on the SID and accepts limitations placed on release of information, albeit grudgingly.

Both sides understand the give-and-take nature of the business. The SID provides a little more information on one story and expects the journalist to follow up on a lukewarm story idea in return at some point. As payback for the same deal, the reporter, on

Building relationships with newspaper reporters is a great way for a sports information specialist to penetrate the local print media in order to garner more coverage for a team or deserving athlete. (Courtesy of Stock.xchng)

the other hand, expects the SID to deliver a useful nugget of information (at the very least) for a major breaking story under deadline and competitive pressures.

The key to working with the media is to always be truthful and honest in all situations. That will build credibility and rapport as the working relationship cultivates.

Working with the Conference/League Office

Just like an SID is a representative of his/her respective organization or team, the conference or league in which the team or organization may belong also has an SID that oversees the entire media operation for that conference or league. For instance, West Virginia University belongs to the BIG EAST Conference and members of the league staff are SIDs who promote the entire 16-team conglomeration. In the professional ranks the same hierarchy holds true. For instance, Major League Baseball has publicity directors that promote the entire league while also working with each team's public relations specialist.

Team SIDs will work closely with league SIDs when it comes to helping them prepare their media guide (when they need a team's vital information), when they go to select weekly league player-of-the-week awards (typically an SID will nominate players based on weekly performances and after getting approval from the head coach), and when compiling the sometimes daily and always weekly updated conference statistics. Those statistics begin with a team's statistics compiled by that team's SID, who submits them to the conference or league, and the league office creates the master daily or weekly conference-wide file.

When it comes to the season's conclusion and it is time to nominate players for conference and national awards, the conference/league SID will assist in the nominations of athletes for everything from All-America or All-Star status to individualized sport-specific awards.

Historian/Record Keeper

An SID is also the chief statistician for their respective sport and is the keeper of all things as it relates to the organization's historical records. As each game is completed, for whatever sport, the statistics are compiled and used to create and update new and existing records for the team and individuals.

In the offseason, SIDs are always researching records that will help enhance the future coverage of their teams. And the longer they are with the team that they're covering, the more point of an historical authority they become.

Rules/Compliance Awareness

While an SID is responsible for myriad tasks, one of the most important jobs is to be aware and keep up-to-date with all rules and regulations that are in effect as it relates to the team or organization. This is especially important, and often difficult, for SIDs at the college level because the NCAA has an abundance of intricate rules. One of the biggest factors as it pertains to rules compliance for an SID is to be aware of national signing day, when prospective recruits become members of the collegiate program. It is imperative to be up-to-date on the rules as it pertains to announcing those signings as well as any other pertinent up-to-date rules that affect an SIDs day-to-day tasks.

Travel

If SIDs travel with their respective teams, and most of them do, they'll take their SID show on the road. While technology has made the SID's job away from the office much easier (prior to the Internet SIDs had to call in scores and key facts/stats from road games), a job still must be done while away from home.

Traditionally, the SID of a visiting team will rely heavily on the host SID to assist in coverage, especially as it pertains to getting postgame information out to visiting media members if the visiting team and SID are departing the arena/venue as soon as the contest has concluded.

On the road, and because technologies are far advanced, SIDs can write their postgame releases and send them out to their media contacts immediately upon the conclusion of the game. Good SIDs will have their statistics file to update their master stats and if there are any interview requests for the coach or athletes, they will facilitate those.

In some sports, such as basketball, the SID is traditionally the visiting score keeper, sitting beside the official scorers or working closely with them during the game should any discrepancies arise.

Various Other Responsibilities

The best way to classify this is as "all other duties/responsibilities as assigned." From writing speeches for coaches and athletes to assisting with a coach's Twitter site or a team's Facebook page, there are countless other activities that an SID will have to complete in the overall promotion of the organization. Other ways to assist the media include helping them obtain photographs and credentialing the media for sporting events. The credentialing process begins with the media applying to cover the sporting event and the SID either granting or denying the request. If the request is granted (all SIDs should have a clearly outlined policy for granting credentials, usually detailed in a media guide, so that no questions of favoritism arise) the SID is responsible for creating a seating chart for the media for the upcoming event.

PROS AND CONS OF THE JOB

As the saying goes, there are two sides to every story. That holds true as it pertains to being an SID. While there are plenty of rewarding moments, there can be times of frustration as well, just as there is in any profession. So let's examine some of the pros and cons to working in the sports information specialist profession?

First, being an SID means you'll get to travel. Depending on the level of your organization or team, your travel could be local, regional, nationwide, or even worldwide. At the small college level, SIDs may only travel within a specific region unless tournaments or postseason plays leads to further destinations. At the largest colleges, SIDs trail blaze the country while they travel with their respective teams, especially for holiday tournaments, bowl games, and other postseason events. In some cases, teams will take international training trips (such as a summer tour) to destinations across the globe. At the professional level, sports information specialists travel much more frequently and the trips are usually further from home and can often last more than a week.

As mentioned earlier, an SID at the collegiate level has a hand in molding the life of a student-athlete. That can be very rewarding and advantageous for many SIDs because they are ultimately having a positive impact on someone's future.

Sports information specialists also traditionally get various free perks, whether it be receiving team apparel or complimentary tickets to sporting events for family and/or friends. Water cooler talk also abounds for an SID. As mentioned earlier, a lot of times an SID is privy to inside information, typically hearing information before the general public. And there's something to be said for being the first to know. Remember, though, that confidentiality must be kept.

Lastly, you'll get out of it what you put into your work, and for many in the profession it's a lifelong enjoyment of promoting whatever school or organization for which they work.

Now, what are some of the cons of the profession? Just as travel was a perk, it can also be taxing and make for a long year or season of constantly being on the go. As previously detailed, SIDs put in long hours that almost always include working late nights and weekends. That makes it difficult to have a normal social or family life in season in this profession.

Lastly, winning and losing marks the best of times and worst of times. If an organization or team is not very successful, the stress levels can reach peaks for SIDs as the frustration level of players and coaches increases. It's important to keep an even keel and remember that a job has to be done win or lose.

HOW TO BECOME AN SID

Now that you have a core background into the sports information specialist profession, how do you become one? First, you volunteer your time immediately with the sports information department at your school in any way, even if that entails being a press row worker (e.g., stat runner), and don't take "no" for an answer. If you're a writer, continue to improve your writing ability and enhance your knowledge by covering as many different sports as possible because that expanded knowledge will be beneficial when it comes to being assigned various sports as an SID.

Tips for Young Sports Information Specialists

1. Learn the philosophy of the athletics program, its missions, its goals, its structure, its personnel, and its athletes—past and present. Doing so will only make your job a lot easier.
2. Know as much as possible about the coaches and the athletes; keep a biographical file, statistics, and pictorial data on each. Also, maintain alumni files if space allows. You'll be called upon to track down information at a moment's notice, so having these at your fingertips is a must.

3. Learn the local media, their missions, their target audiences, their structure, and their personnel. Doing so will only assist you in your pitching of story ideas and the overall promotion of your organization.

4. Know your business. The SID must understand what is going on in the athletic world, the entertainment world, and the media in order to guide journalists to write and tell upbeat, positive stories.

5. Define your public relations target market. Know who should receive information about the athletics program to ensure maximum success. Failure to do so would be a grave waste of time.

6. Learn the production and printing deadlines of local media, and time announcements to attain maximum benefit. Obviously, broadcast media can "break" a story almost immediately. Not so with the print media, which have strict copy and publication deadlines, although most print publications do have websites where they can post breaking news.

7. Encourage coaches and athletes to grant interviews, to return media telephone requests, and to take an active part in the publicity thrust. Guide those who are ill-prepared or inexperienced so they will present a positive image and reflect the appropriate view of the university.

8. Identify and suggest good feature stories and personality profiles to the media, whether the stories concern a volleyball player, a cross country runner, or the star quarterback. This all comes back from items 1 and 3.

9. Know what types of information and messages are likely to generate the most media interest. Also, recognize the potential results from an organized public relations program focused on athletics.

10. Exhibit courage in crisis situations. Be tactful and informative in times of coaching changes, protests, boycotts, drug problems, or any other potentially awkward situations. Be proactive and honest at all times.

11. Remember that credibility, integrity, versatility, and service are the characteristics that define successful sports information directors. An outgoing personality is an asset to an SID, but never can substitute for in-depth knowledge of the school's program and consistent and quality information about the program.

SUMMARY

An SID is arguably one of the most important cogs in an athletic department or sport organization, especially when it comes to promoting its coaches and athletes. The SID is the link and liaison between the media and the athletes and coaches as it pertains to publicity and promotion. During the constant interaction with the players, coaches, and media as SIDs promote their team or organization, they must maintain a professional standard of confidentiality, integrity, and ethical conduct.

There are several essential skills that SIDs must possess, but the core of the profession is wrapped around being able to write and write well, especially under deadline pressures. It's also important to have keen visual skills, strong speaking and interviewing skills, problem-solving abilities, and good interpersonal communication skills.

There are numerous responsibilities that fall under the direction of an SID, including overseeing game management, facilitating interviews and press conferences, working with league or conference SIDs, compiling statistics, and maintaining knowledge of important rules and regulations.

There are several pros and cons to the profession, as with any job, and they range from travel and free perks to working long hours, especially in season. But all told, it's a rewarding profession for those that have a knack for writing, have great time management skills, and have a desire to work towards the overall positive thrust in creating and molding the positive image of organizations, coaches, and athletes.

WVU Media Relations Handbook

The following is part of the West Virginia University Media Relations handbook that is presented to Mountaineer student-athletes at the beginning of each season.

WVU's Sports Communications Office

Because West Virginia does not have any professional sports franchises, WVU athletics is looked upon as the state's leading sports entity. Our varsity teams are under a constant media microscope and are paid attention to very closely, because the state's fans have a vested interest in the Mountaineers. That's why our office exists—to help and continue to promote you and your team and maximize that exposure at the local, regional and national levels. We are the link between WVU's teams, athletes, coaches and administrators and the media. We have an excellent reputation of positive media rapport. Your help in maintaining that is of the utmost importance.

Your sports communications contact handles:

- Processing of all interview requests
- Writing of press releases, feature stories and media guides
- Updating and maintaining the school's official website: www.MSNsports NET.com
- Handling and compiling of team statistics
- Nominations for conference and national athletic and academic awards
- Select travel to road contests
- Hosting the media on game days and subsequent post-game interviews

Remember the following important items as you interact with the media and the public.

1. The opportunity to deal with the media is a learning experience and can help you develop communication skills which can be helpful not only during your time as a student-athlete, but in future professional, business and athletic endeavors.
2. Remember who your audience is. Yes, maybe you're just talking to one reporter or a handful of media members, but remember who they write for: the public that is composed of Mountaineer fans, alumni, fellow teammates, your coaches and your opponents. Create great rapport with the media and the public will love you.

WVU Media Relations Handbook

3. Be punctual. **Always be on time** for a scheduled and pre-arranged interview. Failure to do so is a poor reflection on you, your coaches, the sports communications department and the university. If you are having trouble making it to your interview, contact your sports communications contact immediately.

4. The sports communications office **will not give out your personal phone numbers even if you consent to let us do so.** You have class, practice, athletic events and leading the life of a college student-athlete. You don't need or want media members calling you. That's what the sports communications office is for. Should you get a call from a media member, please direct them to call your respective sports communications contact and set up the interview through them. A proper quote to a media member who calls you would be, *"I'm sorry, but all interviews have to be sent through our sports communications office, and I have not talked to them about this."* Then give them your respective sports communications contact information which is provided in this booklet for you.

5. **Never agree to a phone interview unless arrangements have been coordinated by the sports communications office.** This includes talking to a hometown reporter you grew up with and are comfortable talking to. This policy will help you avoid contact with unauthorized persons who attempt to gain and use information for scouting or gambling purposes. The sports communications office will gladly process and handle all interview requests for you.

6. As a student-athlete at West Virginia University, **you are expected to be available to the media but you do not have to answer every question from the media.** This is extremely important to remember. A proper response to a question you would rather not answer is always, "I'd rather not discuss that subject," or "I don't feel comfortable answering that." *Avoid saying "no comment," as there are negative connotations involved with those two words.* You may always refer a question to your coaches or to a member of the sports communications staff.

7. If you are uncomfortable with questions being asked or the general tone of the interview, contact your respective sports communications contact immediately.

8. Remember that **nothing is "off the record."** While the person you are talking to may not print or broadcast what you say, it could be repeated in conversation and could appear later in a story or broadcast by someone who "heard it from a reliable source."

9. Use good judgment in what you say to the media. You are not only representing yourself, but your family, your teammates, your coaches and the school. A good general rule is **"If you can't say something nice, don't say it at all."**

   • Be confident in your answers but never be ARROGANT.
   • You should *never* say anything about an opponent that could be posted in their locker room and be used against you. The sports communications office is always looking for opponent quotes to be used as motivat-

WVU Media Relations Handbook

ing factors for you in competition. Don't think that your opponents aren't looking at what you say for the very same reason.
- Always have respect for your opponent in interviews regardless if it's the defending national champion or a team that went winless last year because, again, you never want to give them an edge.
- Make sure to accomplish the following with your answers:
  - Illuminate favorable facts
  - Enhance your team or teammates' position
  - Educate the media on what you do
  - Neutralize negatives
  - Correct misstatement or inaccurate characterizations
  - Redirect the focus when necessary
  - Be quotable

10. There is **no need to praise yourself**. If you and your teammates are successful, there will be enough praise for everyone.
11. You may be asked the same question over and over again and in different forms and forums. It can be frustrating, but remember all members of the media cannot be at the same place at the same time. They are only doing their job. Learn to be patient. The rewards will be great!
12. At times you may be asked about personal or family business. You are not required or expected to answer questions of a personal or family nature unless you feel comfortable in doing so. The questions could range from your personal family to your "team" family.
13. What you say, how you say it and how you handle the interview will go a long way in what people think about you, your teammates, your coaches and WVU. **Good media relationships can give you a positive public image for a lifetime. Remember who your audience is!** Use this opportunity to your advantage. It can help you the rest of your life. The media is very influential. What they say and how they portray you is what the public will most likely believe.
14. As a WVU student-athlete, you may have many opportunities to meet and interact with the public, as well as the media. The same suggestions for working with the media can apply to dealing with the public. Be careful what you say and to whom you say it to. Nothing is confidential or "just between us." Once it is spoken it can be repeated and probably will be. Everyone wants to be "in the know" and loves to brag to others about their "insider information."
15. Be particularly careful of well-meaning people who invite you to speak or attend a banquet, parade, etc., even if it is in your honor. NCAA rules regarding these types of events are constantly changing and the least little slip up could cost you your eligibility. Always check with your coach, the sports communications staff or the compliance office before accepting or attending any speaking engagement, banquet or other function.
16. Be careful and conscious of what you do on the Internet (Facebook, Twitter, MySpace, etc.). That's a public forum and anyone, anywhere can access that information and use it against you.

WVU Media Relations Handbook

Guidelines for Working with the Media

The West Virginia University sports communications office takes great pride in having an outstanding relationship with the media that covers WVU's 17 varsity sports. Your help in keeping that high standard is greatly needed, encouraged and appreciated.

1. Only do interviews that have been set up by a member of the Sports Communications Office. Phone interviews will be done from our office or from your contact's cell phone, never from your home or personal cell phone.
2. Don't give out your home phone number or cell number to a member of the media . . . ever! You don't want a reporter catching you unprepared in a time of crisis.
3. If you have an interview scheduled, punctuality and reliability are critical.

Interview Do's and Do Not's

Do

Be Prepared

Knowledge is power. Anticipate the questions. The more you know about the media, the more comfortable and confident you will be. Ask your sports communications contact what the interview is about and what questions you can expect.

Be Positive

Nobody likes a complainer. Whine in private, not in public.

Praise Your Teammates and Coaches by Saying Something Good

Say something good in your interview about a teammate, a coach, an opponent or WVU. Don't brag about yourself. Let someone else do it because if you deserve it, someone will say it.

Make Good Eye Contact

This is extremely important. Show the interviewer that you're interested in talking to them by making and maintaining eye contact. **If it is on camera, look directly at the interviewer, not at the camera.**

Speak Slowly, Be Articulate and Concise

If you're not sure how to exactly answer a question posed to you, take your time in assembling your response or ask the media member to repeat the question. Don't feel that you need to answer a question just for the sake of answering it. Remember what you say is on record. Take your time with your response. Be sure to talk slowly, be concise and articulate your answers.

Think Before You Speak, Keep it Simple and Focus

Once you are quoted, you can never take it back. Put together a clear, concise answer and be polite. Keep your answers short and simple. Avoid over-

WVU Media Relations Handbook

answering. Tell the audience what they need to know, not everything you know on a subject.

Pay attention to what the media is asking you and what your answers will be. Listen to what they say, just don't hear them. Give your undivided attention to the media when in an interview. Turn off cell phones, etc.

Be Friendly, Accommodating and Enthusiastic

West Virginia has a myriad of media members. Be patient with all of them. Have fun with the interview. If you are relaxed, they will be, too.

Use Correct Grammar

Try to avoid using slang or contemporary popular phrases. Remember who your audience is: the general public.

Avoid "Guiding"

Do not let the media "guide" you into an answer you would not normally give. Don't be afraid to voice a different opinion than the one the media member wants you to say. **Example:** They might say "Didn't you feel . . ." or "I know that must be tough."

Emotion

If you are too emotional after a win or a loss and you have been requested for an interview, let your sports communications contact know that you need to cool down a bit before being interviewed.

Be Available

Be punctual. Show up for interviews early. This shows you are dependable, both as a person and an athlete and it shows strong character.

Don't

Don't Say "No Comment"

Find a positive way to answer the question or say "I don't feel comfortable answering that question." There are negative connotations implied with saying "no comment."

Don't Be Negative

The quickest way to lose favor from the public eye is to become a negative influence on your team.

Don't Hide

You can't make the media disappear. Take a positive approach. Learn how to work with the media and reap the benefits.

WVU Media Relations Handbook

Don't Lose Your Cool

The media will test you when adversity comes your way. It's a part of their job. Remember who the real audience is: the fans.

Don't Forget the Fishbowl

You're living in one as a Mountaineer student-athlete. Any of your actions during or after a game or even when you are out socializing may end up on television or in the newspapers. The media are part of your every day life at WVU, including the off-season. Always conduct yourself in a positive manner regardless if you're wearing the Old Gold and Blue or not.

Don't Be Sarcastic

It may be funny with your teammates and friends, but sarcasm doesn't come across well in newspaper quotes or television interviews unless you're a professional comedian.

Don't Use Fillers

Well, you know what I'm saying. It just doesn't, um, like, you know, sound real good, you know what I'm saying?

Don't Cop an Attitude

Nice guys may finish last on the field, but they are definitely winners off the field. You can be tough on the field without being rude or difficult off the field.

Don't Miss the Opportunity

Working with the media can help you develop the people skills you will need in your next career.

DISCUSSION QUESTIONS

1. In your opinion, what is the most attractive part of an SID's daily workload? Why? In your opinion, what is the least desirable?
2. What are some of the facets of the job that would come easy for you and, conversely, where would some of your added attention be targeted or needed?

SUGGESTED EXERCISES

1. Choose your favorite team. For its upcoming event that is about to be played, assemble some pregame notes that you would hypothetically distribute to the media that cover that team.
2. Interview a local collegiate coach and ask about his/her needs from his/her SID. Report back your findings to your class.

5

Developing Interviewing Skills

Interviewing looks so easy on television, but sticking a microphone in someone's face and trying to get a good answer can be extremely difficult. The good interviewers—the professionals who make it *look* easy—actually spend a lot of time in preparation. How the interview ultimately turns out depends a great deal on the time spent before the cameras (or tape recorders) ever begin to roll.

BEFORE THE INTERVIEW

There are several things a sports interviewer needs to consider before sitting down to actually conduct the interview. Primarily, the interviewer must determine issues such as method, audience, agenda, theme, setting, stakeholders, and access. *Method* is simply how the interview will be conducted, either in person, over the phone, or by some other way such as email or text messaging. In situations where there are physical distances involved, or simply sometimes for speed and convenience, interviews will take place over the phone or by email. There is nothing wrong with these methods, but the lack of direct contact sometimes results in answers that are misunderstood or taken out of context. An impersonal interview may also cause the interviewer to miss the subtleties and nuances that go with face-to-face conversation. In this regard, a phone interview is preferable to an email contact, but the in-person interview is the best of all and should be the method used whenever possible.

Audience refers to who will be watching or listening to the interview; it has become especially important in an age of niche sports content where there are potentially dozens of different audiences even for the same media outlet. For example, a local television station may have a sports segment in its noon, 5 p.m., and 10 p.m. newscasts, but all three shows have vastly different types of people watching. Research suggests that more women and casual fans are watching at noon and 5 p.m. compared to other newscasts.

The interviewer needs to consider the type of audience because that will help direct the tone and direction of the interview. Tiger Woods may appear on *60 Minutes* one night and Jay Leno the next, but the interviews will be much different because the audiences and their expectations are different. The *60 Minutes* audience expects hard-hitting questions, while the Leno audience expects more entertainment. If the interviewer does not understand the audience and its expectations it can cause some difficulties (see "A Thorny Rose for Gray" sidebar).

A Thorny Rose for Gray

In October 1999, before a World Series game, NBC sports reporter Jim Gray conducted a live interview with former player Pete Rose. Rose clearly thought the interview was about his inclusion in baseball's "All-Century Team," which was revealed before the game. Rose was honored as part of the team just prior to the interview. But Gray focused the interview more on Rose's alleged involvement with gambling on baseball and his attempts to lift his lifetime ban. The interview created a firestorm of controversy as many thought Gray went too far in his questioning. "It was very venomous, a lot of anger," said Gray, who received death threats and hate mail. "A lot of people were upset. An NBC switchboard operator told me, 'This makes O.J. Simpson look like . . . nothing'" (Martzke, 2004).

JIM GRAY: Pete, the overwhelming evidence that's in that report . . . why not make that step tonight?

PETE ROSE: This is too festive a night to worry about that, because I don't know what evidence you're talking about. I mean, show it to me.

JG: We don't want to debate that Pete.

PR: Well, why not? Why do we want to believe everything he says?

JG: You signed a paper acknowledging the ban. Why did you sign it if you didn't agree?

PR: But it also says I can apply for reinstatement after one year. If you remember correctly in the press conference . . . as a matter of fact, my statement was I can't wait for my little girl to be a year old so I can apply for reinstatement. So you forgot to add that in there.

JG: You applied for reinstatement in 1997. Have you heard back from Commissioner Selig?

PR: No. That kind of surprised me. It's only been two years. He has a lot on his mind. I hope to someday.

JG: Pete, it's been 10 years since you've been allowed on the field. Obviously, the approach you've taken has not worked. Why not take a different approach?

PR: You say it hasn't worked . . . what do you exactly mean?

JG: You're not allowed in baseball, not allowed to earn a living in the game you love, and you're not allowed to be in the Hall of Fame.

PR: That's why I applied for reinstatement and I hope Bud Selig considers that and gives me an opportunity. I won't need a third chance; all I need is a second chance.

JG: Pete, those who will hear this tonight will say you've been your own worst enemy and continue to be. How do you respond to that?

PR: In what way are you talking about?

JG: By not acknowledging what seems to be overwhelming evidence.

PR: You know, I'm surprised you're bombarding me like this. I mean, I'm doing the interview with you on a great night, a great occasion, a great ovation, everybody seems to be in a great mood and you're bringing up something that happened 10 years ago.

JG: I'm bringing it up because I think people would like to see . . . Pete, we've got to go; we've got a game.

PR: This is a prosecutor's brief, it isn't an interview and I'm very surprised at you. I am, really.

JG: Some would be surprised you didn't take the opportunity. Let's go upstairs to Hannah. Congratulations, Pete.

Source: Courtesy NBC/MLB

The public uproar following the interview forced Gray to go on the air the next night and apologize; not for his line of questioning, but for "taking some of the joy out of the moment." Gray was vindicated in 2004 when Rose publicly admitted that he had not only bet on baseball, but had bet on his own team while manager of the Cincinnati Reds. NBC Sports Chairman Dick Ebersol said, "Rose owes an awful lot of people an apology, especially to Jim for the pain and humiliation Rose's lying put him through in the World Series" (Martzke, 2004).

Rose's interview brings up another important consideration, that of *agenda*. For 15 years Rose lied to any and all reporters who directly asked him whether he had bet on baseball, as was alleged in the 1989 report that led to his suspension from the game. "I feel he has embarrassed me," said veteran sportswriter Roger Kahn. "I must have asked Pete 20 times, 'Did you bet on baseball?' He would look at me, blink his eyes and say, 'I didn't bet baseball. I have too much respect for the game'" (Dodd, 2004). Interviewers must understand that the people they talk to have a reason for talking, whether it's to promote their own self-interests, hide damaging information, or achieve certain goals. When Rose finally did come clean about his gambling in January 2004 he had two main goals in mind—to sell more copies of his newly released autobiography, and to try and get lifted his lifetime ban from Major League Baseball. "For the last 14 years I've consistently heard the statement: 'If Pete Rose came clean, all would be forgiven,' said Rose. "Well, I've done what you've asked" (Dodd, 2004). According to sportswriter Hal McCoy, who covered Rose for 31 years, "When it became clear he wouldn't get in (to the Hall) unless he admitted it, he admitted it" (Dodd, 2004).

Interviewers can't do much in dealing with an agenda other than to recognize it and try to push through it. No athlete or coach is going to volunteer difficult or damaging information, which is why interviewers have to keep asking the questions, even if they may be unpopular or even controversial. Regarding the Gray-Rose interview, sportswriter Michael Shapiro observed, "What if Gray had not pushed Rose? What if he had reduced himself, as so many of his colleagues have, to the role of asking, 'So, big fella, heckuva night, huh?' Reporting is neither about deference nor is it always about asking nicely. It is about finding out. We need, we want to know, be it profane or sacred" (Shapiro, 2000).

As an interviewer you must also learn to recognize your own agenda. In other words, there is no such thing as a completely objective, unbiased interview, because every interviewer has his or her own set of personal values, beliefs, and opinions. For example, consider the December 2002 interview between Bryant Gumbel of HBO's *Real Sports* and Martha Burk. At the time, Burk and the National Council for Women's Organizations were pushing for the Augusta National Golf Club to admit female members. Burk and the NCWO tried all kinds of ways to pressure Augusta National, including a threatened protest at the Masters golf tournament (the tactics failed and Augusta National still does not have a female member). The following was part of the exchange between Gumbel and Burk:

BRYANT GUMBEL: I heard it characterized to me one time as whereas women are arguing about wanting to pay the tab at the restaurant, African-Americans can't even get in the restaurant . . . and that's a big difference.

MARTHA BURK: Well, women can't even get in Augusta.

BG: But most Americans can't.

MB: But not because of an immutable characteristic. At least theoretically, you as a man have the ability to get rich enough, powerful enough, or a good enough golfer to get in

Augusta. I, as a woman, do not have that chance. That is the difference; that's the essence of discrimination.

BG: We're talking about maybe one or two rich, privileged women.

MB: Yeah, we are.

BG: So, why all this hoopla to afford one more privilege *(voice rising)* to some already privileged women?

MB: Would you have asked this question at Shoal Creek, Bryant . . . for heaven's sake! Would you say, "Why are we doing this to let one rich, African-American man who's already got it made into the Shoal Creek Country Club?" *(Under pressure from Civil Rights groups, the private Shoal Creek Country Club in Birmingham, Alabama added its first black member in 1990 prior to its hosting the PGA Golf Championship).*

BG: But you don't worry about your safety on this, do you?

MB: No, I don't worry about my personal safety.

BG: See, that's *(voice rising)* . . . another difference between race and gender discrimination.

MB: What? *(voice rising)*

BG: If you were fighting race discrimination, yes, you would be concerned about your safety at all times, because people do get shot over it. Nobody gets shot over women's rights.

MB: Well, I disagree.

BG: Nobody gets beaten or lynched over women's rights.

MB: What do you think rape is, Bryant? It's a hate crime against women.

Source: HBO/*Real Sports* December 16, 2002.

The entire interview lasted about 20 minutes, but in just this short section detailed above you can see the male, minority background Gumbel brought into the interview. As a black and a male, Gumbel had a completely different perspective on the issue compared to Burk. In addition, Gumbel is an avid golfer and a longtime member of the private, all-male Burning Tree Golf Club in Bethesda, Maryland. "The challenge was how do you interject Bryant's private life, and do it in a way that it doesn't taint the journalistic questioning of Martha Burk throughout the entire piece," said Ross Greenburg of HBO Sports. "That became the tricky hurdle to jump over" (Raissman, 2002).

Dealing with personal agenda can be a tricky hurdle for any interviewer. The best suggestion is not necessarily to eliminate any personal feelings (which is impossible anyway), but rather to acknowledge and try to control them. Many people suggested Gumbel would have been better off disclosing his membership either before or during the interview with Burk; Greenburg later admitted that doing so might have prevented "an unnecessary and ill-conceived conflict" (Raissman, 2002). Good interviewers also put themselves in the place of the person being interviewed and try to see things from that perspective. That doesn't mean agreeing with the other person, but rather playing the role of "devil's advocate" with respect for the other position. An interviewer should never ask questions simply to make a point or promote a cause, but at the same time you can't let the person you're interviewing do the same without being challenged.

The *theme* of the story simply refers to what the story is about. Every story should be reducible to one sentence—"The Cougars rallied heroically to win the game," or "John Smith is an inspirational athlete who won't let cancer ruin his career." It sounds overly simplistic, but not establishing the theme of the story before the interview causes all kinds of problems. If you fail to clearly identify a one-sentence theme for the story then the interview can become a rambling, unfocused mess. A clear theme can help the interviewer determine whom to interview and what to ask.

Let's consider the story of a female head football coach at an area junior college. It's important to identify the theme as precisely as possible, so in this case it might be "Female football coach Julie Jones succeeds in traditional man's job." The reason we want as much specificity as possible with the theme is that it will help determine who to talk to and what questions to ask. A less focused theme such as "Julie Jones is a female football coach" doesn't really help clarify these issues. The theme should also reflect what' newsworthy about the story—what makes it interesting or relevant to the audience. It's not just that Julie Jones is a coach, but rather that she is succeeding and doing a good job in what is considered a male-dominated sport.

The focused theme then leads us to determine the *stakeholders* in the story (see Figure 5.1). The stakeholders are the people related to the story who might contribute something to it such as background information or an interview. As you can see from Figure 5.1, there are several potential stakeholders for the Julie Jones story including herself, team players and coaches, school administrators, fans, opposing players/coaches,

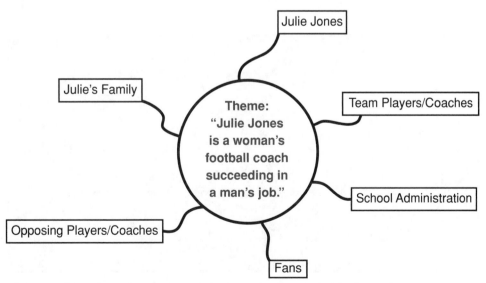

Figure 5.1. List of possible stakeholders for female football coach.

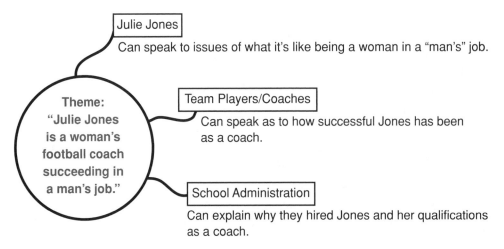

Figure 5.2. Revised stakeholders for female football coach story.

and Jones' family. A long format story such as a magazine feature might include all of these stakeholders, but because of time and space restrictions more than likely you'll need to whittle down this list to just two or three.

This is why having a focused theme is so important (see Figure 5.2). Because the theme is about Jones succeeding in a "man's" occupation we can narrow down our list of potential stakeholders. The fans, opposing players, and Jones's family might be interesting interviews, but they don't really contribute to the main theme of the story (it could be argued that the family perspective is relevant to the theme, but that might actually be a completely different story—"how female coach balances job and family life"). That leaves us with three groups of stakeholders to interview, including Coach Jones, her players and coaches, and possibly the school administration. It also helps us figure out what each of these stakeholders is going to contribute to the story and what

The setting, such as Super Bowl media day, could impact the type of responses received during an interview. (Courtesy of John T. Greilick/*The Detroit News*)

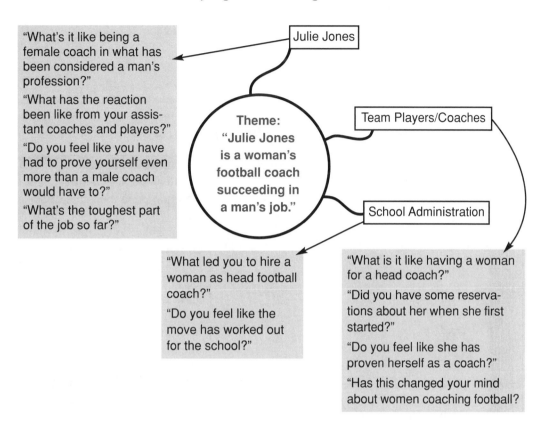

Figure 5.3. Stakeholder questions for female football coach story.

questions to ask them. Instead of fumbling around trying to come up with good questions, the theme leads us to the appropriate questions to ask. The list of questions in Figure 5.3 is by no means exhaustive, but you really don't need to ask more than a few questions from each stakeholder.

Setting refers to where the interview will take place and how much time the interviewer will have. In some cases, this decision is completely out of the hands of the interviewer who may only have a few minutes to talk with a player on his or her way from the locker room to the field. News conferences (see Chapter 8) and locker room interviews (typically where the athlete or coach is interviewed after a game) are also examples where the setting is dictated. These types of events are attended by dozens of reporters if not more (e.g., Super Bowl Media Day) and intimacy is all but impossible. That's one reason athletes and coaches are much less likely to open up or give interesting comments in these group settings.

A good example is the February 2009 interview between freelance political blogger Ken Krayeske and University of Connecticut men's basketball coach Jim Calhoun. Krayeske wanted to talk about Calhoun's large salary (a base of $1.5 million per year; more than the university president or athletic director) in the midst of an economic recession. But Krayeske chose a post-game news conference to ask his questions, and after Calhoun tried to defuse the situation with humor the exchange soon became testy:

KEN KRAYESKE: Considering that you're the highest-paid state employee and there's a $2 billion budget deficit, do you think . . .

JIM CALHOUN: Not a dime back. *(Laughter).*

KK: Not a dime back?

JC: Not a dime back. I'd like to be able to retire some day. I'm getting tired.

KK: You don't think $1.5 million is enough?

JC: I make a lot more than that.

KK: You do?

JC: What was the take tonight?

KK: What's the deal with Comcast worth?

JK: You're not really that stupid, are you?

KK: Yes, I am.

JC: My best advice to you—shut up.

KK: Thank you. That's very polite of you.

JC: No, it wasn't polite of me; I want you to shut up. If you want to talk to me outside, I'd be more than happy to.

KK: If these guys covered this stuff, I wouldn't have to do it. *(Other reporters at news conference begin to audibly groan and complain).*

JC: Quite frankly, we bring in $12 million a year for this university. *(Then, Calhoun's volume really increased).* GET SOME FACTS AND COME BACK AND SEE ME. GET SOME FACTS AND COME BACK AND SEE ME. DON'T THROW OUT SALARIES OR OTHER THINGS. GET SOME FACTS AND COME BACK AND SEE ME. WE TURN OVER MORE THAN $12 MILLION TO THE UNIVERSITY OF CONNECTICUT, WHICH IS STATE-RUN. Next Question (Borges, 2009).

> The Krayeske-Calhoun interview also brings up the issue of *access*. We talked about this at some length in Chapter 2 and don't need to go into much more detail. Obviously, there are going to be situations where interview access is more limited, such as when a player, coach, or organization is dealing with bad or embarrassing news. Access is usually much freer on the professional sports level, where athletes and coaches typically decide for themselves when and where they want to talk. College, and especially high school, athletes are more protected and access is more difficult. Many times, access to an interview will have to be arranged through a sports information person. This is why news conference and locker room interviews are so common—those are the places the athletes and coaches are most available.

The issue is not whether Krayeske had a right to ask the questions (although some suggested that he obtained his press credential fraudulently), but he should have realized that Calhoun was not going to offer any meaningful answers in that particular setting. A more appropriate setting would have been a one-on-one interview that was not conducted in the aftermath of a game. At the same time, there's no guarantee that Calhoun would have agreed to such an interview; Krayeske probably realized that and figured he better ask his questions while he had the chance.

Another type of setting is the on-field or on-court interview, which usually takes place before or after a game, and sometimes at halftime. Before a game or during halftime the interviewer will have a few seconds with a player or coach for some quick analysis, while the end of the game interview focuses more on reaction. In some cases, these interviews can be unintentionally revealing. In the heat of the moment many players and coaches have cursed (on live television) or said something they later regretted (such as the former University of Iowa football player who called the Iowa State coach an unrepeatable name). In order to prevent such incidents and maintain control of their agenda, many teams and schools have banned on-field and on-court interviews in favor of controlled news conferences, which take place after players and coaches have been afforded a "cooling down" period, which by NCAA regulations is 10 minutes after the end of the game.

While the reaction interviews after a big game are sometimes compelling, most on-field interviews are bland and uninteresting. Coaches and players keep their comments intentionally plain, in part because the questions are pretty boring. It's hard to come up with a great question when the team is running on the field and a coach only has 20 seconds to talk. The "celebrity" sideline interviews with former players are similarly uninspired, except for the rare occasions when things go terribly wrong. One of the most famous sideline interviews of all time, a December 20, 2003, interview between ESPN's Suzy Kolber and former New York Jets quarterback Joe Namath, stands out

An on-court interview immediately after a game can be unintentionally revealing due to the emotions of the moment. (Courtesy of George Mason Athletics/John Aronson)

mainly because of Namath's drunkenness (he later apologized to Kolber and admitted he had a drinking problem):

SUZY KOLBER: Joe, it's been a tough season for Jets fans. What does it mean to you now that the team is struggling?

JOE NAMATH: I wanna kiss you. I couldn't care less about the team struggling. What we know is we can improve. Chad Pennington, our quarterback, missed the first part of the season, and we struggled. We're looking to next season, we're looking to make a noise now and . . . I wanna kiss you!

SK: Thanks Joe! I'll take that as a huge compliment . . . *[Namath in background: YEAH!!!!]* Joe Namath, part of the four-decade team. We'll see these guys at halftime ("Top 10," 2004).

To the extent that the setting can be controlled it should be as comfortable as possible for the interview subject. A comfortable, familiar environment automatically puts the subject at ease and makes it more likely that he/she will open up with good answers. Sportswriter and ESPN personality Tim Cowlishaw covered the Dallas Cowboys in 1986 and 1987 and learned this lesson the first time he had a private interview with then-coach Tom Landry. "The man whose answers seemed so predictable in the daily group interviews—although probably no more predictable than our questions—suddenly became expansive as he relaxed on his sofa" (Cowlishaw, 2000). In the case of our story with Julie Jones, the best place for the interview might be her office, home, or even the football field. If possible, avoid a setting that would be unfamiliar or uncomfortable, such as outside with the sun shining in her eyes.

Once the elements of audience, agenda, theme, setting, and stakeholders have been determined the interviewer will likely need to do some additional research and background work. Each sports story has its own unique information that not even the most knowledgeable interviewer can be expected to know. Fortunately, the Internet makes it very easy to access background information, especially related to facts and figures. For more personal information the interviewer might want to contact those with an intimate knowledge of the subject matter. In regards to the Julie Jones story, a quick search of the Internet should provide important information such as age, previous coaching experience, and athletic background. If such information can't be accessed through the Internet a call to the school would be necessary. To get more personal information, such as what kind of coach Jones is, the interviewer could contact the school's athletic director or call athletic officials at schools where Jones previously coached.

Doing the necessary background and research (the "leg" work as older journalists would say) is just as important to the interviewing process as developing the proper theme. The information learned during this process will help the interviewer more sharply focus and frame the appropriate questions. In addition, knowing about your interview subject puts him/her more at ease during the actual interview. People are more likely to open up and give more insightful answers when they can respect and trust the interviewer.

As a corollary, not doing research puts the interviewer at an obvious disadvantage. ESPN's Roy Firestone was reminded of this lesson when he interviewed then-Indiana basketball coach Bobby Knight in the spring of 2000. Knight had come under tremendous pressure amidst allegations that he once choked a former player during practice. A videotape of the incident had circulated in the general media for quite some time, but Firestone never bothered to view the tape and could not question Knight about it. As a result, Firestone came under criticism for not approaching the subject and being too "soft" on the coach.

One of the final things the interviewer may want to do before the actual interview is create a list of questions, which has both advantages and disadvantages. On the plus side, having a list of questions forces the interviewer to focus and narrow down the most important topics he/she wants to address. In some cases, an interview can digress and get off track, and a list can help make sure that the interviewer returns to cover the essential points of the story. However, a list can also make an interview seem scripted and stilted. Instead of an honest conversation, the interview turns into an interrogation where the interviewer is rattling off questions that seem to put the respondent on the defensive. There's also the temptation of not listening to the answers and focusing on the next question on the list. This can lead to some major embarrassment for the interviewer if the respondent says something unexpected. Instead of writing out the questions in the form of a list, you might consider using an index card that includes some short reminders about important topics.

Should you let your interview subject see your list of questions ahead of time? Most sports journalists would say absolutely not. It's fine to tell your subject ahead of time what the interview is about; it may put the interviewee more at ease and allow him/her to develop better answers (e.g., "I would like to talk to you and get your reaction to the reinstatement of Michael Vick to the NFL. Would you have some time for an interview?"). But letting the subject see the list of questions can ruin the spontaneity of the interview and lead to more scripted answers. Worse, it gives the interviewee far too much control of the interview itself. If someone absolutely refuses to grant an interview without seeing the questions ahead of time you might reconsider whether the person is essential to the story. If not, find someone else to interview. If they are essential, you will have to use your best journalistic instincts to determine how to proceed.

AT THE INTERVIEW

The best thing that the interviewer can do at the interview is create an atmosphere of trust and confidence that helps the respondent speak more freely. As we have noted, this is extremely difficult in news conference and locker room situations that include dozens of reporters or more. In those situations, the athletes and coaches have a natural tendency to get defensive and speak more guardedly no matter what the interviewer does. That's why the answers from news conference and locker room interviews often seem cold and uninspired.

If the interviewer has the chance to get a more intimate one-on-one interview there are several strategies for building trust and rapport. The best approach is to already have

Building trust and rapport will enable the interviewee to provide more open and interesting responses. (Courtesy of WVU Sports Communications)

established a trusting relationship with the person being interviewed. If the coach or athlete knows the interviewer and realizes that he/she can be trusted, not only will it be easier to get access, but the answers will also be more honest and open. This is obviously a long-term strategy that can take months or even years to develop, and it works especially well for beat writers who cover a team or player on a regular basis. However, there are more sports media today than ever before and the sheer number of reporters all wanting interviews makes this a difficult proposition.

It is possible to create a certain level of trust even in an interview situation where there is no established relationship. Again, conducting the interview in a place that is comfortable for the interview subject is important. It also helps to engage in what can be called a *pre-interview*, which is nothing more than idle chit-chat with the subject before the real interview begins. Talking about the weather, favorite hobbies, or family is a great way to relax someone and get him/her to feel more at ease. If you see several bowling trophies on the mantle of Coach Jones' office, you might ask her about them and how she got involved in bowling. A pre-interview doesn't have to last long and it can give the broadcast reporter something to talk about while the equipment is being set up. But be sure the interview subject always knows when the real interview starts and his or her comments are officially on the record.

The order of questions can also help put the interview subject at ease. Assuming there is enough time, the interviewer can help "warm up" the subject by asking easy questions first. As already noted, however, this does not work in certain situations where time is more limited. Easy questions at the beginning help the interview subject

The Sacking of Rome

Jim Rome has created a successful career on sports radio and television as the interviewer-provocateur: someone who purposefully tries to agitate and goad interview subjects. To Rome, the interview is spectacle and the idea is not always to get good answers, but to create good television. It's debatable whether the interview Rome conducted in 1994 with then-NFL quarterback Jim Everett qualifies as "good television," but that it is still talked about 15 years after the fact says something. During his interview with Everett on the ESPN show *Talk2*, Rome kept calling him "Chris," as a reference to Chris Evert, a former dominant player on the women's tennis circuit. The name was an implication that Everett lacked toughness—a serious criticism for an NFL quarterback. Rome continually denies that the interview and ensuing studio melee were staged:

JIM ROME: Jim, good to have you on the show.

JIM EVERETT: Good to be here, Jim. Thank you.

JR: Check that. Chris Everett, good to have you on the show.

JE: You know what? You've been calling me that for about the last five years and . . .

JR: Two years actually, Chris.

JE: Let me say one thing. In that game . . . how many sacks did I have that we came back and won?

JR: How many sacks did you have?

JE: Yeah . . . how many sacks?

JR: You see, this was back in 1989. You may have even been Jim Everett back there, but somewhere along the way Jim, you ceased being Jim and you became Chris.

JE: Well, let me tell you a little secret . . . that, you know, we're sitting here right now, and if you guys want to take a station break, you can. But if you call me Chris Everett to my face one more time . . .

JR: I already did it twice.

JE: You'd better . . . if you call it one more time, we'd better take a station break.

JR: Well, it's a five-minute segment, on a five-segment show. We've got a long way to go.

JE: We do.

JR: We've got a long way to go. I'll get a couple of segments out of you.

JE: It's good to be here with you though . . . because you've been talking like this behind my back for a long time now.

JR: But now I've said it right here, so we've got no problems then.

JE: I think that you probably won't say it again.

JR: I'll bet I do.

JE: OK.

JR: Chris.

[Everett tosses aside coffee table and attacks Rome until restrained by studio personnel]

Source: ESPN

relax, so when the harder questions eventually come he/she is more inclined to answer. Asking tough questions right off the top might work for *60 Minutes*, but it runs a higher risk of the interview subject refusing to answer. If the hard questions are asked at the end and the subject refuses to answer, at least you have some quotes/sound bites you can use. Sportswriter Bill Plaschke put this into practice when he interviewed former Major League Baseball player Spike Owen after a game. Owen had hit his first home run of the season in the fourth inning, but committed a costly error in the ninth that lost the game. "Standing in front of several reporters afterward," noted Plaschke, "my first question to Owen was about the home run. Relaxed after talking for a few minutes about the homer, Owen was revealing and insightful when answering my next question about the error" (Plaschke, 2000).

Trust is also a two-way street, which means at the very least you should respect your interview subjects. That doesn't mean you have to like them or even agree with them, but you will have a better interview if you respect their position and point of view. It could be argued that provocateurs like Howard Cosell and Jim Rome (see "The Sacking of Rome" sidebar) were highly successful because of a lack of respect for their interview subjects, but they are the exceptions rather than the rule. Plaschke (2000) correctly observes that "you catch more flies with honey" than you do with vinegar, which is another way of saying that in the long run it usually doesn't pay to be intentionally difficult or argumentative—unless you're Jim Rome.

It's also important not to go too far in the other direction and let the interview subject control the interview. This is more difficult that it sounds for several reasons. Sports figures can be very intimidating figures, whether because of their celebrity status, personalities, or the circumstances surrounding the interview. Consider this June 4, 1976, exchange between former Dodgers manager Tommy Lasorda and Paul Olden of Associate Press radio. Dave Kingman of the Mets had just hit three home runs to help beat the Dodgers. Even though Olden must have felt intimidated, he did not give up on the interview:

PAUL OLDEN: What's your opinion of Kingman's performance?

TOMMY LASORDA: What's my opinion of Kingman's performance!? What the BLEEP do you think is my opinion of it? I think it was BLEEPING BLEEP. Put that in, I don't give a BLEEP. Opinion of his performance!!? BLEEP, he beat us with three BLEEPING home runs! What the BLEEP do you mean, "What is my opinion of his performance?" How could you ask me a question like that, "What is my opinion of his performance?" BLEEP, he hit three home runs! BLEEP. I'm BLEEPING pissed off to lose that BLEEPING game. And you ask me my opinion of his performance! BLEEP. That's a tough question to ask me, isn't it? "What is my opinion of his performance?"

PO: Yes, it is. I asked it, and you gave me an answer . . .

TL: Well, I didn't give you a good answer because I'm mad, but I mean . . .

PO: Well, it wasn't a good question . . .

TL: That's a tough question to ask me right now, "What is my opinion of his performance?" I mean, you want me to tell you what my opinion of his performance is?

PO: You just did . . .

TL: That's right. BLEEP. Guy hits three home runs against us. BLEEP ("Top 10," 2009).

After the 2003 NCAA basketball championship game, Bonnie Bernstein of CBS got a short interview with losing coach Roy Williams, then at Kansas. Speculation was rampant at the time that Williams would soon leave Kansas to coach at North Carolina, but Williams had refused to comment until after the game:

BONNIE BERNSTIEN: Very understandably you didn't want to address this issue during the week, but many people out there, with the game over, want to know what your level of interest is in the North Carolina job, Coach.

ROY WILLIAMS: Bonnie, I could give a flip about what those people want. As a journalist you have to ask that question and I understand that, but as a human being . . . all those people who want that answer right now are not very sensitive.

BB: If they offer you the job, though, would you be willing to take it?

RW: I haven't thought about that for one second. I haven't thought about that for one second. The guy in your ear that told you that you had to ask that question . . . as a journalist, that's fine . . . but as a human being, that's not very nice because it's not very sensitive and I've got to think that in tough times that people should be more sensitive. I don't give a BLEEP about North Carolina right now. I've got 13 kids in that locker room that I love. *(Walks off)*.

BB: Coach, thank you ("Roy Williams", n.d.).

Like Jim Gray with Pete Rose, Bernstein received some criticism for the timing of her comments, but still maintains that "if I had to do that all over, I would do it the same way" (Hruby, 2005). In Gray's case, the problem was one of agenda; Rose kept trying to focus the interview on his All-Century Team honor, while Gray kept pushing him to talk about his gambling. Do Gray and Bernstein deserve credit or criticism for staying so focused? Like the Krayeske interview of Jim Calhoun, their interviews raise questions of venue and appropriateness. All these incidents suggest that there is a fine line between good sports journalism and inappropriateness, and it is extremely difficult to know exactly where the line is and when to cross it.

Questions, Questions

Now we're down to the essential part of interviewing—figuring out what questions to ask. It sounds like a difficult proposition, but it's actually pretty simple if we have carefully figured out our audience, agenda, theme, setting, and stakeholders. Those decisions tell us who will be watching/listening and what they expect from the interview, who we should interview, and most importantly, the main focus of the story. We can now add another important consideration—what kind of answers we want.

Don't confuse expected answers with scripted answers; we're not trying to get the interview subject to say a particular thing or give a pre-ordained response. Many young journalists make the mistake of writing the story ahead of time then trying to goad the interview subject into giving a certain quote or sound bite. The needed portion would then be crammed into the story, which is an approach that works about as well as jamming a square peg in a round hole. When we talk about expected answers we're talking more about what the stakeholder will contribute to the story based on the theme. Refer back to our hypothetical story on football coach Julie Jones (see Figure 5.3). Based on the theme, we already know what we need Coach Jones to contribute—some kind of responses that reflect on her being a female coach in a male-dominated profession. The specific answers Jones gives to these questions don't matter as long as she addresses the topic. So if we asked her, "What's it like being a female coach in what has been considered a man's job?" it's immaterial if she says it's been great, terrible or somewhere in between.

However, there are certain ways to frame such questions to get more meaningful answers. In this context, meaningful suggests an answer that not only supports the theme of the story, but also is memorable and has an emotional impact. Those are somewhat difficult concepts to define, but perhaps an example from our Coach Jones story will help:

Q: Could you tell me a little more about your coaching background and how you got started?

A: "I started out coaching basketball and football at a high school in New Mexico. I eventually dropped the basketball and spent the next 10 years as a high school football assistant, then became an assistant here at Northwest. After six years here I became head coach when Coach Drummond retired.

"I've always loved football, but never dreamed I could ever play or coach. My first coaching job was as a basketball coach at a high school in New Mexico. During my second season one of the football assistant coaches abruptly quit and they needed someone to fill in. I figured they wouldn't have time to hire anyone and would have to fill the job from within. So I went to our athletic director and begged for the job. I told him he would never regret it if he let me coach football, and I don't think he ever did."

Hopefully, you consider the second answer much more interesting and memorable. That's because it relates to the personal perspective of the interview subject; she is telling us something only she can relate from her own experience. You get these kinds of responses by asking certain kinds of questions—"how" and "why" questions as opposed to "who" and "what." "Why is this important to you?" and "How do you feel about this?" are examples of questions that force the respondent to think and come up with more personal responses. In a sports context we hear the same question after every big game—"how do you feel?" It may seem like a dumb question (after all, players on the winning team are certainly going to be happier than players on the losing team), but it's the simplest, most direct way to get a personal answer.

In terms of getting good responses, "who" and "what" questions (along with close-ended questions that can be answered "yes" or "no") are not very strong. Focus more on open-ended questions that can't be answered in a couple of words, and that force the respondent to think about the answer. However, close-ended questions are very important in terms of getting information you need to fill in background in the story. But the answers to such questions should not be used as quotes or sound bites, especially if you have something more meaningful. As an example, refer back to our question about Jones' coaching background. Which of these approaches is stronger?

Story version 1: Coach Jones always wanted to coach football and finally got the chance as an assistant at a high school in New Mexico, where she also coached basketball. "I eventually dropped the basketball and spent the next 10 years as a high school football assistant, then became an assistant here at Northwest" she said. "After six years here I became head coach when Coach Drummond retired."

Story version 2: Coach Jones never thought she would get to coach football, but her career took a surprising turn when she was coaching high school basketball in New Mexico. "During my second season one of the football assistant coaches abruptly quit and they needed someone to fill in," she said. "I figured they wouldn't have time to hire anyone and would have to fill the job from within. So I went to our athletic director and begged for the job. I told him he would never regret it if he let me coach football, and I don't think he ever did." Ten years later she moved to Northwest as an assistant and six years after that took over the program when Coach Ralph Drummond retired.

Version 2 uses the best responses as the quotes, but also incorporates the other responses as background material. If possible, avoid using information (the "who," "what," and "when" information of the story) as quotes or sound bites; the best responses come from the "how" and "why" questions.

As was previously mentioned, it often helps to ask somewhat easy questions at the beginning of the interview to help the respondent relax and loosen up. For our story on Julie Jones the question about her coaching background and history would be perfect—it's an easy question for her to answer and also gets her to open up a little more personally. If need be, the questions can become gradually more difficult, although in this particular situation that probably would not be necessary. The issue then becomes what should follow the opening question. It was previously discussed that having a list of questions can be beneficial and one could be used in this case. But as was already noted, using a list runs the risk of a scripted, interrogation-type interview. Consider these approaches for Julie Jones:

Questions From List

Q1: Could you tell me a little more about your coaching background and how you got started?

A: "I started out coaching basketball and football at a high school in New Mexico. I eventually dropped the basketball and spent the next 10 years as a high school football assistant, then became an assistant here at Northwest. After six years here I became head coach when Coach Drummond retired."

Q2: What has it been like coaching football?

A: "It's been very challenging, but also very rewarding. There have been a lot of hard times; times I wanted to quit, but I stuck with it and I'm glad I did."

MITCHELL LAYTON PHOTOGRAPHY

Coach's CORNER

by Craig Esherick

I've been interviewed by many reporters—after games, a day or two before games, during the off-season, on camera, and in the hallway moments after we've just won or lost a key conference or tournament game. Most coaches understand that reporters have a job to do and are often working on a tight deadline. But whatever the situation and especially when being interviewed by someone I have never met, I want to know that the person interviewing me respects what I do for a living and who I am as a human being. Context is everything when you're asking a coach a question.

A question asked on the first tee of a charity golf outing is a little bit different than a question asked right after a heart-breaking loss to end a tough season. The level of emotion involved and the many thoughts swirling through the coach's head at that moment has to be factored into the question. That does not preclude the asking of tough questions by the press; most coaches understand this. But consider the following example of a question that can be either well received or create friction based simply on the phrasing used by the interviewer.

> "Coach, can you take us through the last possession of the game and talk about what you were trying to do on that last play?"

> "Coach, why couldn't your team get a better shot at the end of the game, especially since you called timeout right before that last possession?"

Unless the reporter is intentionally trying to damage his/her relationship with the coach or is trying to incite an angry response from the coach, the phrasing of the first question is much better. That's the one that will enlighten the audience without alienating the coach. Opting to ask the question phrased the second way will set a tone for the relationship with the coach that will ultimately prove to be unproductive.

As a college coach, I never thought it was a good idea to criticize a player in the press. The relationship between a coach and player at the college level requires the coach, in my opinion, to shoulder the blame for mistakes made by his/her team. This also goes for coaching high school, middle school, and youth league. Interviewers should respect this stance and not attempt to coerce a coach into saying something negative about a player. Professional athletes, however, may not receive such protective treatment.

I always believed that my players deserved to be treated as college student-athletes who played a sport and not as professional athletes who are paid to perform at a high level. I feel very strongly about this and I know that many in the press feel the same way when their own children who are student-athletes are being interviewed.

It's also courteous of interviewers to understand that student-athletes are not as experienced as coaches at being interviewed, so questions should be posed in a manner that doesn't intentionally lead them to say things they will later regret. This consideration should especially be extended when interviewing players immediately after a big game, when emotions are often high and the players haven't had an opportunity to calm down and gather their thoughts.

Q3: What are your football coaching goals? Do you ever see yourself coaching at a big-time college or maybe even in the NFL?

A: "I've often thought of that, because that's certainly a dream of anyone who is a football coach—to move up to the highest possible level, whether that's Division I college or the NFL. But I honestly don't think I have the kind of personality or temperament that would help me do that."

Q4: How long do you think you'll be coaching football?

A: "That's a hard question to answer. I still have a desire and a passion for the game and I love working with these young men. Some of the other stuff might force me out before I'm ready, but otherwise I can see myself doing this a long time."

Questions Without a list—The Conversational Approach

Q: Could you tell me a little more about your coaching background and how you got started?

A: "I started out coaching basketball and football at a high school in New Mexico. I eventually dropped the basketball and spent the next 10 years as a high school football assistant, then became an assistant here at Northwest. After six years here I became head coach when Coach Drummond retired."

*Q: You coached **both** football and basketball? How did that come about?*

A: "During my second season one of the football assistant coaches abruptly quit and they needed someone to fill in. I figured they wouldn't have time to hire anyone and would have to fill the job from within. So I went to our athletic director and begged for the job. I told him he would never regret it if he let me coach football, and I don't think he ever did."

Q: Do you have any regrets?

A: "It's been very challenging, but also very rewarding. There have been a lot of hard times; times I wanted to quit, but I stuck with it and I'm glad I did."

Q: When you talk about hard times what exactly do you mean?

A: "Well, the reception from some of the alumni and fans hasn't always been positive. There's still a lot of 'good old boys' who think a woman has no business coaching a football team. The pressure was pretty intense for awhile, especially when I became the head coach. Winning cures a lot of problems, so it's a situation that has slowly gotten better over time, but there are still some very vocal people who would prefer I find another place to coach."

Q: On that subject, what are your football coaching goals? Do you ever see yourself coaching at a big-time college or maybe even in the NFL?

A: "I've often thought of that, because that's certainly a dream of anyone who is a football coach—to move up to the highest possible level, whether that's Division I college or the NFL. But I honestly don't think I have the kind of personality or temperament that would help me do that."

Q: *What do you mean you don't have the right kind of personality?*

A: "I never wanted to be a trailblazer—a Jackie Robinson or anything like that. Although I think what I'm doing is important for other women, I don't really want to be on the front lines of some great social cause. I just want to coach football."

Q: *How long do you think you'll be coaching football?*

A: "That's a hard question to answer. I still have a desire and a passion for the game and I love working with these young men. Some of the other stuff might force me out before I'm ready, but otherwise I can see myself doing this a long time."

We call the second approach conversational because the interviewer takes time to listen to the answers and adjust the questions accordingly. When Jones mentions about the hard times she has gone through, the skillful interviewer notices and asks a follow-up question. The interviewer going off a list such as in the first approach detailed above simply keeps going to the next question and misses the opportunity to follow up. Notice also that in some cases these follow-up answers are the best, most personal responses. A good interview is like a conversation, which implies listening, dialogue, and feedback. In some extreme cases, a particular response might take the interview in a completely different direction. The interviewer should not be afraid to explore these possibilities, even if it changes the theme of the story. It might be that the response creates a new, better story idea.

Taking a conversational approach can also be effective when the interviewer has to ask difficult questions. Questions can be difficult for any number of reasons; they may be potentially damaging, embarrassing, or conflict with the respondent's agenda. But a conversational interview can help draw out the respondent and make these potentially difficult situations more successful. One strategy is what interviewers call the "Golden Moment," which refers to the interviewer being quiet and letting the respondent fill in difficult dead spaces. Many interviewers tend to talk too much (experts suggest that if you're talking more than 10% of the time in an interview you're talking too much) and they want to fill up all the quiet moments with their own words. Instead, when the interview hits a dead spot after you've asked a question, simply sit back and say nothing. This "Golden Moment" is a nonverbal signal that the respondent should keep talking, and it works surprisingly well. Veteran radio and print reporter Joyce Davis noted, "It is amazing when you shut up how much you get. My normal way of interviewing would be to ask you a question, then as soon as you shut up give you another . . . really pick at you a lot. I tried to ask a question . . . then say absolutely nothing. That was very hard. The person will come up with deepest things if you just let them fill those silences" ("Dealing with," 1993).

SUMMARY

Getting sports interviews can be extremely frustrating, intimidating, and exhausting. Some players and coaches can be very uncooperative, and even the most cooperative of them have usually heard all the questions before. It is a constant challenge for the sports reporter to get access to the people he wants to interview, create an atmosphere conducive to good interviewing, and finally ask the questions that result in memorable answers. There is no magic formula, other than preparing, working hard, and trying to earn the respect of the athletes and coaches you need to interview.

As a final thought, always stay focused on the end result—good answers. In other words, don't spend too much time worrying if your questions are phrased perfectly, whether you asked a dumb question, or how you appeared on camera. Most of the time, your questions aren't even going to be used in the story. If you have to ask a few dumb questions or stumble over asking a certain question, so be it. As long as you get the insightful, memorable quotes or sound bites your need, you have done your job.

DISCUSSION QUESTIONS

1. NBA star Kobe Bryant has been scheduled to give interviews to both Bryant Gumbel of HBO's *Real Sports* and David Letterman of *The Late Show*. How do you think the interview questions will differ? What specific questions do you think each interviewer would ask?

2. How do you think the Martha Burk-Bryant Gumbel interview would have been different if someone else had been the interviewer? How would it have been different if the interviewer had been Katie Couric? Oprah Winfrey?

3. For the same story you have to interview three different athletes; one says he can only do it by phone, another prefers email, and the third has agreed to a sit-down personal interview. Will your approach to these three interviews differ? Do you think the answers you will get will be different? Which do you think would be the more compelling interview and why?

SUGGESTED EXERCISES

1. For each of the following situations identify the appropriate theme, stakeholders, and agendas. Develop a list of questions you would want to ask the people related to your story:

   - Local 80-year old man trains to run in this year's Boston Marathon.
   - Football team reunites 25 years after winning championship.
   - Popular area basketball coach rumored to be leaving to take another job at a rival school.
   - Local high school player sets state record for most home runs.
   - School district declares star player academically ineligible the week before the championship game.

2. If possible, arrange an interview outside of class with a local athlete or coach. (If not possible, pair up with someone in class and interview each other outside of class.) For the interview work on the following:

- choosing the appropriate setting
- establishing a level of comfort
- conducting a conversational interview related to the theme

Write down (or otherwise record) the responses from the interview. What were the best answers? What type of questions led to these good answers?

3. Bob Costas has developed a reputation as one of the best sports interviewers of all time. Access one of Costas's sports interviews, either online or on television, and analyze it in terms of the principles we've discussed. What makes it such a good interview? What makes Costas such a good interviewer?

6

Writing News Releases

PURPOSE AND FUNCTION OF NEWS RELEASES

Writing is much like athletics. Some individuals possess innate qualities that facilitate development of the skills required—a creative imagination for writers, for example—but it takes a lot of practice to excel at a craft or a sport. Any good writer will tell you that the secret to success is practice, practice, practice.

An aspiring sports information director (SID) does not have to be "a born writer." However, anyone in the business of sports information must learn the fundamentals of good writing and practice them diligently to develop proficiency in the craft. A professional cannot succeed without a thorough understanding of the parts of speech, sentence structure, grammar, spelling, punctuation, and theme development. A knowledge of writing techniques—use of description, direct quotations, analogies, similes, and metaphors—is also helpful.

Although creativity is an asset, writing for the media is more like theme or report writing than creative writing. James Stovall, author of *Writing for the Mass Media*, draws these distinctions between writing for the media and other forms of writing:

Subject matter. Writers for the mass media must take on a wide variety of subjects, including news stories, feature stories, advertisements, letters, editorials, and so on.

Purpose. Writing for the mass media has three major purposes: to inform, entertain, and persuade.

Audience. Mass media writing is often directed to a wide audience, and this fact dictates not only the subject matter but also the way in which something is written.

Circumstances of the writing. Writing for the mass media often takes place in the presence of others who are doing the same thing. The writing is frequently done under deadline pressure, and often several people will have a hand in writing and editing a particular item for the mass media. (2009, p. 8)

A news release is very similar to a news story written by the print or broadcast media. Both may emphasize the *hard news* angle of a story, such as the announcement of the selection of a new coach, a scholarship recipient, or a new facility. Both also may take a *soft news* approach, as in a personality profile of the new coach. In simplest terms, hard news generally centers on issues, events, actions, and their consequences. Soft news usually revolves around people such as athletes and their connection to the event or issue.

The purpose of a news story, however, is significantly different from that of a news release. The primary objective of a news story is to inform (i.e., to present information in a fair, objective manner). A secondary function (though no less important) is to entertain, so the sports journalist works hard to inform and entertain an audience. The primary intent of a news release is to persuade (i.e., to present the organization's message or image in the most favorable light). Secondary functions may be to inform, to entertain, and in some cases, to educate. So the SID strives to use information to persuade—to enhance indirectly the image of the organization in the public eye—rather than simply to inform for information's sake.

In *Becoming a Public Relations Writer*, Ronald D. Smith says all public relations writing seeks to influence a reader in some way:

> All public relations writing is an attempt to influence people in some way. If you aren't trying to make an impact on your readers, why write? Without intending to affect readers in some way, you're just wasting time, because you won't produce anything useful. . . . As a writer, you have a particular effect in mind when you write. You want to increase your public's knowledge and understanding about something, you want them to feel a certain way about this information, and you probably want them to respond to that information in a particular way. (2008, p. 7)

Sports information specialists usually structure news releases like news stories, with some modifications, to enhance their publication or broadcast prospects. Hard news

Writing a press release about a team's departure to the NCAA men's basketball tournament's Final Four could lead to media coverage of the team's trip. (Courtesy of George Mason Athletics/John Aronson)

stories generally follow a simple but rigid *straight news* format designed to deliver key information quickly, whereas soft news stories may take a variety of creative or *feature* approaches that emphasize the people in the story as much as the information.

The most common structure for hard news is called the *inverted pyramid* because it places the most important information at the top and the least important at the bottom. The lead of the story quickly summarizes the basic news elements: *who, what, when, where, why,* and *how* (known as the *5Ws and H* in journalistic jargon). It emphasizes the most important element of the news and presents the details of the six elements in descending order of importance. The story does not have a conclusion, but ends with the least important detail:

Most Important Information or Element

Quick Summary of 5Ws and H

Most Important Details

Less Important

Least Important

No Conclusion

The information or "news" drives the story in the inverted pyramid. The structure is effective for two reasons. First, it quickly delivers the information readers are most likely to want. Even those who do not read more than a couple of paragraphs will obtain a quick summary of the facts, with emphasis on the most important details. Second, the story is very easy to trim if it is too long to fit the space allotted on a newspaper page or the time allotted on a newscast. The journalist sacrifices only the least important—and least read—details.

(LEAD) MORGANTOWN, W.Va, March 4, 2004 (WHEN)—West Virginia University women's basketball coach Mike Carey (WHO) was named BIG EAST Conference Coach of the Year (WHAT), as voted on by the league's head coaches (WHY) today at the BIG EAST Conference's annual banquet. (WHERE)

(BODY) Carey, in his third year at WVU, guided the Mountaineers to their best record in more than a decade and led them to their third NCAA Tournament (HOW) in school history.

"This award is a culmination of a great coaching staff, excellent student-athletes and a very supportive administration," Carey said. "I'm appreciative of the honor as it has been bestowed upon me by my peers."

West Virginia returns to action when it takes on Ohio State in opening round action of the NCAA Tournament next weekend, Saturday, March 11, in Morgantown.

The inverted pyramid approach is most appropriate for stories such as announcements, meetings, and breaking news because the reader does not already know most of the basic information. Sports information specialists most often use the inverted pyramid

NEWS TERMS

advance—a story written before an event, such as a preview

alternative structure—any one of several literary formats, including a circle and an hourglass, utilized to organize information in a story

5Ws and H—the six questions (who, what, when, where, why, and how) that all news stories must answer

feature release—a news release that spotlights, or "features," a particular athlete

follow—a story written after an event, such as coverage of a game or an update to an earlier story

game advance—a news release that offers a preview of an upcoming game

header—information at the top of a news release that provides contact information and suggested release time for the story

hometown release—a news release about an athlete that is sent to media in the geographical area in which the athlete lives

inverted pyramid—a story format in which the writer organizes information in descending order of importance

lead—the first sentence or paragraph of a news story

news peg—a phrase or sentence that connects the story to the most important news element or news event

tieback—a phrase or sentence that explains how a story relates to an earlier news event

weekly preview/review—a weekly schedule of all the organization's athletic teams

approach for game advances, news releases, and announcements. Sports information personnel also use the inverted pyramid style on stories they submit to the news media immediately following a game.

Journalists use a number of variations of or alternative to the inverted pyramid for soft news stories in which the basic information will not "hook" the reader. For example, the reader already may know the basic details—the 5Ws and H—of last week's football game, so the journalist looks for an entertaining angle to encourage people to read further in the story. The journalist often starts with a literary device that emphasizes the drama, the suspense, the irony, or some unusual or intriguing facet of the topic. The story may open with a narrative lead, a re-creation of a key play, an anecdote, a quotation, an ironic twist, a question, or some other common literary technique that engages readers.

The rest of the story also may take a variety of forms, depending on the technique utilized in the beginning. A story that opens with a scene-setter might relate the rest of the action in chronological order. A story that begins with a re-creation of the turning point in a game might move from one key play to another. A story that features the star player might move from one key play by the star to another. Such stories generally require more description and detail than do stories that follow the inverted pyramid format. They also require greater creative writing skill.

No matter what technique the writer uses, stories that follow the alternative structure *do* have several common organizational elements. They use a literary device to establish a theme or focal point and then follow with a *news peg* or *tieback*. A news peg connects the story to the most important news element like the first sentence of a story written in the inverted pyramid style. It also may summarize the 5Ws and H to remind the reader of the basic news details. A *tieback* explains how the story relates to a previous news event (i.e., it ties the opening back to the original news announcement or news event). The body of the story adds details in a logical order and wraps up the story with a conclusion that reinforces the theme. The alternative styles may take more of a circle approach in that they "come full circle," or conclude with the emphasis on the same point as the beginning.

Feature Opening—Theme

News Peg or Tieback

Points in Logical Order

Conclusion—Reinforce Theme

Alternative approaches put greater emphasis on the people and the drama of the event. As a result, they usually contain more description that re-creates the scene or event and more quotations that give voice to the "characters" in the stories. They are most effective for stories about athletes in which most readers already know the basic information or the news details are secondary to the person or theme of the story. Journalists utilize alternative styles most often on personality profiles, human-interest features, and *follow* stories—stories printed a couple of days after an event. The alternative styles are also becoming more prevalent by newspaper writers for game stories, because by the next morning most fans already know the essential details of the game from TV, radio, and Internet coverage. Sports information directors use them for feature releases and weekly reviews or previews.

A journalist actually can use either or both approaches to tell the same story. Here's an example of an inverted pyramid lead and an alternative lead and news peg on the same story:

Inverted Pyramid

MORGANTOWN, W.Va.—West Virginia University's women's basketball team used a 41-8 run in the first half and never looked back, holding Towson scoreless for more than 11 minutes, en route to a 79-42 victory over the Tigers in opening round action of the Preseason WNIT Friday night, in front of 3,581 fans, at the WVU Coliseum.

WVU shot 56.3% from the field (18-32) in the first half and forced 14 Towson turnovers in taking a 43-13 first-half lead. WVU's defense held the Tigers to 3-22 shooting in the first half and just 30% (15-50) for the contest.

For the game. . . .

Alternative

MORGANTOWN, W.Va.—West Virginia felt the pressure early.

Nearly 3,600 fans filled the WVU Coliseum to watch WVU's season opener against Towson in the preseason WNIT, Friday night at the WVU Coliseum.

Towson got out to an early 5-2 lead in the opening minutes while WVU tried to find its offensive rhythm.

Twelve minutes later, however, the Mountaineers led by 20, 34-14, and all was right by the partisan crowd.

Broadcast journalists use a modified, and abbreviated, inverted pyramid approach to most news stories. Because listeners or viewers are hearing the story rather than reading it themselves, stories for broadcast often open with a catchy word, a phrase, or a sentence designed to catch one's attention—to give the ear time to listen for the important element. The rest of the story is written in a conversational style, just as in telling a story, but generally follows the inverted pyramid style.

The TV or radio story emphasizes the same basic news elements as those of a newspaper story. Because of time limitations and the emphasis on immediacy in broadcast journalism, a story may cover only the *who, what, when,* and *where.* The accompanying video in TV news may provide the details in a couple of highlight film clips. In fact, the video, or visual images from the video, serves as the attention grabber.

Radio reports generally cover only the results and, if time permits, some quotes (sound bites) from the coach or a player who starred in the game. Broadcast news reporters have to write stories to fit a specific time allotment. According to Kohler (1994), most radio stories are 10 to 45 seconds long, 25 to 110 words. Most TV news stories run 15 seconds to 2 minutes, or no more than 300 words. That means broadcast journalists often do not have time for the *why* or the *how* unless those are the most important angles of the story.

NEWS RELEASES

Sports information specialists can enhance the possibility that a newspaper, a radio station, or a TV station will use the information in a release by writing in a style similar to news formats. Of equal importance is providing the name and telephone number of a contact person a reporter can call for additional information or clarification.

Editors generally prefer releases on standard, 8½"-by-11", white paper in black ink and a standard computer font such as Courier, Arial, or Times New Roman because they are easy to read. Stories on eye-catching colored paper with computer "clip art" incorporated in the text smack of promotion—anathema to objective journalists. Editors also prefer stories that are double-spaced, so they can insert editing notes and symbols between the lines for the reporter who next handles the release. An editor rarely will run a news release without making some changes in style, structure, content, or length for policy or space reasons. For those that do, it's imperative that the SID be on top of his/her writing game.

From a structural standpoint, the SID must pay close attention to two primary elements of a release: the *header* and the *story.* The header at the top of the page identifies the organization and provides other information useful to a reporter or editor. The story, of course, is the release.

Header

The header on a news release generally includes the following information:

1. College or team's name and address—to identify the sender.
2. Contact person—the SID or the person who wrote the release.
3. Telephone numbers—day, night, and fax, if desired.
4. Release date—a requested publication or broadcast date. "For Immediate Release" means the media are free to use the information whenever they wish. "Embargoed until 7 a.m. Aug. 18" or "Not for release until 7 a.m. Aug. 18" indicates a preference that no one print or broadcast the information prior to the specified time. However, the "embargo" is not legally binding on the media. It is only a polite request.

   "Release" means the media are free to use the information whenever they wish. "Embargoed until 7 am Aug. 18" or "Not for release until 7 am Aug. 18" indicates a preference that no one print or broadcast the information prior to the specified time. However, the "embargo" is not legally binding on the media. It is only a polite request.

Public relations firms often attempt to embargo or to dictate a release time out of a sense of fairness. They hope to give all a chance to release the information at the same time, to nullify any competitive advantages. However, differences in newscast times and newspaper deadlines make it impossible for all to release the information at the same time, although if it is an important news item the media outlet will usually put the release on its website. Public relations personnel may also send information they plan to reveal at a press conference to the media in advance so the media can gather background and other details. The objective is to give reporters a head start on a story that might be released on their deadline.

Use embargoes carefully. Remember, the media are under no obligation to honor them. Some reporters do not honor them, as a matter of policy. They argue that their job is to disseminate news as soon as they are aware of it. Competitive pressures lead others to break embargoes. They can get the jump on the competition as well as on the story by breaking an embargo before a press conference.

Story

Although a good news release is similar to a news story, it contains additional elements designed to serve the purposes of the sport organization. Two parts of the story are optional:

1. Suggested headline: A newspaper seldom will use a headline suggested by the sender. Reporters do not write the headlines at most newspapers. Copy editors write the headlines to fit a given type size and space dictated by page-design considerations. However, the headline may give a reporter or editor a quick idea of the subject matter.
2. Dateline: The dateline identifies the city in which the release originates. It is printed in all-capital letters, followed by a dash (—), at the start of the first sentence. Newspapers traditionally use datelines on stories that originate from cities

outside their circulation areas. From the perspective of the SID, a dateline quickly gives the media a clue to the proximity of the sender.

The majority of news releases follows the inverted pyramid structure but may add a concluding paragraph that provides direction on how to obtain additional information. The most common structure contains the following components:

1. Lead (5Ws and H)
2. Details
3. Background
4. Sport organization tag

The lead starts with the element most important to the audience, or the readers. For example, a release announcing an award would emphasize the "who."

MORGANTOWN, W.Va.—West Virginia University junior running back Joe Smith has been named the BIG EAST Player of the Week for his efforts in guiding the Mountaineers to a 35-13 victory over Pittsburgh last weekend.

The lead also zeroes in on the strongest "news" characteristic. Although journalism texts offer anywhere from five to eight criteria, most include these six: *timeliness, proximity, prominence, impact* or *consequence*, the *unusual* or *odd*, and *conflict*. The sports information specialist can improve a release's publication or broadcast prospects by emphasizing the same elements.

Emphasizing the *timeliness* would be effective in the lead on a story announcing the selections on an all-star team.

PROVIDENCE, R.I.—The 2009 CoSIDA/ESPN The Magazine all-District II academic first team was announced today and West Virginia University junior point guard Sarah Smith was named to the team for the second consecutive season.

The SID most likely will focus on *proximity* in a hometown release. Note how the SID might change the Sarah Smith release sent to the *Baltimore Sun*.

MORGANTOWN, W.Va.—Baltimore native and West Virginia University junior point guard Sarah Smith was named today to the 2009 CoSIDA/ESPN The Magazine all-District II academic first team for the second consecutive season.

Prominence would be significant in a release announcing a speaker or a new employee.

MORGANTOWN, W.Va.—Former Mountaineer All-American Mike Taylor was introduced today as the 35th men's lacrosse coach at West Virginia University.

Emphasizing the *impact* or *consequences* might be effective in the lead on a story about the upcoming season.

MORGANTOWN, W.Va.—West Virginia University's women's basketball team's 2009–10 season schedule was released today and will feature 14 games on national television, a first in program history.

"We are excited that our young ladies will be on national television so many times this season," head coach Mike Carey said. "It's a testament to the rise of our program and will certainly help in the recruiting efforts next season."

The *odd* or *unusual* might catch editors' and readers' attention in a news feature.

MORGANTOWN, W.Va.—Just call him the "Diamond in the Rough." For senior West Virginia University men's swimmer Justin Taylor, when he's not in class or practicing with his nationally ranked teammates, he's preparing for his internship next summer in the South African diamond mines as part of his major's study abroad program.

Conflict could come into play in a story about resignations, conference alignments, or suspension of players for rules violations.

MIRAMAR, Fla.—Riptide State University soccer coach Jack Johnson today announced the indefinite suspension of four student-athletes for a violation of team rules.

The body of the story should begin with details that elaborate on the basic news elements in descending order of importance. Obviously, the first details should provide amplification of the news element emphasized in the lead. The writer should put times, dates, and other specific information in the body.

A story that leads with the announcement of the selection of a coach, for example, should go on to provide more information on the coach's experience, coaching record, reasons for accepting the job, quotes, etc. Background on the circumstances that led to the search for a new coach, on the outgoing coach, and on team record for the season would follow. Newspaper editors who do not want to run the entire story or do not have space for all of it can easily eliminate the background, the information that followers of the team already will know.

An announcement about ticket sales, scheduling, or other matters about which readers might want additional information should close with a paragraph that tells them how to quickly find it.

Times for all West Virginia University basketball games will be announced at a later date. Season tickets for all 18 home games are on sale at the WVU Ticket Office at the WVU Coliseum, online at WVUGame.com, or by calling 1-800-WVU GAME.

An alternative lead uses a literary technique to emphasize the theme or news element of a story. It incorporates the peg or tieback that explains the news connection.

MORGANTOWN, W.Va.—Kansas State gave Bob Huggins a second chance. Now West Virginia is doing the same.

Five years after initially turning down an offer to coach WVU, Huggins resigned after one year at Kansas State, which hired him after a year away from coaching, to return to his alma mater and coach the Mountaineers.

The body of an alternative story is similar to that of an inverted pyramid. However, it flows in a logical order appropriate to the style. Because the emphasis is on people, the story may contain more direct quotations from those included in the story. The writer must be careful to attribute the direct quotation to the speaker. The story may close with a direct quotation, an example, additional details, or a technique that reinforces the theme.

TYPES OF RELEASES

Different types of releases naturally lend themselves to an inverted pyramid or alternative style. News releases fall into five broad categories.

Game Advance

An advance is a preview of an upcoming game. The story is designed to provide basic details on time and ticket information, as well as a rundown on team records, star players for both teams, series records/information, and coaches' quotes about the matchup.

For the news media, the release provides useful information about the game for readers. From the perspective of the SID, the advance may help to stir interest among readers and to draw a crowd.

A game advance is sometimes written in the style of a feature story (i.e., an alternative approach). One popular supplement is a *fact box*, which is a format that lists basic facts (similar to the 5Ws) in a brief and punchy writing style. This technique makes it easy to find the primary information. The reporter or editor who receives the advance (fact box) can immediately gather information of importance.

If written in essay or narrative form, the release should take the inverted pyramid form, with the most important information on top and the least important on the bottom. All releases must contain the basic news components. For example, an advance on a football game should include the following:

1. What is the event? (conference game, nonconference)
2. Who is participating? (teams, players, etc.)
3. When will the event take place? (date and time)
4. Where will the event take place? (stadium and city/state)
5. How do they match up? (records for each team, style of play of both teams, strengths and weaknesses, and assessment by coaches/players)

The story should give information about which radio or television stations, networks, or cable outlets will broadcast the game, and include the time. Other important details on both teams are injuries, notes and statistics on key players, coaches' records, team records, and notes and statistics on the rivalry. The advance also may include a brief preview of the style of play of both teams. Further notes about the sender's team and athletes should be included.

The timing of the release of a game advance is most important. It should be in the hands of the media five days in advance of the event for football and, depending on

Types of News Releases		
Game advance	Hometown release	Feature release
News release		Weekly review/preview

the schedule, two days in advance for other sports that may have more than one contest per week.

Hometown Release

A hometown release is a story about a student-athlete that is sent to the media in the player's hometown. Weekly newspapers that do not have the staff or resources to write about stories outside their circulation area often will run a hometown release as submitted.

Hometown releases generally are no more than six or eight paragraphs and follow the inverted pyramid style. They identify the athlete, the sport, and any honors earned. They could also list the student's major field of study and a cumulative grade point average if noteworthy.

A hometown release includes a brief background of the high school the student attended and athletics achievements there. Information about the parents or guardians and other family members also goes into the release. A photograph is included, if possible. Most sports information departments shoot pictures of all the athletes on a team on media day or at the first practice, then keep them on file for use in releases.

Feature Release

A feature release is intended to spotlight a student-athlete. The student does not have to be the most visible or talented athlete on campus. The SID can highlight some unusual or interesting facet of the athlete, such as hobbies or academic activities.

Because the emphasis is on an athlete rather than an event, and the purpose is to entertain as well as to inform, most feature releases use an alternative lead. The first paragraph must "grab" the reader immediately. A feature release should include the basic news details, such as the student's sport and performance. The body might follow the inverted pyramid style, or it might develop an interesting angle. In either case, the presentation should be "bright" and "tight," because the primary purpose is to entertain.

News Release

The basic news release is newsworthy because it provides information that most readers do not yet know. It may announce the hiring of a new coach, the signing of an outstanding high school athlete, the firing of a coach, or the groundbreaking ceremony for a new facility.

The release often supplements information announced at a news conference. The emphasis on timely and new information calls for an inverted pyramid approach and a concise explanation of the details. The release also may include quotations from appropriate coaches or university officials that elaborate on the news or put the significance of the announcement into perspective.

Weekly Review/Preview

The weekly review/preview is a necessary evil for sports information directors. This type of release amounts to a weekly schedule of all the institution's athletic teams. It gives a summary of the records, opponents, and key players as well an upcoming preview of events to come during the week.

While somewhat taxing to formulate (the assistance of graduate and student assistants is key) the entire review/preview can be sent via e-mail as a PDF file.

AUDIENCE AWARENESS

Regardless of the type or structure of a news release, it should conform to strict media standards of accuracy, clarity, and brevity. A media organization's credibility and professional reputation depend to a large extent on the accuracy of news reports. A reporter who consistently submits stories with errors or inaccuracies will not last long with a newspaper, magazine, radio, or TV company. Likewise, a sports information specialist who consistently submits releases with errors will soon find that no one in the media will trust or use any of the information.

Accuracy means the story is correct in every detail. To ensure accuracy, the SID must double-check to make certain that all times, dates, numbers, etc., are correct. The SID should check the spelling of all names, addresses, and titles; he/she should also take care to list the titles of (or to otherwise identify) all people in the story and to attribute all direct quotations and statements that contain opinion. It's also imperative that someone else edit the story if at all possible. There may be glaring errors or omissions that the writer just doesn't see since he/she has been working on the material constantly. A fresh set of eyes will certainly help.

The writing style should be clear and concise. Remember, both the media and sports information specialists are writing for a mass audience. The reading ability of members of the audience may vary widely; some may not read at more than a sixth- or seventh-grade level. To reach the broadest audience possible, the journalist or SID must write in a simple style that is easy to understand.

Stories with short, simple sentences, shorter and simpler words, and short paragraphs are the easiest to read and understand. Numerous studies have shown a correlation between sentence length and readability. The longer the sentence is, the fewer the people are who can understand it in its entirety. Journalists disagree on the optimum sentence length, but sentences averaging 15–25 words will pass most readability tests. In addition, journalists prefer one- and two-syllable words to longer ones that are more difficult to understand. The SID should avoid the use of jargon or technical terms the reader might not understand. For example, a recruiting story that refers to a "Proposition 48" recruit should briefly explain the term or substitute a phrase that specifies the restrictions on eligibility.

Long paragraphs are a barrier to readability. Readers mentally interpret long paragraphs as dull and tedious, so journalists arbitrarily limit stories to two or three sentences per paragraph.

Print journalists generally use third person and past tense; broadcast journalists favor present tense because of the emphasis on immediacy. The SID should avoid "we" or "you" in most stories.

The SID should be particularly careful with both opinion that is not attributed and interpretive adjectives. They compromise the objectivity of the story because they suggest bias in favor of one side. It is better to forget the self-serving praise. The SID should avoid the superlatives and interpretive adjectives; for example, "Matt Smith, the best player in the conference, is approaching a school record." Clichés ("a classic game," "a coach on the field") are another thing to be avoided. An editor will purge all of them, or pitch the release in the trash.

The SID can make certain a story conforms to news style by stocking the office with reference guides used by the media. Here are some of the most popular:

- *The Associated Press Stylebook.* The stylebook provides guidelines on news style for titles, addresses, numbers, dates, etc. It also includes tips on word usage, grammar, and punctuation. One chapter is devoted exclusively to sports and is usually updated every year. It is a must for any SID or PR practitioner and is often referred to as "the journalist's Bible."
- *Broadcast News and Writing Stylebook.* The guide not only offers tips on style, but also addresses leads, endings, and story forms for both radio and television.
- *The Elements of Style.* This book has served as the authority on grammar, spelling, style, and usage for years.

COMMON ERRORS

Lack of Newsworthiness

The story fails to emphasize the most important news element or buries it in the middle of the story.

WRONG:

West Virginia University will play a basketball schedule this season, including 13 teams that appeared in postseason play.

The Mountaineers will play 10 non-conference contests and face the usual 18 league members in BIG EAST play.

New coach Bob Huggins will lead WVU when the season kicks off as he was named WVU's 21st men's basketball coach Monday.

RIGHT:

Veteran coach Bob Huggins was named the 21st men's basketball coach at West Virginia University Monday.

He takes over a team that will face 13 teams that appeared in postseason play last year, and a schedule that includes 28 contests, 18 of which are in BIG EAST Conference play.

Lack of Objectivity

The story promotes instead of reports. It sounds like a sales pitch for the school instead of an objective news story.

WRONG:

Riptide State leads the country in fewest points allowed, through 19 games this season, allowing just 61.7 points per contest.

Unfortunately for the Man-O-Wars, they are only averaging 49.6 points a game themselves but are a scrappy, hard-working squad that gives their all every game. But they just can't seem to buy a bucket or get the right call from the officials when the time arises.

"I don't think the officials like me or my team," Coach John Armstrong said. "If they did, we might have won a few more games."

RIGHT:

Despite leading the country in fewest points per game allowed, the Riptide State Man-O-Wars are off to their poorest start in school history.

Opponents are outscoring the RSU by nearly 12 points per contest and are still looking for their first victory 19 games into the season. Poor shooting has hurt the Man-O-Wars all season. They are only connecting on 29 percent of their attempts while the opposition is shooting 46 percent.

Too Many Superlatives and Interpretive Adjectives

The story attempts to create hype by using superlatives and interpretive adjectives rather than letting the subject matter speak for itself.

WRONG:

Sharpshooting guard Chip Glass has been uncanny this basketball season.

With the touch of a safecracker and the precision of a diamond cutter, he has led Cincinnati Poly to a break-even season, standing at 12-12 at the three-quarter mark of the campaign.

Glass will duel Curly Grimes of Indiana Tech when the two teams meet Wednesday night, and while Grimes is a first-team all-conference selection, Glass is better, according to CinPoly coach Sam Cameron.

"I will take Glass over Grimes every day of the week," Cameron said. "Everyone should come out and see for themselves that Glass is the best guard."

RIGHT:

Arguably the two finest guards in college basketball will face each other Wednesday night at Riverfront Arena when Cincinnati Poly meets Indiana Tech.

	The Eight Most Common Mistakes in New Releases		
1	Lack of newsworthiness	5	Emphasis on the obvious
2	Lack of objectivity	6	Lack of a local tie (on out-of-town releases)
3	Too many superlatives and interpretive adjectives	7	Unnecessary background
4	Self-serving quotations	8	Wordy

CinPoly's Chip Glass will trade shots with all-conference choice Curly Grimes when the Pollys hope to snap a five-game losing streak.

"It will be interesting to see the guard matchup," said CinPoly coach Sam Cameron. "Each is a skilled player, and they both know how to score lots of points in a basketball game."

Self-Serving Quotations

The direct quotations aim at self-promotion instead of at explaining and providing perspective on the subject matter.

WRONG:

"I firmly believe we have the finest college basketball team in all of Division II," said Baltic University coach Kelly Smith.

"We have great shooters, we are quick, and we play tenacious defense. I say we have it all and it's a shame we are only 5-12 this season. We have so many injuries, and they have hurt our chances."

BU will try to snap a nine-game losing streak tonight when the Overseas take on Wharton University, which is 19-1.

"We have played a much tougher schedule than Wharton, and we are a better team than the Stockbrokers," added Smith.

RIGHT:

Baltic University will try to snap a nine-game losing streak tonight when the Overseas play host to Wharton University.

BU, which is 5-12, has not won since defeating Baker Barber College, 112-111, on Nov. 11. Wharton, meanwhile, is 19-1.

"We have our job cut out for us, and we know it will not be easy, but the Wharton players put their shorts on one leg at a time, just like we do," said BU coach Kelly Smith.

Emphasis on the Obvious

The story leads with information the reader already knows or with obvious information that does not encourage the reader to go further.

WRONG:

Jane McIntyre, of Hoboken, N.J., plays on the Ashoil University basketball team.

RIGHT:

Jane McIntyre has been the unsung hero for the Ashoil University women's basketball team this season.

McIntyre, the only player from Hoboken, N.J., on the Eagles, leads them in steals and blocks and her calming influence on the court has helped carry Ashoil to a 12-0 record going into conference play.

Lack of a Local Tie (on Out-of-Town Releases)

The story does not quickly make clear that some aspect of the story has a local connection (proximity).

WRONG:

Release sent to the *Plain Dealer* in Cleveland.

FORT WORTH, Texas—The Texas Christian women's basketball team will play host tonight to Southern Methodist for the tournament championship of the Southwest Conference.

The Lady Horned Frogs are led by sophomore Becky Lane of Houston, who has averaged 25.4 points per game this season.

RIGHT:

Release sent to the *Plain Dealer* in Cleveland.

FORT WORTH, Texas—Sophomore Becky Lane of Cleveland, Ohio, will lead the Texas Christian Lady Horned Frogs into tonight's Southwest Conference championship women's basketball game against Southern Methodist.

Lane, who attends TCU because her aunt lives in suburban Fort Worth, averages 25.4 points and 12.7 rebounds per game for the Frogs.

Unnecessary Background

The story contains too much "old news" at the top of the story, obscuring the new or important elements.

WRONG:

Freshman Jane Schmidt came to Miami University on a basketball scholarship with plenty of previous acclaim.

She was a middle school phenomenon before she starred in high school, when she was named an All-American, and then played a key role for a team that won the Amateur Athletic Union (AAU) 16-18 title. Now in her first year at Miami she has continued her solid play with a 22.1 scoring average.

Schmidt exceeded her scoring average with 25 points last night as the Lady Hurricanes defeated Georgia 77-71 in the first round of the NCAA tournament.

RIGHT:

Jane Schmidt, who has been one of the nation's top women basketball players for nearly a decade, scored 25 points last night to lead the University of Miami to a 77-71 victory over Georgia in the first round of the NCAA championship tournament.

Wordy

Long sentences filled with clauses that cover two or three ideas confuse and lose readers.

WRONG:

Johnny Jones, who is from Paducah, Ky., is one of the finer young golfers in the nation who play on Wednesdays and Fridays during July and August in preparation for the National Junior Golf Championships.

Jones, who is a southpaw, and James Johnson, another teenager, will compete with Bill Brown, who has a very good game, and George Green, a former standout basketball player from Athens, Ga. This group, which has a combined age of 98 years, is, as a group, quick on the draw, and each one, when the climate is right, can putt with the tour professionals.

These young golfers from the Midwest also are very good students, and several of them, when not playing golf, work out in karate classes. This helps them develop the arm strength needed to be good golfers. His long drives are one of the reasons Jones is one of the favorites in the tournament and the person many pros think will win.

RIGHT:

Johnny Jones, a smooth-swinging teenager from Paducah, Ky., is the odds-on favorite to win the National Junior Golf Championships.

The primary competition Jones will face for the trophy include James Johnson, Bill Brown and George Green. All four are good putters, but the long drives of Jones is what many professionals believes sets him apart from the rest of the field.

DISTRIBUTION OF RELEASES

Two considerations figure into decisions about who should receive a news release: the news organization and the target audience. A news organization's story selection depends on its mission and audience. That is why *USA Today* offers a comprehensive

Selecting the sports media outlets in which to send a news release is determined in part by the target audience of the specific release. (Courtesy of Dan Mendlik/Cleveland Indians)

sports section every day, whereas the *Columbus Dispatch* seldom sends sports reporters outside the state. Similarly, a news organization shapes its coverage to meet the interests of its viewers or readers. College athletics are big in the Midwest; pro sports are the draw in New York City. Stories on local athletes are more interesting than information about athletes outside the circulation/coverage area.

A Cleveland, Ohio, sportswriter will have little use for a Texas Christian University football review/preview or a feature release about a women's basketball player at Louisiana State University. Unless the athlete is from Cleveland, or LSU plays an Ohio team, the information in the release likely will offer little or no benefit to the Cleveland media. Sending the release is a waste of the SID's time.

It is imperative for the sports information specialist to know the sports reporter and the editor or director who supervises sports coverage for each of the local media. It is also important to know the types of sports and the types of stories each uses most frequently. Finally, it is helpful to keep directories in the office that provide names and addresses of sports editors and directors to whom the SID might send hometown releases. Two such directories are the *Editor and Publisher International Year Book* and the *Broadcasting/Cablecasting Yearbook*.

The personal contacts and yearbooks make it possible for an SID to keep a mailing list up to date and use it to his or her best advantage. In trimming the list to get the most out of releases, the SID can determine who is sincerely interested in receiving a specific kind of release. It would also be beneficial to update the contact list every year. The SID should ask if the sports department still wants to receive releases, if the names, email addresses, and other contact information are accurate, and what types of releases they will consider running. The use of email has now become the most prevalent method in submitting news releases, particularly in conveying news with a tight time frame.

The SID should be careful not to overwhelm the local media in the primary target market who regularly cover the school. Too much of a good thing can work against the SID, too.

Simply put, the SID or public relations director must know the target market and the media market, then use common sense about the distribution of releases.

In every case, the SID should send the release to a specific person. Releases addressed to generic titles like "Sports Editor" are often treated as junk by journalists. Sending the release to a specific person takes on added importance in fax releases and electronic communication because releases of every type may pour into a common pool.

Timing is another critical factor. If the information arrives too early, it may wind up buried at the bottom of a pile of submissions. If it arrives too late, it is worthless to the media and the sport institution.

SUMMARY

Sports information specialists and sports journalists enjoy an interdependent relationship. The SID or public relations director is a source of sports information for the media. The media are the channels through which the sport organization or team reaches followers and potential fans. The most common means of communication is the news release, a prepackaged story distributed to the media in hopes they will pass the information on to the public. Because printed releases are the most common form of information distributed by sport organizations, strong writing skills are essential to success for SIDs.

News releases are similar to news stories, although their primary objectives differ. News releases attempt to persuade—to create a favorable image of an athlete, a team, or a sport organization. News stories attempt to inform—to present a balanced view of a topic to readers or viewers. They also entertain. The structure of a news story depends on the information or entertainment value of the story. The inverted pyramid puts emphasis on the information in the story, pushing the most important details to the top.

Alternative structures emphasize the human-interest angle or entertainment features. They are used most often when readers already know most of the basic facts or when the news value is minimal.

A sports information specialist can increase the chances that the media will use a news release by writing in a style similar to that of journalists. Game advances, hometown releases, and news releases follow a standard format—lead, details, background, and where to call for more information—built on the inverted pyramid model. Feature releases and weekly reviews/previews often will take an alternative approach. The SID will add information at the top of a release that provides contact information to reporters seeking additional details. The SID can request that the media withhold publication or broadcast of the information until a specified time, but the media are under no legal obligation to honor an embargo.

The most effective releases emphasize the characteristic that makes the story newsworthy, whether it is the announcement of a new coach or the success of an athlete from the media's city. Because the media reach a broad, mass audience, effective releases also are clear and concise. Short sentences, simple language, and short paragraphs are the most readable. Guidebooks such as *The Associated Press Stylebook* provide direction on how to write according to news style. The most important consideration for every release is accuracy. The SID must check and recheck every name, date, number, and fact to maintain credibility and cooperation among the media.

SIDs maintain up-to-date mailing lists and information on the types of releases specific news organizations use. SIDs also pay close attention to deadlines and the timing of releases. A release that arrives too late is of no value. The SID who knows the target media, the target audience, and news structure can write a release that emphasizes the same elements a sportswriter would emphasize. A well-written release may be utilized by both print and broadcast media in different locales, with little alteration.

DISCUSSION QUESTIONS

1. When making an announcement, plea, or request in the form of a release, how do you persuade your audience to take the action you desire?
2. What are the criteria used to determine what angle will be taken when preparing to write a news release? Create an illustration and discuss it.

SUGGESTED EXERCISES

1. Write four one-page releases (hometown, feature, news, and weekly review/preview).
2. Apply a readability formula to a story you have written and determine the reading level at which you write.

7

Creating a Media Guide

A sports organization's image is one of the most important aspects to its success. How the organization is perceived and portrayed is very important and vital to ensuring success in its future endeavors. A positive image portrays success. That perception starts with the organization's director (i.e., athletic director in college, general manager, owner, or president in the professional ranks) and it trickles down through the department's hierarchy to and through the sports information specialists.

Part of the organization's image is portrayed through its media guide, and creating and maintaining that guide is arguably one of the most important duties of an SID. While their names have evolved through the years, as well as their content, length, size, and even method of delivery, media guides are still recognized as one of the backbones to the SID's profession. Some sport organizations still refer to them as media guides. Others refer to them as recruiting guides, information guides, or just guides because they now serve many different purposes.

In the 1960s and 1970s, media guides at the collegiate level were nothing more than a handful of pages, especially for football, usually in a small booklet or pamphlet format that included the most vital of information about an individual sport: schedule, roster, basic profile information, a brief outlook of the upcoming season, and any pertinent records.

Today, primarily because technologies have evolved so much, media guides have morphed and they now serve many different purposes: providing a basis of information to the media (which was the original concept in the development and creation of media guides), serving as a tool by coaching staffs in the recruitment of prospective student-athletes, and generating income and interest because they are often sold to the general public to allow fans and alumni to feel an even greater connection to their team or organization. Keep in mind, however, that the primary audiences are the media and the coaches' potential recruits.

In a contemporary guide, there is all sorts of information that fulfills the needs of its audiences:

- schedule
- roster

- coaches' bios
- players' bios
- conference/league information
- historical records such as single-game, season, and career records for both individuals and teams
- the previous season in review
- the upcoming season's prospects and notes
- opponent information
- honors and awards
- basic information about the organization (e.g., at West Virginia University it is an in-depth look into the entire university and the city of Morgantown)
- basic information for the media (e.g., SID contact information, directions to athletic facilities, radio and television affiliates, and rules and regulations pertaining to obtaining interviews with coaches and athletes)

Simply put, it's a one-stop point of reference for everything that a recruit, a coach, a member of the media, or a fan would need to know about that organization or team.

THE BASICS OF A MEDIA GUIDE

"The SID . . . is in charge of all aspects of the media guide from planning, writing, layout, proofreading, the bid process where applicable, budgetary considerations and production" (Shutt, 1998).

Depending on the structure of the organization, most SIDs are in fact their own writer, planner, editor, designer, and point of contact in terms of production and costs. But there are also other institutions or sport organizations that have their own separate sports publications department that works closely with the SID, decreasing the SID's work load and assisting with the production, layout and design, advertising, and overall structure and presentation of the guide. Despite the structure in place and its impact on the creation of the media guide, the SID is still the "editor in chief" and is responsible for ensuring that the project comes to fruition.

While ensuring that the needs of the guide's audiences are met, the SID must discover how much of the guide will be devoted to recruiting, how much to the players and coaches, the record book, and overall basic information about that specific sport and or sport organization's entire department or program. How much of it will be a conglomeration or crossover of both, fulfilling a multitude of needs all in one swoop? While all those questions are kept in mind, the SID will also continue to work closely with the coaches to ensure the eventual finished product is to their liking.

Once the blueprint for the guide has been cultivated and the SID knows exactly what is going into his/her guide, there are rules implemented by the NCAA that must be implemented and followed when it comes to the guide's creation.

"NCAA rules currently allow institutions to print a recruiting brochure or media guide, but not both. The publications are limited to one color (except for the front and back covers) and may not exceed 8.5 × 11 inches in size or more than

208 pages in length. Schools typically devote the front half of the media guide to recruiting information and the back half to records, historical data, and key player and coach biographies more relevant to media covering their athletics teams." (McKindra, 2009)

Know that media guides are rarely ever started or created from scratch (unless an institution or sport organization begins to sponsor a new sport). Media guides are usually an evolution from the previous year's version. And as the previous season unfolds, updated information is kept in the SID's Word files of the guide—keeping track of pertinent game-by-game information for players' and coaches' bios and the updating of any team records or game, seasonal and career marks set by the organization's players. It is imperative to point out, again, that the guide evolves from the previous entry.

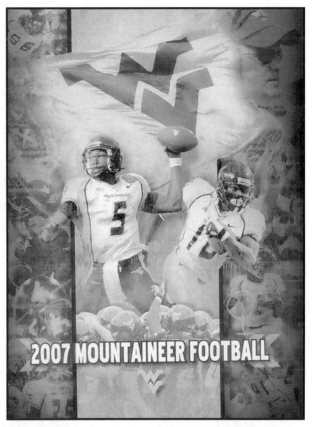

Collegiate media guides serve as part information guides and part recruiting tools. (Courtesy of WVU Sports Communications)

It should also be pointed out that media guides at the professional sports level are just that, actual media guides. There are no recruiting tools, but they are simply full of factual information that the media use at their convenience. There are no page-count limitations (more on that later on in this chapter) and the guides are usually smaller pocket guides such as 5.5 × 4.25 inches as opposed to the traditional collegiate guides that are 8.5 × 11.

What follows are some key components that the SID must be aware of before delving into the media guide.

Budgeting

The budget generally is determined by university administrators (or in the professional ranks, by front office personnel). The SID receives an annual allotment for publications and supplements it through advertising. The SID, in concert with public relations or athletics administrators, decides how to divide the publications budget among various sports. Higher-profile sports will have a larger guide and more are distributed, necessitating a much larger publications budget than lower-profile sports.

Advertising

The more advertising the SID can acquire for media guides, the more attractive the guide. Consequently, the sports information office may solicit advertising to supplement the budget allotment. The advertising rate depends on the cost of production per page and the number of pages earmarked for advertising. The SID at a larger university or organization may have an advertising manager oversee solicitations of advertising; however, sports information personnel will proof the ads (i.e., read them and note any corrections needed).

Written Content

The sports information or public relations director oversees all the written material in the guide. Sports information personnel will write most, if not all, of the information and compile the statistical sections. That written content will then be edited by everyone in the SID's office to ensure there are no grammatical or spelling errors or factual mistakes.

Photographs

The sports information or public relations director also arranges for all photographs. The SID selects action pictures from the previous year and arranges for new head shots of coaches, team members, and athletics officials. A staff photographer, a freelancer, or a studio photographer may shoot the pictures. All of these photos are then archived in the SID's permanent files and can be referenced for future guides, historical picture requests by media members, or supplementing the photographs in future guides.

Art and Graphics

The SID will arrange for all charts, drawings, and illustrations or obtain initial art and graphics designs and review those with members of the current staff and the coaches to ensure the look is appropriate and accepted. The artist may be a volunteer, a member of the art department, an in-house professional, or a hired studio artist.

Page Design

The page design may be created by members of the sports information or public relations staff, personnel in the college's printing services offices, printing company employees, or outsourced to a paid graphics designer. As in the case of advertisements, the SID or sports information staffers read and mark corrections on proofs of all pages.

Page Limitations

In 2005, the NCAA mandated that all media guides, regardless of the sport, would no longer exceed 208 pages in length. The rules were set in place to create an even playing field as it pertained to recruiting prospective student-athletes. Think about why these restrictions were imposed. If you're an SID at a major Division I institution, chances are your operating budget for your media guide would almost seem limitless. In knowing that, media guides, prior to the 2005 NCAA mandate, were astronomical in size, especially when it came to major, traditional football and basketball powers (e.g., Missouri's 2004 football guide was 614 pages). If bigger is better, then potential future student-athletes might have made their decisions on attending a school based on the size of its media guide, at least in theory, since their first encounter with said school might very well be by looking at a 600-plus page guide.

Now, consider those same recruits who might be getting recruiting attention from smaller Division I schools that don't have as large a budget for their guides. The smaller schools just couldn't compete because of budgetary limitations, hence the rules that took form in 2005.

So under the 208-page restriction, the SID must choose what goes in a guide and what does not. For smaller varsity/Olympic sports (such as soccer, baseball, lacrosse, etc.), however, those media guides will rarely reach the full 208 pages, freeing the SID from determining whether certain information will or will not appear in the guide. But for major sports, such as Division I football and basketball, it is imperative that the appropriate information is provided, while keeping the delicate balance in place in terms of meeting the needs of the varying audiences: recruits, media, and the general public.

Information that is left out, and there will be information that doesn't make the media guide's final cut, can easily be placed in a supplement to the actual guide. That information can be bound and serve as an accessory. Information that could appear in the supplement would include additional all-time records that are an important piece of the overall media guide puzzle, but not the most important or they would be in the guide itself.

But, again, those supplements are usually just for sports such as football and basketball. The smaller varsity/Olympic sports will have plenty of room to contain all of that information in their own guides.

Printing

Most colleges contract with professional printing companies for multicolor, magazine-style guides. Local print shops or university printing services often can handle small brochures. The SID or an athletics department administrator negotiates the printing contract or oversees competitive bidding for the contract.

Once those areas are recognized it is important for the guide to include every detail about the players, coaches, team, and sport organization that will aid the media in their coverage of the team. Because the media often work under intense deadline pressure, they may need to check a record, a past score, or a player's hometown. The more easily they can find the information in the media guide, the better the media guide will have served one of its purposes.

MANDATORY CONTENT ITEMS FOR A FUNCTIONAL MEDIA GUIDE

Many media guides take on the personality of its author and sport organization. Some have used movie themes consistently through the guide, while others use "team themes" created by the coaching staff (e.g., research Tennessee women's basketball and its yearly publication). Others will use the guide as a tie-in with the preseason promotion and publicity of an All-America candidate.

Some guides will also use all of its allotted pages, filling any "holes" with added fillers such as an overview and outlook of the institution and an in-depth listing of the organization's entire staff. Others will fill holes with advertisements from the organization's sponsors. While these are nice to add if space is available, there are mandatory and essential sections of a media guide that must be included in order for it to be a functional guide.

Table of Contents

This usually appears in the opening pages of the media guide and includes a complete listing of the contents of the guide, including page numbers, from the front to the back of the publication.

Schedule

The schedule should be as up-to-date as possible with a list of every game that includes the opponent, date, location, starting time, and, if available, television information.

Alphabetical and/or Numerical Rosters

Every media guide, regardless of sport, should contain an alphabetical roster that lists every member of the team. It may be beneficial for some sports' media guides to also include numerical rosters. The rosters will vary slightly depending on the sport and whether the guide is for a collegiate or professional team, but essentially they should include name, height, weight, position, age, class, experience, hometown, and high school or college.

Sample Pronunciation Guide	
First Names:	
Akeema	uh-KEEM-uh
Asya	Asia
Ayana	Eye-yahn-uh
Korinne	CORE-inn
Madina	Muh-DEAN-uh
Tonia	Toe-Knee-uh
Last Names:	
Bussie	Bus-E
Repella	Re-PELL-uh

Pronunciation Guide

The pronunciation guide is a must for those that cover the team via the radio or television medium. If an athlete's name is pronounced differently than it appears on the roster or is one that may create problems, it is important that the phonetic spelling of the name be provided.

Last Year's Results

The previous year's results will play a vital role in the coverage of the contemporary team. Therefore, a capsule of each game in the previous season, including both individual and team statistics, is required. Results will also include the entire compiled statistical results such as season highs and lows, statistical trends, player and team seasonal averages, and scores from each contest.

2009-10 West Virginia University Women's Basketball Roster

ALPHABETICAL

No.	Name	Pos.	Ht.	Class	Hometown	High School/ Previous School
44	Madina Ali	F	6-0	r-Jr.	Williamsport, Pa.	Daytona Beach CC
35	Natalie Burton	C	6-5	So.	Perth, Australia	Carine
20	Asya Bussie	C	6-4	Fr.	Randallstown, Md.	Seton Keough
21	Korinne Campbell	G/F	6-0	Jr.	Princeton, N.J.	Notre Dame/Minnesota
3	Jessica Capers	F	6-1	r-Fr.	Gastonia, N.C.	Forest View
33	Ayana Dunning*	C	6-3	r-Fr.	Columbus, Ohio	Eastmoor/LSU
12	Vanessa House	G	5-7	r-Jr.	Fresno, Calif.	Fresno City College
5	Sarah Miles	G	5-7	Jr.	San Antonio, Texas	Sam Houston
10	Liz Repella	G	5-11	Jr.	Steubenville, Ohio	Steubenville
15	Akeema Richards	G	5-9	Fr.	Baltimore, Md.	Western
32	Tonia Williams*	G	6-1	r-Fr.	Warner Robbins, Ga.	Houston County/South Carolina
23	Antishia Wright	G	5-11	Fr.	Boynton Beach, Fla.	Lake Worth Christian

NUMERICAL

No.	Name	Pos.	Ht.	Class	Hometown	High School/ Previous School
3	Jessica Capers	F	6-1	r-Fr.	Gastonia, N.C.	Forest View
5	Sarah Miles	G	5-7	Jr.	San Antonio, Texas	Sam Houston
10	Liz Repella	G	5-11	Jr.	Steubenville, Ohio	Steubenville
12	Vanessa House	G	5-7	r-Jr.	Fresno, Calif.	Fresno City College
15	Akeema Richards	G	5-9	Fr.	Baltimore, Md.	Western
20	Asya Bussie	C	6-4	Fr.	Randallstown, Md.	Seton Keough
21	Korinne Campbell	G/F	6-0	Jr.	Princeton, N.J.	Notre Dame/Minnesota
23	Antishia Wright	G	5-11	Fr.	Boynton Beach, Fla.	Lake Worth Christian
33	Ayana Dunning*	C	6-3	r-Fr.	Columbus, Ohio	Eastmoor/LSU
32	Tonia Williams*	G	6-1	r-Fr.	Warner Robbins, Ga.	Houston County/ South Carolina
35	Natalie Burton	C	6-5	So.	Perth, Australia	Carine
44	Madina Ali	F	6-0	r-Jr.	Williamsport, Pa.	Daytona Beach CC

* Will sit out season in compliance with NCAA transfer rules

Head Coach: Mike Carey (Salem, '80)—9th season

Associate Head Coach: George Porcha (New Haven,'95)—1st season

Assistant Coaches: M.L. Willis (Iowa, '98); Donchez Graham (Morgan State, '91)

Season Prospectus

The upcoming season can be discussed via a brief overview of the previous season and a general preview of the upcoming season. The overview should include comments from the head coach. The growing trend with this section is shifting toward quick hitter information broken down into short paragraph notes.

Quick Facts

Quick facts are the first glimpse into a program or sports team. They are an informational listing about the institution/organization and the team, which should include the location of the organization, head coaching information, key elements about the current team such as starters returning and lost and basic contact information for the SID.

Biographies of Coaches

A complete biography of the head coach is required, including an up-to-date coaching record with any notable achievements, all-time great victories, players in the profes-

Sample Quick Facts	
General Information	**Sports Communications**
Location: Morgantown, W.Va. **Nickname:** Mountaineers **Colors:** Old Gold and Blue **Conference:** BIG EAST **Enrollment:** 28,840 **Arena:** WVU Coliseum (14,000) **President:** James P. Clements **Athletic Director:** Ed Pastilong	**Assistant SID/WBB Contact:** Phil Caskey **Office:** (304) 293-2821 **Work Cell:** (304) 276-4105 **e-mail:** Phil.Caskey@mail.wvu.edu **Fax:** (304) 293-4105 **Press Row:** (304) 293-2821 **Website:** www.MSNsportsNET.com
Coaching Staff	**Team Information**
Head Coach: Mike Carey (Salem, 1980) **Record at WVU:** 150-101 (.598) **Years at WVU:** Entering ninth season **Career Record:** 438-203 (.683) **Years Coaching:** Entering 23rd season **Associate Head Coach:** George Porcha (New Haven, 1995; George Mason, 2006) **Assistant Coaches:** M.L. Willis (Iowa, 1998); Donchez Graham (Morgan State, 1991; Goucher, 2003) **Director of Basketball Operations:** Toni Kay Oliverio (West Liberty State, 2001) **Graduate Assistant:** Kyle Cooper (West Virginia, 2008)	**2008–09 Record:** 18-15 **Conference Record/Finish:** 5-11/11th **Postseason:** WNIT Second Round **Letterwinners Returning/Lost:** 3/2 **Starters Returning/Lost:** 3/2 Liz Repella—G (Jr., 16.5 ppg, 8.1 rpg) Sarah Miles—G (Jr. 12.2 ppg, 5.3 rpg) Natalie Burton—C (So., 4.8 ppg, 4.9 rpg) **Newcomers:** 6

sional ranks, etc. Biographies on assistant coaches, athletic trainers, strength and conditioning coaches, and other key support personnel are helpful, but not vital. Photographs of the coaching staff help dress up a media guide and create a favorable impression.

Profiles of Players

Arguably the "meat" of the media guide is the player profiles section, which is especially pivotal in the preseason prior to competition. This section contains a detailed profile of each player, including photographs and statistics for each season the athlete has performed for the organization. The bio will also include season-by-season statistics and individual career game highs. Due to the nature of sports, player profiles have a short lifespan; however, the media frequently use them for reference.

No.	Name	Pos.	Ht.	Class	Hometown	High School/ Previous School
5	Jane Doe	G	5-7	Jr.	San Antonio, Texas	Sam Houston

Extremely talented combo guard . . . came into her own last season as one of the team's go-to players . . . excellent perimeter player . . . great quickness with a lightning first-step . . . good on-court vision . . . has tremendous scoring potential.

At West Virginia (2008–09): Named BIG EAST's Most Improved Player after a vote of the league's coaches . . . 25th in BIG EAST scoring average . . . 15th in league field goal percentage . . . fifth in leage minutes per game . . . third on the team in points . . . second on squad in assists . . . team leader in free throw percentage . . . third in rebounds . . . second in minutes per game average . . . 22 double figure scoring efforts . . . 11 perfect free throw shooting games . . . six 20-point efforts . . . two double-doubles . . . 13 straight double-figure scoring efforts from Dec. 30 to Feb. 15 . . . BIG EAST Player of the Week (Feb. 9) after guiding Mountaineers to victory at No. 5 and national runner-up Louisville during regular season . . . victory was highest-ranked road team the Mountaineers had ever defeated in program history . . . scored 22 points, on 8-13 shooting and a perfect 6-6 from the free throw line, with 10 rebounds in 39 minutes of action against the Cards . . . career-best 27 points with 10 caroms in home win over Mercyhurst . . . 21 points, on 8-15 shooting, with eight rebounds in narrow loss to DePaul in second round of BIG EAST Championship . . . 23 points on 8-17 shooting and 7-7 from the free throw line in win over Marshall . . . 22 points on 10-14 shooting with seven rebounds in Longwood win . . . 20 points against Seton Hall . . . 19 points, including career-best 10 free throws against Indiana . . . 19 points with eight rebounds in home win over Providence.

At West Virginia (2007–08): Appeared in 16 games as a backup . . . averaged 1.8 points in 5.4 minutes per game . . . career-high 10 points on 5-5 shooting in home win against Presbyterian . . . four assists and two points in home win against St. Francis, Pa. . . . three points and three assists in home victory over Canisius in season-opener.

In High School: Averaged 15 points, four assists and six rebounds as a senior at **Sam Houston High** . . . guided Hurricanes to 30-5 record including a perfect 13-0 mark in conference play . . . team advanced to second round of AAAA playoffs . . . SAISD tournament MVP, All-District MVP and TABC All-Region as a senior . . . Northside LoneStar All-Tournament Team . . . *San Antonio Express-News* "Super Team" . . . four-time first team all-district . . . SAISD All-Tournament Team . . . rated among the top 250 prep players according to *All-Star Girl's Report*.

Personal: Daughter of Janet Doe . . . birthday is July 5 . . . majoring in design studies.

History

This section will include a history of each series with every opponent on the schedule in the form of a series records. Some guides will also include a detailed history of the sport organization from inception to present day, noting great moments throughout its existence. They can be rather detailed and written in flowing paragraph form or broken down into a series of bullet points.

Honors and Awards

The honors and awards section is a complete listing of all honors and/or awards that the team's players and coaches have received throughout the program/sport's history (e.g., all-conference accolades, major academic honors, honor roll information, all-tournament players, players of the week, All-America honors, etc.)

Team Records

The team records section is a statistical rundown on the season-by-season records of the team and individuals, dating back to the first year of the program. From those, career records are created and maintained. The good SID will also compile opponent records against his/her team.

Stadium or Arena Layout

Key information about the stadium/arena in which the team plays is also important. A diagram and information are interesting, if not essential, and will prove helpful to both the media and fans.

Media Information

The media information section explains how members of the media obtain credentials, the procedures to be followed by broadcast media, parking information, working media room facilities, and interview request procedures for pre- and post-event. Contact information, such as mailing addresses, phone numbers, and e-mail addresses, for the sports information specialist are also compiled in this section.

PRODUCTION SCHEDULE

We've already discussed that the SID is the chief operating officer for the media guide. Keeping that in mind, it is imperative for a timeline to be established by the SID for the entire project to be complete, creating and maintaining deadlines so the media guide is printed and delivered prior to the season's first game, or sometimes even a month or so prior to the start of competition. A lot of the production schedule depends on when the coaching staff wants the finished product in hand. Some are fine with it being delivered right before competition starts, but a more ideal timeline would be to have the guide available for the team or league's media day, which can be four weeks prior to the first contest.

By knowing the final delivery date, the SID can work backwards from that point, setting deadlines for text/copy to be written, having the text edited by members of the

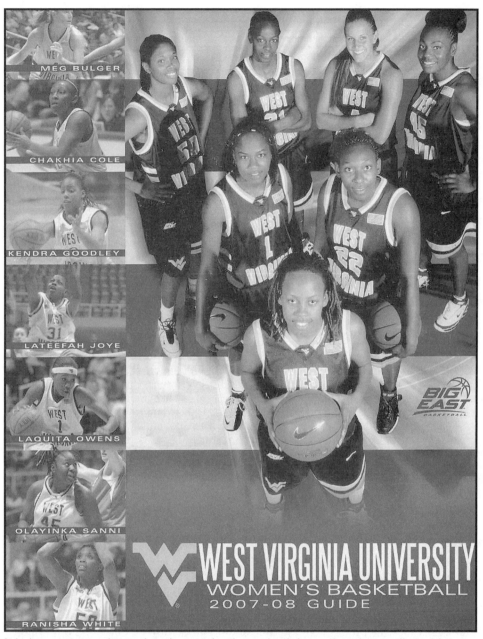

It is important to determine the production schedule so that the media guides are back from the printer and available prior to the start of the season. (Courtesy of WVU Sports Communications)

SID's staff, as well as the coaches for their overall approval (especially of their biographies), pulling photographs, setting the budget, selling advertisements (if necessary), and having the look and feel of the guide created by graphic designers or in-house colleagues. Typically a guide will need to be sent to the printer about three weeks prior to your desired delivery date, so plan accordingly using that basis.

MITCHELL LAYTON PHOTOGRAPHY

Coach's CORNER

by Craig Esherick

A coach looks at the media guide not only as a means to impress the media, but also as a tool to recruit potential players and their parents. The media guide often becomes the first look a potential recruit will have of the school and campus the coach represents. While it might be called a "media" guide, the publication is often a handbook for recruits and their parents to learn about the coaching staff, check out photos of the locker room, and get a view of campus life through an array of photos and descriptions of students, staff, and faculty.

Members of the media sometimes need to be reminded of this dual use. So while several pages of the media guide outlining pricey renovations to the weight room might seem like a waste of ink to reporters, it is of great interest to the high school player looking to bulk up for the move from prep star to college standout.

And this is where communication between the coach and his or her sports information director (SID) is key. A well-informed SID is an invaluable asset to a coach. An SID who understands the recruiting process (i.e., when the contact periods begin and end, when the signing period starts, and when letters of intent are due) can also be instrumental in setting up the media guide's publishing schedule to take full advantage of this process. The SID who understands the needs of his or her coach will take the time in the offseason to gather current photos and images of the campus, community landmarks, members of the team, and write interesting feature stories or captions that enhance the recruiting value of the media guide. A list of the games that will be televised is always a great handout to a parent/coach or recruit.

Recruits and their families want to know if any former players are playing in the pro ranks. A page or two of pictures featuring alums that are in the NBA or NFL can grab the attention of a recruit. A story on a former player that is playing professionally or a list of the "players in the pros" is also effective.

The cover of the media guide is equally as important as what is inside. Are the players featured on the front or should the coach be on the cover this year? Which players and how many should appear there? Is one player a potential Player of the Year? Is there a theme for the upcoming season? Is there a new building on campus or a landmark in town that carries special meaning, recruiting, and promotional value? The answers to these questions and others will influence the final product but it all begins with good communication between the coach and SID. Additionally, with the emphasis on "going green," should the SID create a media guide this is available exclusively online, there are some innovative uses of video that can be implemented along with the media guide. Producing some video clips that help the media, fans, and recruits get to know the players is a great way to use video to enhance an online media guide.

Finally, it goes without saying that many players, parents, and high school coaches are keenly interested in a school's academic reputation, its offerings, graduation rates, and other metrics of success. The media guide is a great place to feature a signature academic program or discipline, to promote an elite faculty, and highlight the achievements both on and off the court or playing field of the student-athletes.

There's little question that a well-designed, lively, and informative media guide can be a coach's best friend when selling the program to recruits.

Once a season is completed, the SID can certainly update the entire record book section, if he/she hasn't already done so during the course of the season. A season review, coaches' biographies, and the history section can also be updated, which would include honors and awards for players and coaches. From there, the SID will create long-term deadlines for updating player information, especially for newcomers, writing the preseason outlook/notebook, and generally working on the guide every day as to ensure the deadlines are met.

For football, the guide information may be used for the spring prospectus, thus the SID has but four months (pending a bowl game or playoffs) to finalize the specifics. Should a spring prospectus not be warranted, the football SID should allot five to six months of continual media guide work to ensure the tangible product is in hand by its deadline, which is usually a month and a half prior to the start of season.

For basketball, the guide may be requested for the conference's media day, thus bumping up the deadline. If an SID is continually updating information in-season, approximately two or three months should be reserved for producing the guide. For varsity sports guides, a couple of weeks would be the normal time frame for completing a guide.

GAME-DAY PROGRAMS

In most instances, the SID is responsible for—or at least will assist in—the creation of the game-day program. Why is this included in a chapter about producing a media guide? Because the same steps that are used in creating a media guide are also used in the formation of the game-day programs that are sold primarily at football and basketball events. While the game programs are heavy on advertisements, the sports information specialist still plays a primary role in its production. The programs typically include feature stories on contemporary athletes and coaches/administrators, often times written by the SID, updated player and team statistics as the season progresses, and updated schedules/results.

For football, a new game program is published and sold for every home contest. Much of the program will remain unchanged from game to game (these pages are known as "standing pages") but sections described earlier (i.e., player features, statistics) will be changed and a new cover will be used. For basketball, because home games are often played more frequently than once a week, the same program could be sold for a two- or three-game span with all the same information, just different opponents and updated rosters/stats.

For smaller varsity sports that have programs, a flip card with rosters and an athlete feature will suffice, and that responsibility will usually fall on the SID.

FUTURE OF MEDIA GUIDES

The future of media guides appears uncertain, at least in terms of a printed tangible item. "A trend is afoot in college football to do away with printed media guides, which . . . have been published for decades by the publicity wing of each school's athletics department. But cost-cutting measures and the Internet have made media guides an expendable relic in the eyes of some" (Milian, 2009).

Milian points out that the move to go away from a printed media guide is a cost-cutting venture and, in truth, it is. All of a guide's information is usually already available on an organization's website, readily attainable by potential recruits, coaches and support staff, the media, and fans. By eliminating a printed media guide, a sport organization would save thousands of dollars. Former Ohio Valley Conference commissioner Jon A. Steinbrecher oversaw the elimination of the conference's football and basketball media days and eliminated the printed media guides in a cost-cutting measure (Belson, 2009).

It's not just smaller conferences that are moving in the direction of making printed media guides extinct. The ACC has also discontinued printing its conference media guides (Parsons, 2009), and in 2009, ACC member Maryland eliminated printed media guides and saved an estimated $150,000 (Stevens, 2009). Other highly recognizable schools such as Michigan, Ohio State, Oregon, Texas A&M, and Wisconsin have also discontinued publishing their media guides.

The Pac-10 actually submitted a proposal to the NCAA to eliminate all printed media guides (Murschel, 2009). The SEC submitted a proposal to the NCAA to allow printed media guides, but prevent schools from sending them to recruits (Schroeder, 2009). In April 2010, the NCAA Legislative Council approved changing the language in the bylaws concerning sending printed media guides to recruits in order to prohibit that practice. Schools now are only able to send prospective student-athletes complimentary digital versions of the media guides (e.g., via CD, jump drive). This could potentially eliminate the need for as much information in the guides that is geared toward recruits, thus returning them to being true "media" guides, but most likely it will just mean that the guides are sent to recruits in a digital format that is allowed under the new NCAA guidelines.

More and more schools are already choosing to instead provide their media guides on jump drives or CDs in order to deliver them to the media in a much less cumbersome and costly fashion. And, of course, the guide can be accessed via the Internet, with whatever desired pages simply being printed out by the user.

Interactive features, full color (without the printing cost), and a potential limitless amount of pages are the positives for the Internet-only move. The negatives would certainly be alienating media, boosters, and others that would still prefer a hard copy of a media guide. Media members love having a readily available reference, especially when it comes to in-game coverage, and a printed guide provide that. In addition, there's a potential for lost revenue from advertising that is sold for printed media guides.

Regardless of the future of media guides, the SID's role will essentially remain the same. A media guide, whether it's printed or not, will still need to be created.

SUMMARY

Media guides are the look and feel of a sports organization and serve many functions, from recruiting future student-athletes (at the collegiate level) to assisting the media during sporting events as it pertains to media coverage. They are a one-stop shop in assisting the media with everything they need to know about that sports entity.

The guide is comprised of essential information about a team, including player and coach bios, information on the sport organization, records, a history section, opponent information, and other general pertinent information that is a reference point for the media that cover that team. The guide does have size restrictions at the collegiate level, which creates an equal playing field as it pertains to recruiting prospective student-athletes in terms of fairness between schools with varying budgets.

The SID is the ultimate point person in the guide's production and will oversee the writing, advertising, photograph selection, and overall content considerations for the entire project.

Guides differ between the professional and collegiate level. Professionally, the guides are not bound by the same principles as that of the collegiate level, such as the 208-page limit and coloring. Professional guides are usually smaller in trim size, but bigger in page count and they have no recruiting information in them that the collegiate guides would have.

Done properly, the guide will represent a key cog in an organization's overall PR thrust and will be a vital tool in portraying the organization's overall positive image.

DISCUSSION QUESTIONS

1. In your opinion, what is the most important part of the media guide? Why? Conversely, what are a few items that could be omitted from the guide? Why?
2. As technologies continue to shape the future of media guides, do you think there will eventually be no need for a guide at all? Defend your argument.

SUGGESTED EXERCISES

1. You are an SID for a very small Division II school and you have a limited budget for your football guide. Due to financial restrictions, you are only able to produce a 48-page guide. Create an outline for the guide consisting of all the essential items and the order in which they will appear.
2. After doing research and as much fact finding on your favorite collegiate or professional athlete, write a sample media guide bio. Remember to provide as much useful information as you can to assist the media with the coverage of the athlete.

8

Event Management

Event management for a sports information director encompasses a wide array of duties. The duties can be categorized into three primary events: game management/game-day operations, press conferences/media days, and special events. They all have some similarities while each also possesses unique aspects. Regardless of whether it is an actual game or a different occasion, all eyes will be on the SID's organization during the event. That is why it is of the utmost importance for an SID to excel at preparation, organization, and communication, all while being a hospitable host.

GAME MANAGEMENT/GAME-DAY MEDIA OPERATIONS

When fans of any sport, regardless of level, attend a contest, they typically enter the venue shortly before the game starts, enjoy the show, and then leave in a timely fashion upon its conclusion. What they typically do not realize is the amount of behind-the-scenes effort that is required in order to host the event without a hitch, especially from a publicity standpoint. Enter the SID.

Depending on an SID's sport and the coverage that it receives, the days leading up to and the day of the event may be very hectic. And once the game is over there's no rest for a public relations specialist, who must turn right back around and repeat the same process all over again in preparation for the next event. The game itself is the premier showcase for the SID and will be a culmination of all the hard work leading up to and following the event.

For SIDs that cover football, there are numerous tasks that must be accomplished in order to effectively host a successful game day. Many times the actual game is an afterthought. You read that right. There are times where so many things need to be accomplished leading up to kickoff that the actual game itself is no where near as stressful. It's very similar to the long-time cliché in sports that practices are sometimes more difficult than the games themselves.

There are three types of operations as it pertains to hosting a sporting event: pregame, in-game/game-time and post-game.

Pre-Game Preparation

Weeks before the season-opener it is imperative that the SID ensures the press box/press table is functional: stocking of media guides for both his/her school and the opponent, seeing that enough accessories are ready (paper, pencils, working copy machines) and ensuring the Internet is available for the media that will be using it either via wireless or Ethernet connections. The SID will also plan for the food that will be served in the press box/press row during the season. An SID's budget will dictate many of the decisions regarding food but meals for each home game are determined well in advance.

The press box/press row food for the professional ranks often includes treating the media to sit-down dinners before games, and snacks at halftime. High-profile Division I schools often do so as well. Small schools can provide niceties, too, without stretching budgets. Small colleges typically offer coffee, soda, and donuts in working media areas. Others, with a bit more money to spend, add hot dogs, pizza, or submarine sandwiches to the pregame fare. The budget should be the guiding factor in formulating the menu. Remember, the press area is a workplace, first and foremost—not a restaurant.

An in-season game work week begins on a Sunday (when a traditional Saturday game is played) when the SID will update the team statistics from the previous day, nominate any of his/her players for conference, regional, and national players of the week awards (should any be worthy), assist the coaches with any media responsibilities (e.g., conference calls or press conferences) and prepare the weekly game notes for the upcoming game.

The game notes, as mentioned in Chapter 4, are usually a conglomeration of key statistical trends, notes on players to watch, the team's season statistics, updated player information that supplements the media guide that came out at the beginning of year,

Sports reporters rely on the media relations staff to provide a clean and efficient working press box. (Courtesy of Dan Mendlik/Cleveland Indians)

and any and all other pertinent information the SID believes that belongs in the notes. If an SID's game notes are very good, they'll make it in some form to the television or radio broadcast during the contest. For example, in 2007, former West Virginia University fullback Owen Schmitt, a future NFL draft pick of the Seattle Seahawks, was known for his bruising playing style. During his career, Schmitt mangled and broke numerous facemasks on his helmet. The WVU sports communications department inserted a running counter of his career broken facemasks in its game notes. During numerous WVU football games that were broadcast, announcers frequently referenced Schmitt's number of broken facemasks when discussing his toughness, which was a direct result of good work by the SID of including an interesting and useful tidbit in the game notes.

During the days leading up to kickoff, the SID will issue credentials to any local, regional, or national media that request to attend and report on the upcoming game.

The sports information staff should develop a written policy for working press credentials. The SID can avoid confusion and mute complaints by including in the media guide and on the back of the credentials themselves the policy and procedures for arranging credentials.

The policy should address eligibility for credentials, limits per media or other organization, and arrangements for travel companions. The eligibility requirements should specify what types of publications or broadcast media are not eligible for credentials. For example, a university might choose to exclude gambling publications; Internet-based publications; free publications, such as advertising tabloids; and publications that do not regularly cover sports events. The policy should explain how the university will handle requests from scouts (i.e., general admission, VIP, or working press credentials). It also should explain accommodations (credentials or tickets?) available for any spouses. Most college and professional organizations do *not* give working press credentials or seats in the working press area to spouses, though some do provide guest tickets and special seating sections depending on the event and seating availability.

The credentials policy should spell out differences in press passes for reporters, photographers, announcers, videographers, and other broadcast personnel, as well as the limit for each media organization. The SID may set limits on the number of reporters and photographers from a single media organization based on the print or broadcast company's size, coverage area/audience, and proximity to the school or city.

Newspapers and magazines typically send a beat reporter and a photographer to a college or professional game. They also may want to send a columnist or general assignment reporter and a second photographer to games between rivals and games with post-season playoff impact. A radio station usually will send a two- or three-man crew—a play-by-play announcer and color man, and sometimes an engineer/technician that takes care of the equipment. However, a television production crew may need upwards of 25 press passes—including two for talent (announcers), one for a statistician, one each for a director and a producer, two or three for videographers (camera people), and perhaps a couple for technicians in the truck (who might need to come and go in the stadium/arena).

The credentials policy should specify the work areas to which each person with credentials has access. The *press pass* or working credential issued to each person should provide direction—by written or color code—that aids university officials monitoring access. For example, a football pass might enable reporters to walk around freely in the press area, in the locker rooms, and on the sidelines for a football game. Colleges and professional teams often issue armbands to photographers that define access to the field, the court, and/or the locker rooms. The passes and armbands might limit access strictly to the field or only to the press box.

The SID is in charge of issuing the credentials and keeping a running count to avoid overbooking the work space, realizing that establishing a cutoff point and sticking to it is more important than trying to accommodate everyone who wants a credential. The cutoff policy can create conflicts with a journalist denied a credential, but the media organizations at the bottom of the priority order are the least important to the school or team. Assigning a reporter to a seat behind a pole or crowding everyone to squeeze in a few more journalists may cause greater relationship problems with those media organizations that regularly cover the team. It is better to deny access to low-priority journalists at the outset than to provide substandard work space and assistance to all. Media organizations recognize that space is limited, particularly for high-profile events, and accept decisions of the host organization when those decisions are backed up by printed policy.

The SID should assign a staff member to prepare the credentials, each of which should include the name of the individual and the organization represented.

From his/her master credential list the SID will create that week's seating chart for the press box or press row. The seating chart is compiled based on space availability and the demand for the upcoming event. Usually the better seats in the facility (i.e., between the 40-yard lines at football or between the foul lines in basketball) are given to the media that frequently cover that organization on a daily basis. Visiting media can be added around the core media and the seating chart will go from there. Professional scouts should not be seated with the media or with the statistics staff. Rather, they should have their own areas. For away games, sometimes the SID will compile a list of media that cover his/her organization and are requesting credentials and submit that to the host SID rather than having the visiting media contact the host SID individually to request credentials.

Also during the week of a game, a schedule of interview availability for the organization's coaches and players should be distributed so that any of the media planning to follow the SID's organization that week are aware of interview opportunities.

The SID will also ensure any technical concerns are addressed: making sure the statistics crew personnel are in place for the upcoming contest andthat an internal press box announcer has been secured. The SID must arrange for spotters as well as *runners*, who act as utility infielders, performing whatever chore is needed. Lining up the SID's staff and any press box assistants (stat runners, etc.) is a must as the job of this magnitude can't be done alone. He/she will also want to ensure the media has the opportunity to file/post their stories via the Internet (be it via Ethernet or wireless) from the press box/row.

The primary personnel needs for serving the media during game management are as follows:

- Sports information director: The sports information director serves as the controller and troubleshooter. The SID should act as overseer and manager rather than performing a specific job.

- Statistical crew: The most important permanent unit of the press box/row team is the statistical crew, which may consist of several people for football and around three to four for men's and women's basketball. The stats crew for football should consist of one play-by-play typist, spotters for both sides of the ball and a spotting coordinator. The spotters advise the typist on the name of the ball carrier, the tackler(s), yardage gained or lost, and down and distance to go for a first down. For all sports the tasks are similar but they may be accomplished with far fewer members of the stats crew.

The SID may supplement the basic crew with specialists who keep drive and tackle charts, information that aids in identifying the star performers as well as the statistical differences in the game. Many times those are requested by television and radio. A drive chart is a schematic drawing of a football field that shows the starting point and progress on each play of a drive. A tackle chart is a compilation of the number of tackles, sacks, fumble recoveries, and interceptions by each player on the defense. *(Text ontinues on page 154)*

Scoring Summary (Final)
The Automated ScoreBook
#8 PITT vs WEST VIRGINIA (Nov 27, 2009 at Morgantown, W.Va.)

PITT (9-2,5-1) vs. WEST VIRGINIA (8-3,4-2)

Date: Nov 27, 2009 • Site: Morgantown, W.Va. • Stadium: Milan Puskar Stadium Attendance: 56123

Score by Quarters	1	1	1	1	Total
PITT	0	3	3	10	16
WEST VIRGINIA	0	3	10	6	19

Qtr	Time	Scoring Play	V-H
2nd	03:21	PITT—HUTCHINS, Dan 37 yd field goal, 11-54 4:16	3 - 0
	00:05	WVU—BITANCURT, Tyler 20 yd field goal, 10-37 0:58	3 - 3
3rd	09:18	WVU—BITANCURT, Tyler 43 yd field goal, 10-48 3:57	3 - 6
	04:52	PITT—HUTCHINS,Dan 30 yd field goal, 8-46 4:18	6 - 6
	04:34	WVU—DEVINE, Noel 88 yd run (BITANCURT, Tyler kick), 1-88 0:12	6 - 13
4th	10:05	WVU—BITANCURT, Tyler 39 yd field goal, 5-39 1:08	6 - 16
	07:37	PITT—HUTCHINS,Dan 36 yd field goal, 7-33 2:19	9 - 16
	02:54	PITT—BALDWIN,J. 50 yd pass from STULL,Bill (HUTCHINS,Dan kick), 3-75 1:14	16 - 16
	00:00	WVU—BITANCURT, Tyler 43 yd field goal, 10-42 2:48	16 - 19

Kickoff time: 7:05 • End of Game: 10:15 • Total elapsed time: 3:10

Officials: Referee: Dennis Hennigan; Umpire: Bruce Palmer; Linesman: Steve Matarante;

Line judge: Kevin Codey; Back judge: Gary Dancewicz; Field judge: James Smith;

Side judge: Howard Curry; Scorer: Mark DeVault;

Temperature: 36 • Wind: WSW 5mph • Weather: Cloudy

id-771084

(Continued on next page)

Team Statistics (Final)
The Automated ScoreBook
#8 PITT vs WEST VIRGINIA (Nov 27, 2009 at Morgantown, W.Va.)

	PITT	WVU
FIRST DOWNS	15	18
Rushing	8	10
Passing	7	8
Penalty	0	0
NET YARDS RUSHING	146	205
Rushing Attempts	29	43
Average Per Rush	5.0	4.8
Rushing Touchdowns	0	1
Rushing Touchdowns	0	1
Yards Gained Rushing	160	231
Yards Lost Rushing	14	26
NET YARDS PASSING	179	164
Completions—Attempts—Interceptions	16-30-2	19-32-0
Average Per Attempt	6.0	5.1
Average Per Completion	11.2	8.6
Passing Touchdowns	1	0
TOTAL OFFENSE YARDS	325	369
Total offense plays	59	75
Average Gain Per Play	5.5	4.9
Fumbles: Number—Lost	0-0	0-0
Penalties: Number—Yards	2-20	6-46
PUNTS-YARDS	3-136	5-216
Average Yards Per Punt	45.3	43.2
Net Yards Per Punt	43.3	41.4
Inside 20	0	1
50+ Yards	1	1
Touchbacks	0	0
Fair catch	0	0
KICKOFFS—YARDS	5-330	5-293
Average Yards Per Kickoff	66.0	58.6
Net Yards Per Kickoff	47.6	29.8
Touchbacks	0	0
Punt returns: Number—Yards—TD	3-9-0	2-6-0
Average Per Return	3.0	3.0

(Continued on next page)

	PITT	WVU
Kickoff returns: Number—Yds—TD	5-144-0	4-92-0
Average Per Return	28.8	23.0
Interceptions: Number—Yds—TD	0-0-0	2-6-0
Fumble Returns: Number—Yds—TD	0-0-0	0-0-0
Miscellaneous Yards	0	0
Possession Time	29:47	30:13
1st Quarter	6:02	8:58
2nd Quarter	7:17	7:43
3rd Quarter	9:09	5:51
4th Quarter	7:19	7:41
Third-Down Conversions	2 of 13	9 of 19
Fourth-Down Conversions	1 of 1	1 of 3
Red-Zone Scores—Chances	3-3	1-2
Sacks By: Number—Yards	2-19	1-10
PAT Kicks	1-1	1-1
Field Goals	3-5	4-4

Individual Statistics (Final)
The Automated ScoreBook
#8 PITT vs WEST VIRGINIA (Nov 27, 2009 at Morgantown, W.Va.)

PITT Rushing	No.	Gain	Loss	Net	TD	LG	Avg	WVU Rushing	No.	Gain	Loss	Net	TD	Lg	Avg
LEWIS, DION	26	158	3	155	0	30	6.0	DEVINE, Noel	17	137	3	134	1	88	7.9
GRAHAM, Ray	1	0	1	-1	0	0	-1.0	CLARKE, Ryan	10	30	1	29	0	8	2.9
STULL, Bill	2	2	10	-8	0	2	-4.0	BROWN, Jarret	13	43	22	21	0	10	1.6
Totals	29	160	14	146	0	30	5.0	STARKS, Brad	2	13	0	13	0	13	6.5
								SANDERS, Jock	1	8	0	8	0	8	8.0
								Totals	43	231	26	205	1	88	4.8

PITT Passing	C-A-I	Yds	TD	Long	Sack	WVU Passing	C-A-I	Yds	TD	Long	Sack
STULL, Bill	16-30-2	179	1	50	1	BROWN, Jarrett	19-31-0	164	0	35	2
Totals	16-30-2	179	1	50	1	TEAM	0-1-0	0	0	0	0
						Totals	19-32-0	164	0	35	2

(Continued on next page)

Individual Statistics (Final)—*Continued*
The Automated ScoreBook
#8 PITT vs WEST VIRGINIA (Nov 27, 2009 at Morgantown, W.Va.)

PITT					WVU				
Receiving	No.	Yards	TD	Long	Receiving	No.	Yards	TD	Long
BALDWIN, J.	8	127	1	50	ARNETT, Alric	7	71	0	35
SHANAHAN, Mike	2	17	0	10	SANDERS, Jock	3	15	0	8
LEWIS, DION	2	14	0	14	AUSTIN, Tavon	3	12	0	9
DICKERSON, Dorin	2	12	0	6	LYONS, Wes	2	44	0	24
McGEE, Cedric	1	6	0	6	STARKS, Brad	2	16	0	11
HYNOSKI, Henry	1	3	0	3	URBAN, Tyler	1	4	0	4
Totals	16	179	1	50	DEVINE, Noel	1	2	0	2
					Totals	19	164	0	35

PITT						WVU					
Punting	No.	Yds	Avg	Long.	In20.	TB.	Punting	No.	Yds	Avg.	Long	In20.	TB
HUTCHINS, Dan	3	136	45.3	50	0	0	KOZLOWSKI, Scott	5	216	43.2	52	1	0
Totals	3	136	45.3	50	0	0	Totals	5	216	43.2	52	1	0

PITT

	Punt			Kickoff			Intercept		
Returns	No	Yds	Lg	No	Yds	Lg	No	Yds	Lg
SMITH, Aaron	3	9	7	0	0	0	0	0	0
SADDLER, Cameron	0	0	0	2	81	42	0	0	0
GRAHAM, Ray	0	0	0	3	63	29	0	0	0
Totals	3	9	7	5	144	42	0	0	0

WVU

	Punt			Kickoff			Intercept		
Returns	No	Yds	Lg	No	Yds	Lg	No	Yds	Lg
SANDERS, Jock	2	6	6	0	0	0	0	0	0
AUSTIN, Tavon	0	0	0	2	39	21	0	0	0
TANDY, Keith	0	0	0	0	0	0	1	6	6
RODGERS, Mark	0	0	0	2	53	29	0	0	0
SANDS, Robert	0	0	0	0	0	0	1	0	0
Totals	2	6	6	4	92	29	2	6	6

(Continued on next page)

Individual Statistics (Final)—*Continued*
The Automated ScoreBook
#8 PITT vs WEST VIRGINIA (Nov 27, 2009 at Morgantown, W.Va.)

PITT

Field goals	Qtr	Time	Dist	Result
HUTCHINS, Dan	1st	08:52	46 yards	Missed
HUTCHINS, Dan	2nd	03:21	37 yards	Good
HUTCHINS, Dan	3rd	04:52	30 yards	Good
HUTCHINS, Dan	3rd	01:36	53 yards	Missed
HUTCHINS, Dan	4th	07:37	36 yards	Good

WVU

Field goals	Qtr	Time	Dist	Result
BITANCURT, Tyler	2nd	00:05	20 yards	Good
BITANCURT, Tyler	3rd	09:18	43 yards	Good
BITANCURT, Tyler	4th	10:05	39 yards	Good
BITANCURT, Tyler	4th	00:00	43 yards	Good

PITT						WVU					
Kickoffs	No.	Yards	Avg	TB	OB	Kickoffs	No.	Yards	Avg	TB	OB
BRIGGS, Luke	5	330	66.0	0	1	BITANCURT, Tyler	5	293	58.6	0	0

PITT

All-purpose	Run	Rcv	KR	PR	IR	Total
LEWIS, DION	155	14	0	0	0	169
BALDWIN, J.	0	127	0	0	0	127
SADDLER, Cameron	0	0	81	0	0	81
GRAHAM, Ray	5	0	63	0	0	62

WVU

All-purpose	Run	Rcv	KR	PR	IR	Total
DEVINE, Noel	134	2	0	0	0	136
ARNETT, Alric	0	71	0	0	0	71
RODGERS, Mark	0	0	53	0	0	53
AUSTIN, Tavon	0	12	59	0	0	51

Fumbles	Pitt	None	WEST VIRGINIA	None

(Text ontinued from page 149)

A basketball crew consists of a play-by-play typist; a spotter who records points and fouls for players for each team; a spotter who tracks rebounds, turnovers, and assists; and a spotting coordinator.

- Duplication/copy specialist: The duplication specialist makes the predetermined number of copies of statistical information, ranging from quickie stats at halftime to books of final statistics.

- Runners: The runners distribute duplicated materials and other information to everyone seated in the press box. Football runners pass out "quickie" stats (summaries) after each quarter of a football game, halftime statistics, and final statistical packages. The same holds true for basketball, but on the collegiate level, quickie stats are provided at halftime.

- Pool reporter: The SID may assign one assistant to each locker room to gather quotations from players and coaches to distribute to the media. SID assistants can type the quotations and deliver them to the duplication specialist.

- Telephone person: This person is responsible for handling all national phone requests that arrive during a contest. National media will want score updates and other information often in order to pass it on to its customers.

- News conference aids: The SID may assign an assistant to bring players and coaches from each team to the designated room for the news conference. The visiting SID usually handles his/her requests. The SID may rely on assistants or volunteers who perform other duties during the game, as long as the duties are completed by game's end.

- Media spotters and runners: A radio station sometimes will request a spotter, especially for football, although many radio crews will provide their own spotter. Television production crews frequently will request a couple of runners—a statistician and someone to manage the cords for videographers who move about the sidelines. The same will hold true for basketball.

The SID should ask about personnel needs when radio or television media request credentials. It also is a wise policy to keep a volunteer or two on standby if media interest is high, to handle any last-minute requests. Merle Levin, a former SID at Cleveland State University, says student volunteers are acceptable if they are "absolutely dependable." A dependable pool may be found in the university's communication, journalism, and/or electronic media departments. Many of those may be knowledgeable about the media's needs as a result of course work and previous field experience.

- Hospitality and concessions: The SID should assign a volunteer or two to assist with food and other amenities. The volunteer can advise food service personnel of supplies running low, spills, etc. In many cases, the caterer or university food-service people will take care of this responsibility.

While budget and the pool of volunteers available may limit personnel resources, the SID should keep in mind that efficiency is inseparable from the size of the press-box staff. Mistakes are more likely to happen if people are assigned multiple duties, particularly if the timing for different responsibilities is tight. Service is more likely to falter if flexibility is limited by insufficient personnel at the site.

The SID also should bear in mind that efficiency is inseparable from preparation. The SID should train statisticians ahead of time, even if that involves practice with videotapes. Sports information personnel should schedule volunteers well in advance and call to confirm their participation a couple of days in advance of the game. A walk-through and check of equipment is also good practice.

Remember, a satisfied reporter is likely to speak highly of the accommodations. Word of mouth inside media circles spreads like a wildfire. Good news can spread as quickly as bad news.

If the contest is on television, Thursday or Friday of game week sees the television talent and director/producer meet with some of the team's notable players and its coaches to follow up on story lines they may have found in the SID's game notes. It's a unique opportunity to further promote the athletes and the team and all of this is arranged through the SID. A lot times the information the announcers acquire in those meetings is used in the subsequent broadcast.

On the day of the game, the SID should arrive no later than two to three hours before the start time to assist with any media issues that may arise. Those would include myriad tasks including checking the starting lineup with TV, setting up press row for a smaller sport, passing out the game notes packets and media guides, and assisting the statistics crew with preparing the game file. Sometimes seating chart issues arise and the SID has to think on his/her feet (e.g., two media members that don't get along are seated beside each other). The SID will also field questions for story ideas from the media and assist in facilitating those story lines.

For away games, the SID should meet with the public address announcer and any radio and TV broadcasters to ensure pronunciation of their players is accurate.

In-Game Operations

Once the sporting event has begun, the well-prepared SID has the school's, conference's, and NCAA's (should it be a collegiate game) record books readily available should any statistical feats from the contest set new standards. And if that happens, the internal and external public address announcers, television (if the game is being broadcast), and the home radio broadcasters should immediately be informed so the general public and the media are aware of the record-breaking information. Game notes should be readily accessible for player game-, season-, and career-high marks that may be achieved. An ongoing tally of notes should also be kept and distributed to the media after the contest's conclusion. In-game, a contest's statistical play-by-play and box score from each quarter is distributed to the media via the SID's support staff to ensure the media is able to effectively cover the contest. Other responsibilities would include the gathering of coach and player names for post-game interviews, being on call should an injury occur and the media request information about the injury, and generally just being available. Some games go on without a hitch. Others that may be high-scoring, record-breaking affairs will keep the SID's nose buried in the record book. For smaller sports that don't receive the same amount of coverage as football or basketball, the SID will be responsible for writing the post-game press release, and the good SID will constantly be writing as the contest goes on in order to have the release ready as soon as possible following the outcome of the contest.

Also in-game, and with today's technology, the sports information department can Twitter up-to-the-second records and notable achievements, as well as blog or Facebook the same information. Both are unique ways of keeping the fans roped in tight to the organization by giving them quick and interesting insight they might not receive until well after the game.

Post-Game Duties

The primary duties of an SID in the post-game involve managing the head coach's press conference, win or lose, and bringing the requested players into the press conference once the coach has finished. For football, there are usually two areas, one for the visiting team and players and one for the home school, because the event will have so much media coverage. For basketball and other sports, traditionally the visiting team's coach and requested players appear first in the interview room, followed by the home team's coach and requested players.

Post-game is arguably one of the most challenging aspects of the job on game days. It can be a stressful time, especially if media are on deadline and the head coach is slow in wrapping up his postgame chat with his/her team. Should the SID's team lose, his/her players rarely want to be interviewed, yet the media still have a job to do. In these situations it is imperative to let the student-athlete who is resisting the interview know that true character is shown in both good times and in bad. The media will respect players even more if they speak after a loss, especially if, when times are good, they are more than willing to be in the limelight. As mentioned in Chapter 4, now is the time the athlete would best utilize the tips and strategies the SID gave the athletes for being interviewed. By heeding the lessons taught by the SID and knowing that all eyes are on them at that very moment, giving a great interview will only give the athletes, team, and organization a lasting, positive image.

The quotes from the entire press conference should be recorded, transcribed, and distributed with the contest's entire statistical package to the media as quickly as possible after the game. A press release/news story needs to be written for the organization's website and for immediate distribution to members of the media that were unable to attend the contest.

One of the responsibilities of a sports information director is to ensure that athletes are made available to media for postgame interviews. (Courtesy of George Mason Athletics/ John Aronson)

The final statistical packages for football games typically consist of these items:

- A scoring summary.
- Team statistics, including first downs, net yards rushing, net yards passing, total yards, etc.
- Individual statistics, including rushing, passing, pass receiving, punting, field goals, and returns.
- The contest's starters, on both sides of the ball, for both teams.
- Individual defensive statistics, including tackles (assisted, unassisted, and tackles for losses), quarterback sacks, fumble recoveries, fumbles forced, pass interceptions, passes broken up.
- A drive chart showing the starting field position and time, and end result of the drive for each team.
- A participation chart showing each player that performed during the contest.
- A play-by-play rundown from coin toss to final play.

The final statistical packages for basketball contests typically consist of these items:

- Final Box Score, which includes starters.
- First and second half play-by-play.
- First half box score.

For SIDs in charge of basketball, the same process is to be used when it comes to pre-game, in-game, and post-game management. The big difference, though, is that the entire process is usually repeated two to three times a week because basketball games are played more frequently, so the turnaround time for game notes, interview requests, credentials, etc., is far shorter and the SID is under constant pressure for five months during basketball season.

For varsity/Olympic sports that don't receive the same amount of attention as football and men's and women's basketball, the same responsibilities are still required. The tasks may vary depending on the media coverage of those sports and the frequency of which the sport is played. The most noticeable difference with other sports is that the SID is usually self-sufficient and will probably be the lone official scorer if it's baseball or soccer, or be a part of a statistics crew if needed. There may be no press box food, like with football or basketball. Instead, snacks may be provided, which would have a minimal impact on the overall budget. For sports that require a crew, such as a public address announcer and scorekeeper, etc., the SID will be charged with securing those workers.

Event Management on the Road

When the SID is on the road with his/her team—depending on the sport—many of the same principles described above will generally apply. The SID may keep the statistics, assist with a radio broadcast, run his/her postgame press conference (should there be a need), and deliver the event's statistics and press releases to his/her media outlets that aren't in attendance. It is imperative that the news of the event still make it into the hands of the media that cover the team but do not travel to the event. Host SID's may assist in the coverage, but the growing trend, especially with technology advancements such as wireless air cards and wireless Internet, is that the visiting SID has now become self-sufficient.

Do's and Don'ts in Press Box

The *NCAA Public Relations and Promotion Manual* lists these MUSTS, DO'S, and DON'TS regarding press boxes. While some of these are a bit-outdated, they serve as an excellent start for the SID to focus on when it comes to game-day management:

MUST'S

- Must have adequate space for working media
- Must be functional before making it fancy
- Must be heated in cold climate
- Must keep non-workers out of working area
- Must have adequate area for service and statistical crews and equipment
- Must have an electrical outlet at every seat
- Must have adequate space for home and visiting coaches' phone booths
- Must have adequate space behind writers for traffic

DO'S

- Do have food service available
- Do have adequate toilet facilities for men and women
- Do have water fountains
- Do have pay telephones available for emergencies
- Do have adequate storage space for stats crew materials
- Do have easy access to field and dressing rooms
- Do have adequate communications between stats crew and working media
- Do have adequate lighting, power, and telephone cables and outlets
- Do install a bank of telephones throughout the working media area to assist writers filing a story
- Do have specially designed television booth and camera spaces
- Do have conduit of sufficient size to handle television cable
- Do have an elevator

DONT'S

- Don't have poles, pillars, posts, or lattice-work windows that obstruct view
- Don't have so many entrances to the press box that policing is a problem
- Don't mix scouts and other necessary fringe workers with working media
- Don't lead VIPs and other non-workers into the working press area
- Don't put food bar in main stream of press-box traffic
- DON'T CHEER—THERE IS NO CHEERING IN THE PRESS BOX

The last point is especially important to point out. The press box/press row is a working environment, home to SIDs of both organizations, the working media, press box assistants, and other members working to make the game go off without a hitch. It is imperative that it is kept a work place and no cheering will be allowed as it is an unbiased work place. Any violators will be removed from the premises.

The responsibility for running a clean and efficient media work area belongs to the sports information or media relations staff. The press table is the "office" for the working media. To be of real service, the sports information staff must efficiently provide the materials and assistance the media need to perform their jobs. Good intentions and "I'm sorry" mean nothing to the football announcer who just stumbled through player identifications for four quarters because no pronunciation guide was available. What makes a difference is anticipating every problem that might arise and resolving it quickly.

When the games begin, the SID or public relations director is the managing partner in the working relationship between media and sport organizations. The press table or press box is the work area. "Work area" is the operative phrase. The space reserved for the media at athletics events is a work area, not a social club or party room. Press boxes are not places for VIPs and friends of the university to watch the contests and enjoy free food and drink. That is not to say the press box should be off limits to everyone but the working media; it is to say that the sports information staff should restrict access and eliminate any activity that is not work related.

The press box can double as a mini-dining room for the working media, and no one will complain if university administrators and special guests share the refreshments. However, the SID should seat them away from the areas in which the media will be working during the game. After the game, staff members should ask outsiders to leave, because the press box, press table, or media room immediately turns into a very busy and hectic place—like a subway station when the train arrives. Everyone scrambles to get to work quickly.

At no time is the partnership between journalists and sports information personnel under greater pressure and strain than during postgame. The sports information staff often must cater to the needs of a large group of media with diverse interests. Broadcast journalists must deliver their stories live. Many print reporters must file stories within 20 to 30 minutes after completion of the game. All must work quickly in a setting with little margin of error and few advantages of the home office. Finishing the job before the deadline takes precedence over social graces and professional amenities.

Even during hectic times, however, remember that the SID's overall responsibility is to always create a favorable image of the organization and team. So it's imperative for SIDs to ensure that in the days and hours leading up to a game, they are fully prepared for the event. After all, games are arguably the most important opportunity to convey the most positive image of the organization.

NEWS CONFERENCES AND MEDIA DAYS

The most common types of managed events, outside of game days, are news conferences and media days. Sport organizations set up news conferences to make major announcements (usually positive) such as trades, signings of new players or coaches, changes

MITCHELL LAYTON PHOTOGRAPHY

Coach's CORNER

by Craig Esherick

The fans' demand for more information has led many media outlets to request interviews with coaches and players hours prior to a game. This is relatively common with professional athletes, with NBA locker rooms, for example, being opened to the media a couple of hours prior to tipoff. In college athletics, however, coaches and SIDs should work together to develop a procedure for handling requests for game-day interviews.

Some coaches believe that game-day interviews are a distraction for them and the players; other coaches don't have a problem doing these interviews. If the game is on national TV, the network may not have a camera available until the day of the game. In that instance, an SID may want to encourage the coach to be more flexible in granting an interview prior to a game. A good SID will always have the best interest of the coach, players, and team/organization in mind, and if the SID thinks that it is important that a player or the coach be available for an interview on the day of the game, he/she should convey this to the coach.

It is important that the coach have an understanding of who is at the game and where they will be sitting, too. If pro scouts have asked for a press pass to a collegiate contest, the SID should let the coach know this because the coach may want to use this information to motivate the team or a particular player. If the SID knows that the coach has a less than cordial relationship with a particular member of the press that occasionally attends games (e.g., a newspaper columnist), he/she should inform the coach prior to the postgame press conference.

It is extremely important for a coach to have a discussion with the sports information director (SID) about postgame interviews. There is no question that an athletic contest is an emotional event for players and coaches. Things happen during games that stay with the participants a long time after the game is over. A good working relationship between the SID, coaching staff, and players can help to prevent emotional outbursts that could be damaging to the reputation of the team or organization.

It is always a beneficial practice for the coach to say a few words of caution to the team after a game that may have ended with a controversial call by an official. It usually is not in the best interests of an athlete or coach to criticize the referees/officials in the postgame press conference. In fact, in many cases, this criticism can lead to sanctions (e.g., fines, suspensions) from the league office. A word of caution from the coach after the game may help to put in perspective the result of the game.

The SID also can caution the coach before he/she talks to the press about the value of self control. Another rule of thumb is to never criticize an opponent in the press after a game. Humility is a valuable character trait. A gentle reminder to some of the key players after the game is always good practice.

Preparation is also important in this area. A discussion before the season starts with the team, either individually or together by the SID, outlining postgame interview procedures is always helpful to the players, particularly those that are new to the team. When I was at Georgetown, we had a policy that freshmen were not available to the press until the end of the first semester. There were a few in the press that did not like this, but the logic was that the new players should have an opportunity to learn about the school, program, and college basketball before they were asked to expound on these subjects by "seasoned" members of the media. I am sure the press would appreciate the same for their sons and daughters.

of ownership, or details on a new facility. They use media days primarily to kick off a new season. Reporters who attend can interview coaches and players. College conferences also organize media days prior to the start of a season. Each college sends a coach and selected players to a joint media day, giving the media access to representatives of each team in the conference. Reporters can gather information, media guides, and pictures they can use in stories throughout the season.

News Conferences

News conferences are one of the most important means through which sport organizations communicate with the media and the public. Managed events, such as news conferences, enable sport organizations to distribute the same information to large groups of reporters at the same time. However, the announcement must be worthy of a news conference. News conferences also give the media the opportunity to ask questions and to obtain information from key players, coaches, and team or athletics department officials at one location and at one time.

On the professional level, most news conferences concern the hiring and/or firing of front office personnel or coaches; player trades or signings; injuries and other personnel matters; and ticket, stadium, and franchise issues. Professional sport organizations are more likely than colleges or high schools to schedule news conferences to address negative issues such as the punishment for a player who violates the organization's substance-abuse policy.

Colleges and universities typically call news conferences to make announcements in high-profile sports such as football, men's basketball, and women's basketball. News conferences may also be necessary in other sports if there is a large enough following (e.g., LSU in baseball, Georgia in women's gymnastics, and Iowa in wrestling).

High school administrators seldom arrange a news conference for anything other than the introduction of a new coach or administrator or the signing of one of their star athletes to a major Division I institution.

Planning the News Conference

Planning a news conference is a team effort that may involve many administrators, coaches, and sports information personnel. The roles and responsibilities vary according to the makeup of the sport organization. A team owner may instruct the public relations director to arrange a news conference when the owner fires a general manager (GM) or manager. The GM may order a news conference to announce a trade. The president of a university or the athletics director may request a news conference to announce the hiring of a coach or the announcement of a large donation to the department.

The sports information or public relations director must work with administrators to create a chain of command and a roster of responsibilities for news conferences. The document should spell out the roles and responsibilities of each person in the chain. It should specify who decides when to call a news conference and what information to release, who makes the physical arrangements, who prepares the information released at the meeting, who makes the announcement, and who answers questions.

MITCHELL LAYTON PHOTOGRAPHY

Coach'S CORNER

by Craig Esherick

It is important for coaches to plan for press conferences and media days, both with their coaching staff and sports information specialist. Class schedules need to be evaluated for open time slots and conflicts with labs, classes, and exams. It is also important not to schedule a media day on a date that will conflict with another sports event in the area that may tamp down turnout. The sports information director (SID) wants the press at the event, so a coach should make it easy for the SID to get them there.

With some teams, it may be necessary to have a weekly press conference because of the media interest in a team. Most Division I football and men's basketball programs have a weekly press conference. In addition, most teams usually have a season opening press conference to give the local media an opportunity to meet and interview key team members, talk about the prospects for the season, and watch a workout. During these preseason media days, coaches and players alike should realize that many members of the media from outside the immediate coverage market will be in attendance and may not be extremely familiar with the team. This will most likely lead to some questions being asked that may seem silly or redundant, but coaches and players should do their best to answer them in a straight-forward manner without becoming frustrated.

Coaches should sit down with the sports information specialist and prepare for any press conference or media days that they will host. Issues that may come up during these media opportunities should be discussed so that a coach is not caught off guard with a topic that the media may want to discuss. The SID should have some ideas as to the main topics to be discussed and the coach may have a few ideas that he/she wants to promote relative to his/her team.

If a school has just built a new practice facility or a meeting room that a coach wants the press to see, maybe that should be where the press conference or media day is held. If the day of a press conference is a heavy class day for students, the coach and SID may decide to hold the media opportunity right before practice on the gym floor. It may also be important for the local TV to get footage of a team conducting drills, so the gym floor may be the best place for that reason, too.

I also think it is important to take a look at how players are presenting themselves the day of the press conference or media day. Should they wear a team or school dress shirt or jacket instead of a T-shirt? If the team will practice immediately after the press conference, however, it will be more practical just to have the players wear their practice jerseys. It is important to realize that most college student-athletes will be in the job market soon. The coach and SID should continually put the players in the best position to be employable. Making them wear a coat and tie from time to time may not be popular with college students, but it may make a potential employer take notice.

At the press conferences and media days, student reporters will usually be present. It is important that players are counseled that these "students" are reporters and should be given respect and taken seriously as members of the media. Many college athletes have said something they regret because there was an impression that the conversation was "off the record" with a fellow student.

Typically, sports information personnel begin notifying the media of a news conference as soon as possible, usually a day in advance. The objective is to give reporters sufficient time to make arrangements to attend the meeting, but not enough time to gather enough information to "break" the story before the announcement. In an age of high-intensity investigative reporting by the media, keeping the name of a coach or other major news absolutely secret is almost impossible. In all probability, the media have speculated for days on the most likely candidates for a coaching position, but the sports information or public relations director still should make an attempt to keep the information confidential until the formal announcement. But even if a media outlet does get a "scoop" and reports the information that was planned to be announced during the news conference, the sport organization should go ahead with the news conference—including providing the news release, biographical information, and statements from relevant university or team personnel.

Here is a list of suggestions for SIDs to follow in organizing effective news conferences regardless of the size of the organization.

1. Make certain the announcement is newsworthy.
2. Inform all members of the media. The timing of the invitations should allow reporters enough time to arrange schedules, but not enough time to find out and to report the particulars of the announcement.
3. In the case of a "blockbuster" announcement, issue verbal invitations three to five hours in advance of the news conference. Blockbuster announcements would include the naming of a coach, the completion of a trade, or a decision to build a new stadium. In the case of a "soft" announcement, such as a groundbreaking ceremony for a new stadium, the SID should mail, fax, or email invitations three to five days in advance.
4. Make certain that sufficient parking space is available close to the meeting room.
5. The room for the news conference should be large enough to handle the crowd but small enough to create an atmosphere of intimacy and importance. A handful of reporters in a large room has a hollow feel, perhaps creating an impression that not many reporters showed up or felt the announcement was important enough to attend. The announcement should be made on the organization's own turf—campus, stadium, office, gymnasium, or conference room.
6. The facility should be attractive and functional. Provide an adequate number of chairs and easy access to restrooms and telephones. Also, make certain sufficient working space is available to reporters. You should incorporate the institution's name and logo in the backdrop or place them on the front of the speaker's podium.

   Remember, the SID's job is to put the university or organization in the public eye. One of the simplest and most effective ways to do so is to display the institution's name and logo in such a manner that they appear prominently in photographs or video clips from the news conference.

7. Make the media feel welcome by offering refreshments, such as cookies or donuts along with coffee, tea, and soft drinks. Do *not* serve alcohol. In today's society, news conferences are work sessions, not social get-togethers. Do not spend more than you can afford on refreshments. If a modest lunch fits into the budget, a meal is more than acceptable to members of the media. Coffee, soft drinks, and pastry generally are sufficient, however.

8. Provide the media copies of the news release. The release should supply all basic information but not all the details.

9. Allow enough time in the schedule for media questions. Do not let the question-answer session run longer than 30 minutes.

10. Supply photographs to the print media if they will enhance coverage.

11. Following the news conference, allow 15–30 minutes for additional one-on-one interviews, which are typically needed by TV and radio reporters. If you let the questions continue for more than 30 minutes, you may infringe on the time available to media representatives to prepare their stories for publication or broadcast.

12. The SID should always remain on-hand after a news conference in order to facilitate any further interview requests and answer any questions.

Media Days

Media days are popular and effective publicity-generating events for Division I universities and for professional teams. In Divisions II and III in most parts of the country, media days usually are limited to college football and/or basketball. Colleges and conferences may organize media days for other sports depending on the visibility of the sport in a particular area.

The sport organization gives the media the red-carpet treatment on these days, so careful planning and attention to detail are essential. A poorly organized media day can be a disaster and can result in poor public relations that may take a long time to overcome.

The fall, or football, media day is the first opportunity each year for reporters to visit a college campus or professional team's facilities and interact with the athletes in person. In the case of a conference, the fall media day gives journalists a chance to meet new coaches, athletic directors, and sports information directors, too. Of particular importance is luring journalists new to the school or conference beat. There is perhaps no better opportunity to treat the journalist to a taste of the school and to begin to establish a favorable one-on-one relationship.

College conferences also arrange media days prior to the start of the football and basketball seasons. Such events typically include a luncheon, comments from the men's and women's coaches for each team, opportunities for interviews with coaches and selected players, and announcement of the results of preseason voting on the top teams and players in the conference. Gifts are usually given out to the media as a "thank you" for attending the event.

The Big East Conference has one of the most well-known and respected media days for its football and men's and women's basketball days. For the eight-team football

The Big East Conference's women's basketball media day is held at ESPNZone in Times Square, offering a unique setting for the event. (Courtesy of WVU Sports Communications)

league, the media day centers around a clambake in Newport, Rhode Island, creating a unique atmosphere for coaches and players to mingle with the media.

For the 16-team basketball league, the men's Big East Conference media day is held at Madison Square Garden, the world's most famous arena and the site of the conference's postseason tournament. For the women's media day, the Big East Conference uses ESPNZone in Times Square as its venue, offering a unique setting. The Big East Conference media days are memorable experiences for the media, coaches, and players alike, and it has created great rapport between coaches, players, SIDs, and the media, while also garnering plenty of positive exposure for the league.

Planning the Media Day

As in planning for a news conference, preparing for a media day is a team project. The planning, however, starts much further in advance and involves more people because of the multi-faceted nature of the event. The media day amounts to multiple announcements and interviews all rolled into one package.

The planning typically starts many months in advance. As in the case of news conferences, the effective sports information or public relations director must develop an organizational chart that spells out responsibilities for administrators, coaches, and others. The plan should include a budget and a timetable that lists deadlines for completion of specific tasks and dates for particular steps, such as the date for mailing out invitations. Here's a rundown on the most important steps in the process.

1. Choose a date and a starting time.
2. Choose and reserve a place to hold the event.

Typical Media Day Timetable

- Nine months (before the event)—Begin the planning process.

- Two months—Announce the media day. Send a memo to coaches, sports information personnel, and other athletics officials to provide the date, time, and agenda of the media day. Also release to the media the date, time, and agenda. (If a reporter calls earlier for planning purposes, it is OK to tell the reporter about the event.) Arrange for preparation of composite photo sheets for distribution at the media day. It usually takes a month to get back an order.

- One month—Send invitations and event schedules, preregistration forms, and maps to print and broadcast media, coaches, and sports information directors. The invitation can be as simple as a sentence atop a preregistration form or as formal as a printed invitation. The preregistration form should include
  - place for the person to respond yes or no
  - place for the person's name and affiliation
  - deadline for preregistration
  - person to whom to return the form
  - address to mail or email, or telephone number to send the form by fax.
  - a map with written directions
  - One week—Call the caterer or food service director with the final count for luncheon or brunch.

Send an email message to selected TV stations. Send another reminder message three days before the event. Call two days in advance to ask if someone will attend. The more persistent you are with the television media, the more likely you are to get results.

3. Choose and reserve a caterer if the school or the facility selected does not have one.
4. Determine the schedule of events for the day.
5. Announce the media day and send out invitations, preregistration forms, and maps.
6. Prepare a preregistration list and add names as they come in.
7. Prepare information packets (press kits) for the media and for others who attend.
8. Prepare a biography sheet on the coach(es) who will attend.
9. Notify the caterer of the final count for the meal.
10. Create a checklist of duties to be performed the day of the event.

SPECIAL EVENTS

A special event encompasses in-house promotions tied to scheduled games or sport seasons as well as one-time events in which the host team/organization may or may not participate. Both are promotional, designed to enhance the image of the sport organization, and/or to increase revenues.

Colleges and cities collaborate on bids to host preliminary and championship rounds of NCAA regional or championship tournaments and meets in men's and women's basketball, swimming, wrestling, track, gymnastics, golf, tennis, etc. At the professional level, special events embrace everything from all-star games to sites for professional tour events or league championships, such as the Super Bowl.

The common denominator among special events is promotion. The objective of an in-house promotion or a single, special event is to advance the financial goals of the sport organization and/or sponsors. An in-house promotion for a game may aim at generating media interest in a team or sport in hopes that increased publicity may result in additional ticket sales.

In the late 2000s, West Virginia University (WVU) placed bids to host the men's and women's Big East Conference soccer championships at Dick Dlesk Soccer Stadium, because WVU had a new facility that the school wanted to showcase. The university also wanted a platform to announce that it was now a major player in collegiate soccer. In that sense, hosting the special event enabled WVU to garner more attention to its soccer facility and teams while also generating revenue. WVU also played host to opening-round action in women's basketball's 2009 Preseason WNIT. In its home opener a slew of special promotions were offered that the general public took advantage of and, as a result, the game drew more than 3,500 fans, more than triple the attendance for a typical women's basketball game.

Although boosting attendance and revenue at events may not be the direct responsibility of the SID, the marketing function and public relations thrust often mesh in staging special events. As in many other aspects of the business of sports, marketing and promotions specialists may lead the way in identifying target audiences and determining the best ways to reach them.

The marketing and public relations functions vary according to the type of event. The university development or professional marketing departments play the larger role in events with a heavy emphasis on identifying audiences, conducting advertising campaigns, and selling tickets and sponsorships. Promotions and marketing people generally handle direct mail, telemarketing, personal contact, group ticket discounts, game-day promotions, and paid advertising or sponsorships. For example, a university promotions specialist or athletics director would most often negotiate the sponsorship of an invitational tournament and halftime giveaways/contests by local businesses. Those assigned promotional duties also would oversee individual game promotions. For example, they would take care of a promotion that promised free admission to a college women's basketball game to youngsters wearing T-shirts from the university-held sports camp the previous summer or the first 50 students to attend the game would be provided with free pizza from a university sponsor.

The sports information or public relations departments play the larger role in events with heavy emphasis on generating publicity and assisting the media in information delivery. The emphasis on media management is why the sports information department takes the lead in news conferences and media days. The objective of each is not to sell tickets, but to deliver information through the media that will heighten interest and indirectly boost ticket sales. Likewise, the sports information office will play a significant role in the awards banquet, postseason playoff events, and all-star games.

Special events essentially can be categorized as either *informational* or *promotional* activities. Informational activities are directed primarily by sports information personnel and include news conferences, media days, news releases, awards banquets, postseason playoffs, all-star games, programs for special events, tournament press operations, tournament all-star teams, and awards. Promotional activities are directed primarily by marketing personnel and include opening day festivities, single-game promotions, ticket discount promotions, advertising campaigns (including posters, flyers, billboards, etc.), tournament sponsorships, halftime giveaways, and contests.

Planning the Special Event

When an amateur organization, an institution, or a team decides to stage a special event, everyone must get involved: coaches, athletics directors/general managers, business managers, marketing/promotions directors, advertising managers, sports information directors, and even the athletes. Successful events are the result of well-coordinated efforts by specialists in a variety of fields. Each specialist contributes expertise in one area of a multifaceted plan.

The planning process for a special event is similar to the preparations for media brochures or media days, but it is far more extensive. It calls into play all the skills and functions of the sports information specialist—for example, news releases, managed news events, media brochures, interviews, and press-row operations. Planning news releases, news conferences, and other pre-event publicity is part of the job, but the SID may have to think in multiples, scheduling releases and news conferences over a one- or two-year period to maintain public interest and to coincide with the start of ticket sales, selection of teams, etc.

Planning for a special event is a multifaceted process. The primary planning concerns, in order of importance, are as follows:

1. Scope and size of the event
2. Budget
3. Planning committees
4. Operations manual
5. Timetable of duties and activities

The first considerations are the scope and size of the event. They will dictate the budget, the number and nature of planning committees needed, and the timetable for performing duties. The second consideration is the budget. The budget will have a bearing on everything from advertising efforts to promotional activities to paid staff to media operations. If existing budget resources *may* limit the scope and size of the event, organizers should create a fundraising or sponsorship committee to come up with additional financial resources. The event itself should dictate the budget, not vice versa. If the event is billed as a special attraction, the final product cannot be sophomoric if it is to send a

Hosting a special event such as a postseason game requires mutli-faced planning and coordination. (Courtesy of WVU Sports Communications)

positive message. It must be *special*. Organizers should consider the financial obligations *before* deciding to host an event, not afterward.

Creating planning committees and assigning responsibilities follow development of the budget. The budget will identify the paid staff members. Organizers then can determine the number of volunteers needed. The organizers or executive committee will delegate responsibilities to each committee. Individual committees will decide how much volunteer help they will need and how they will fulfill their assigned responsibilities. Each will come up with an organizational chart, complete with group and individual assignments and responsibilities.

Once the budget, organizational structure, and human resources are in place, the real work of planning can begin. All planners must become "detail conscious." Lack of attention to details can destroy a major event. In this case, an old cliché proves true that states that big things can only be accomplished by attention to little details. Paying close attention to details can make an event successful because planners are anticipating and preparing for snafus that might occur.

Preparing a timetable for completion of duties and activities is an effective way to organize details, in three respects. First, it can serve as a logistical tool, identifying needs and the timelines to fulfill them. Second, a timetable can double as a calendar of activities that ensures that organizers keep the event in the public eye in the months and days leading up to the event. Marketing personnel and sports information staff can time advertising efforts, promotional gimmicks, news conferences, and news releases to appear at regular intervals. The calendar of activities also provides a checklist or deadlines that aid organizers, planners, and volunteers in time management.

Third, a timetable facilitates the coordination of the work of all committees. Putting together the timeline requires adjustments within committees, to mesh their efforts with the overall plan. Development of the timetable helps the promotional unit and sports information personnel to coordinate advertising and news releases in particular.

Effective planning and preparation may ensure that a special event runs smoothly, but they will not guarantee a large audience. Promotion and publicity are the keys to building excitement for a special event and boosting spectator and media participation. Promotional activities should be structured much like a seven-course dinner—they should start with appetizers and work up to a sumptuous main course. In short, each activity should create a hunger for more that entices the media and fans to attend.

The promotional activities and publicity plan should be established early in the planning process. They should be incorporated into the operations manual and/or timetable, and they should be structured in such a way that they periodically remind the public of the upcoming event, its significance, and its entertainment value.

Publicity serves a dual purpose. First, it provides both the public and the media with information about the special event. The nature or significance of the event alone may be sufficient to attract spectator and media interest. Second, publicity complements promotional activities. It calls attention to activities and entertaining aspects of the event. In that respect, the objective of the publicity is to drum up fan and media support.

Promotion aims at selling tickets. Although promotional activities may incorporate publicity and information materials, the primary objective is to persuade people to attend the event.

Publicity

One way or another, organizers should work to maintain a steady stream of publicity about the event. News releases, features, and news conferences should build until the final advances are written and broadcast on the day of the event. Here are the key components of a typical publicity plan.

MEDIA LIST

Sports information directors use their working media list for local special events, such as awards banquets or game promotions. They expand the list to include the appropriate media in geographic areas for regional or national events. Sponsoring organizations such as the NCAA, USGA, LPGA, and NFL, etc., provide hosts with media lists and telephone numbers.

Key Components of a Publicity Plan			
Media list	Announcements		Timed releases
Interviews	Media Days	Dinner	Press packet and program

ANNOUNCEMENTS

The SID should send out an announcement for any special event when plans are finalized. If time allows, sports information specialists also should call a news conference to announce the event. They should invite both print and broadcast media members who are involved and potentially interested in the event. The news conference should be timed to get maximum coverage. Mid-afternoon of a *slow news day* is ideal. A slow news day is a day, typically early in the week, when the calendar of scheduled news events is smaller (i.e., a day with a light activity schedule and/or little breaking news). The mid-afternoon announcement will make both the 6 p.m. and 11 p.m. television newscasts, and will give reporters for morning newspapers plenty of time to prepare their stories.

Although most of the attention focuses on television and major print media, the SID should not neglect weekly and school newspapers. They, too, are very important because they may reach audiences (potential ticket buyers) not served by the larger media.

Sports information directors do not always send out releases or call news conferences for annual events or game promotions. They may send out a release covering all the promotions for a sport or team for a year; they may distribute a release with a list on a monthly or weekly basis; or they may include information about the special promotion in game advances or notes releases. However, any one-time or special event, such as a playoff game or a tournament, should receive special treatment, meaning an announcement and a press conference, if possible.

TIMED RELEASES

The publicity plan should include a schedule for releases to selected media. The releases must be newsworthy to be effective. The most effective timed releases are those that relate to details of the event or information about the event. Timed releases include stories about the teams involved, features on the athletes competing, and announcements about the program speakers. Stories on teams and players always should include photographs. Every release should include the pertinent facts of the event: date, time, and location, along with ticket prices and locations of purchase.

INTERVIEWS

If possible, periodically arrange telephone or in-person interviews with the top athletes for the local media. Such interviews are most popular among the media and most effective for the host organization in the month prior to the event.

MEDIA DAY

A media day prior to the event can generate a load of publicity. The sports information or public relations director can draw a good audience by including participants in the event on the program. Setting up a round of golf or other activity involving participants may lead to photographs or video on the local TV news as well.

DINNER

Sport organizations often schedule a welcome ceremony, including a dinner, the night before a major special event, such as a tournament. The dinner provides an opportunity to orient the media and the participants; it also may generate additional media coverage on the opening day of the event.

If organizers are hosting a dinner, they should establish a menu equal to the status of the event itself. In the case of a professional championship game, a full sit-down meal is in order. If it is a small college basketball tournament, pizza is satisfactory.

PRESS PACKET AND PROGRAM

Depending on the time they are distributed, press kits and programs may not produce much pre-event publicity. However, they provide useful information for advance stories immediately preceding the event, and they unquestionably help reporters prepare accurate and thorough stories once the event begins.

The number and scope of publicity efforts should correspond to the stature of the event as well. A single release may be sufficient for an awards banquet or a game promotion. A full-scale campaign may be more appropriate for an event with nationwide interest such as the Major League Baseball All-Star game.

Promotional Activities

The sports information or public relations staff's involvement in promotional activities will depend on the size of the sport organization. Athletics officials may have to take care of both publicity and promotion for high schools and amateur organizations. Sports information personnel may have to assume some promotional duties at the collegiate level, particularly at the Division II and III levels. At the Division I and professional levels, separate departments generally take care of most promotional responsibilities.

Most of the promotional activities involving SIDs and public relations directors are informational, not marketing oriented. The SID seldom will be involved in advertising and ticket sales, unless the advertising is for the program prepared by the sports information staff. However, sports information personnel may be called on to help with posters, flyers, and other printed materials.

Major special events generally are an easy sell. Promoting annual events and games is far more challenging, particularly for low-profile sports and losing teams. Obviously, a team in competition for a championship year after year or a team in a city with no other major sports should draw good crowds. The real challenge in marketing is to attract large crowds for less well-known products.

Marketing a losing team takes plenty of work. Promoting a losing professional team is often more difficult than promoting a noncompetitive team at the collegiate level. At the collegiate level, a pool of loyal students and graduates will generally attend regardless of the team's record; however, their interest will also increase dramatically as the victories increase. Game giveaways and other promotions also may fuel interest.

Common Promotional Activities				
Posters	Prize Giveaways	Banners	Flyers	Promotions on back of tickets
Event T-shirts	Billboards	Placemats	Bumper stickers	Portable signs
Grocery stuffers	Free merchandise	Direct mailings	Complimentary tickets	PA announcements at other events
	Public service announcements		Speakers at civic clubs	

At the Division III collegiate level, the most important "sell" is on campus even if the tickets are free. Although the major purpose of attendance is to generate revenues, the sports information and marketing people can push other attractions, such as school spirit and support.

The following are general suggestions that relate to increasing attendance at games as well as at special events:

1. Establish a budget for promoting attendance, and set realistic goals for the budget. If goals are met, the budget for the next season may be increased.
2. Make ticket buying easy. Set up a number of ticket outlets with clear information about when, where, and how to secure tickets. This is important not only for professional teams but also for amateur contests.
3. Work with local banks, department stores, gas stations, or other businesses to help in promotion and ticket sales.
4. Keep a mailing list of potential ticket buyers. Included on this list should be graduates, new students, area businesses, and past ticket holders.
5. Keep the people on the mailing list informed regarding schedules, ticket prices, season ticket availability, special ticket packages, and special events such as Community Day or Homecoming.
6. Do not overlook less visible or nonrevenue sports on the collegiate level. Any publicity and promotion may bring a few more people into the stands.
7. Utilize students in promotional activities at the collegiate level; the results can be most worthwhile.
8. Design publications that are not only valuable to the media but also act as promotional literature that will help boost attendance in recruitment of athletes.
9. In addition to media guides, flyers and posters should be designed to increase attention and attendance.
10. Contacts with the media should include invitations to promotions and special events. Unexpected positive publicity can result from bonds forged among the media, graduates, and coaches at a golf outing or other activity in connection with a special event.

Media Operations

Considerations in planning for media coverage of a special event are identical to the pregame, game management, and postgame preparations for a press-box/press row operation. The planning process must address credentials, work space, work crews, working materials, and food.

The differences between planning for a game and planning for a special event are a matter of degree—primarily, differences in logistics and in numbers of media to serve. The needs for an annual event, such as an awards banquet, are fewer because most information distributed to the media can be prepared in advance. The setup for a game promotion or postseason playoff match is virtually identical because it is linked closely to the game and the playing field or court. The details and duties for a major event, however, expand a hundredfold, in some cases, because far more members of the media attend. For example, requests for media credential for the 2009 Super Bowl exceeded 4,500 ("Super Bowl media," 2009). Additionally, some events, such as a golf tournament, may last more than one day.

SUMMARY

Event management encompasses three main categories: game management/game-day operations, press conferences/media days, and special events. They are each unique in their own ways and put the SID's organization in the limelight differently, but each also possess some of the same characteristics.

Game days are the culmination of a week-long effort of hard work, time management, and organization. The days leading up to the game find the SID working closely with the media, overseeing interview sessions, preparing game notes, and being available for any and all needs from media and facility personnel. The day of the game, the SID is at the forefront of the organization's publicity thrust, and game days are arguably the most important opportunity for a team or organization to project a positive image.

Post-game duties for an SID usually are highly stress because deadlines must be met by both the media and the SID. Post-game duties include everything from facilitating coach and player interviews to writing releases and game notes. Depending on the sport, the entire process is duplicated the very next day in preparation for the next sporting event.

News conferences and media days are a great way to provide the media with a large amount of information at one time and in one location. News conferences usually have a "business-like" atmosphere while media days offer more of a social gathering atmosphere. Both are used as informational gathering tools for the media. News conferences could be called for any number of reasons: the hiring of a new coach, the announcement of a large donation to the sport organization, plans to renovate a facility, or a team's selection and inclusion into postseason play. The planning for the news conference is usually minimal and the entire process can be performed in a day.

Media days usually involve more intricate and advanced planning, sometimes as much as six to nine months in advance, and could involve an entire team or representatives from every team in a conference in a "meet-and-greet" setting with the media. For media days, a wider selection of food is usually provided to attendees.

Special events encompass an entire spectrum of offerings from a one-time hosting of a post-season tournament, to a week-long playoff. They involve special planning, involving a budget and planning committees, and a lot of hard work from the SID focusing on organization, time management, and communication.

DISCUSSION TOPICS

1. Of the three types of event planning, which one looks the most appealing? Why? Conversely, which one looks the least appealing? Why?
2. What are the main differences between game-management, special event management and media days/press conferences? What are the similarities.

SUGGESTED EXERCISES

1. Shadow a local SID or home-game administrator on game-day and report your findings to class.
2. Create a detailed plan for your school's hosting of next year's men's basketball NCAA first and second rounds. What steps will you have to take to ensure that the event goes off without a hitch?

9

Publicity Campaigns

In 2001, the University of Oregon found a unique way to push the promotion of its star quarterback, Joey Harrintgon. At a cost of $250,000 to its boosters, a 10-story billboard of Harrington was erected in New York's Times Square, promoting the rising senior quarterback's candidacy for the Heisman Trophy. While Harrington didn't win the Heisman Trophy that year, the promotion achieved its desired result, garnering national attention for Harrington while also gaining notoriety for the school and its football program.

Fast forward nearly a decade later to West Virginia University, where the that school used a completely different, and far less expensive, approach, in its publicity campaign of star quarterback Patrick White. The university created a website (PatWhitePlays Here.com) to assist in the overall promotion of White.

While there is no right or wrong plan in the promotion of either quarterback, both examples are unique and different ideas in the creation of a publicity plan. When unique ideas meet cutting edge technology, the end result, at least in the contemporary sports information specialist's world, is a wealth of opportunities used in the promotion of an organization's star athlete.

Unique ways for garnering attention are redefined seemingly every year and the limits are endless, bound only by the lack of creativity one might possess.

Because of the creative freedom and endless possibilities of publicity campaigns, there are no step-by-step directions that must be followed. There are, however, some core principles and processes that every sports information director (SID) should be aware of regardless of the publicity campaign being employed.

EARLY STAGES OF CAMPAIGN DEVELOPMENT

There are several considerations pertaining to creating a publicity campaign. The early stages of communication within the organization are of the utmost importance and should include the SID, prospective candidate or team, and the coach.

Some coaches are "team" coaches and believe any and all accolades earned by individual players are a direct result of the overall success of the team. Their logic is that the better the team does, the more accolades the individuals will receive. Thus, those coaches are not big fans of publicity campaigns.

Other coaches believe a unique publicity campaign will bring notoriety to the entire team, program, or organization. If an athlete deserves it, and they are granting permission, those coaches are completely in favor of creating a publicity campaign.

Neither opinion is right or wrong. In either regard, both of the opinions represent why it is important that the coach be involved in initial discussion before any further planning or promotion of the athlete or team can begin. If a coach resists a publicity campaign in these preliminary discussions, the SID should strongly consider dropping the campaign.

The campaign is a unique venture outside of the realm of the standard or traditional publicity an SID would normally do. Making the athlete and coach aware that added attention, and thus the added media stressors, will result if the campaign begins is of the utmost importance. The sports information or public relations director should consider both the candidate's athletics performance and his or her personal behavior. If the athlete is unreliable, isn't punctual, and/or is generally just not a good person, then the SID should consider looking for another candidate to promote, or cancel the campaign. An athlete featured in a publicity campaign must fulfill more interview requests and have added media responsibilities that go above and beyond the norm. The campaign may require conducting many more interviews with the media, answering fans' questions in an internet chat, and just generally being more available than usual. Those not willing to put forth the required time and effort, and those that may not be reliable enough to meet the demands, may only hamper the campaign after it has already become irreversible. Again, campaigns are for the benefit of the athletes. If they don't think they can fulfill the added obligations, then the campaigns should not be created.

If the coach and star athlete are in agreement that a publicity campaign is a good idea, the SID should alert the athlete to the dangers of dishonesty, a lack of cooperation with the media, and personal indiscretions. By the end of the conversation, the athlete should be well informed and forewarned of all that may occur once the campaign begins. If the athlete is not fully comfortable and cooperative, the plan should be dropped. Pressing the idea will not serve the athlete or the organization well.

The campaign has a greater chance of succeeding and less chance of backfiring if the athlete's integrity is on the same level as his or her performance. In publicizing an athlete, school officials should never go overboard on a player they know is not worthy. Be sure the

West Virginia University created an interactive website as a centerpiece of its publicity campaign for star quarterback Pat White. (Courtesy of WVU Sports Communications)

player is really as good as the coach, the SID, and others believe the individual to be. Remember, the reputations of all involved are on the line. Making a decision on the worthiness of a candidate is not as easy as it sometimes appears to be.

The publicity campaign also has a greater chance of success if it promotes an athlete or team in a high-profile sport. If the object is to achieve high visibility, the potential gains are minimal if the media pay little attention to the sport anyway. For this reason, football and basketball players most often are the focus of publicity efforts on a college or high school campus. An SID often will focus on an outstanding athlete from one or both of these sports. The SID may achieve success in promoting an athlete in another sport if the campaign identifies and motivates a receptive media audience. For example, a campaign promoting a soccer player should aim at media in cities with all-star voters and consistent soccer coverage as well as at the local media.

In the summer of 2008, West Virginia University opened its campaign for Pat White, not necessarily in order for him to be mentioned among the preseason Heisman Trophy candidates, but rather as a way to further promote one of the school's all-time great football players. Any and all accolades that came as a result of the campaign would be an added bonus. The sports information staff at the school, led by director of football communications Mike Montoro, pitched the campaign ideas to White and Coach Bill Stewart, who both agreed it was a good idea to move forward. What resulted was an interactive Internet site that included facts, statistics, video clips of White's greatest highlights, and an interactive area where the future NFL quarterback could answer questions posed to him from fans. The campaign was well received and accentuated White's performances on the field.

If, after discussions with the coach and player, the campaign is to proceed, preparations must begin well before the start of the season for the sport in which the athlete participates. The push must start in late spring for athletes in fall sports such as football, in summer for winter sports, and in fall for spring sports. The SID must organize the campaign and compile and prepare the avalanche of information well before the particular season is underway; consequently, the SID must evaluate candidates well before the season begins. Was the junior who blossomed in postseason play at the end of last year enjoying a short-lived stretch of success or is he/she a superstar in waiting? Is the lone senior on the team, an all-league caliber player, really ready for the added stressors that will be imposed on him/her?

The SID should meet with the coach and player to develop a strategy to increase the star's national visibility. In the case of Joey Harrington, "Joey Heisman" evolved from the campaign, a unique nickname that fit for the Ducks' quarterback, playing to the alliteration of his last name. The nickname created an image of Harrington as a legitimate Heisman Trophy contender and had a catchy ring to it. And it stuck.

In other cases, unique story ideas showing a player's humility, character, or personality; a rare human interest story; or a story detailing an athletic lineage may well be the route to go when kicking off the campaign. If the SID shows a different side of an athlete, that of compassion or of public service, it may do wonders in terms of allowing the media and public to gain new insight on the player.

The SID should conduct an informal but in-depth personal interview with the athlete being featured in the campaign in order to find out as much as possible about the athlete's personal background, likes and dislikes, hobbies and other interests, church and community activities, goals and dreams, and attitudes and beliefs about athletics, education, and other pertinent subjects. The interview will serve two purposes. First, it will give the SID a fuller portrait of the athlete and insight into personal strengths and weaknesses that may affect the campaign. The interview may also forge a strong personal relationship between the athlete and the SID, which is important during those trying times when the pressure becomes unbearable for both the athlete and the SID. Second, the interview may generate a lot of ideas for story angles to develop or to suggest to the media during the publicity campaign.

The next step is for the SID to prepare a budget that will cover cost of extra printed materials, photography, artwork, videotape, and postage. The budget will dictate the size of media kits, the number of mailings, and even the scope of the campaign. A small school with a limited budget, for example, would not have the financial means to place a banner in Times Square as the University of Oregon did with its campaign for Harrington.

All photographs used should be of high resolution quality, for use in newspaper and magazine stories as well as the Internet. Video footage should show only the best of the athlete's plays, particularly those showing the skills or strengths of the campaign's target so that TV stations may use the clips packages in addition to other video archives of the athlete they may already have.

The SID should complete the bulk of the printed materials prior to the season. Anything that can be done in advance lightens the extra burden the campaign will create when the season commences. The SID should write an introductory news release, prepare a biographical sheet, compile statistical charts and comparisons, and compose hometown and news features for inclusion in media kits and for distribution to journalists who request information during the season.

Any area of excellence can be supported with selective use of statistics. How the athlete's ranking, scoring, yardage, and other averages stack up nationally, in the conference, and on the career school charts always provides evidence of excellence. The SID can devise new stats to fit a story idea. Statistics are very good supportive material.

A media kit for distribution to selected media (and voters for postseason honors and awards) should include photographs (action, informal, and posed), biographical information, feature stories, a statistical history, video highlights provided on a DVD, and other pertinent information regarding the publicity of the individual. If an organization's budget is tight, the material that makes up the media kit could be made available online rather than mailing the entire media kit to what could be hundreds of journalists or voters. It would be a much cheaper venture on a tighter budget and in the end could produce the same results as that from a program with a substantially larger budget the mailed the media kits.

In addition to creating media kits, there are other ways in which the campaign subject could be prominently featured through various items produced by the school or organization.

The Publicity Campaign Media Kit

The media kit that focuses on the athlete at the center of the publicity campaign typically will include a packet of information and artwork that emphasizes the *selling point*, the single element that best illustrates the athlete's excellence. The kit will include some combination of these items:

News release	A story introducing the athlete, built around a news angle.
Suggested stories	A list of story ideas/angles for the journalist who receives the kit. Make it easy for the journalist to pursue a story.
Biographical summary	An information sheet similar to a résumé that includes records set or about to be broken during the upcoming season.
Reprints	Copies of newspaper or magazine articles that extol the excellence of the athlete.
Quotations	A list of quotations drawn from what opponents (players and coaches), scouts, and analysts have said about the athlete. These have great value.
Fact sheet	Quick facts on the athlete, team, conference, and school. The fact sheet should include telephone and fax numbers as well as the name of a contact person in the SID office.
Statistics	One or more statistical lists with individual statistics and rankings (career, school, conference, nation).
Head shot	A professional, portrait-style photograph.
Action shots	A couple of posed or candid shots of the athlete in competition.
Poster	A glossy poster of the athlete in action.
Other promotional items	Giveaways the coach, athlete, and SID agree upon such as a notepad containing the athlete's image and campaign slogan.

Media Guides

The campaign subject should receive special attention in the media guide, as long as the coach approves of the idea. The SID can supplement promotion of the star by using a color photograph of the player on the cover of the media guide and including a more comprehensive biography than the brief sketches of other players inside the guide. In other words, the guide should feature the star in as many ways as possible.

Websites

Arguably the easiest and most cost-effective tool in the publicity campaign is creating a website for the star athlete. The Internet is the contemporary one-stop shop used by all. The website is usually created by the sports information staff and is hosted by the school's official athletics webpage, which will include a link to the promotional player page. Using a clever URL, such as "PatWhitePlaysHere.com" will make it easier for visitors to remember the web address of the page. Once it is created, much of the material contained in the media kit should be incorporated on the website, including statistics, biographical information, and photography and video archives.

Mailers

Mailers are a form of publicity by which the university can promote an athlete through a vehicle that is, in effect, an advertisement. The mailer should model the format of advertising on high-quality paper and could take the form of a pamphlet or brochure. The contemporary growing trend is for the mailer to resemble a post card.

For a mailer to be effective, it must catch the eye and command attention. The nickname and poster might be used individually or collectively in a mailer. Sending out mailers is expensive, and the money should be spent wisely. Mailers are used where the budget allows. The SID should send mailers only to members of the media or coaches who vote for postseason honors and awards.

Several printings of the mailer, with updated bi-weekly or monthly information as well as any information on the candidate's website, can be distributed to the same mailing lists, effectively keeping the voters abreast of the athlete's updated performances.

After the media kit has been compiled and products such as media guides, websites, and mailers have been created, the sports information staff devises a publicity strategy, with news releases timed to coincide with career milestones for the athlete. The SID creates "Countdowns" and "Watches" (with logos) for insertion in game advances and notes columns. Perhaps a newspaper will print an updated chart with each game

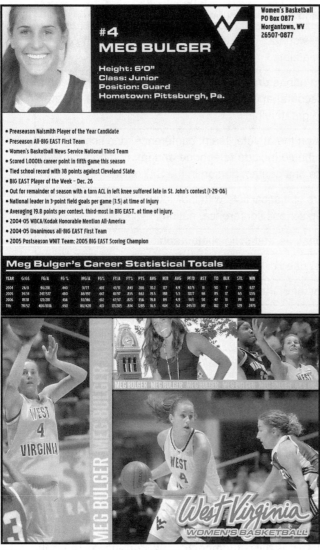

This mailer was used by WVU Sports Communications and assisted in Meg Bulger garnering All-America honors during her sophomore season. (Courtesy of WVU Sports Communications)

story, or a TV producer will flash the graphic on the screen with the results of each game. These types of mentions are invaluable in terms of exposure and what it means for the underlying theme of the campaign. Focusing on small details such as this will result in greater things down the line, especially in the campaign.

CONTINUING THE CAMPAIGN

Once the season begins, and a foundation for the campaign has been created, the SID changes modes from planner to facilitator.

A good SID will work daily with the star athlete that is at the center of the publicity campaign, fulfilling any media requests as best as possible. The SID could also set the standard for interviews, pre-arranging the athlete's availability into block times. The SID must remember, especially at the collegiate level, that the athlete at the center of the campaign also has class, strength and conditioning, study hall, practice, and a social life. So it is imperative that interview times and requests be granted with the athlete's best interest at heart. Being organized with a timetable and sticking to the schedule is a must. Once the schedule is set, distribute it to the media so they know when the athlete is available to be interviewed.

It is also imperative that the SID never give out the athlete's phone number, or the phone number of any athlete, for that matter. Should the athlete be contacted by members of the media, instruct the athlete to request that the reporter arrange the interview through the SID.

Sports information personnel should take care to keep interviews to a minimum close to game day—the further from game day the better, in fact. Disruptions can affect an athlete's mental preparation for the game. Coaches, SIDs, and the media should respect and honor requests for privacy on game day. If a particular writer wants an in-depth interview, the SID should set it up at the convenience of both parties, but well in advance of the next game.

It also maybe appropriate for the SID to "coach" the athlete with regard to fulfilling interviews (for more on this see Chapter 4). In addition to being a media manager and time organizer, the SID continues to serve as a publicity mill during the season. The SID can recycle the printed materials, photographs, and artwork that was produced in the early stages of the campaign's development in a variety of ways as the season unfolds. He or she can also put together individual packets for journalists or others who call to inquire about the athlete. The publicity campaign can also include a schedule of timed releases to media on the original mailing list. The SID can send out features on different angles at prearranged intervals. Sports information personnel can also time releases to coincide with achievements during the season. For example, a new release would be timely when the athlete sets a personal, school, or conference record.

As the season progresses, the SID will continue to update all the factual information regarding the candidate, such as updated statistics, news clippings, photography, and video footage. Should a request be made from an out-of-town media member, the SID will have all that information readily available.

Coach's CORNER

by Craig Esherick

Managing egos is often a coach's most delicate responsibility. And launching a publicity campaign featuring a single athlete is especially difficult if the "star" athlete is on a team sport. So it's important to keep a couple of things in mind: prepare the other members of the team for the added attention focused on the star and counsel the "star" to appreciate the contributions his or her teammates bring to the team.

Since everyone likes attention and to tamp down feelings of jealousy by others, photo shoots and interviews with the featured athlete should, whenever possible, be done away from the other members of the team. Nothing affects team chemistry more than a diva in the midst! Having said that, don't forget to include the subject of the campaign in the planning of it. Sometimes the most creative idea for a publicity campaign will come from the athlete to be featured in the campaign. An experienced sports information director who understands good communication skills can use ideas from the player to develop a successful publicity campaign.

Promoting the "student" in student-athlete also will pay dividends. Featuring your "star" studying in the library, sitting in a lecture hall, or walking across campus with a backpack and jeans stresses the importance of your program as part of a larger academic institution—one that is goal oriented, disciplined, and future minded. And never underestimate the power of business attire. Even in this day and age where dress codes seem quaint, the image of a conservatively dressed student-athlete never fails to impress.

Finally, a well-orchestrated publicity campaign is a great recruiting tool for the coach. Potential recruits and incoming players look forward to seeing their names and images in print, on TV, or on the web. Media savvy youngsters appreciate a sports information professional who gets his or her athletes featured in the news. And successful media campaigns featuring an outstanding athlete compiled over the years not only builds and preserves a program's history, but also comes in handy when the coach is selling his or her program to potential players, their parents, and their high school coaches.

ETHICAL CONSIDERATIONS

The SID who undertakes a publicity campaign functions in a foggy area between sports information and *press agentry*. Press agentry is a term applied to publicists in the early days of public relations who promoted a client with all types of gimmicks and tricks. Some of the techniques were intentionally misleading. Others attracted attention because they were so outrageous. The publicists would promote their clients by any means possible. The SID can avoid straying into these areas by measuring every aspect of the publicity campaign and every action in carrying it out by two standards: *honesty* and *information value*.

First, no one associated with the campaign can engage in any deceit or appearance of deceit (such as providing misleading information). The SID cannot hope to hide negative information about the athlete's past or performance, hence why it is important to select a reputable and worthy candidate for the campaign. The SID must not distort any information or statistics. Using statistics selectively to support a point is acceptable; juggling or adjusting statistics to fit the point is not. For example, a statistician yearns to "help" a linebacker set a record for tackles and earn individual honors, so he or she gives the player credit for an assisted tackle any time he's near the football, even though

	Ten Rules in Creating a Publicity Campaign
1	Pick a worthy candidate. Never promote an athlete you do not believe is deserving of recognition (athletically or personally).
2	Seek approval of the coach and the athlete before launching any campaign. Explain the demands and dangers in detail to each when seeking approval. Drop the idea if either has objections.
3	Orient the athlete on what to expect during the campaign. The athlete's athletic and academic standings are at stake.
4	Help the athlete set up a schedule that absorbs the additional time demands as effortlessly as possible. Make an effort to control media contact and to coach the athlete on handling interviews.
5	Remember that you put the athlete in this high-pressure situation. The SID has a responsibility to help the athlete get through it with as little stress as possible.
6	Borrow techniques from advertising for publicity materials, but do not go overboard. Creative presentation is OK. Exaggeration and flattery are not.
7	Clearly identify promotional elements such as bumper stickers and posters as advertising. Use them as such, not as information.
8	Selective use of statistics is acceptable. Distorting or doctoring statistics is not.
9	Treat the media with courtesy and respect.
10	Never tell a lie. No breach of honesty is acceptable. Always tell the truth in the promotion of your athlete.

a teammate may have been responsible for the tackle. Judgment call or well-intentioned manipulation? It will be deemed a deception if the totals differ markedly from the statistics kept by the opponent, and word will spread quickly that someone is "cooking the numbers" if it happens in more than one game. Such accusations will undermine the publicity campaign, taint any record the athlete sets, and damage the reputation of the team and the university.

Second, the SID should consider the information value of all materials prepared for the publicity campaign. Certainly, the objective is to "sell" the athlete, but the techniques employed must use legitimate information to do so. The SID may borrow from advertising, using promotional items such as bumper stickers, posters, nickname gimmicks, or giveaways. However, such tools should be clearly identifiable as promotional items and openly distributed as such—that is the honesty in the promotion. Furthermore, all printed materials, photographs, and videotapes should revolve around a core of information consistent with the criteria of news. The media are more likely to use the information if it has news value. The SID should not stage a news conference just to gather a media crowd for the athlete; he or she must have real news information to deliver, or the pseudo event will cross the boundary into misleading manipulation.

SUMMARY

The creation of a publicity plan is a multi-faceted process that involves creativity, cooperation from the athlete and coach, and a resolve to see the process through to its fruition. If done correctly, the attention garnered for the athlete at the center of the publicity campaign will gain instant notoriety. And if the accolades earned on the playing field back up the exposure the campaign provides, then the chances are great that the athlete will receive some sort of national or regional recognition.

Several factors are initially involved in selecting the athlete, informing him/her of the added responsibilities and stressors the campaign may have, and seeking the approval of the coach. If the coach or athlete waiver in the initial discussions of creating a campaign and have reservations about the process, then the campaign should go no further. If the athlete and coach agree to participate in a campaign, further attention is given to the athlete by the SID in the areas of handling, assisting with, and processing the additional daily, weekly, and monthly media stressors that the campaign will bring.

Once the campaign has begun, the SID switches gears from planner to facilitator in assuring that all the plans that were created in the beginning stages are executed while attempting to alleviate as best as possible the stressors of the campaign that the player will experience.

Ethical considerations are to be understood and followed in terms of the athlete's statistics and their presentation during the campaign. The SID should simply state the facts and avoid misleading or misrepresenting the athlete's accomplishments.

The campaign is a unique tool and a special presentation for the organization and the athlete at the center of it. It will create added work for the SID and athlete, but if implemented properly, the publicity campaign should prove to be an enjoyable, and hopefully successful, experience.

DISCUSSION QUESTIONS

1. What tools used in the publicity of an All-American would you use in running your own campaign? What one tool would, in your opinion, be the most effective?
2. Review the Ten Rules in Creating a Publicity Campaign. Which one do you believe is the most important?

SUGGESTED EXERCISES

1. Choose a local collegiate athlete and create an All-American campaign for the athlete using the information in this chapter.
2. Research successful All-American campaigns. What went right and why did they work? Conversely, in hindsight what could have been done better in the promotion of that athlete? Discuss with your class.

10

Crisis Management

It's a Monday morning in the height of the offseason and you just arrived to work in the sports information office at 9 a.m. to start some work on your media guide. Not even five minutes after you're comfortably at your desk, a member of the print media comes in with last night's police report that unfortunately lists your school's star quarterback as having been arrested for DUI. The reporter asks to speak to both the player and the coach. How do you handle the request?

A few minutes later, a broadcast media member calls to confirm an interview that had already been arranged with the same quarterback for later that afternoon with regard to his offseason community service work. Knowing that he's just been arrested, what do you do in that situation?

Lastly, as you begin to gather facts about last night's incident and contact the football coach to discuss the situation, you begin to hear rumors from student interns that work in the sports information office that two of the school's men's basketball players were involved in a car accident. What do you do now?

All good sports information and public relations directors will tell you that you should have planned—well before the problem(s) arose—what you would say, what you would do, and how you would deal with a crisis. In today's society, athletes, coaches, and teams perform under a media microscope. The spotlight is constantly on, and it often gets very hot under the lights very quickly. Trouble does arise occasionally, even in the best of sport organizations. High school and college athletes behave immaturely at times, no matter how hard everyone in the institution tries to guide them properly. Coaches and boosters cross the boundaries of NCAA rules, sometimes intentionally and sometimes inadvertently. Some professional athletes believe they are immune to the law, because they have been pampered and protected. Others succumb to temptations such as drugs, gambling, and domestic violence.

When trouble arises, the spotlight shines brightly on the sport organization as well as on the athlete or coach. Revelations about NCAA or NFL investigations, disclosures about athletes' indiscretions, and speculation about business matters (e.g., the firing of a coach) can evolve into crises that damage the public image of the organization and its relationship with the media if the matter is not handled quickly and efficiently. The responsibility for effectively filtering the light of media scrutiny and for effecting favorable public reaction rests heavily on the SID's or the public relations director's shoulders. The media expect assistance, or at least cooperation, in gathering information quickly. Team owners and athletics administrators demand limits on information released and control of the content; consequently, sports information specialists often find themselves in the middle of a conflict between administrators who do not want to say anything and aggressive journalists who dig out details of the story on their own.

A person who cannot cope with the heat in the middle of a flash fire (or who does not want to deal with it) should not pursue a career in sports information. Crisis situations are challenging, frustrating, and stressful—they are the public arena in which SIDs prove their mettle and earn their pay and keep. If they do not act quickly and decisively, the reputations of athletes, coaches, teams, and owners/administrators may be hurt. If SIDs do not respond tactfully and aggressively, the relationship between the media and the sport organization may deteriorate. If they do not serve both sides effectively, they may find themselves looking for another job.

A CLIMATE OF COOPERATION

Sports public relations is challenging, exciting, and rewarding when the work involves interviewing athletes, writing features, creating media guides, managing media days and press conferences, running press-box operations, and directing publicity campaigns. Working with the media, outstanding athletes, and witty coaches during good times and winning seasons is enjoyable. Unfortunately, the business of sports information is not always about distributing positive information and promoting cordial relationships. Sometimes it requires dealing with negative news, losing seasons, and strained relationships.

The relationship between the media and sport organizations is always a push-and-pull association, because their objectives differ. In the case of sports journalism, those who control the media not only select which sports and which events will be covered, but they also decide what will be emphasized in that coverage. The emphasis may be positive or negative. As much as the SID would like to control the flow of positive information at all times, the media ultimately will decide what is the best route for their coverage be it positive or not.

The sport organization also presents a selective version of information—a version that promotes the organization's philosophy and goals. The emphasis is always positive, or as positive as circumstances permit. The sport organization attempts to push the selection of events and the emphasis in coverage in the direction it favors. Push comes to shove when the media's selection and coverage emphases are unfavorable or unfair.

The challenge for the sports information specialist is far broader than simply controlling negative news that reflects unfavorably on the sport organization. The media's coverage selections, particularly as they relate to women's sports and men's low-profile sports, also create a challenging issue for the SID. Shove comes to confrontation most often on issues of commission, rather than those of omission. The primary flashpoints are events or issues that generate information that appears to contradict the image the sport organization intends to present to the public. However, any threat to the organization's public image represents a potential public relations crisis, and lack of media coverage of men's low-profile sports and women's sports creates an incomplete portrait of the sport organization. Its omission may even suggest the organization is not as committed to those sports as administrators claim.

A crisis for a sport organization is any event, incident, or issue that falls outside the realm of everyday management activities and poses a threat to the reputation of the organization. Crises can strike at any time—crises such as the arrest of an athlete, the dismissal of a coach, or an upset loss in a key game. Crises can also develop slowly over a period of time; for example, frequent criticism of a coach by a disgruntled reporter. Crises also can grow out of long-standing issues, such as lack of coverage of men's low-profile sports and women's sports.

Each type of crisis may demand a different type of response from sports information directors, athletics administrators, or team officials. However, three general truths apply to every crisis:

1. The battle for public support during the crisis is usually won or lost in the first 24 hours.
2. The sport organization will probably lose the battle of public perception if representatives of the organization fail to develop specific procedures for early and regular communication with the public during the crisis.
3. The more complex the crisis procedures, the less likely they are to succeed.

The timeframe is critical. First impressions are most difficult to erase, so the sport organization must develop a course of action and implement it quickly. When possible, providing the media with the maximum amount of information in a minimal amount of time is key. The athletics director, general manager, sports information director, or public relations director will serve as head of the emergency response team that implements the procedures. Even if the SID or public relations director does not lead the team, he/she will be called upon to guide a critical part of the procedure—the part that decides the battle of public opinion.

The SID must balance the objectives of the organization and the needs of the media in implementing crisis-management procedures; in so doing, he/she must serve two bosses, each of whom is operating on a different schedule. The decision-making cycle generally moves slowly in the world of academia; administrators appoint committees to study an issue, to gather data to formulate options, to analyze and test options, and to choose a course of action. The process can take months.

In the realm of the media, the decision-making cycle moves at whirlwind speed and at deadline intervals—for example, 24 hours between daily newspaper editions; 4–5 hours between morning, noon, evening, and late-night newscasts; 30 minutes between radio newscasts; 30 minutes between updates on all-news radio and TV channels; and instantaneously on the Internet. Because of the intense competition among the media, reporters, editors, and producers must decide quickly whether a snippet of information is news, how much information they can gather before the next deadline, and what element to emphasize in their presentation of the story.

It is important to remember that the objective of the media is not to analyze the facts and draw conclusions. The role of the media is to present information to the public—to present *all the facts that are known at the time of publication or broadcast*. Therefore, the media first will churn out facts about the arrest of an athlete on sexual assault charges—whether or not the athlete is guilty. They will attempt to interview people on both sides of the story but if people on one side do not want to talk, the media will report the information they were able to obtain now and continue to try to get the other side for the next news cycle. As a result, the facts of a story may unfold over the course of several news cycles. Reporters usually will not hold a report in order to wait until the story runs its course (judgment on guilt or innocence) unless they are assured no competitor will get the information. A reporter might be persuaded to hold a story on an internal investigation by the athletics director, but no amount of cajoling, stonewalling, or withholding comment will stop a story that comes from a police blotter or from any other record open to public inspection.

Sports information personnel, school administrators, and team executives must understand that the decision-making models they typically follow move much too slowly to keep up with fast-breaking stories and even faster-breaking rumors. Whether the crisis is a legitimate story or an unfounded rumor, for example, of an NCAA investigation of an athletics department, news travels swiftly in the community. The media assuredly *will* report legitimate news, and the private lives of public figures such as athletes and celebrities fit the media/public criteria of news. The media also will address rumors if they find some factual basis to support them, many of them turning to blogs or Twitter accounts if it's a rumor that at that point in time doesn't warrant an entire story. Sport organization personnel cannot prevent publication or broadcast of a story simply by refusing to talk about it.

Once one accepts the premise that the media dictate the selection and emphasis of news, it is easy to understand why a climate of cooperation is the best response to public relations crises. Sport organization personnel who provide prompt and direct answers to questions stand a far better chance of forestalling rumors than do those who stonewall. Sport organization officials who avoid the media or offer "no comment" run the risk of fueling suspicions, turning a tidbit of fact into a tidal wave of rumor and speculation.

The starting point for effective crisis management is a relationship with the media that is built on a foundation of cooperation. Charges against a school athletics program, whether they are true or false, should be answered as soon as possible to protect the integrity of the athletics department or the institution. When trouble strikes, coaches, athletics directors, college presidents, and members of the board of trustees may find themselves swept into a controversy. They must realize that expediency in responding to the charges is the best course of action. The longer charges go unanswered, the larger the problem of combating negative perceptions.

Three Guiding Principles

An effective climate of cooperation can be built on three simple principles: honesty, availability, and fair play. Strict adherence to these principles by all representatives of the sport organization will enhance the relationship with the media and will put the organi-

zation in a positive position from a public relations point of view. In the world of
sports, the cooperation must come not
only from the SID or the public relations staff, but also from all coaches, athletes, athletics directors, administrators,
and support staff. If all are honest, open,
and fair, the media are far more likely to

How to Create a Climate of Cooperation	
1	Deal honestly with the media
2	Be available
3	Treat all members fairly and cordially

give the organization the benefit of the doubt when facts are in dispute; they are more
likely to emphasize the positives, from the institution's perspective. For example, a story
about suspension of athletes for team rules violations might focus more on the forth-
right manner in which the coach and the university dealt with a disciplinary problem
than on the violations themselves.

PRINCIPLE NO.1: DEAL HONESTLY WITH THE MEDIA

Less than complete honesty will return to haunt those who are not straightforward.
Mistrust will feed suspicion and give credence to rumors of wrongdoing or deceit. Honesty is especially important when dealing with sensitive or negative situations. Keith
(1985) compares an SID to a successful team possessing speed and quickness; such attributes are assets when dealing with the media in a stressful situation.

An honest approach does not require sports information or other representatives of
the institution to tell the media everything they know about a given situation. The institution definitely should exercise some control over the release of information; after
all, the objective of the sport organization is to influence public opinion favorably
through the selective release of information. However, honesty demands that the sport
organization avoid deception in the posture it takes when responding to questions or requests for information. If SIDs are forbidden to comment regarding a question or situation because of university policy, they should say so. If they cannot comment because of
the sensitive nature of the issue, they should say so. The SIDs should give a reason for
their refusal to comment, in every case. Honest, hard-working members of the media
will accept a "no comment" without rancor or suspicion if an SID explains why. Reporters will work around "no comment" responses and search for other sources or documents to complete the factual puzzle.

The SID should establish specific ground rules for release of information in the
course of casual conversation or discussion of an issue and should make clear to all reporters the organization's policies on off-the-record comments and anonymous sources.
Sometimes an SID or a representative of an organization may need to provide some
background information or an explanation to clarify the response to an inquiry. The
background or explanation may give the reporter some facts the organization is not
ready to announce or disclose. *Before* discussing the information, the SID must make it
clear to the reporter that such information is off the record. *Off-the-record* is a journalistic handshake—an agreement that the reporter who accepts comments off the record
will not use the information in the story.

MITCHELL LAYTON PHOTOGRAPHY

Coach's CORNER

by Craig Esherick

While the focus of this chapter is how sports information directors must deal with public relations dilemmas, specifically with regard to dealing with the media and coaches, it should be noted that coaches must also deal with public relations problems, particularly as it relates to the actions of their players. Potential PR problems could result from anything from arrests, academic failures, or injuries.

When you are coaching college student-athletes, a reality of the job is that your players will behave like college students. And from the dawn of the higher education enterprise, college students have tested the limits of their parents, teachers, coaches, and sometimes the local constable. When college student-athletes push the limits, sometimes their actions create public relations nightmares. Coaches can never predict when something bad will happen, which is why excellent lines of communication between a coach and the SID will help to produce the best outcome for the player, coach, and school, regardless of the public relations dilemma..

It is important to keep in mind that much of the information the media may want access to may be restricted by the federal government under the Buckley Amendment. Athletic accomplishments, statistics, height, and weight are all able to be provided to the media and public, but public release of grades, disciplinary proceedings, or other "personal information" is regulated by statute. Health information is also a sensitive area; be careful when releasing information about a player's health without permission.

If a player is arrested, understanding the legal situation is very important for all parties and if the player has retained counsel, this adds another layer of complexity. A coach may be in communication with players, parents, police, lawyers, the athletic director, and the SID, in addition to being bombarded by the media, who want the coach to comment on the situation. The player's lawyer may advise the coach and SID not to comment at all, but the coach and SID must always do what is in the best interest of the player, team, and organization, but often times those interests conflict with each other. In those situations, it may be wise to talk to your school's General Counsel about how to properly handle a legal situation. Remember, though, that the long-term interests of the player should always be a concern of the coach and the sports information specialist.

Some players may be confronted with academic issues during their college career. Suspensions for lack of attention to academic responsibilities are common. Coaches will also suspend players for less than diligent classroom attendance. Without detailing specific grade reports, the coach and the sports information specialist can release general information to the press in order to satisfy their curiosity of why a player has

(Continued on next page)

COACH'S CORNER—*Continued*

been suspended or disciplined. If it's an issue such as class attendance, some coaches may prefer to administer different forms of punishment to the player. If the punishment doesn't involve a suspension (e.g., running stairs after practice for two weeks) it's best to tell inquiring members of the press that the matter is being handled internally rather than detailing the specific form of punishment imposed on the player.

Injuries to star players can also have the potential to create a PR dilemma. However, if a coach, SID, player, and the player's family are all communicating regularly and are on the same page, no problems should arise.

Regardless of the problem a coach must deal with regarding players, it goes without saying that players' parents must always remain informed. I can't imagine any parents would enjoy being informed by the local TV station about their son or daughter's arrest, suspension, or injury. A coach and SID should always work together to ensure that information is released to the media in an appropriate manner, because in this age of blogs and Twitter, once information is obtained, it is spread instantaneously.

Some organizations attempt to control public reaction by releasing selected information through anonymous sources. Perhaps someone in the organization feels compelled to reveal certain facts but worries about how the public will view the disclosure if the source were revealed. The person may agree to reveal the information provided the journalist attributes it in a manner that shields the name of the source, for instance as "a source close to the athletics department." The technique is common practice in Washington political circles, where "an anonymous source" leaks selective information to test public reaction. If the public reacts negatively, no harm is done if the source is anonymous. A member of a sport organization under public assault for firing a coach with a losing record might attempt to douse the negative response by anonymously disclosing private factors (such as a drinking problem) that contributed to the dismissal.

Neither off-the-record remarks nor anonymous attribution is recommended. Both practices raise ethical questions. Although off-the-record comments are acceptable, representatives of sport organizations must remember that they cannot control information once it is disclosed. The organization risks revealing information unintentionally or prematurely through off-the-record statements. The sport organization should not stake its integrity and reputation on the honesty of anyone else, including that of journalists. If a journalist violates the agreement, the sport organization should complain about the breach of ethics and trust to the appropriate editor or station executive. Honesty is a two-way street, essential to a positive working relationship on both sides. If the reporter violates the agreement, however, the damage is already done.

Ethics policies for journalistic associations and trade organizations discourage the use of anonymous sources. From the standpoint of the reporter, such sources compromise the credibility of the story somewhat. How can readers or viewers evaluate the accuracy and validity of the information if they do not know the source of the information? Identification of sources helps readers and viewers draw conclusions about conflicting information. Certainly, there is a difference between charges of recruiting violations from a player who quit the team and those from a private detective hired to investigate allegations. Journalistic organizations also recommend against the use of unnamed sources because anonymity provides a shield of protection. It is far easier for a source to make wild and exaggerated accusations under the cover of anonymity than to risk the exposure of identity and accountability. Anonymity gives the source an opportunity to distort or lie about the facts and to leave the reporter to take the fall if the information is incorrect. From the standpoint of the sport organization, a source's attempt to hide behind anonymity raises questions about motives and public posture. From the standpoint of both journalists and representatives of sport organizations, anonymity is, by nature, deceptive—a bruise on the apple of complete honesty.

PRINCIPLE NO. 2: BE AVAILABLE

The sport organization does not have an opportunity to influence the facts or the focal point of a story if no one talks to the media. Instead of avoiding contact in times of crisis, the designated representatives of the institution or organization should make themselves readily available. The best approach is to remain in the office as much as possible when a crisis arises. If no one can be available to meet with a reporter, speak on the telephone, or return an email a representative should get back to the reporter as soon as possible. A message should be recorded on voicemail stating the times when someone will be available to answer questions or supply information. The representative should be sure to return all telephone calls and emails. In addition, he/she should show up for interviews on time and answer all questions as thoroughly as possible without compromising the organization's crisis management objectives.

Administrators, athletics directors, coaches, and sports information specialists should collaborate on a crisis management policy. The plan should outline steps to follow when a crisis occurs and should spell out the responsibilities of all who make contact with the media. In fact, the plan should specify which members of the organization can speak to the media under which circumstances and any restrictions on what they can say. It should establish a chain of command that details the role of each member in addressing the crisis and should offer guidelines on availability to the media. The plan also should provide direction on the judicious use of "no comment" and tactful responses to typical probing questions. Finally, the crisis management plan should thoroughly explain procedures to follow immediately after the story breaks—news release, news conference, interviews, and so on.

The SID must remember that the decisive battles in the war of public opinion occur in the first 24 hours. The best way to win the battle is to present the positive aspects to the public before the negatives stack up into an insurmountable barrier. A prompt response usually is received favorably by both the public and the media, even if the news is negative; additionally, a prompt response suggests the organization is well organized and accountable, rather than being caught off guard or ducking responsibility.

Officials in the organization must decide quickly whether to answer or to quell rumors. A prompt response may limit speculation and exaggeration. If one journalist runs wild with a story without knowing all the facts, the institution and involved individuals may be hurt even if 99 responsible reporters ignore it. Careers may be ruined and reputations damaged beyond repair if a reporter reveals the name of a player under investigation for gambling on sports events. The SID who is available can at least say to the reporter, "You are off base on that story, because that player is *not* under any investigation."

Dispelling misinformation is an important reason for sport organizations to respond promptly to accusations of wrongdoing. If a university with an athletics program is under investigation, the SID should urge the administration to report exactly what happened as soon as the inquiry is made public. In the case of an NCAA investigation, the SID should release the facts as soon as they are known rather than sitting on the story and letting competing media dispense partial and piecemeal information. They should be given a full story from the outset. When a crisis erupts, many sport organizations quickly issue a news release spelling out the facts. Whether the athletics program is guilty or innocent, the SID should present the organization's version of the facts to the media and, by extension, to the public. Administrators in the forefront of the investigation should make themselves available to the media. In a situation involving serious charges of wrongdoing, many people in the school's hierarchy must be informed before news releases can be written and disseminated to the media. In fact, for a story as potentially damaging as one dealing with NCAA penalties for rules violations, a news conference should be scheduled as soon as possible after the story breaks.

Every member of the media, of course, will want an exclusive interview with everyone involved. Setting up exclusive interviews for a large number of journalists is impossible. A news conference both appeases competing reporters and creates an atmosphere of cooperation that may help to place the stories written and broadcast in a brighter light. If administrators and sports information directors are not available, the opposite is likely to occur. The media will begin to ask about accountability and to question the motives behind the secrecy. The silent organization sets itself up for a public flogging in the media. The same rules apply to revelations about individuals, including criminal activity, alcohol or drug abuse, and in-school disciplinary actions. The federal Family Educational Rights and Privacy Act prohibits disclosure by high schools and colleges of names and other information about students (for more on this see Chapter 12), but institutions can discuss rules and penalties; that gives the SID some control, though not much, over information disclosed. The media can still get the names from police reports or other public documents in some cases, but addressing the issue, even with limited information, is far better than sitting on the story.

PRINCIPLE NO. 3: TREAT ALL MEMBERS FAIRLY AND CORDIALLY

Competition within the media is always intense. It is even more cutthroat when the print media compete against equally aggressive broadcast journalists. An exclusive or "scoop" on an important story, such as an NCAA investigation, is the ultimate badge of achievement for a reporter. It is not surprising, then, that an inexperienced, overeager, or unscrupulous reporter occasionally blows a story out of proportion in an attempt to get a scoop.

According to Chamberlin (1990), it is imperative that the SID establish a strong working relationship with the media. Positive attitudes are essential in this communication; the SID must accept the failings of inexperienced and overeager reporters and not shut those reporters out. Sports information personnel must not allow minor mistakes, disagreements about story emphasis, and criticism about athletics programs to damage the working relationship. They also must take care not to get caught in the crossfire of competing media, favoring reporters they trust and ignoring journalists most likely to focus on the negative aspects of a story.

Sports information personnel must treat all media fairly in times of crises, when the competition among them is most fierce. First, SIDs must be sure to send news releases to all the media at the same time. Second, they must schedule news conferences at times that are as advantageous, from a deadline standpoint, to as many journalists as possible. Deadline differences necessarily create some inequities, but reporters cannot legitimately complain if the sport organization gives all members of the media the information at the same time. Third, SIDs must not give one reporter any piece of information that they do not give to all the others. Any slight—real or imagined—threatens the SID's working relationship with all the media. Despite their competitive nature, the media are a close-knit community. A slight to one is a slight to all. A tidbit of information disclosed to one creates suspicion among all others.

Additionally, the SID must remain impervious to the negative publicity (as long as it is fair) during a crisis and avoid complaining about minor problems. Words look worse in print than they sound when spoken. The temptation is to complain about being misquoted or having comments reported out of context by the media if an administrator criticizes something you said. The temptation is to blame the media if the words do not come out exactly as the SID intended. During contentious public relations crises, the SID is wise not to accuse reporters of misquoting or of taking information out of context unless he/she can verify it. Good reporters write what is actually said, not what they think someone meant or what someone should have said. By whining, the SID suggests he/she really is mad about the content of the story, and his/her complaints are just a way to dismiss the facts in the story. On the other hand, the SID must demand corrections for misquotes or mistakes that can be verified or confirmed.

Negative news does not necessarily reflect poorly on the sports information specialist or organization. Harsh criticism of athletes, coaches, or organization policy is not an indictment of everyone in the organization. The SID must be careful not to overreact to stories with a negative slant, particularly to stories prepared by newspaper columnists, radio and TV announcers/analysts, and talk-show hosts. Part of the job of the columnist, commentator, or talk-show "expert" is to second-guess the institution or organization. These analysts attempt to represent the sentiments of the reading or listening public when providing commentary. When a member of the media levels criticism at an institution, at an event, or at individuals, it usually is intended as honest, constructive criticism. Granted, a few reporters and talk-show hosts are controversial for controversy's sake, but honest journalists abide by an unwritten rule of fair play. When they skewer a team, coach, or players, they give the subjects of their criticism an opportunity to state a position or to take a written or verbal counterpunch. If critics remain aloof from their subjects, professional relationships can deteriorate beyond repair.

A Climate of Cooperation

The first line of defense in a crisis is a climate of cooperation. Here are a few guidelines to consider in coping with crises:

1	Do not underestimate the value of daily communication. Foster a positive working relationship through periodic contact with media representatives year-round, not just in times of crisis.
2	Get to know the strengths and weaknesses of reporters. Some are better at digging out information. Some are more likely to favor the organization's side or to tell the story thoroughly. Consequently, some actually may help in a crisis situation.
3	Getting people to listen after the fact is difficult. You must catch their attention early.
4	Rumors usually are worse than reality. Tackle each issue head on, tracking down the *facts*.
5	The entire organization—not just the public relations department—must be ready for a crisis.
6	All constituencies are equal. Keep all fully informed from the beginning of the crisis.
7	A good lawyer can be the best ally of a public relations operation in a crisis. A lawyer who understands both the legal system and the court of public opinion can provide sound advice.

When a crisis occurs within a sport organization, if the media relations staff has already established a climate of cooperation with the media, negative publicity can often be kept to a minimum. (Courtesy of Cleveland Browns)

In any event, the SID should never get into a battle with a journalist in the media. A minor story could turn into a major story if public complaints are made about the coverage. Political promoters caution against fighting with someone who buys ink by the barrel. In other words, the journalist always has the last word. Furthermore, crisis management and the reputation of the institution may suffer if the working relationship deteriorates into a public squabble in the media.

CRISIS MANAGEMENT

Crisis management is not easy. Trouble can strike when least expected and twist in unforeseen directions. Each twist may bring a new topic of inquiry, another round of media scrutiny, and renewed public concern—particularly if resolution of the issue comes slowly. It is not uncommon for the media to draw conclusions as incriminating facts come to light, even if all the facts are not yet known. Investigations by the NCAA, conferences, or university officials usually drag on for a long time, from several months to a couple of years. During the process, representatives of the sport organization may feel as if they are running from one brushfire to another to stem the spread of negative speculation. If investigators ultimately uncover wrongdoing and a penalty is forthcoming, no magic formula or crisis contingency plan can prevent damage to the institution's reputation.

However, effective institutional response and crisis management may blunt the impact of negative information. If a sport organization allows the media to exercise complete control over the release of the information, the winds of public opinion may fan the brushfires into a firestorm that permanently damages the institution. If the organization openly acknowledges the problem and resolves it professionally—in the public's estimation—the damage may be temporary. In fact, effective crisis management and controlled release of information by sports information or public relations directors may restore public confidence. The public ultimately will judge the organization on how well its response matches its philosophy and standards; that is, public opinion will hinge on how well the organization "practices what it preaches." Although negative publicity may be unpleasant, it seldom is fatal if handled effectively.

Of course, crisis prevention is the panacea for public relations dilemmas; that is, SIDs must try to stop problems before they start. For times when there is no doubt that the information will come out, crisis management limits the damage, at best. The best PR plans as it pertains to crisis management are the ones never heard or made public because they were tackled and solved before the crises had legs to run on.

Crisis prevention can head off dilemmas, and it is the responsibility of everyone in the sport organization. Team owners or school administrators set the standards for the organization and hire people to maintain them. General managers, athletics directors, and coaches implement the standards. They select the players and provide whatever indoctrination is necessary regarding the team or university's philosophy. General managers, coaches, and players also establish and enforce the rules of decorum, discipline, and punishment that maintain the standards. Sports information directors can offer direction on the most effective ways to communicate the standards to the public through word and action.

Clues to a Budding Crisis
The campus and public rumor mills are hyperactive.
The news media are showing interest in the story, or in the rumors.
Customers, business associates, and friends are inquiring about the situation.
Murphy's Law seems to be at work (if anything can go wrong, it will go wrong).
The situation requires action on several fronts at the same time.

The sports information or public relations director also can help by setting up a system to monitor what is happening on campus. The staff can be trained to listen for signs of trouble when they interact with students, faculty, athletes, and other constituencies. Contemporary locals for such a place to listen to the "chatter" would be Internet message boards and chat rooms. If a player mentions a "big hit" on the professional football games over the weekend, perhaps it is a warning signal that someone is gambling on the NFL. The SID also can cultivate internal sources by informing everyone from the university president to physical plant technicians that the sports information staff wants to know what is going on, including rumors, in the interest of crisis prevention. The SID should make it clear that he/she will not disclose the names of people who provide information. Additionally, the SID should put his/her name on every campus mailing list.

No number of internal watchdogs can spot every danger signal; however, sport organization officials can anticipate common problems and be on the alert for warning signs. The staff can study Internet message boards for anything that might suggest impending trouble. They also can read trade journals, NCAA literature, and sports magazines to keep up with the kinds of problems popping up on other campuses and in colleges.

Of course, not every danger sign points to an impending crisis. A missed practice and one-game suspension are hardly an impending crisis; if the SID makes too much of it the media will suspect there is more to the story than the sport organization is revealing. Wilcox and Cameron (2009) suggest that in developing a strategic management plan for crises an organization should brainstorm about potential crises, "rating both the 'probability' of a particular crisis and its 'impact' on the organization" (p. 263).

It is wise to begin a crisis management plan early rather than late. The gestation period is unpredictable. A day? A week? A month? The speed at which the crisis grows depends on the nature of the situation and the enterprise of the media. The safest approach is to implement the organization's crisis management plan when two or more warning signs appear. It is better to start too early than to start too late.

It is imperative that everyone in the organization is also on the same page with the plan and there is an organized, proactive, unified front as it pertains to the message that is presented to the media and the general public.

That strategy applies to the crisis management plan, as well. Representatives of the team or university should establish or review procedures prior to the start of each season or school year. The emergency plan should outline a proactive course of action for dealing with the dilemma and the media for specific problem situations (e.g., dismissal of a coach, criminal charges against an athlete or a coach, an investigation by a governing body such as the NCAA). The document should identify the primary spokesperson for the sport organization for each type of problem. The objective of any plan should be twofold:

1. To quickly and accurately communicate information that will assist in managing the crisis, saving lives, or protecting property.
2. To stabilize the damage to the institution's reputation until the crisis subsides.

Most public relations scholars recommend an open communication policy with the media and all audiences and constituencies in times of crisis. Wilcox, Ault, and Agee (1992) identify three common approaches to crisis management in *Public Relations: Strategies and Tactics:* stonewalling, denying the problem, and refusing to talk to the media; information management, releasing partial and misleading information while concealing damaging facts; and open communication, providing the media with all the facts as well as background information to put the facts in the proper context. Stonewalling may foster an image of arrogance and lack of concern for the public, and information management may smell of "cover-up" when concealed facts appear (Wilcox et al.). They cite Johnson & Johnson's handling of the Tylenol cyanide deaths in 1982 as a case study in effective corporate crisis management. Someone replaced the medication in Tylenol capsules with poison and put the boxes back on store shelves. Following an emergency plan and corporate principles, company public relations officials quickly gathered as

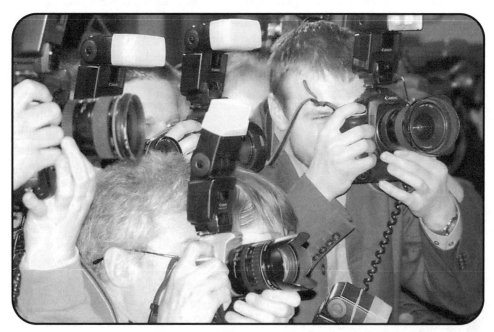

A sport organization that follows the open communication model and keeps the media informed will have a better chance of preventing the growth of speculation and negativity. (Courtesy of Stock.xchng)

much information as possible and set up a phone bank to answer media questions. Company officials cooperated fully with the media, consumers (toll-free number to provide information and to give out capsules in new, tamper-resistant packages), and investigators. The company unveiled the new packaging with a 30-minute videoconference and followed up with an intensive advertising campaign. Tylenol eventually recaptured most of the market share it had lost (Wilcox et al.).

A sport organization that follows the open communication model will keep the media fully informed at each stage of a criminal case, an NCAA investigation, or the search for a new coach. The organization will not sit on any information unless that information would be detrimental to the investigation or the search.

Development of a crisis management plan should begin with interviews of executives and an examination of the organization's philosophy or mission statement. The planning process should include consideration of potential threats, communication channels, notification procedures, and the chain of command. Once the plan has been completed, the principals involved should conduct a dress rehearsal to determine what works and what needs revision.

CREATING A CRISIS MANAGEMENT PLAN

Research

This should include interviews with the president, the provost, deans, and other appropriate administrators for information on the university's mission, philosophy, and standards. Consulting with other schools and viewing their policy is a good idea as well.

It should also include review of all documents related to ethical policies and legal regulations—student and staff codes of rights and responsibilities, NCAA regulations, Family Educational Rights and Privacy Act, and so on. A code of conduct typically spells out prohibited conduct on campus, an alcoholic beverage policy, and a sexual harassment policy. It also includes regulations related to disciplinary action and appeals. For a professional team, research entails interviews with the president, the chief operating officer, the general manager, and directors of key functional areas. The document examination encompasses league regulations as well as team policies and philosophy.

Assessment

This involves a brief situation analysis and an evaluation of common crisis situations. The situations may differ among amateur organizations, high school and college athletics departments, and professional teams.

Communication Channels

It is important to outline all types of communication channels—news releases, news conferences, phone banks, and so on—to be utilized for each type of potential threat. The outline should specify roles for the president, general manager or athletics director, coaches, athletes, sports information personnel, and anyone else in the organization or institution that will have contact with the media.

When creating a crisis management plan, it's important to establish which representatives of the organization, such as the head coach, should be speaking to the media. (Courtesy of Melinda Dove. Image from BigStockPhoto.com)

Notification Procedures

This is a procedure to be followed for notification of each member of the crisis management team when an emergency arises.

Communication Control Center

This is the central location for preparation and release of all information to the media. The location also may serve as the strategy room for meetings of the crisis team as needed.

Crisis Kit

This packet lists all items needed to be set up in a communication center quickly. One list would include telephones, copy machines, materials, and other logistical needs. The packet should also contain a media relations checklist with guidelines for dealing with the media in the first hours of the crisis.

Policies and Procedures

This requires a synopsis of key policies, regulations, and positions on issues, drawn from the document research. Copies of all documents reviewed during the preliminary research should be kept in a designated location listed in the crisis kit.

Appendices

Appendices include lists of addresses and telephone numbers of executives, managers, employees, media contacts, and others needed for consultation or for distribution of information.

Rough Draft

A rough draft incorporates the areas mentioned above. One person should prepare the draft; all others on the crisis response team should review it. Include the president, team owner, and board of directors or trustees if they are not assigned duties in the plan.

Final Draft

This is a revision based on input from all who have reviewed the plan. Following approval of the final draft, the SID should send copies to all members of the team and to other appropriate members of the sport organization.

Dress Rehearsal

The dress rehearsal is a test of the plan. The SID should conduct hypothetical exercises or a dress rehearsal to troubleshoot the plan of action, noting the strengths and weaknesses and adapting as needed.

TOUGH PUBLIC RELATIONS PROBLEMS

Public relations problems fall into two broad categories: emergency situations and ongoing issues. Emergencies are unexpected threats to the image and reputation of individuals or organizations. These generally concern actions or events arising from the behavior of members of the organization, as in the dismissal of a coach. Ongoing issues relate most often to policies and procedures that affect the working relationship between the organization and the media. Common issues range from coverage selections by the media to dressing-room policies of the sport organization.

Emergency Situations

These are situations involving the behavior of members of the organization with the potential to generate negative news. Common stories include the firing of a coach or manager, the release or trade of an athlete, unruly fan behavior, player indiscretions, tragedies (e.g., death of an athlete), internal investigations and disciplinary action against members of the organization, criminal charges against members of the organization, and investigation of individuals or of the organization by regulatory bodies.

Ongoing Issues

These issues involve policies and procedures that damage the working relationship between sport organizations and the media or that distort the image and reputation of either party. Common issues include coverage of men's low-profile collegiate sports, coverage of women's sports, refusal of athletes to speak to the media, and verbal or physical abuse of reporters by players or coaches.

A well-designed and well-rehearsed crisis management plan can help a sport organization take charge of the story in emergency situations. With a plan in place, members of the organization can take a proactive approach to dissemination of information. Development of the plan will provide a blueprint for handling the media, training for all institutional officials, and guidelines on how to answer certain questions. The organization and preparation will help members of the sport organization gather facts quickly, recognize and define the problem in their own terms, and come forward with information promptly.

The primary component of the crisis management plan for the sports information or public relations director is the checklist for dealing with the media (see "Media Relations Checklist" sidebar). The list enables the organization to update the media quickly and to advise them of actions being taken to resolve the issue.

Most ongoing issues deal with problems that have simmered for years with occasional movement in positive or negative directions. Although such issues may be as critical to the image of the sport organization or to the working relationship with the media in the long term, dealing with them lacks the communication dynamics of an emergency situation. Because such issues seldom affect sports events per se, they are of less immediate interest to the public as a whole; consequently, a crisis management plan and quick-response procedures are of little value in dealing with them.

Ongoing issues demand a well-organized plan designed to create immediacy in the minds of the public and interest on the part of the media. Of course, immediacy in the

	Media Relations Checklist
1	Prepare a one-page guide outlining steps to take in the first few hours of an emergency situation. Remember to use the "max-min" principle giving the maximum amount of information in the most minimal amount of time.
2	Choose an institutional or team spokesperson and a backup. The designated person should release all key information to the media. To ensure a consistent response, no one else should talk to the media without approval and if asked to, should defer to the spokesperson.
3	Think about more than the obvious implications of the problem. Come up with 10 questions the media are most likely to ask and prepare answers for them. Also, consider tangential areas into which the media may probe.
4	Deal with the crisis head-on. Do not hide from the media. Face the media quickly and openly.
5	Gather the facts before the meeting. Assign people to gather information on specific aspects of the situation. They should report to the SID or the designated spokesperson from the scene, from the hospital, from the police station, or from any other point the crisis touches.
6	Respond to every media question. Return every media telephone call and email within 10 minutes, if possible. Return calls or emails in this order: radio, TV, newspapers.
7	Never lie—not so much as "a little white lie." Once you lie to one reporter, you leave a permanent crack in your credibility. If you don't know the answer to a question, don't make one up.
8	Do not babble. Review what you want to say in advance and make sure it conforms to the team philosophy or university mission statement. Say exactly what you mean, and mean exactly what you say. Do not leave your comments open to interpretation.
9	Never volunteer negative information.
10	Avoid off-the-record comments. Stick to the facts. Do not speculate in response to hypothetical questions. In short, do not tell the media anything you do not want to see in print or to hear on radio or television. Even off-the-record comments can be repeated. If you do not want to see it in print, do not say it. You can gain the confidence of both athletes and media by avoiding cat-and-mouse games about what is OK to use and what cannot be repeated.

mind of the audience will help generate interest on the part of the media. At any rate, a plan of attack on ongoing issues requires a combination of marketing and publicity strategies, much like creating a publicity campaign. Like the publicity campaign, management of ongoing issues is both purposeful and planned. It may include advertising elements, marketing promotions, publicity releases or activities, and meetings with individual members of the media. Unlike crisis management, in which the SID responds to the media, management of ongoing issues requires the SID to take the institution's message to the public and to the media. The sports information director must prod and persuade in order to generate movement on ongoing issues such as gender equity in coverage decisions.

The SID bears a responsibility to attack ongoing issues as vigorously as he/she attacks emergency situations and should deliberately prepare strategies for resolving the problem, including techniques to be utilized and a timeline for implementation. Sports information personnel can adapt and adjust as circumstances dictate. They also should involve members of the organization at all levels. For example, they can enlist the development office or marketing department in promotional activities. They can stage events on campus that call attention to a particular team, such as a women's basketball clinic. They can include members of the sport organization in the plan, perhaps by setting up a speaker's bureau that sends coaches into the community to sell their sports.

Coverage of women's sports and low-profile men's sports is among the most important ongoing issues at the amateur, high school, and collegiate levels. For women's sports, the SID should collaborate with administrators and athletics officials on a plan to "sell" events and teams to the public and the media. Before preparing the plan, organizational officials should analyze the current differences in attendance, coverage policies of various media organizations, and emphasis on women's sports by the institution. Planners can use the information to devise "selling points" and strategies.

The SID should do everything possible to encourage and help the media publicize men's low-profile and women's sports. Calling or emailing the media with game reports and statistics is a good strategy; it is hard to turn down a story that is already prepared. At the very least, it may get a paragraph in a roundup in a newspaper or a spot on the list of sports scores displayed on the TV screen during a newscast. The SID can pitch features on athletes' standout performances and records to selected reporters and media organizations. The sports information department can also pass along conference standings and individual statistics. The most effective sales techniques are one-on-one. Pitching stories and statistics to selected media members is more effective than blanketing the media at large. It also is less expensive, and it helps the SID identify and cultivate journalists who show some interest. When targeting media, SIDs must remember this old public relations adage: "If you throw enough features on a wall, some of them are sure to stick."

Whereas publicity efforts depend on the media, advertising and promotional activities may take the pitch directly to the public. An SID may plan a schedule of public service announcements for radio to coincide with key games or events. In collegiate women's basketball, the recent trend in promoting key events that draw interest to the sport is the Women's Basketball Coaches' Association "Think Pink" weeklong contests. The initiative is centered on raising breast cancer awareness and some institutions couple it with other promotional events to draw large crowds.

Amateur sports organizations should put public relations strategies right next to fundraising on their lists of responsibilities. Directors or managers should establish communication with the local media, assigning a staff member or volunteer to deliver announcements to the local media about grand openings, facility expansions, special events and tournaments, new equipment, and programs.

What Not to Do	
As an SID, there are 10 critical errors you can make that may have a far-reaching impact.	
1	Do not divide the media into groups—that is, opponents and proponents, essential and nonessential, large and small. Pigeonholing suggests unequal treatment.
2	Do not put up roadblocks. Dealing only with selected media members, withholding information, or refusing to discuss an issue makes it more difficult for all concerned to do their jobs.
3	Do not ignore phone calls and emails or wait to return them until the next day. Failure to return a telephone call or email promptly gives the impression you do not think the person is important.
4	Do not scream about negative information in a story. You cannot expect the news media to ignore negative aspects of a story.
5	Do not talk down to reporters. Do not tell reporters, "There is no story here." Do not lecture reporters on their thirst for negative news and tendency to sensationalize stories or to blow them out of proportion. They've heard it already . . . often.
6	Do not insist that reporters clear all information with the organization before using it. They will ignore you. "No prior restraint" is one of the legal principles in a journalist's creed.
7	Do not promise exclusives to several reporters. Giving information to one reporter that you do not give to all others assuredly will damage your reputation. Giving the same information to all and calling it "exclusive" will have the same effect.
8	Do not torpedo the energetic reporter. Do not badmouth the reporter who breaks a new angle on the story in front of other members of the media. Reporters prize enterprise, even from a competing journalist.
9	Do not threaten to pull advertising. If you threaten to pull advertising over a story, not only do you compromise your integrity, but you also increase the odds the journalist will run the story, too.
10	Do not violate any of the these rules. You may gain a temporary ally or two if you favor certain members of the media or criticize competitors, but you ultimately create more enemies.

Whether the dilemma is an emergency situation or an ongoing issue, representatives of sport organizations should avoid actions that intentionally or unintentionally strain the working relationship with the media. They should guard against procedures or comments that belittle members of the media, give one member of the media an advantage over another, or impede composition or presentation of a story.

SUMMARY

Working with the media during crisis situations and ongoing public relations problems is the most challenging, stressful, and joyless part of the job of sports information. The sports information specialist's job shifts from publicizing positive news to combating negative information or rumors. The working relationship with the media may change temporarily from that of a partnership to that of a protagonist or antagonist. A misstep or false step may do far more harm; it may hurt an individual, a group of people, or the organization itself. However, the SID's performance in the midst of a public relations dilemma may do more to enhance the image of the organization than a ton of publicity brochures and media days.

Any event, issue, or incident that poses a threat to the reputation of the sport organization represents a potential crisis. A crisis may arise quickly as a result of the behavior or activities of members of the sport organization. A dilemma may develop slowly in connection with an unresolved issue related to coverage decisions, working relationships, or organizational policies.

Regardless of the origin or nature of the crisis, the sport organization should quickly respond to inquiries and implement procedures planned in advance. The quicker the response, the better; the battle for public opinion is usually decided within the first 24 hours. The simpler the emergency plan, the better, because response time is critical. The SID may have to convince superiors of the need for expediency, because the decision-making process moves at a much slower, more measured speed in upper-level management. In the news media, decision making operates on a deadline cycle, which may be as little as 30 minutes. To deliver its side of a story to the public, a sport organization must be prepared to move at the same speed. Because of deadline demands and competition among the media, a journalist seldom will wait until the sport organization is ready to print or broadcast the story.

An SID or public relations director can project a positive image and reinforce the organization's reputation by maintaining a climate of cooperation in all situations. The foundation for a positive atmosphere, even in times of turmoil, rests on three principles: honesty, availability, and fair play. To be effective, representatives of the sport organization must be open and honest, must make themselves available to the media, and must treat all journalists fairly and respectfully. They must attempt to answer all questions honestly, without relying on crutches such as anonymity and off-the-record comments. They must give information to all the media at the same time through news releases and news conferences. They must return telephone calls and emails promptly, within 10 minutes if possible. They do not complain about the negative elements of stories in the media.

A crisis can arise at any time, and some negative news is inevitable. A crisis seldom is fatal, however, particularly if the sport organization takes control of the story. To put themselves in position to take charge of the situation, members of the sport organization can monitor warning signs of trouble. They can watch Internet message boards, campus publications, and trade literature for hints of danger. They also can pay attention to what faculty, staff, students, athletes, and fans are saying. Excessive rumors, heightened media interest, and unusual inquiries from customers, boosters, and other supporters are among the signals that a crisis is imminent.

To respond quickly in a crisis, members of the sport organization should prepare a crisis management plan. The plan should reflect the philosophy, standards, and ideals of the organization. The primary objectives should be to accurately communicate information to the media and public that will assist in managing the crisis and to stabilize damage to the institution's reputation until the crisis subsides.

The sports information expert and school administrators or team officials should work together to develop the plan. The plan should address potential threats, notification procedures (for members of the organization), communication channels, procedures to follow, and media and institutional contact lists. The procedures should specify the responsibilities of everyone on the crisis management team, particularly those of the individual designated as primary spokesperson. What others are permitted to say to the media, if anything, also should be defined.

A crisis management plan is most effective for dealing with emergency situations that involve behavior or actions detrimental to the image of the organization, as in the firing of a coach or an NCAA investigation. Such plans are of little value in handling ongoing issues related to the working relationship with the media, such as coverage choices and access to athletes. The media come to the sport organization in times of crisis. The sport organization must go to the media to address ongoing issues. Such issues lack the obvious expediency and public interest intrinsic to emergency situations. As in crisis management, however, the most effective strategy for dealing with issues is a predesigned plan.

In every type of crisis, honesty and open communication are the best policy. The organization's response to an investigation, player discipline, or contract negotiation may reinforce the image the organization intends to project. The positives may outweigh the negatives in the media and public reaction. The same is true regarding athletes who are in trouble, whether the problem is crime, drugs, alcohol, or discipline. Open communication and early intervention give the SID and the sport organization some control over the flow and focus of information—perhaps not much, but some. Unquestionably, the sport organization stands a better chance of winning the battle of public opinion by employing a proactive plan rather than by sitting on information and conceding control to print and broadcast journalists.

DISCUSSION QUESTIONS

1. How does an SID develop a climate of continued cooperation with the local media?
2. Explain in detail how an SID is able to work effectively with his/her two bosses—the institution and the media—in a time of crisis.

SUGGESTED EXERCISES

1. Place students in groups in a role-placing scenario where an organization is dealing with a potential crisis. One student acts as the sports information director, another as the coach, and others as reporters. Examples of scenarios might include illegal recruiting, gambling on sports, or drug charges against an athlete. The reporters should then interrogate and write a story.
2. Have students write news releases announcing that an institution has been accused of cheating in regards to athlete recruitment. They should use the three principles of crisis management.

11

Global Sport Media Relations

Sports journalists, broadcasters, and communications directors across the United States will be asked by their superiors to cover sports events outside the borders of the United States. The US has become part of a global economy, and a big part of that global economy is the sport and media industries. If you are in the sport communication business and don't have a passport, you better go apply for one now.

Authors John Naisbitt and Tom Friedman have each chronicled in separate books how advances in technology have made our world smaller. Naisbitt has a background in research and is a business writer and futurist. Friedman has traveled around the world as a foreign affairs columnist for *The New York Times*. He has also written several best-selling books about international issues. Naisbitt's first best-seller, written in 1982, was called *Megatrends*, in which he made many observations that Friedman expounded on more than 20 years later in his book, *The World is Flat*. Our society has moved away from agriculture and manufacturing to an economy based on the creation and distribution of information (Naisbitt, 1982).

In *Megatrends*, Naisbitt outlined two stages of US economic development. The engine for the first great jump was the invention and use of the telegraph and the railroad for communication and transportation (Naisbitt, 1982). In the late 20th century, the two inventions that helped to spur globalization were the jet airplane and the communication satellite. Tom Friedman noted the next stage of economic development in his aforementioned book. The creation of a global fiber-optic network along with the refinement of software and new applications has made everyone around the world next-door neighbors. (Friedman, 2005)

These improvements in transportation, communication, and technology have made it necessary for the sport industry and the media business to expand their horizons. The editor for the *Atlanta Constitution* now has no problem assigning the newspaper's professional basketball reporter to follow a former NBA player from the Atlanta Hawks who is now playing for the basketball club Olympiakos in Greece. Another newspaper's hockey correspondent will be assigned to write a feature on the burgeoning professional hockey league in Russia (KHL). *Sports Illustrated* will send its soccer expert to cover a soccer story in Honduras.

The telephone system in the early 21st century is so advanced that a reporter sitting at his/her work station in Chicago has no trouble calling a contact in Johannesburg, South Africa, to find out background information on World Cup preparations in that country. In fact, the reporter does not have to be at his/her desk; he/she can be walking home from work while talking on a cell phone, and so can the source in Johannesburg. A local South African can send a picture that he/she just snapped with his/her cell phone that can provide evidence to that reporter in Chicago of the progress workers have made in building one of the new soccer venues for the World Cup.

GLOBAL MEGA-EVENTS

The World Cup and the Olympics are global mega-events, watched by a huge number of sports fans around the world (Amis & Cornwell, 2005). The cumulative TV audience for the 2004 Athens Olympics was 40 billion viewers; for the 2002 World Cup, 28.8 billion watched (Amis & Cornwell, 2005). FIFA reported that the cumulative audience for the 2006 World Cup was 26.29 billion viewers who watched from 214 countries over 374 channels ("TV data," n.d.). This number was less than the 2002 World Cup only because China, the world's most populous country, did not qualify for that World Cup.

The Beijing Olympics in 2008 drew 11 of the top 25 audiences of daily US sports programming in that year (Brown & Morrison, 2008). Nielsen reported that more than a third of the world's population watched some of the opening ceremonies of the Beijing Olympics; estimating just over 2 billion viewers ("Beijing Olympics," 2008). The website for the Sydney Olympics drew 11.3 billion hits (Wamsley & Young, 2005).

Thousands of media members from around the globe are credentialed to cover the Olympics, including hundreds working for the network televising the mega-event.
(Courtesy of US Army)

This fan interest generates a similar interest in the coverage of these events by news organizations around the world. The World Cup in Germany saw 18,850 members of the media descend upon the soccer venues in that country. Most of these were employees of the many television networks that covered the Cup; however, there were 4,250 print and Internet journalists and editors in Germany accredited by FIFA ("Germany 2006," 2006).

These events have also become big business for the countries that host them (Shipley, 2009). Thus, the selection process to host the Olympics or World Cup draws tremendous media attention (Blitz, 2009). That media attention is primarily from those reporters based in the countries that are pursuing the right to host the event. In the year leading up to the selection of Rio de Janeiro to host the 2016 Summer Olympics, there was tremendous media interest in Spain, the US, and Japan, the other three countries that joined Brazil as finalists ("Rio wins," 2009). You can bet there was even greater media interest from the newspapers and local television networks in the cities who were the four finalists—Tokyo, Madrid, Chicago, and Rio.

The sports media weren't the only ones paying close attention to these developments; so, too, did the political and business writers in these cities. For weeks, newspapers and other media outlets across the US speculated whether President Barack Obama would fly to Copenhagen, where the vote to select the 2016 host took place, to help lobby the International Olympic Committee on behalf of the US/Chicago bid (Nicholas, 2009). The business writers analyzed the amount of new investment, tourism spending, and sponsorship money but also attempted to put a dollar value on image creation if their respective city was selected as an Olympic host. How much is all that worldwide publicity worth? (Cashman & Hughes, 1999).

The 2010 Vancouver Winter Olympics drew the attention of 10,800 media representatives from around the world (Vancouver, 2010). NBC broadcast these games to the US and had a significant number of their employees in Vancouver working to produce this mega-event. It has been estimated that this Olympics drew a total audience of 3.5 billion TV viewers (Vancouver). In a nod to new media, 1.1 million Facebook fans logged onto the Vancouver page—four times the number that did so for the Beijing Games (Vancouver).

BEYOND THE BORDERS

The professional sports leagues based in the United States have many teams across the border in Canada. The Toronto Blue Jays, Toronto Maple Leafs, Toronto Raptors, Toronto FC, Montreal Canadians, Vancouver Canucks, Edmonton Oilers, Calgary Flames, and Ottawa Senators are the Canadian professional teams that play in the MLS, MLB, NBA, and NHL. Journalists and sports information specialists throughout the US will be assigned tasks when, for example, an NBA team travels to Canada to play the Raptors, but will also draw assignments when their local team travels outside the US for overseas exhibition games. NBA Commissioner David Stern has voiced his intent to have expansion teams in Europe in the next decade ("Have game, will travel,"

2008). The NFL plays games in Europe from time to time to try and promote the league to fans across the Atlantic. The Buffalo Bills played some of their home games in Toronto in 2009. The New England Patriots played the Tampa Bay Buccaneers at Wembley Stadium in October of 2009. The NFL has also played games in Japan, Mexico, and Germany.

Many Americans are playing professional sports overseas and this can produce a travel assignment and story for reporters in the US. Former college basketball stars from men's and women's programs in the United States are on rosters for professional clubs all over Europe; many of the top women play in both Europe and the WNBA. Beat writers covering professional golf and tennis and sports information specialists working in these sports may be asked to travel to the Ryder Cup, Davis Cup matches, the British Open, the French Open, the Australian Open, Wimbledon, etc.

The United States will send a team to the Men's World Cup in South Africa in 2010. The US team had to play many qualifying matches in their Confederation (North America, Central America, and Caribbean-CONCACAF) before they officially qualified for the World Cup. Some of these matches were in the US but World Cup representatives for the US also had to travel to Barbados, Guatemala, Cuba, Trinidad and Tobago, Honduras, Mexico, El Salvador, and Costa Rica. The US soccer reporters assigned to cover all of these games had to develop a comfort level for travel outside of the US as well as developing international experience to do their jobs. The trip to Cuba presented challenges that the communications professional would not face covering the Raptors in Toronto, Canada.

Traveling abroad to compete isn't just relegated to professionals or teams/individuals in mega-events such as the Olympics. More and more college teams, especially in basketball, are taking overseas trips during the summer. Others are participating in holiday tournaments such as one in Puerto Rico. Notre Dame will play the Naval Academy in a college football game in Ireland in 2011; a large contingent of professionals in sport communication will make that trip.

All-star teams that represent a league or USA Basketball will also take its contingent abroad. Jamie Dixon, head men's basketball coach at the University of Pittsburgh, led a US Under-20 team to victory in a tournament in New Zealand in the summer of 2009. Dixon's team was composed of 12 collegiate basketball players, thus keeping many college sports information directors at those schools busy during the summer updating their school's fans about this tournament halfway around the world. College basketball beat writers in Pittsburgh as well as some of the cities where these players went to college kept tabs on these players with stories while the competition was going on in New Zealand.

Each one of these sports and professional and collegiate leagues and organizations recognizes the value of the new markets outside the borders of the United States. The globalization of sports presents new opportunities for leagues, television networks, advertisers, and professional athletes who can now play in more than one professional league.

EXPANDED MEDIA COVERAGE

Global media companies have emerged to televise these teams and leagues all over the world. ESPN, BSkyB, Star Sports, Brazil Globo, Direct TV, NBA TV, Eurosport, Televisa, China Central TV, Canal France International, and Fox Sports all bring games from one side of the world to the other. Al Jazeera, the Qatari financed pan-Arab network, now televises NBA games and other sporting events from Europe and Asia.

ESPN signed an agreement in 2009 with the Bangladesh National Cricket Federation to broadcast their games on ESPN3 (ESPN's web-based video channel). The contract is for three years and calls for ESPN3 to show Bangladesh home cricket matches with some of the finest national teams in the world. For example, Bangladesh will host India and Sri Lanka, England, the West Indies, and Pakistan ("ESPN 360.com and Nimbus," 2009). Another division of ESPN, Star Sports, has signed a multi-platform rights deal with Cricket Australia. ESPN will provide coverage of these matches on the Internet, television, mobile devices, and radio ("ESPN Star Sports," 2007). Several global media companies have submitted bids for the Chinese rights to the best professional soccer league in the world, the Premier League of England (Blitz & Fenton, 2009).

With this globalization, new challenges and opportunities are presented to the journalists and sports information directors of today. It also must be noted that with these developments, there are more job opportunities for broadcast journalists and former professional athletes interested in TV careers. Each of these broadcasts usually has a studio host as well as a play-by-play announcer and color commentator. Al Jazeera has seven sports correspondents working for their Al Jazeera English division as well as a fully developed English language sports news website. ("Sport," n.d.). Those students that speak a second language will find themselves in even greater demand, but they will also face stiff competition for those jobs from graduates outside the United States. This growth in sports programming outside the borders of the United States will help to grow networks like Fox Sports and ESPN. It is important for students to understand this new market that is constantly changing and growing and also know how they can put themselves in the best position to take advantage of these exciting new opportunities.

NATIONAL SPORTS ORGANIZATIONS

Many of the US national governing organizations or national sports organizations (NSOs) hire full-time staff members to provide content to their websites and/or to prepare their athletes and coaches for media opportunities with members of the press from all over the world. These members of the media may be covering foreign competitions such as the Pan Am Games, Olympics, and World Championships in sports such as basketball, track and field, and swimming. The communications director with these sports federations will also interact directly with the media in arranging interviews for coaches and their athletes, scheduling press conferences at events, and also providing background information for their national teams in the form of bios, press releases, and statistics. International sports federations like FIFA (the governing body of soccer) and FIBA (the governing body of basketball) also have fully developed communications departments.

One of the busiest sports federations in the United States, USA Basketball, employs several sport communications professionals that have developed extensive experience working at global sports competitions and with the global media that are assigned to cover those events. Craig Miller, Caroline Williams, and Jenny Maag all play vital roles in USA Basketball's communications strategy.

Miller is the chief media officer for USA Basketball. He has worked six Summer Olympics, four World Championships, and four Pan American Games. Prior to his current position, Miller was the sports information director at Villanova for 10 years, including 1985, when Villanova won the NCAA Basketball national championship.

Williams is the director of communications and she has been with USA Basketball since starting as an intern in 1985. Like Miller, Williams has an SID background; she worked in that department at George Mason University, where she graduated with a bachelor's degree in speech communication. Williams has worked three Olympic Games and three World Championships, where she was the primary media contact for the women's USA Basketball team.

Maag is the manager for communications with USA Basketball. She has a bachelor's degree in journalism from Western Washington with experience in TV and radio, as well as public and media relations with the Seattle Supersonics franchise. Maag and Williams are heavily involved in the updating of USA Basketball's website along with compiling press releases and the occasional newsletter that USA Basketball publishes ("Staff bios," n.d.).

USA Basketball has a full plate of international basketball events in 2010—the men's World Championships in Turkey, women's World Championships in the Czech Republic, NIKE Hoop Summit for high school aged boys from around the world in Portland, Oregon, and the FIBA Under 17 women's Championships in France ("Inside USA Basketball," n.d.).

A COMMUNICATIONS DIRECTOR'S PERSPECTIVE

Caroline Williams

In order to fully appreciate and understand the job of a communications director for a national sports federation, Williams was interviewed about her role with USA Basketball and was asked to describe some of her experiences during the last 15 years with the organization.

Q: How many different countries have you visited since you started with USA Basketball?

Williams: Probably more than 20 countries; I have to think about this by region. In North America and the Caribbean, I have traveled to Canada, Mexico, the US Virgin Islands, Cuba, and Puerto Rico. On the continent of Asia, I have been to Japan, China, and Thailand. I have been to Australia several times; they like their basketball and have had very competitive men's and women's teams at many age levels. The Sydney Olympics in 2000 also was a reason to travel to Australia. I have been all over Europe with our national team: Monaco, Croatia, Serbia, Hungary,

Poland, Russia, Slovakia, Czech Republic, Italy, Greece, Germany, Spain, and Portugal. On the continent of South America, I have been to Brazil, Argentina, and Chile.

Q: In general, what type of press coverage does the USA team receive at some of these events?

Williams: When I am working a basketball event in a basketball crazy country like Brazil or Argentina, you can expect a very crowded press area during and after games. The local press will be there in force as well as representatives from many of the other countries that are participating. We had an Olympic qualifier in Chile in 2007, and basketball is not that popular in that country; however, because this was considered an historic event, the local press covered this tournament extensively. When I have been to Serbia and a country like Australia, where basketball is as popular as it is in Brazil or Argentina, there is also a very large local and regional contingent covering the event.

The general rule is that when you have NBA/WNBA players on your roster, the press interest will increase both from the local press and the amount of reporters outside of the host country assigned to the event. When I have worked an international tournament for our U19 women or U19 men, there is definitely a drop-off in press coverage. For example, I covered a U19 women's tournament in the Czech Republic where there were maybe two or three reporters at the post-game press conference. I also must add that recently, with the economic downturn, many media companies have hired local stringers to cover the event, or just relied on a wire service like *The Associated Press* to send out a game story.

Q: How does the USA Basketball Communications department staff these international events?

Williams: We sent five people to the Olympics in Beijing. For the World Championships, we will send three or four but at the age events like the U19 Worlds I may be it. Recently I covered our U19 women's national team at an event. I was the photographer, I did play-by-play, and I posted video to our website along with photo galleries. I also wrote game stories, put together quotes for every game, helped to manage some of the hometown media, and also did some off the court features.

Q: What is a typical game day like for you?

Williams: I usually end up waking up too early after going to bed too late, particularly when I am covering our men's or women's national team at an Olympics or World Championship. At the Olympics, because we are all (USA Communications staff) covering both teams, we have 16 straight nights of games. Since our national teams are also popular, they usually play the last game or the next to the last game of the night.

For the age group events (U17 and U19) we usually have a few off days over the course of the tournament. The reason for this is that while the U19 or U17 worlds are held for men and women in the same year, they're hosted at different times by different countries. It's a singular tournament so to speak with 12 or 16 teams competing for the gold medal and there are off days built into the schedule. Only in the Olympics, Pan American Games, and World University Games do our men's and women's teams compete across the same time period in the same city.

In the morning on a typical game day, I will wake up and immediately check email to see if I have any media requests. I travel with my own coffee and coffee maker, so once I have made a cup or two, I will also start work on the day's game notes. We will then travel to the gym for the game day shoot-around, which usually lasts just an hour. We will return to the hotel, eat lunch, and finish up the game notes. Hopefully there will be a few free hours in the afternoon and I typically will either take a nap, exercise, or try and visit a local tourist attraction. My last working trip to Berlin, we had enough of a break to visit the Checkpoint Charlie Museum.

I usually attend the pregame meal with the team and will then travel to the gym on the team bus. Even though the team arrives early, there will be plenty for me to do, particularly at an Olympics or World Championship. There might be a request for background information for a story on one of the players, a scheduling request for an interview with a coach or player, a quick review of our game notes, or a logistical discussion with the TV crew regarding pregame, halftime, and postgame interviews.

The media will have questions or need help during the game, so we all will be working through the end of the game. We will then put together a recap of the game and start collecting quotes from individual interviews and the postgame press conference. If the event is an Olympics where there are five of us, we may end up with 6–10 pages of quotes. These quotes become valuable to those reporters that may have to cover the entire Olympics for their newspaper. They might have been over at the swimming venue watching Michael Phelps in one of his gold medal winning races or at a track and field event. Other newspapers can't afford to have their reporters stay all the way through an entire World Championship and they might arrive in time for the final rounds. Once

Governing bodies have differing rules for postgame interviews. FIBA, for example, has a "mixed area" for interviews, which can cause chaos for sports information and reporters. (Courtesy of USA Basketball)

all of these quotes have been loaded onto our website, it can be anywhere from midnight to 3 a.m. and we are ready to get some sleep.

Q: What are the postgame press conferences like for these international events?

Williams: The governing body for basketball, FIBA, has a few rules governing the press for these events. Postgame, each team must bring one player and their coach to the formal end-of-game press conference. The locker rooms are not open to the press like they usually are in the NBA or at most colleges around the country. These press conferences will last somewhat longer than in the US because of the many different languages spoken by the global press as well as the different international teams in these tournaments. The questions and answers sometimes have to be interpreted and re-interpreted based on the language of the person asking the question and who answers the question.

The players that don't go to the formal end-of-game press conference will go into what is called the "mixed area" before they board the bus for the ride back to the hotel. This mixed area is a large room or hallway separated by a short fence—similar to a parade barrier. Players will be on one side and press on the other. At an event like the Olympics, the mixed area is organized chaos. Since we have a staff of five, one of us will go with the player and coach to the press conference while the other four fan out in the mixed area, recording player quotes and helping the hometown press connect with players that they may cover regularly. For example, I will make certain that the *Denver Post* writer has the opportunity to interview Carmelo Anthony as soon as he enters the mixed area. If a reporter is doing a feature piece on Diana Taurasi, I will bring Dee to that reporter when she is ready to leave the locker room.

In the mixed zone, picture taking and autograph requests are common at these events, particularly the Olympics with all of the NBA stars on the USA team. Our communications staff attempts to shut down the paparazzi and autograph hounds early so the working media can do their jobs. In Beijing, with LeBron James, Kobe Bryant, and Dwyane Wade, this was a full-time job.

Q: You mentioned an interpreter at the press conference. How does FIBA and the host country deal with the many languages spoken by reporters, players, and coaches at one of the global basketball events?

Williams: At the Olympics, there is a dedicated interpreter for basketball and that interpreter usually is fluent in three or four languages. FIBA or the host country will sometimes hire specialists when needed as well. At the smaller FIBA events, the host country will usually make some arrangements but not all languages will be covered. As an example, when I was at an event in Russia, there was no one to translate Japanese but a coach for the Japan team could speak English, so that coach served as the interpreter for the players that did not speak English and then in turn the Russian press attaché translated the English translation to the local press.

I did an event in Spain once and we had a coach for our team with a deep southern accent. I had to interpret his English for the interpreter and then the interpreter would convert my version to Spanish for the media.

The Olympics usually have three official languages: English, French, and the language of the host country. Thus, if we're in China and there's a press conference with the Brazilian team, the Brazilian's answer will be translated from Portuguese to Chinese, French, and English. Oftentimes, however, the player for Brazil will just conduct the interview in English.

Q: What opportunities are out there for students to work in the international sports area?

Williams: USA Basketball, the United States Olympic Committee, and most of the other national governing bodies and NSOs have internship opportunities. All of these organizations work with their counterparts in other countries as well as the International Olympic Committee and their respective international sports federations. The international sports federations also hire interns. The pay is horrible for many of these internships but the opportunities are endless.

Also, there are a large group of people from many different countries that work at the Summer and Winter Olympics. They can be hired to work for a few months, for the two or three years leading up to the Olympics, or they may just be hired to work a few days before, during, and after each Olympics. They can work at a particular venue (e.g., track and field or swimming), in the hospitality area, for the operations staff, or at the press center. Jobs like these are tremendous networking opportunities for future jobs in the sports world.

Q: If you could offer one or two thoughts to students with regard to a career in sports communication or sports journalism, what would they be?

Williams: Real world experiences are incredibly valuable to your development. My internship at USA Basketball and my work with the sports information department at George Mason University helped to prepare me for my current job. It also made me realize what I wanted to do for a living after I graduated.

I was very fortunate to work for Carl Sell when I was at GMU. He was proud of the fact that many of his interns went on to work for other colleges and professional teams. Carl had me write features, edit game notes, and other jobs of substance; he gave me real responsibility. My timing was also good. We had just hired Paul Westhead to be our coach and this attracted a tremendous amount of media attention. The experiences gained by internships or simply volunteering at an event are huge in my opinion. They allow prospective employers to find out if you can cut the long hours, whether you work on the weekends without complaint, and if you can get along with others; personality comes into play when you're in close quarters with people for long periods at a time. Even if it's as simple as volunteering for the long Final Four weekend and taking flash quotes, the more experiences gained and the more people with whom an intern/volunteer interacts, the more likely it is that s/he will get an opportunity somewhere down the line. Always strive to make a good first impression (and second and third).

TRAVELING ABROAD

A trip to cover the Toronto Maple Leafs will be somewhat more complicated than a trip to cover the Washington Capitals if you are the NHL beat writer for the Philadelphia

Flyers. Despite the good relations with their neighbor to the north, US citizens must go through customs when traveling to any city in Canada. You will not need a visa but you will need a passport.

However, if journalists have been assigned by their editors to cover the 2010 World Cup in South Africa, they will face a few more complications because a visa is required to enter South Africa. The visa process can sometimes be expedited but it is important to plan ahead. A great majority of the countries where someone in the profession may travel to have websites with very easy instructions on how to apply for a visa; if one is a US citizen, there are some countries where a visa is not required. This process has also been made much easier by adding the online application as well as express delivery. To apply for a visa, it goes without saying that you will need a U.S. passport. Common questions when applying for a visa will be the purpose of the visit, the date of entry, and the date of departure. If one doesn't have a passport, it can be obtained from most post offices in the US as long as a birth certificate is supplied when applying for the passport.

After reporters have contacted the embassy of the country they will be visiting to secure a visa, it might be a good idea to check with their health insurance providers or with the U.S. State Department to determine if they need any inoculations/immunizations prior to the overseas assignment. Contracting malaria for the flight home is not a good way of recovering from jetlag. Matching current medical records with the suggested immunizations of the host country can prevent a visit to the hospital at home or abroad. When checking for immunizations, it is also important to find out what is suggested in the way of food, beverage, and water consumption. While staying in some countries, it may be best to brush one's teeth using bottled water.

Assuming the country reporters will be visiting has no problem with them (or their media outlet or organization), they must make plane and hotel reservations. Advice from an experienced reporter can come in handy at this point in the planning process. It is also important to understand the nuances of the sports venues in which the events will be held. There are several questions to consider. How difficult and expensive is the trip from the hotel to the stadium or arena? Does the city have reliable public transportation? Is there a press bus that can be used to travel to each event? Are taxis reliable and plentiful? How easy will it be to pay with a credit card? Are ATMs available and accessible in order to access extra cash?

If a reporter is covering an event such as the Olympics, will he/she be at one venue the entire time, or will he/she be expected to cover four or five different events located in different venues? In the past, many Olympic Games have venues that are located in a neighboring city that is miles away. This has the potential to cause problems if a reporter hasn't planned ahead and arranged to rent a car or arrange for alternate transportation. The host country usually has a local organizing committee that is typically, although not always, helpful to the working press. They usually provide bus service for the working press, but the ability for reporters to leave and move to another location or return to their hotels for some rest may be restricted by the bus schedule.

The hotel location is important but equally important is that the hotel has the necessary Internet connection to meet one's communication needs. A reporter will usually be able to file stories from the venue but it is important that if it is necessary, he/she can also file from the hotel. When checking for an Internet connection, it is also important to ask what type of electrical plug is needed for laptops, shavers, chargers, etc. For the frequent world traveler, this is a suggested purchase. Some hotels have these alternate plugs for sale or for use for their hotel patrons but some hotels don't. For the frequent traveler it would make sense to own several adapters.

Another note is that telephone service in many foreign countries is much more expensive than in the United States. A boss would not be happy to receive a receipt for phone calls in the thousands of dollars. It is important for reporters to communicate ahead of time with their business office. If they have to make calls to talk to their editors, a suggestion would be to find a cheap Internet phone service. There are several that offer the ability to make inexpensive phone calls online. A cell phone capable of calling back to the United States may be a necessary rental or purchase. Additionally, if a reporter is responsible for providing content to a blog or a Twitter account, it is important to be certain he/she can tweet and update the blog from the venues.

Another important issue for sports communication professionals to consider is the time zone of the city where they will be during the event. For example, Beijing is 12 hours ahead of the US Eastern time zone, Vancouver is three hours behind, and South Africa is seven hours ahead. Those journalists from the US covering the London Olympics in 2012 will have to recognize that London is five hours ahead of the Eastern time zone.

A *New York Times* reporter covering the 2010 Winter Olympics should be cognizant of the fact that if a figure skating competition wasn't scheduled to conclude until 11 p.m. Vancouver time, there is no way the reporter would be able to submit a story in time for the next day's edition of the newspaper if the paper's deadline is prior to 2 a.m. On the other hand, a reporter covering the 2012 Summer Games in London would have some additional time to write the game story and notes for a basketball game that concludes at 11 p.m. local time because of the five-hour time difference. When posting stories to the Internet either via a media outlet or organization's website, blog, or Twitter account, time zone differences obviously aren't a factor. The information will immediately be made available for readers around the world regardless of which time zone they reside.

As Caroline Williams of USA Basketball said earlier in this chapter, there may be some free time for sport communication professionals to visit some tourist attractions while in another country. However, U.S. State Department travel advisories may be helpful in providing alerts as to parts of the host country that should be off limits for touring. The USOC, U.S. Soccer Federation, and USA Basketball are American-based NSOs that can give sport communication professionals guidance when they are working at the Olympics, World Cup, or basketball World Championships. It is important to remember that the respective US sports federation and/or the international sports federation are very good starting points for information when working at an international event.

A JOURNALIST'S PERSPECTIVE

Steven Goff is a *Washington Post* reporter that covers all things soccer for the *Post* as well as college basketball. He has traveled to 25 countries during his 20-plus years as a sports reporter. Goff has covered many World Cups and many World Cup qualifiers as well as club teams and other soccer matches outside the US. Goff also covers college soccer, Major League Soccer, and DC United for the *Post*. Goff talks about his experience covering soccer around the world.

Q: Where have you traveled to cover the sport of soccer around the world?

Goff: I was in France for the World Cup in 1998, South Korea and Japan in 2002, and Germany in 2006. Previously I was in Costa Rica four times, Jamaica and Mexico three times, El Salvador, Guatemala, and Honduras twice, and Barbados, Cuba, Panama, and Trinidad and Tobago to cover our national team. I have had some other international soccer assignments that have taken me to England, Ireland, France, Belgium, Holland, Spain, and Greece.

Steve Goff

Q: How would you characterize some of the differences in attitude toward the press in some of these countries?

Goff: My first reaction is that we have been spoiled in this country—"we" meaning the press. When you cover an event at a college/university or for one of the professional leagues, these sports entities are trying to present to you a positive impression of their enterprise. You are fed, you are given game notes, a nice typed list of quotes, there are people working to service you at every break in the action, and most of these venues have a very secure and comfortable place to watch the game and file your story during and after the action is over. At some of these venues I have traveled to cover the U.S. Soccer Team, if you are with the working press, you are on your own.

As an example, at one of the venues during the qualifying rounds in the summer of 2009, we had about 12 reporters covering the match between the US and their hosts. All of us had laptops but we could not connect to a power outlet. The only power outlet was in a locked room. Many of us at this venue were contemplating how we were going to break down the door to this locked room so that we would be able to charge our laptops that were all running out of power. We couldn't do our jobs. Finally, about two minutes before the game was ready to start, a maintenance worker came into our "area" with an extension cord about 100 feet long, with a power strip big enough for all of us to power up. He ran the cord through the crowd, up some steps and around a corner to a power source we could not see. The bottom line is we were up and running, but all of us were very close to running out of battery power before the game had even begun.

Q: What other "press box issues" have you encountered?

Goff: Well, the first press box issue is that in many locales, there *is* no press box. You are assigned a seat in the stands at some of these qualifying venues with no table top, no security, no privacy, and in many cases you are with the paying public when it comes to finding a restroom. You better have an extra battery for your laptop.

I have had beer thrown on me more than once, so I am prepared. When I suspect that I am covering a game where there could be flying beer, I will bring a towel with me just in case. I also sometimes have brought a baseball hat with the logo of the local team; this will sometimes permit me to be able to watch the game "unmolested" by the more rabid fans. They see the hat and they decide we are going to leave this guy alone.

I did a game once in Guatemala where I lost my Internet connection halfway through the game. I ended up filing my story on my blackberry. Try putting a 300-word story together on a Blackberry sometime.

Q: Describe a typical postgame press conference during this last qualifying swing for you and the US team.

Goff: The postgame press conferences in Central America are usually formal for coaches' comments—often in a cramped room with a stage, chairs, microphones, sponsor mascots hanging around with the working press (a giant chicken once), product placements all over (water, cell phones, sodas, etc.), scantily clad sponsor girls, aggressive/opinionated radio reporters, and no air conditioning. The players and coaches for some of these teams don't feel any obligation to answer questions from the press. Essentially, it is chaos.

Q: How has the visa process worked for you when traveling to all of these countries?

Goff: I have received some help with visas through the U.S. Soccer Federation and it also does not hurt that the *Washington Post* is so close geographically to the embassies of all of these countries in Washington, D.C. When you cover the U.S. soccer team, you can sometimes piggy back on the visa applications of the team and staff that travels to games outside the US. Our newspaper has consistently followed both the US men's and women's soccer teams.

The toughest visa issue I have had was when the US had to play in Havana for the most recent World Cup qualifiers. The game was in Cuba in the fall of 2008. The visa process took months. I had to alert the U.S. Soccer Federation that I wanted to travel to cover the game. The Federation then sent my request to the U.S. Treasury Department. You have to receive permission from Treasury because of the economic embargo we currently have with Cuba.

The Cubans issued me a visa but they rejected the visa application from the sports reporter at the *Miami Herald*. Evidently they don't appreciate how the *Herald* has covered Cuba recently. The *New York Daily News* wanted two reporters to attend; Cuba would only grant the *News* one visa. There were probably about 10 reporters from the US at the Havana match, including reporters from the *New York Times, Daily News, St. Louis Times-Dispatch*, and *Sports Illustrated*.

When we landed in Havana, each one of us had to report to the International Media Center, where we were credentialed as journalists in Cuba. We were all charged about $85 for this credential and you better have it with you when walking around the city.

Q: Did you encounter any other issues when you were in Havana?

Goff: The most difficult "issue" logistically in Cuba is the amount of cash you have to carry. Your American-issued ATM cards and credit cards are not accepted there, and you can't write a check. I was there for four days and by the night on the third day, I was scrambling. I ended up borrowing some cash from one of my fellow journalists. We were all lucky we could pay for our hotel in advance.

Q: How was the game?

Goff: Cuba wanted the journalists covering the match to be pleased, so we were treated very well by the game management staff. There was plenty of power for our laptops and the wireless connection was very good. The US ended up winning the game 1-0. The game was played in an old baseball stadium that was also used for soccer. The field was not in good shape and the lights went out a few times because of a rainstorm before and during the game.

Q: Are you are going to cover the 2010 World Cup in South Africa?

Goff: Yes, the *Washington Post* will probably send three of us over to South Africa. Since the pairings have been set, we have started working on the logistics of that trip. The hotel space is limited so it is important to find a room soon. The hotels are pricey and travel in between game sites is not going to be easy. When I covered the World Cup in 2006 in Germany, the trains were a great way to travel inside the country to the different venues. The flights to South Africa are also going to be very expensive.

We will probably bring one reporter that will write a blog, bring a camera to file video, and just stay a limited amount of time. I will cover the majority of the games, write stories, update my blog, and also send out tweets on my Twitter page. We will bring a third reporter who will probably have had experience covering events or politics in Africa. That reporter will help to set the scene for the *Post* readers inside South Africa.

Q: You mentioned Twitter. Do you tweet during games?

Goff: I do send out tweets during games, both when I cover games in the US and overseas. My Twitter traffic during one particular game was off the charts because the game was not picked up in the United States by any network. ESPN had negotiated with the Honduran Soccer Federation and decided the asking price was too much. So if you were a soccer fan and wanted to actually see the game, you would have had to find a local sports bar that had bought the closed circuit rights for those games. An independent production company out of Spain bought the rights to the game and then offered closed circuit rights to sports restaurant/bars in the US. If you were an owner of one of these establishments, you were charged a fee close to $15 times the capacity of your restaurant/bar.

Those that were not watching at the local sports bar wanted updates during the game; I was their source for updates. It turned out that this was the game that the US qualified for the World Cup, so the result was pretty important to the soccer fans in the US.

Q: Have you ever had any trouble finding a place to stay on these assignments?

Goff: I did have a big problem finding a hotel in Trinidad and Tobago a few years ago. The only other country that does carnival better is Brazil, which meant that there were zero hotels available. A few other reporters were in the same boat I was. We ended up staying at a yacht club in Port of Spain, about 30 miles outside the city itself. Obviously this was not ideal, but the rooms were clean and I was able to cover the game.

SUMMARY

The 21st century is an exciting time for those involved in the sport industry. The Olympics has become a truly global entertainment event, followed on TV, in newspapers, and online around the world. The World Cup, a celebration of the world's most popular sport, rivals the Olympics in its reach around the world. Fans from all over the globe descend on the host cities and countries of these events. The stories of these events are told by the television, radio, newspaper, and online journalists from countless countries. These teams also have their own communications professionals that act as liaisons with the global press but also must tell the stories of their teams and their athletes. These communications professionals must learn to work in this new international wonderland.

When these events have concluded, it does not lessen the mobility of today's sporting events and today's athletes. European soccer players regularly play in the MLS. The best tennis players and golfers travel the world competing on a tour that is a test of stamina just in the travel necessary to make each event. Major League Baseball has websites in English, Japanese, Spanish, Chinese, and Arabic. The best basketball players from Europe can be found on NBA teams. The professional women's teams in Europe are loaded with former NCAA female college stars. The world's best professional soccer league, the aptly named Premier League, has developed a regular following all over the world. Fans around the globe follow the games of Manchester United and Chelsea. World media companies are now vying for TV rights outside their borders, looking to take advantage of the burgeoning interest in sports programming. All of these developments offer opportunities for the sports journalist and communications professional that is prepared for this global marketplace.

Steve Goff, the *Washington Post* writer featured above, has developed a comfort level with the sport of soccer but he also can cover that sport anywhere in the world. The student that wants to become a sportswriter can develop an appreciation for travel while still in college. There are numerous study-abroad programs at virtually every college and university in the United States. There are volunteer and internship opportunities at all of these world athletic events. The Summer and Winter Olympics, Pan Am Games, and Commonwealth Games all rely heavily on volunteers and interns looking for interesting work experience in the sports and/or media industries. The final total of all workers, both paid and volunteer, at the Vancouver Olympics was 50,000 people (Vancouver, 2010).

Caroline Williams emphasized taking advantage of internship opportunities while still in school. The United States has many national governing bodies like USA Basketball that hire interns in the communications field. Because the United States Olympic Committee headquarters is based in Colorado Springs, Colorado, many of these NGOs are also located in that city. All of the professional leagues in the US want to take advantage of the global economy, so there are opportunities in those organizations to learn some valuable lessons about doing business overseas and traveling outside the United States. Your value also increases when you learn to speak a second language. Both Goff and Williams talked about being able to maneuver in places where English was not the primary language. Taking a minor in Spanish, French, or Chinese may set you apart from other job seekers.

With all of these new opportunities and challenges available in the sports communication industry, it is also important to remember that story telling is still important. While broadening your horizons is important, the ability to write and communicate with the spoken word is the "nuts and bolts" of sport media relations.

DISCUSSION QUESTIONS

1. Should FIFA standardize press box and media arrangements at all venues that host official FIFA national team events? Explain your answer.
2. Why do sports federations around the world hire communications staff? What are some of the skills you think are necessary to succeed in that position?
3. What are the differences between Steve Goff's position as a journalist for the *Washington Post* and Caroline Williams's position as a director of communications for USA Basketball? Any similarities? Is it more important to know how to write or to know your sport in these jobs?
4. London is the host of the 2012 Summer Olympics. What problems will that cause for the TV broadcaster? The journalist that has a daily column to file at a newspaper? The online journalist that blogs and also is in charge of keeping the newspaper's website updated during the Olympics?

SUGGESTED EXERCISES

1. Go to the website of one of the international sports federations, such as FIFA or FIBA. Who works in their communications department? Critique their website. How do you like the format and appearance? Are the stories well written?
2. Go to the website of one of the United States' national sport organizations, other than USA Basketball. Identify its communications director. Analyze the content on its website. Determine what types of media it uses to tell its story. Take a look at its media page. How would you contact the organization if you wanted to write a story about one of its coaches or athletes?
3. Do some research on one of the major global media companies in the United States or in another country. What work does it do outside of the borders of the country where it is headquartered? Does it broadcast sporting events? If so, in how many countries? Who is its sports chief executive? What, if any, major sports rights properties does the company own?
4. Do some research on one of the Central American countries that Steve Goff visited. Compare the US economy to the country you choose (e.g., GDP, per capita income). What are that country's major newspapers and TV network or stations? What sports are televised inside that country? Can you watch American pro leagues, college sports, and Premier League soccer if you lived there? How much is the cost for sports programming?
5. Go to the websites of the IOC and USOC. Take a look at their communications departments. How are their websites organized? If you wanted to interview someone from each organization, what are your instructions for contacting them?

12

Law and Ethics

I n the dissemination of sports information and the profession of sports journalism, law, ethics, and regulations play a big part in not only governing the behavior of the profession but also providing subject matter for countless articles. NCAA regulations, coaches' contracts with buyout clauses, Title IX compliance, collective bargaining agreements, antitrust lawsuits, and defamation claims—not to mention drunk driving charges, handgun charges, and performance enhancing drugs—cry out for at least a cursory understanding of the legal system in this country for those that cover sports. These legal issues lead to broader discussions of ethics and the role of sportsmanship in athletic contests and behavior outside the lines of competition. In fact, ESPN produces a show called "Outside the Lines" that discusses these very issues.

In the first half of this chapter we will examine the various laws and regulations that sport information specialists and journalists should be aware of in order to successfully perform their duties. Once the legal and regulatory framework has been examined, we will take a look at what the ethical obligations should be of the sports journalist and the communication professional. Where can the journalist look for guidance when there is an ethical dilemma? Fortunately for sport communication students and professionals there is plenty of guidance in this area from professional organizations and also from media companies. Sports information directors (SIDs) can look to the College Sports Information Directors of American (CoSIDA) for suggestions in the form of a code of ethics (see also Chapter 4). The common components of an ethical code will then be further examined.

LAW AND MEDIA RELATIONS

While you don't need a law degree to be in sport communication, it is a good idea to have a basic understanding of some of the specific federal statutes that loom large in the coverage of sports. A reporter may experience some sleepless nights if there has not been some exposure to certain prohibitions of the publishing of personal or private information.

The First Amendment of the U.S. Constitution is most often cited as extremely important with regard to members of the media and communication industries. In part, the First Amendment says: "Congress shall make no law . . . abridging the freedom of speech, or of the press . . ."

So why did the framers of this amendment include this very explicit protection in the Bill of Rights? The founding fathers studied history and, in particular, English history. They had all operated under the thumb of the British monarchy before the Declaration of Independence and the Revolution. James Madison, for example, knew that there was a tax on periodicals in England. He also knew that the monarchy had refused to introduce printing presses to the colonies and that there was an aggressive enforcement of the criminal law of seditious libel (Carter, Dee, & Zuckman, 2006). Newspaper printers and editors were controlled by the power to tax, they were controlled by the power of the English government to license publications, and they were further controlled by the seditious libel laws that punished even the printing of truth.

Truth was *not* a defense under the laws of that time, because it was argued that the King was "justice" and it was necessary for the people to have a high opinion of the King. Truth in fact aggravated the offense and endangered the public peace (Brandt, 1965). Any criticism was tantamount to treason. The printing press was thought by some as a dangerous invention to be used as a weapon by enemies of the state (Cohen & Varat, 1997) Hundreds were convicted under the seditious libel laws during the 1500s and early 1600s; in some cases the Star Chamber was the forum for these prosecutions. John Twyn was hanged, drawn, and quartered because he had the temerity to say that the crown was accountable to the people (Cohen & Varat, 1997).

With this background in mind, Madison and the other leaders of this new government recognized that a free press could act as a further check on a powerful government. Just as government had been divided into three branches and further diluted by granting very broad powers to state governments, it was also necessary to equip the people with the power to criticize their government. The press functioned as a source of information for the electorate. True democracy needs information. The press is in the very important (and powerful) position of supplying the citizenry with this information.

In today's world, if an owner of a Major League Baseball team wants the local taxpayer to shoulder the cost of a new stadium, the press has the job of informing that taxpayer what the benefit will be to the owner and what the benefit and burden will be to the taxpayer. In many of these cases, the baseball owner has the support of the local government. The job of the sports reporter or the reporter that covers local politics is to present the taxpayer with information that may be relevant the next time that taxpayer goes to vote for those politicians that support this public stadium subsidy to the baseball team owner. Is there information that would lead the local populace to believe that this decision is good for most people, or just a very privileged few?

Certainly Madison did not know anything about baseball or professional sports for that matter, but he did understand that if local politicians had the power to license the press or could censure their publications, the citizens would lose their ability to receive valuable information about how government is functioning and what interest groups are exerting influence over public officials. Only a truly independent media can provide this service.

The rights granted to the press in the First Amendment have been debated and massaged since this amendment was ratified along with the other nine on December 15, 1791. Many states wrote similar "freedom of the press" clauses into their constitutions. The passage of the Fourteenth Amendment and a subsequent landmark Supreme Court decision established that this freedom and the other freedoms in the First Amendment are checks on state governments, too (*Gitlow v NY*, 1925). The marketplace of ideas coupled with every citizen's power of thought is the best way to keep voters informed; a free press encourages this trade in ideas from a diverse group of people (Brandt, 1965). Courts also must be able to protect the acquisition of information by the press. Citizens need accurate information in order to understand the issues they have been asked to vote upon (Powe, 1991).

Laws and regulations that effect sport communication professionals the most can be broadly broken down into two categories that will be further discussed: legal issues and access to information.

LEGAL ISSUES IN SPORT COMMUNICATION

While most colleges and universities have a team of lawyers as well as compliance officers that a sports information specialist can go to for help, an SID can't rely solely on others because they must act quickly and capably due to the immediacy of news. A basic understanding of some of the more common laws and regulations that members of the sport communication industry will deal with on a regular basis is essential.

Defamation

The First Amendment's protections are an important foundation to our public discourse but our system of laws and court decisions also protect citizens, both public and private, from over-reaching by the press in the form of state defamation laws. Defamation falls under tort law; a tort is a civil wrong, other than breach of contract, for which the complainant may be compensated by damages or protected by an injunction against a defendant (Garner, 2009). Defamation can take two forms—*slander* or *libel*. Slander is the use of the spoken word to injure reputation. Libel is the written form of defamation. To defame someone, you must diminish their self-esteem, take away from the respect they are held in the community, damage the goodwill they may have acquired, or insert a lack of confidence into their reputation among the members of the community where the statements have been published.

Sports communication and journalism students don't need to go to law school to have an understanding of this area of the law. However, this area is important enough that some study is necessary to prevent problems in the future. Dissemination of information will be your business. Hopefully, careful review of this information before anything is published will become a habit. This careful review applies to emails and Twitter posts as much as feature-length magazine articles or news releases. As it is noted below, a libelous statement just needs to be "published" to one person to meet one of the requirements of defamation.

Defamation statutes are mostly civil in nature, but there are some states where you can also commit criminal libel. The most famous of the defamation cases as they relate to the First Amendment and the press, is the U.S. Supreme Court case of *NY Times v Sullivan* (1964). Sullivan was Mr. L.B. Sullivan, the city of Montgomery's (AL) Commissioner in charge of the police and fire department. Sullivan claimed he had been libeled by an ad in *The New York (NY) Times*. He sued for damages and won a large judgment in two state courts in Alabama. *The NY Times* appealed to the U.S. Supreme Court, which decided in favor of *The NY Times* and the press.

This case outlined what a plaintiff must prove in order to secure a defamation judgment against the press. However, the court limits this standard to cases where a public figure was the plaintiff. Was there actual malice involved in the publication of the story? In other words, *should* the newspaper, editor, or writer have known that the story was false or, *did they know* that the story was false? Was there a reckless disregard for the truth? In analyzing these questions, the court will ask if there were good faith journalistic judgments made in deciding to publish this story (Feinman, 2006).

Debate about public issues should be robust and uninhibited when it comes to the criticism of public officials (Barron & Dienes, 2005). Four years after the *NY Times v Sullivan* case, the Supreme Court also included an athletic director (AD) in the definition of a "public figure." Wally Butts, the AD at the University of Georgia, sued *The Saturday Evening Post* magazine for libel (*Curtis Publishing Co. v Butts*, 1967). Because the AD at a major university like Georgia had inserted himself intentionally into a position that had a great amount of public interest, he would not be given the same protection that a private individual would when seeking redress for defamatory statements. However, the court did rule in Butts' favor. They held that the *Post* had departed from normal investigative standards of journalism, the magazine had inflicted harm upon Butts in their story, elementary precautions in preparing the story had not been taken, and the reliability of the primary source was called into serious question by trial testimony (*Curtis Publishing Co. v Butts*).

Later, Supreme Court decisions as well as these two just discussed have held that a public official or public figure voluntarily enters into the hurly burly of criticism that is the life in the media's eye. A private individual that has been thrust into a temporary position of public awareness will be given greater protection (*Gertz v Robert Welch*, 1974; *Time, Inc. v Firestone*, 1976). The private individual is more vulnerable to defamation and thus more deserving of relief (*Gertz v Robert Welch*, 1974).

The basic elements of *defamation* are

- a statement has been made,
- that statement was heard or published to at least one other person, and
- the plaintiff was identified in the statement (Carter et al., 2006).

Publication implies that others were intended to hear. A private conversation between two people is not libel. The defamer also must be the one that publishes the statement. The law does not consider it libel if the plaintiff published the statement (Carter). Truth is a defense in a libel action. There is also an absolute privilege of debate in a legislative forum; legislators must be permitted to vigorously debate issues without fear of defamation lawsuits (Carter). Those participating in judicial proceedings and members of government involved in executive or administrative session also receive similar protection. If you have been assigned by your editor to cover one of these proceedings, you will be protected by a qualified privilege. If your report is fair and accurate you will fall within the protections of this privilege (Carter).

A well-known defamation lawsuit in the sports arena was brought in state court by a member of the Oklahoma football team who claimed he was defamed by an article in *True Magazine* (*Fawcett Publications, Inc. v Morris*, 1962). The article was titled "The Pill That Can Kill Sports" and the writer alleged that the Oklahoma football team was using amphetamines. The court found that the entire team had been libeled because each individual was subject to public ridicule. The court also found that even though the player was not specifically named in the article, each member was defamed.

This case is important for future sports journalists to consider. Many articles will be written that cover subjects involving behavior off the field or court of play. An experienced editor can help in this area, but in the modern era of blogs, tweets, and the constant updates of websites each journalist better have a clear handle on the words used in a published story. Also, the reach and permanence of the internet can exacerbate the defamation. The useful life of the daily paper is much shorter than a story on the web.

As has been noted in the two Supreme Court cases just detailed, the press will be protected when they have behaved in a reasonable manner, particularly when the story they are covering revolves around an individual deemed a public figure. However, courts do not like shoddy reporting or assumptions not based on solid facts. The First Amendment and freedom of the press don't grant "the publisher of a newspaper . . . special immunity from the application of general laws. He has no special privilege to invade the rights and liberties of others" (*Curtis Publishing Co. v Butts*, 1967, p. 150).

Right to Privacy and Right to Publicity

Consistent with the protections against defamation, we also enjoy a right to privacy that is recognized in common law, constitutional law, or statutory law in each state in the US. Part of the freedom that we have been promised by the founding fathers is the right to remain free from unnecessary intrusion into our private lives by the government. The right to publicity was an additional method to protect our right to privacy as well as a way to establish a property right in our name, picture, and likeness.

Privacy concerns can be found in the First Amendment, the Third Amendment, the Fourth Amendment, and the Fifth Amendment. Justice Louis Brandeis and his law partner, Samuel Warren, wrote a pioneering article aptly titled "Right to Privacy" for a law journal in the early 1900s that was cited by judges for many years thereafter. Brandeis described this right in his dissenting opinion in the *Olmstead* case as the "right of every citizen to be left alone by their government" (Mabunda & Mikula, 1999, p. 505).

Coaches should be made aware by their sports information specialists of what can and cannot be publicly revealed with regard to a student-athlete's academic, medi-cal, and personal information. (Courtesy of WVU Sports Communications)

A string of Supreme Court cases in the 1960's and 70's have outlined a zone of privacy around the individual. The Privacy Protection Act was passed in 1974 and this provides citizens with protection regarding data collected by the government. A citizen has the right to challenge information or correct inaccurate information that the governmental agencies collect. Under this act you also have a right to inspect personal records main-tained by any governmental agency. You also have a zone of privacy surrounding your credit records after the passing of the Fair Credit Reporting Act of 1970.

The right to privacy and to be shielded from the intrusiveness of the press merged into the right to publicity and to prevent unauthorized business use of your likeness, your name, and your picture. A New York statute provided for a right to privacy in 1903 as well as penalties for unauthorized use of a citizen's name, portrait, picture, or likeness for advertising or any other commercial purposes. A New Jersey judge held that a man's likeness and name were his property, thus it was his decision how to use both (Yu, 2007). A pharmaceutical company had put Thomas Edison's likeness on a medi-cine bottle without his permission.

With the invention of new media like radio, TV, and sound recordings in the early and middle 1900s, celebrity became a manufactured commercial value. Entertainers and athletes were in great demand to lend the celebrity of their name, likeness, picture, or voice to the promotion and marketing of companies and products. Like the right to privacy, this right to publicity is recognized in every state, although how it is defined is different. Many states also recognize the publicity right as descendible to the heirs of the celebrity's estate.

The company CKX paid the estate of Elvis Presley $100 million for an 85% share of the rights to his image and likeness (Yu). A year later, the same company paid Muham-mad Ali $50 million for an 80% share of his name and likeness (Yu). There are many rationales offered for this right. Everyone is entitled to the fruits of their labor. You should be able to prevent others from "free-riding" on your reputation and likeness. There is an economic incentive to create, to achieve, and be successful in order to be able to profit off of your image.

These arguments all assume that everyone that is a celebrity is "successful." We have many cases today where celebrity is achieved without any measure of accomplishment . . . other than being able to acquire "15 minutes of fame." In sports, the desire to acquire celebrity-sized endorsements has led to any number of cases of attention-grabbing behavior that have nothing to do with winning games or demonstrating the value of teamwork or sportsmanship.

Intellectual Property, Copyright, and Trademarks

This area of the law is designed to protect the creation of fixed forms of expression or inventions by their creators. Copyrights, patents, and trademarks all fall under this definition of intellectual property. A sportswriter who creates a screenplay, one who writes a book, or produces an investigative piece for a national magazine receives copyright protection for his or her work. The well-known logo of NBC, depicting a multi-colored peacock, receives trademark protection under the Lanham Trademark Act of 1946. The innovative shoe design of the latest NIKE football cleats can be patented by filing the proper paperwork with the Patent and Trademark Office. If the patent is approved, NIKE will receive protection for a certain number of years as to the exclusive manufacture of this shoe. It is important to note that NIKE owns this particular patent, not the designer that works for NIKE in that department.

The foundation for future federal legislation in this area of intellectual property can be found in the U.S. Constitution. Article I, Section 8, Clause 8 states: "Congress shall have the power to . . . promote the Progress of Science and useful Arts, by securing for limited Times to Authors and Inventors the exclusive Right to their respective Writings and Discoveries."

The U.S. Constitution was signed in 1787 and soon thereafter the Copyright Law of 1790 was passed by Congress. This law granted authors the exclusive right to reprint and sell their works for 14 years. Fines were included for those that copied original works without permission. The intent of the legal protection for these works was to motivate the creation of works of art, literature, and music as well as inventions that can be put to commercial use. The author, musician, playwright, or inventor would be given a special reward for a limited period of time and after that time lapsed, the public would have access to the use of this work or invention unencumbered by patent or copyright law.

The law was also intended to preserve a publisher's incentive to disseminate copy-

Subject Matter of Copyright
Literary works
Musical works, words
Dramatic works, music
Pantaomimes—choreographed works
Pictoral, graphic, and sculptured works
Motion pictures
Sound recordings (Subject matter, 2005)

righted works as well as a manufacturer's incentive to contract for an exclusive right to produce an inventor's latest creation (Johnston, 2008). For a work to be copyrighted, it must be an original work and be fixed in a tangible medium of expression ("Subject matter," 2005). The owner of the copyright has the right to produce the work, to distribute copies of the work, to display the work, and to perform the work created. Current law extends copyright protection for the life of the author, plus 70 years after the author's death ("Durations of copyright," 2005). Copyright protection is *not* extended to news reporting, comment, research, or any other educational uses of the copyrighted work; these exceptions are called "fair use" ("Limitations," 2005).

Trademark protection was a direct result of technological improvements in transportation and communication. Business transactions were no longer face-to-face matters. Individuals and businesses needed a system to identify products and businesses. Consumers needed to be able to have confidence in the products they were purchasing (McManis, 2009). The Lanham Trademark Act was passed in 1946 to help consumers identify a business and to identify products produced by that business. In order for a mark to receive protection that mark must be in use in the flow of commerce and the mark must be distinctive. A trademark is a valuable asset of any business and can be a symbol of goodwill to consumers (McManis).

In the field of sports there are many examples of trademarks—the team name Yankees and the distinctive NY you see on baseball hats are one example. The name of the newspaper the *New York Times* with its distinctive typeset is a trademark representing many years in the newspaper business. College or university names, their team nicknames, and their logos all can be trademarked and licensed for sale. The NIKE swoosh is a trademarked symbol of the sporting goods company based in Beaverton, Oregon.

Texas Tech University, a member of the Big 12 Conference, had to sue a local business that had made unlicensed use of merchandise with Texas Tech trademarks. The university had licensed its mark to companies selling pens, book ends, knit caps, coffee mugs, flip flops, and a host of other merchandise. The court found that the marks that the local business was using clearly belonged to the university and that the business was making commercial use of the distinctive nickname, colors, and logos of the university and its athletic teams (*Texas Tech v Spiegelberg*, 2006). The court also protected nicknames and phrases unique to Texas Tech—"Red Raiders," "Wreck'em Texas Tech," and "Raiderland."

Like Texas Tech, many of the owners of these trademarked goods aggressively protect them from counterfeiting. The NFL wrote to several local businesses in the New Orleans area asking them to stop selling T-shirts that combined the Saints fleur-di-lis logo with the distinctive expression "Who Dat," which became popular in reference to the New Orleans Saints in previous seasons (Sayre, 2010).

Several government agencies are involved in the discovery and prosecution of those that traffic in counterfeit goods. They also have the power to seize items that have not complied with U.S. trademark law ("Destruction," 2009). Agents from the Immigration and Customs Enforcement (ICE) agency seized $197,000 worth of counterfeit basketball jerseys, T-shirts, hats, and other merchandise from local merchants at the Dallas NBA All Star weekend in February 2010 ("ICE seizes," 2010). ICE also seized more than $430,000 worth of counterfeit goods during the days and weeks leading up to the 2010 NFL Super Bowl in Miami ("ICE's operation," 2010).

Due to a flood of cases like this involving the importation of "knockoffs" manufactured overseas, the Trademark Counterfeiting Act was passed in 1984. Congress established criminal penalties including substantial fines for repeat offenders as well as large fines for corporations caught in violation ("Recovery," 2009). Injunctive relief can be sought and in the most egregious cases attorney's fees and treble damages can be granted by the court.

The National Intellectual Property Rights Coordination Center is a key weapon in managing the many organizations that protect the creators of intellectual property in the United States ("National Intellectual," 2010). Federal agencies like the FBI, the Department of State, Homeland Security, and the Department of Justice combined with private groups like the International Intellectual Property Institute and the International Intellectual Property Alliance to attempt to devise strategies together to combat this problem.

Copyright law has evolved over the years due to advances made in technology. Motion pictures were granted copyright protection by the Copyright Act Amendment of 1912. Sound recordings were specifically covered in 1971 and broadcasters of TV content were protected in 1976 from the unauthorized use of their signal. The 1976 Act was a direct result of lobbying from the National Association of Broadcasters after two different court cases had been decided in favor of cable television operators.

The Digital Performance Right in Sound Recordings Act of 1995 was an attempt to protect the copying of original music. Advances in digital recording technology and peer-to-peer sharing of files have put a huge dent in sales of music CDs. Record labels, recording artists, songwriters, and music publishers were all lobbying Congress to do something (Lincoff, 2009). The Digital Millenium Copyright Act of 1998 prohibited the removal of locks on copyrighted works as well as the sale of anti-circumvention devices. Internet service providers were also protected from infringement liability on behalf of third parties. Copyright protection was extended to all parts of a website; computer programs, HTML code, sounds, designs, video text, and computer programs.

The Sonny Bono Copyright Term Extension Act of 1998 extended copyright protection for creative works 20 more years. The World Trade Organization has become involved in enforcing copyrights and trademark law. They have a dispute resolution mechanism when an infringement complaint has been brought. There have been a series of worldwide conventions attempting to standardize intellectual property law around the globe. Great progress has been made, but there are also still some significant problems in this area for owners of intellectual property.

The move from analog transmission to digital, the ease with which copies of music and video can be now be made, as well as the explosion of the use of the internet around the world has increased the frequency of copyright complaints coming from creators of music, broadcasters, and the motion picture industry. Google has drawn the attention of copyright owners and regulators around the world regarding the aggregation of previously published literary works.

A Chinese author sued Google, Inc., for the unauthorized publishing of her book extracts online (Chao, 2009). A French court sided with a publisher in a recent suit filed by La Martiniere against Google that was very similar to the Chinese author's suit (Chao). Google has also been negotiating with the Authors Guild and the American Association of Publishers to scan a very large number of books and publish them to a Google Digital Library (Kang, 2009). A settlement was renegotiated after the original deal had drawn the attention of the Department of Justice as well as a few of Google's competitors, most notably Amazon and Microsoft (Kang).

The books that have been included in this latest settlement are from Great Britain, Canada, the US, and Australia. France and Germany were not happy with the first settlement; their copyright laws are even more protective than those in the United States. The EU has also publicly funded their own book digitization project called Europeana; they want to digitize four million volumes (Googlemania, 2009).

Rupert Murdoch and Microsoft have been in discussions to put all of the News Corporation content up on a Microsoft site for a fee and ban Google and other aggregators from using their content without paying for that use (Murdoch, 2009).

Google argues that being included in their search engine is good for business for these newspapers, their writers, other media companies, and book authors. Google also says that they will gladly take down any content if asked to do so by the owner or creator. Sun Jingwei, the lawyer for the aforementioned Chinese author, thinks that Google's position is unreasonable. "You should settle the issue first and then scan and upload the books, not committing infringement first" (Kang, 2009).

Sun has an ally in the Irish rock star Bono. He has called for tougher controls to prevent the unauthorized use of intellectual property over the internet (Bono, 2010). Bono pointed out in an op-ed piece in the *New York Times* the damage that has been done to the music industry and newspapers around the world because of the ease of the sharing of files. He also predicted that the movie industry will soon face the same fate as creators of music and literary copyrights because the technology of file sharing will rapidly improve to the point of allowing quick downloads of entire movies (Bono).

Access to Information

Federal and state laws, the rules of regulatory agencies, and institutional policies can both assist and derail attempts by sport journalist to acquire information and for sports information specialists to control the release of information. The following are some of the most common types of laws, regulations, and policies relating to access of information for sports information and communication personnel.

FREEDOM OF INFORMATION ACT

The Freedom of Information Act (FOIA) was passed in 1966 by Congress and signed into law by President Lyndon B. Johnson. FOIA has since been amended a few times

It is important for those in sport communication to understand the various laws in place with regard to access of information. (Courtesy of Dan Mendlik/Cleveland Indians)

based on historical circumstances and also technological advances in the storage and communication of information online. There was an amendment in 1974 in response to some of the abuses that occurred in the Nixon Administration during the Watergate scandal. FOIA was amended in 1996 in response to the recognition that the US was becoming a nation of computer databases and email, not a nation of paper file cabinets and surface mail. This amendment established that computer databases were records that could be included as the subject of FOIA requests. In 2002, in response to the 9/11 attacks, some protections were implemented to prevent FOIA requests by foreign agents. President Barack Obama released an "Open Government Plan" in December of 2009 that requires agencies to publish information in a timely manner and also make it easily accessible to the public in the form of an easy-to-use website. The order has guidelines for those agencies that have backlogs to reduce them in a timely manner (O'Keefe, 2009).

The purpose of FOIA, as expressed by President Bill Clinton when he signed into law one of the FOIA amendments, was to firmly recognize that we are a "country . . . founded on democratic principles of openness and accountability" (Woolley & Peters, 1996). Currently all federal agencies must maintain a webpage that outlines FOIA guidelines for that agency. For example, if you log onto the website for the Federal Communications Commission, you will find a short explanation of the Freedom of Information Act, what files are available at the FCC without a FOIA request, how you can submit a FOIA request, what is available at the FCC under FOIA, what is not available, how much the FOIA request will cost, and many other guidelines to help those seeking information (FCC, 2010).

Indiana's FOI statute expresses the purpose for this legislation in its opening section:

Sec. 1. "A fundamental philosophy of the American constitutional form of representative government is that government is the servant of the people and not their master. Accordingly, it is the public policy of the state that all persons are entitled to full and complete information regarding the affairs of government and the official acts of those who represent them." ("Public policy," 2006, p. 162).

Arizona's FOI statute states that "[p]ublic records and other matters in the custody of any officer shall be open to inspection by any person at all times during office hours." (Inspection, 2001)

Connecticut provides that "[e]xcept as otherwise provided by any federal law or state statute, all records maintained or kept on file by any public agency . . . shall be public records and every person shall have the right to inspect such records promptly." (Access, 2000)

These freedom of information statutes at both the federal and state level have been invaluable to the reporter looking for information about government actions and information about public officials. FOI statutes have also helped the sports reporter gather information relative to the actions of athletic officials at state institutions. However, FOI statutes are expensive policies to maintain. There have been tremendous backlogs to comply with these requests, many requests made seem to have no useful purpose, and there is a lack of resources at many federal and state agencies to comply with these requests in a timely manner (McMasters, 2009).

Florida State University was involved in a FOI request in 2009 regarding ongoing NCAA Enforcement proceedings that concerned 61 of their student-athletes and a few athletic department employees. The school had been penalized by the NCAA for academic fraud relative to an online music class and improper help from staff members. A Florida state court judge issued a decision that ordered copies of Florida State documents relative to their appeal of NCAA sanctions turned over to *The Associated Press* and other members of the media. The NCAA challenged this ruling but the Florida appellate court sided with the trial judge (Kaczor, October 1, 2009). The NCAA argument was that secrecy was necessary for their enforcement process, that the documents were created by a private organization (NCAA), and that the fees paid to join the NCAA were actually paid by the Florida State Foundation, a private entity. Both state courts ruled that these documents were public records and needed to be released immediately. They said that if the NCAA rationale were accepted, the "state's public access laws would be emasculated" (Kaczor, August 21, 2009).

GOVERNMENT IN SUNSHINE ACT

The Government in Sunshine Act, passed in 1976, mandates that government agencies open up their meetings to the public. The public must be given notice of when and where meetings will be held as well as what will be covered at these meetings. Except in rare cases, a transcript of the meeting must be made available to the public as well. Exceptions to this open meeting requirement can be made if defense issues are being discussed, personnel matters, criminal matters, conversations of a personal nature regarding members of the agency, or any conversations relative to ongoing legal proceedings

("Public information," 2007). When meetings are closed, these decisions are also subject to judicial review by the federal district courts.

All states have some form of FOIA and Sunshine Laws. The purpose of these state laws is the same as the federal purpose—to allow citizens to know what their elected officials are doing. These statutes permit citizens and the press to attend meetings and to request information from state and local legislatures and state agencies. All states have started to provide information online. In fact, as part of "Sunshine Week," a movement sponsored by *The Associated Press* and other media organizations, states were rated as to the ability to find information online about government. Texas was ranked number one for access in 2009, followed by New Jersey and Kentucky. The bottom three states for lack of transparency online were South Dakota at 48, Wyoming at 49, and Mississippi in last ("Sunshine weekly," 2009).

As an example of specific state legislation in this area, Colorado passed an Open Records Act and an Open Meetings Law. Both of these pieces of legislation would fall under the heading of Sunshine Laws. Their purpose is to assure that the workings of government are open to view by the public and that the public is fully informed on the important issues of the day. "It is declared to be the public policy of this state that all public records shall be open for inspection . . ." ("Legislative declaration," 2001). Any Colorado citizen can ask to inspect and copy those records that fall within this statute. The Open Meetings Law declares that it is "matter of statewide concern and the policy of this state that the formation of public policy is public business and may not be conducted in secret" ("Declaration," 2001). Notice must be given when and where these meetings of public interest will be conducted.

There are exceptions to information requests as well as exceptions to open meetings in the various 50 states. There are some fairly consistent clauses that often will permit state agencies to deny access to information or to meetings. States do not like to disclose personal information of their citizens; phone numbers, home addresses, and social security numbers are usually not going to be disclosed. Meetings surrounding criminal prosecutions or investigations, meetings or information housed on databases relative to personnel decisions, or discussions or meetings surrounding preparation for legal proceedings will usually not be given to the public. Confidential records, trade secrets, or financial information that are either personal or can be used to trade in the open market are usually exempt from disclosure requirements under these statutes. Personal medical history is usually not released to the public. Many of these states also have penalties to discourage the release of private information to the public.

State sunshine laws have been used by many enterprising sports reporters to gather information about state sponsored and/or funded athletic programs. Private organizations like professional sports teams and private universities don't have these requirements that state taxpayer funded universities do. But when an NFL team is asking for the taxpayer to fund the building of a new stadium or improvements to an old one, there are many meetings and related information where the taxpayer and the well-prepared reporter will be granted access. Knowledge of your state's laws in this area is

REGULATIONS

Federal agencies will draw up regulations to implement legislation. These regulations will have the full backing of the federal government. One example is the regulations to implement Title IX. The Department of Education drew up regulations that must be followed by schools when funding male and female sports teams. Those that work for high school and college athletic departments must stay on top of these regulations when making decisions related to squad size, funding and the addition or subtracting of men's and women's sports teams.

The Federal Communication Commission (FCC) also issues regulations governing who can own media companies. If you own a newspaper can you also own a local TV station or a radio station? Many of the FCC regulations can have a significant impact on sports television programming around the country.

Governing bodies in college sports like the NCAA, NJCAA, and the NAIA have rules and regulations for their respective member schools. These relate to recruiting, eligibility, academic performance, squad size, length of sport seasons and number of team's needed to qualify for each association.

These regulations don't have the force of law but there are enforcement penalties and compliance issues that can cost teams and players eligibility. Also, major violations can be a reason to suspend or fire coaches or athletic department personnel. Sports information specialists have a set of rules governing their behavior too including the release of recruiting information to the media.

important. Also, with the continued pressure from First Amendment groups as well as other voters' rights groups that favor "open government," information will continue to become more available online.

FERPA AND HIPPA

These two acronyms are nothing to be afraid of for the aspiring sports communication professional. A quick understanding of what is in these two pieces of federal legislation will help in the information process and also keep you out of hot water with your boss and an angry plaintiff looking to sue you for invasion of privacy.

FERPA stands for Federal Educational Right to Privacy Act and is commonly referred to as the Buckley Amendment. ("Family," 2010) The law was passed in 1974 and its major purpose is to protect students from the disclosure of statute defined private records to any individual or group not given permission to view those records. Private information includes grades, standardized test results, disciplinary actions, and records from the school health office. Directory information can be released without the consent of the parents and this information includes many facts and figures that are of interest to sports reporters. The height and weight of the student can be released. Sports statistics and records of participation in other extracurricular activities can be released. A student's date of birth, place of birth, and major field of study can also be released without permission.

FERPA also permits private information to be released to colleges where that student has applied for admission, to teachers and academicians for legitimate educational reasons, to authorized representatives of the local, state, and federal governments, as well as those conducting legitimate educational studies. If information is released to researchers, biographical information must be deleted. Parents are also given the right to inspect all records that the school keeps on file pertaining to their child under the age of 18. Eighteen-year olds have full access and now become the person to whom the records are released; at universities and colleges, parents don't have the right to inspect or receive a copy of student records unless this permission is specifically given by the student (Alexander & Alexander, 2003).

A note to those covering high school and college athletics regarding the application of this statute; be careful that the school is not hiding behind FERPA in responding to your questions. FERPA does not prevent the release of ANY information. Chris Herring wrote about this very issue in the *Wall Street Journal*. "Some critics say a number of schools are deliberately misreading the Family Educational Rights and Privacy Act in order to keep scandals and other unflattering news from hitting the media." (Herring, 2009) The shielding of grades, test scores and financial aid records is not disputed, but student conduct issues and enrollment status are areas where reporters can push for the disclosure of information. (Herring)

HIPAA operates like FERPA but protects private information held by health care providers and insurance companies; this information relates to the health of the individual, not academics. The Health Insurance Portability and Accountability Act became law in 1996. The Act permits the disclosure of information necessary for a patient's care but also protects the privacy of the patient in relation to unnecessary disclosure of private health information. The act protects electronic, written, and oral information as well as permitting the patient a right of inspection and correction. Health records held at elementary and secondary schools are actually considered "educational records" and therefore fall under the protection of FERPA (Health information, 2010).

These laws are must reading for the sports information director who is in the business of providing information to the public about college students. Sports reporters also must be careful how they report on academic and health information when covering high school and college athletes. In the overwhelming number of cases the disclosure of an injury suffered during the course of a game or practice will not be a violation of these two federal statutes. In many cases, the college athlete has signed a waiver that permits disclosure of this type of "injury" information to reporters (Conrad, 2006). However, if a university sports information director posts on a website that one of the star football players is out for the season because he has HIV-AIDs or the local sports reporter writes a newspaper article about the highly recruited basketball player at the local high school that is being treated for drug addiction and depression; these disclosures of very personal and private information will be treated differently. Where does this information come from? Who authorized disclosure? Was that authorization made by an adult or a 17-year-old minor? Are we talking about a high school student, college student, or professional athlete?

STUDENT-ATHLETE RIGHT TO KNOW ACT

The Student-Athlete Right-to-Know Act was signed into law by President George H.W. Bush in 1990. The bill was the brainchild of two former NBA players that were serving in the U.S. Congress at the time of passage; Bill Bradley, a Senator from New Jersey, and Tom McMillen, a member of the House from Maryland (Berry & Wong, 1993). The bill publishes the graduation rates of college athletes receiving athletic-related financial aid for all NCAA Division I, II, and III institutions, separating out the rates by race, sport, and sex, too. The NCAA requires this information to be given to all athletes before they sign their commitment letters to the school as well as being disclosed to the guidance counselors of high schools around the country.

The intent of this legislation is to give accurate academic performance information to parents and athletes that are being recruited by NCAA schools. Recruited athletes can see what percentage of students at a particular school graduate and then compare that percentage to scholarship athletes, scholarship athletes in their sport, and also scholarship athletes of a particular ethnicity or sex.

The NCAA also releases three different reports on member schools each year. These reports reveal the Academic Progress Rate (APR) for each school, the graduation success rate (GSR) for each Division I school, and the academic success rate (ASR) for each Division II school (NCAA academic reform, n.d.). The GSR and the ASR are both barometers of how schools have performed in the classroom and don't bring with them penalties for schools that have not met a benchmark established by the NCAA. These two rates are opportunities for those schools that have outperformed their rivals to trumpet these results in their media guides, alumni magazines, and websites.

Sports information directors at all Division I and Division II programs will be very aware of the publishing of this information by the NCAA. Sports reporters that cover college athletics will also generate a story or two about the performance of a particular team at the local school and its impressive or less than impressive score under this NCAA report. Columnists and reporters that work for national news organizations also generate stories when these reports are published by the NCAA. Trends are discussed in those stories and there is usually commentary around reforms that have been recently proposed by coaches, faculty, and concerned groups like the Knight Commission.

The APR is different from the GSR and ASR in that it actually carries with it penalties for underperformance (NCAA academic reform). The APR takes into account eligibility of athletes, the school's retention rate of their players, and also the graduation rates of each team. Schools can lose a scholarship in a particular sport, be banned from postseason play, have their practice time restricted, or even face department-wide sanctions for continued underperformance (NCAA academic reform).

ETHICS AND MEDIA RELATIONS

Each student has been influenced by many common factors that contribute to the values they will take with them into the field of sports communications. Influences include parents and family members, religious beliefs, school teachers, and the prevailing cultural values of the student's immediate geographical environment. In addition, once students enter the work force, they will be influenced by the values of their supervisors, colleagues, and professional associations. Editors, journalists, and broadcasters all have very specific published ethical guidelines.

Is your company for profit? Are you funded by the state? Are you a non-profit like a PBS station? Do you work for a newspaper? A television network? An online website? A radio station? Were you raised in a household where the press is the enemy of the state? Did you have an elementary school civics teacher that thought the freedom of the press was God's gift to mankind? Do you have an editor that is from the school of Machiavelli? Get the story by whatever means necessary! Do you work in China where the laws for dissemination of information are much different than the laws of the United States? Does this present a legal as well as ethical dilemma for you as a journalist?

Are Ethics Important?

A very practical answer to the above question is that, of course ethics are important. And if you don't know journalistic ethics or the professional values that your company holds dear, you can get yourself fired. On a purely business level, the public does care about ethics. If your newspaper, radio station, or television network is perceived by the public as unethical, it can damage the company's reputation. Low ratings or a drop in subscriptions means budget cuts, which means job cuts, so the very health of the enterprise of sports communication does depend in some way on your ethics and whether your operation is perceived as an ethical actor. Philip Meyer, a journalism professor at the University of North Carolina at Chapel Hill puts this another way. "Without clear standards, journalism can't be trusted. If it can't be trusted, it won't be influential. If there is no influence, there is nothing to monetize" (Meyer, 2009).

Another important consideration is the journalist's role in evaluating and commenting on the ethics of a sport organization, player, coach, or owner. The adage of the glass house and those that throw stones comes to mind. If you have been assigned to cover a story on the use of performance enhancing drugs in baseball, would your story carry less weight in the community if you are perceived as a cheater yourself?

The ethics of journalists and other communication professionals are also important because of the tremendous responsibility the First Amendment places on the press and those that speak and write for a living. Communication professionals are granted wide latitude to publish and broadcast because of the role a free press plays in our democracy. The freedom to provide robust debate, wide-ranging opinion from various sources, and criticism of those in power hopefully come with a sense of responsibility that members of the media are accurate, truthful, have done their homework, have no conflicts of interest, and have reflected on the possible ramifications about what is about to be published or broadcast. Language is powerful and words matter. Words can wound and those wounds can fester (Carter, 1996).

Lastly, an ethical professional life will carry with it a greater sense of respect for what you do and why you do it (Merrill, 1997). Providing information to the public is a great service. The satisfaction that this service is accomplished with the highest ideals in mind will provide you with a reason to work long hours and look forward to arriving on the job each day.

Ethical Codes

Many professional communication and journalism organizations and companies have their own codes of ethics. The American Society of Journalists and Authors, the American Society of Newspaper Editors, and the Society of Professional Journalists all have their own code of ethics. The *BBC*, the *New York Times*, the *Associated Press*, the *Washington Post*, and *Al Jazeera* to name just a few, have also composed a code of ethics for their respective company's newsgathering professionals. The Sports Information Directors of College and University Athletic Departments in the US have a professional organization called CoSIDA, which publishes an ethics code.

There are also many "think tanks" that offer free advice to the media in the form of ethical guidelines. Accuracy in Media, the Center for Media and Public Affairs, the First Amendment Center, the Freedom Forum, and Fairness and Accuracy in Reporting (FAIR) all weigh in from time to time to report how the media rate in relation to their ethical practices. The Department of Justice has an Office of Information and Privacy that deals with the administration of the Freedom of Information Act as well as the Privacy Act. Federal government employees also have their own Ethics in Government Act as well as the Public Officials Integrity Act that will check illegal or unethical impulses.

There are many journals that publish regular commentary on ethics—*Journal of Mass Media Ethics*, *Public Integrity*, *Journal of Ethics*, *Journal of Moral Philosophy*, and *Online Journal of Ethics* all provide great discussions about real issues journalists and communications professionals must wrestle with in their practice.

Ethical Issues in Sport Communication

When examining the various commentaries and codes on ethics, there are a few themes that are consistently discussed. These themes are not only relevant for sport communication professionals, but for everyone involved in mass media.

TRUTH

Don't write, publish, or broadcast anything that you know is not true. The First Amendment of the U.S. Constitution, coupled with many Supreme Court interpretations, grants the press wide latitude in the performance of their public function to inform citizens. How could the media possibly be executing this function if they are lying to the public in what they are writing, publishing, or broadcasting? Truth also relates to photos. Two examples of less than "truthful" images of sports personalities involved the airbrushing out of body art in separate pictures taken of Allen Iverson, the NBA star, and Danica Patrick, the well known race car driver. Iverson's photo was taken for the NBA magazine *Inside Stuff* in 1998. Patrick's tattoo of an American flag was airbrushed out of a photo shoot for *Sports Illustrated*. As a general rule of thumb, if photographers and publishers want to change or alter what is in a photo, they should choose another photo.

Honesty is one of the basic foundations of the modern world. Our laws and values are based on the ability to believe in public institutions, individuals, and private companies. Criminality and unethical conduct is associated with dishonesty. Without honesty, our ability to make contracts, to educate, to inform, and to govern breaks down at every turn. In *The Book of Virtues*, William Bennett says that "to be honest is to be real, genuine, authentic and bona fide. To be dishonest is to be partly feigned, forged, fake, or fictitious" (Bennett, 1993, p. 599). Can there be a more damning criticism of a media story than it is feigned, forged, fake, or fictitious?

Truth must be a fundamental principal of every communication professional and every media company that is charged with informing the public. It must become a habit, exercised every day and a periodic reminder from managers and supervisors is always a good practice in the business of communication and information.

ACCURACY

Right behind truth is the ethical requirement to get the story right. This implies a minimal level of attention to detail and hard work. Stories must be proofread for grammar, spelling, fact checking, incorrect quotes, the wrong name associated with a published photo, incorrect statistics, etc. It makes good business sense to be accurate if you are selling news for a living, but it is also the right thing to do. Competition and cost cutting makes this job more difficult but the fact that a newsroom is understaffed is not an excuse for journalists to not do their homework. With all of the blogs on the internet, a journalist's mistake will show up quickly. You are not doing your organization or your profession any favors if this becomes a habit. Accuracy also calls for not omitting information that would be helpful to the understanding of a particular story by the reader; an accurate story is also *objective*.

A recent internal study conducted by the *New York Times* resulted in some suggestions to decrease the frequency of errors in its newsroom. The first recommendation was to establish a policy and enforce the policy that the writer is ultimately responsible for his/her story. The writer should double check facts with sources when necessary. A system of identifying patterns in inaccurate reporting was also a recommendation to be set up by the organization. Editors were also charged with a responsibility for accuracy when editing and also enforcing and encouraging basic fact checking on behalf of *ALL* of the writers they edit.

In order to be accurate, you also may have to do some quick work in the library or on the internet. What you know is important. In order to inform the public, as the communicator, you have to be informed. The ethic of a "lifetime learner" is a good one for a sports reporter or sports information specialist. You may have to know antitrust law, psychology, contract law, sociology, labor law, geography, history, physiology, chemistry—the list is endless (Neff, 1987).

In Tom Wicker's book *On Press*, he talks about the perils of competitive pressures to rush a story to print and the effect that this can have on the media's credibility.

When faulty stories do get into print, and turn out to be false or misleading or overstated, not only their unfortunate subjects are damaged; so is the general credibility of newspapers. Lack of credibility with readers, of course, is a profound limitation on the power of the press; if people don't believe what they read or hear or see, then the supposedly prodigious ability of the press to shape public opinion comes to little. To the extent that the press discredits itself with inaccuracies and wild swings, it ironically limits its own theoretically vast powers—and those inaccuracies and wild swings often are the direct result of competition. (Wicker, 1978)

The British Broadcasting Company groups accuracy and truth together in its editorial guidelines. "Accuracy is more important than speed and it is often more than a test of getting the facts right. We will weigh all relevant facts and information to get at the truth" (BBC editorial guidelines, 2010).

FAIRNESS

Another common ethical requirement is that the media respect the dignity of all who they cover or involve in their stories. Children that are the subjects of news stories can't be treated like adults. Their inability to defend themselves changes the dynamic and increases the ethical responsibilities of the press. High school athletes will be held to a different standard than professional athletes. Their age and connection with an educational institution will call for less exposure to public scrutiny. A 16-year-old athlete's ability to run, jump, and throw like an adult shouldn't obscure the fact that he or she is still a child.

Fairness dictates that the press will not use deception or coercion when covering a story. A reporter should not hide the fact they are covering a story for a news organization. There are rare exceptions to this requirement and the use of those exceptions will inform the public as to the values of that news organization or reporter.

Those who cover the sports landscape must also be aware of the legal presumption of innocence. An arrest is not a conviction. A charge or allegation is not a prison sentence. Competition, a deadline, or sensationalism should not pressure a reporter to forget this very important part of the U.S. Constitution. Get familiar with the term *allegedly* and use it often when reporting on such stories.

Another right to be respected is each citizen's right to privacy. In this age of Chad Ochocinco and Paris Hilton, it is difficult to believe that there are people that don't want fame, but there are plenty of people out there that have no desire to be featured in the headlines. Respect for an individual's desire to be left alone is important for every communication professional to remember.

ACCOUNTABILITY

Letters to the editor, opportunities to comment online, and the role of an ombudsman all speak to the ethical responsibility of the media to allow readers a chance to ask questions as well as air grievances. Most newspapers publish a "corrections" section of the paper when necessary to explain mistakes that were made in previous issues. "News magazine" television programs have used this practice as well, broadcasting letters to the

editor and corrections at the end of programs from time to time. These letters are sometimes highly critical of a particular show or an individual broadcaster. A news organization's website can be corrected much easier and quicker if a mistake is found. This type
of editing happens all the time on the web. In addition, writers or editors are able to
provide updates when a new set of facts needs to be reported to make the story more
complete. The public will take note of companies and reporters that don't hide from
mistakes; this is a habit that will build trust.

Broadcasters and writers regularly publish an email address where the public can respond to stories. This type of accountability not only is consistent with many codes of
ethics, it is also good business. An opportunity to respond can breed a very loyal following. This interactivity has become much easier with online news and the ease of email
communication. Many newspapers and other media outlets also offer online chats with
readers and their popular commentators. A topic may be introduced for that day's chat
but the commentator may also respond to other concerns brought up during the online
chat. The public must also feel that they are not being ignored by the media. Do the local media companies cover the entire community? This question will come up regularly
in sports coverage decisions by media companies. Why don't you cover more high school
games? You never have women's basketball box scores. Why not? How about soccer?
The public's source for information must attempt to answer these questions. Shared
norms and values will demonstrate trust and accountability, which is an ongoing process (Belmas & Vanacher, 2009).

Another codified ethical mandate under accountability is the right of an individual
to respond to a critical story. An athlete, coach, or owner that is the subject of a less
than flattering news story should be given the right to know what will be said about
them in the newspaper or on the nightly news. The subject should have the opportunity
to rebut facts or at the very least present their version of events.

CONFLICTS OF INTEREST AND INDEPENDENCE

The consumers of information expect to be delivered an accurate and truthful version
of a story but there is more to the building of a trusting relationship between the media
and the reader or listener. There must be an understanding that the reporter or the
broadcaster does not have a personal interest in the story. And if a personal interest is
unavoidable, the public deserves to be informed of what that interest is, so as to make
an independent assessment as to whether the conflict has upset the credibility or objectivity of the author's version of the facts. A perfect example of this is who employs the
color commentator or play-by-play announcer for an NBA or MLB game. Do they
work for the Lakers, the Yankees, or the Trailblazers, or for ESPN, TNT, or NBC? The
public should be told who pays them and also if each professional team has the right to
"approve" the announcers that receive their paycheck from a television network.

The New York Times Company Policy on Ethics in Journalism specifically prohibits
sports reporters from accepting "tickets, travel expenses, meals, gifts or other benefits
from teams or promoters" (The New York Times Company, 2005). There are many

other proscriptions under this code that warn against the appearance of a conflict for all reporters that work at the *New York Times*, including accepting speaking fees or meals from a source, or potential source, and also covering stories where a spouse, a family member, or a close personal friend is involved (The New York Times Company). The *Times* organization places a high value in this code on the goal of protecting the neutrality of its function as a news source.

News judgment, story lines, and how particular stories are chosen by editors can all come into question when readers, bloggers, and media critics analyze the relationship between a writer or media company and a particular story. Advertising considerations, competitive influences, personal relationships, personal financial interests, romantic entanglements, and pressures from ownership are just a few examples that help to break down trust in the media. In the Radio Television Digital News Association Code of Ethics, these conflicts are called "unprofessional connection[s]" (Code of ethics, 2010). Under the Australian Journalists Association's Ethical Code, these influences are discussed in three different sections; advertisement as well as commercial pressures are dissuaded. Conflicts, if unavoidable, must be disclosed. Furthermore, none of the aforementioned conflicts should impact a story's "accuracy, fairness or independence" (Australia, 2010). It is also important to note that the sport communication professional must steer clear of accepting "freebies" during the performance of their duties from those whom they must write or talk about. A free meal at a ball game is one thing; unlimited alcohol and expensive gifts go too far and should not be accepted.

Another measure of independence is the public's ability to separate the media's news stories from commentary and opinion pieces. These pieces have become a popular staple of the sports media. Can the media consumer easily see the difference? And will the sports media be as accurate in their opinion pieces with the use of facts as they are when writing a pure news story? When the press runs opinion pieces, will those opinion pieces favor those in power? Or will the everyday fan feel their voice is being heard? Is the public being informed or is a sports reporter that wants to write a biography burnishing the image of an athlete that is far less than what he seems? The proximity to athletes, coaches, and owners that the press enjoys is understood by the public. That understanding does not make the public blind to the abuses that this proximity can bring to a truthful, accurate, and independent accounting of the day's news.

SUMMARY

The media and sport industries around the world have grown by leaps and bounds in the last 25 years. The size of the newspaper has shrunk and many magazines have either folded or moved strictly to the internet, but think about how many television stations we have now. How many more websites do we have in just the last few years? How many more blogs? How many more TV networks devoted solely to sports?

This explosion of information comes with a legal responsibility to ensure the integrity of the process of information gathering and publishing. As we discovered in this chapter, the First Amendment grants the reporter and broadcaster freedoms but also ensures that the disseminators of information take into consideration the individual. Like the checks and balances discussed in our constitutional government, the law of defamation provides a check on an overly aggressive or an irresponsible press.

Our system of copyright, trademark, and patent law provides property rights to the sports biographer, the sportswriter that has a talent for creating feature length films, and the sports teams that want to market their names and logos to their fans. It will be interesting to see the development of copyright law concerning publication of material on the internet. The pervasiveness of the web and the accessibility of so much information online will provide challenges to those writers that want to be paid for their creativity. News organizations also must deal with this issue. Will newspapers permit Google or the Huffington Post to aggregate stories without compensation to the company or the writer?

A basic understanding of the law is important but so is a grounding in the ethical principals associated with the gathering and dissemination of information. Ethical precepts are the foundation of legal principals like defamation, freedom of the press, and the property protections surrounding intellectual work. The US legal system penalizes dishonesty both in its libel laws and in copyright protections for works like books and screenplays.

I am sure there are many students that look at the newspaper industry in the 21st century and wonder why we would we devote any words at all to the topic of ethics when "our" future livelihood is dying right before our eyes. There is a Machiavellian segment of the industry that feels editors and reporters are too concerned with ethics and not concerned enough with circulation, ratings, and sensational reporting that will draw eyeballs to the TV, the magazine page, or the newspaper. This concern with news and stories that draw advertising dollars has recently become much more acute.

The increased focus on advertising, profits, and searching for "new" pay models for newspapers, magazines, and websites does not need to interfere with the bonds of trust that always need to be strong between consumers of media and the disseminators of media. Those that consume news still need to be able to pursue and find accurate information to meet their daily needs of news, entertainment, politics, and information about current events. Trust truly has an economic value to newspaper companies like the *New York Times* and television networks like the BBC. There will always be pressure from the business/accounting side of media companies, particularly those companies that are traded on stock exchanges. Those in the media must also be vigilant that competition "between" reporters and different companies does not help to break down trust in the entire industry (e.g., MSNBC and Fox News).

Periodic ethics training can be effective to reinforce the values that have been codified in the various ethical guidelines touched on in this chapter. It is difficult to leave each ethical decision up to the individual. Refresher courses and direction from supervisors, professors, and professional organizations are all valuable methods to encourage communication professionals to engage in an aggressive and *ethical* pursuit of the truth as well as an *accurate* publishing of what was discovered.

DISCUSSION QUESTIONS

1. Of the federal statutes discussed in this chapter, which statutes should sports information directors be aware of and why? How can SIDs make use of this information to promote their school's academic and athletic profile? Why would the local beat reporter want to keep track of this information when covering the college football and basketball programs in his/her area?

2. We are seeing more and more consolidation in the media industry, with companies becoming bigger and bigger and controlling more and more of the media landscape. Is this good or bad for the citizen consumer? For the sport industry?

3. What ethical dilemmas would you have had as a *Sports Illustrated* reporter if you had been assigned to cover the Beijing Olympics in China?

4. You are a producer for ESPN and you have given an assignment to one of your new reporters. That reporter tells you that their religious beliefs prevent them from carrying out this particular assignment. What do you do?

5. ABC is owned by Disney. NBC is owned by General Electric. What ethical issues could this raise for journalists at these two television networks? Is this a regulatory issue for the Federal Communication Commission?

SUGGESTED EXERCISES

1. Read the *NY Times v Sullivan* Supreme Court case. Do you think the case was correctly decided? Should the press be held to a higher standard? What do you think of the dissenting opinion? Is your local college football coach a "public figure" under the *NY Times* standard? How about your local high school basketball star?

2. Read a few stories about how injuries have been reported in the newspaper or on a news/sports website that publishes this type of information. Also read stories about coaches that have taken leaves due to illness. How much information has been revealed? Do you think these federal regulations are much ado about nothing? Have we gone to far in protecting an athlete and coach's privacy?

3. Go to the websites for CoSIDA and the Association of Professional Journalists. Compare their ethical codes; note the similarities and the differences.

4. Read a recent post by the ESPN ombudsman. Note the issues that he raises that we have discussed in this chapter. Do you think the ESPN reporters and producers pay attention to him?

13

New and Emerging Technologies

Sports and the media have traveled a great distance since the newspaper and magazine days of the 1800s and the days of radio in the early 1900s. What would those that worked for the sports media in the early 1900s think of streaming video, blogs, Twitter, the iPhone, and Facebook? Would Ring Lardner send out better tweets than Grantland Rice? How do you think Edward R. Murrow's podcast would compare to listening to him live on the radio? Do you think Howard Cosell would have been a blogger? What type of Facebook page would Damon Runyon have had?

Every year, every month, sometimes every week there seems to be a new innovation that can make a sports journalist's job easier but at the same time make it easier for a professional athlete, organization, or sports information director to bypass the beat writer and talk directly to the sports fans of the world. Newspapers and sports departments are shrinking, yet advances in technology create new platforms for sport communication professionals. AOL has separated from Time-Warner and has launched many new sites that need content. One such site, Fanhouse, has hired many former newspaper sports reporters (Carr, 2009).

Forty years ago, a family watched ABC, NBC, CBS, or a local over-the-air station. Fast forward to today and the choices are absolutely endless once you turn on the television. Not only do we have many choices for our news and entertainment, but we have seen an explosion in sports networks. ESPN, ESPN 2, ESPNU, CBS College Sports, the Big Ten Network, and the list goes on. Each one of these networks hires sport communication professionals. Many of these networks have also expanded their presence on the web, which signals greater demand for competent communication professionals to provide stories, videos, and podcasts.

The dramatic growth of the Internet and the movement of advertising dollars from TV and newspapers to the web have caused a sea of change in these industries. People still appreciate good writing, good TV, and radio commentary; where they go to find that information has changed. In 1995, only 15% of adults in the US used the Internet (Mills, 2010). Pew Research has found that in 2009, 74% of this same group used the

Internet. The International Telecommunications Union announced that at the end of 2009, 1.9 billion people had access to a computer (ITU, 2010). We don't just connect to our favorite sports page via a laptop or PC. We now have smart phones that permit us to find an article by our favorite sports writer while riding on a bus to the office or we can watch that same writer who moonlights on ESPN or Comcast Sports Net in that same seat on that same smart phone. It has been estimated that by the year 2013, one billion people will be surfing the web with their smart phones and by 2020, that same device will be used more than any other to go on the Internet (Wilcox, 2009). To further show the importance of mobile phones, a recent survey indicated that almost 92% of Americans keep their mobile phone within three feet of them 24 hours a day (Filoux, 2010). Not only are more and more people canceling their newspaper subscriptions, they are also getting rid of their landline phones at home.

In the following sections, some of the latest innovations to emerge that have effected how sport media professionals and athletes alike communicate will be examined.

SOCIAL MEDIA

Twitter and Facebook

Twitter and Facebook have become more and more popular as social media sites with each passing day. These two websites are the top two queries on the Google search engine (Rao, 2009). By the end of 2009, Facebook had 350 million users worldwide and Twitter had passed the 60 million thresholds (Boulton, 2009). Twitter recorded its 10 billionth update in March of 2010 (Parr, 2010). Twitter was established in 2006 as a social media tool by Biz Stone, Evan Williams, and Jack Dorsey (Johnson, 2009). Communications sent out on Twitter use just 140 characters to send messages (tweets) over the Internet. Facebook was started at Harvard by a student as a way to meet fellow students on campus. That student, Mark Zuckerberg, expanded to other Ivy League campuses and now it is a widely popular social forum used by the young and old.

With this rapid rise in the use of social networks such as Twitter and Facebook, media companies have attempted to take advantage of this popularity and build audiences with these tools. Many sports journalists use Twitter and Facebook to post stories or informational updates and also to comment on games, athletes, teams, and other events during the course of the day. The goal is to drive traffic back to your media outlet. The communication arms of all of the major professional sports leagues also use both of these social networks to create interest in their games, teams, and leagues. College athletic departments use Facebook and Twitter to promote their programs; these platforms are used by the marketing and the sports information departments.

Players and coaches have also become active in using social media. The information they provide has created many news stories for reporters but has also created controversy because tweets and Facebook posts are viewed by some as an attempt to cut out the press. *USA Today*'s Thomas Emerick wrote that Twitter gives athletes even more power "to circumvent the modern sports writer [and to leave] journalists further out of the brawl" (Twitter, 2009). Some members of the Italian and English speaking media had announced that they would no longer report the updates that cyclist Lance Armstrong tweeted because the seven-time Tour de France winner had refused to speak directly to the press during the 2009 Tour of Italy (Taciturn Armstrong, 2009). Golfer Tiger Woods posted a message to the media and public on his own website months before he had a press conference or submitted to one-on-one interviews with the Golf Channel and ESPN in early 2010. Woods attempted to use his website to shape the public debate about the state of his marriage and the published reports about his personal life. Many in the press resented this tactic and even Arnold Palmer, one of the great golfers and sports icons of our time, thought Woods needed to get out and talk to the press (Ferguson, 2010).

Kevin Love, an NBA player for the Minnesota Timberwolves, tweeted that his coach Kevin McHale had been fired (Pucin, 2009). Unfortunately, the Timberwolves had not announced this new development. NFL wide receiver Chad Ochocinco announced on his Twitter feed during training camp that the Bengals' first-round draft choice, Andre Smith, had just signed. This was not accurate, so Smith's agent had to use Twitter to refute Ochocinco's tweet (Wilner, 2009). When he was with the San Diego Chargers, Jets defensive back Antonio Cromartie announced on Twitter that the food at training camp was not good; this drew a fine of $2,500 from management (Wilner). NBA star Shaquille O'Neal has used Twitter to criticize Orlando Magic head coach Stan van Gundy and center Dwight Howard, and to announce to the Twittersphere that he was going to attempt to visit President Barack Obama at the White House without an appointment. Needless to say, Shaq's tweets have become popular and as of February 2010 he had more than 2.8 million followers on Twitter.

The Big Ten Conference has a Facebook page as well as five different conference-sponsored Twitter feeds. One Twitter feed is for general conference news (@Conf). The Big Ten Championships feed (@BigTenChamps) provides detailed updates when the conference is holding its championships in each of its sports. Three of the conference communications professionals also update feeds that cover various sports. Scott Chipman, the Director of Communications, has detailed updates for football, men's basketball, and baseball (@BigTenScott). Latonya Sadler, the Associate Communications Director, provides regular tweets on men's basketball (@BigTenLaTonya). The Assistant Big Ten Communications Director, Valerie Todryk, provides regular coverage on Twitter of Big Ten volleyball, women's basketball, and baseball (@BigTenVal). The Big Ten's Facebook page offers game stories, video, pictures of recent Big Ten events, sport-specific announcements like the All-Big Ten women's basketball team, and regular plugs to visit the Big Ten website.

The NBA has a large Twitter and Facebook presence. The league has Twitter feeds from the WNBA and the Developmental League. Announcers like Ernie Johnson (@TurnerSportsEJ) and Kenny Smith (TheJetonTNT) have their own Twitter feeds and these are linked on the NBA website. Also linked to the NBA site are the Twitter feeds for many of the NBA's players. You can find Shaq on Twitter @THE_REAL_SHAQ, Steve Nash @the_real_nash, Paul Pierce @PaulPierce34, and Dwight Howard @DwightHoward. Facebook pages can be found for the NBA, the WNBA, the D League, the NBA Store, the NBA on ESPN RV Tour, and the NBA on TNT.

When reporters such as John Feinstein got into the industry, they weren't asked to blog, tweet, and write separate web stories in addition to writing the traditional game stories when covering athletic events. (Courtesy of George Mason Athletics/John Aronson)

Twitter and Facebook can be valuable resources if you need to find game times, if you just want to see how your favorite team did in their last game, or if you want to feel connected to your favorite player. These social media sites also can be used by the local beat writer to follow their assigned teams, to learn what a player is up to, as well as to find new story lines about the NBA. Leagues like the NBA and the Big Ten also post video highlights of recent games on their Facebook pages as well as references to their main website to try and encourage friends to log onto the website. Each of these leagues uses their website as a major promotion for e-commerce opportunities like the purchase of T-shirts, jerseys, game tickets, and hats.

Twitter and Facebook updates from a league like the Big Ten or the NBA are written by communications professionals hired by each of these leagues. The posting of these stories, video, audio, and pictures is a full-time job. Well-written tweets, interesting stories written by league-employed communications professionals, and eye-catching pictures and video all serve the marketing interests of these sports leagues. However, the communications professional is also writing and posting for the benefit of the large press contingent that "follows" these leagues, their players, owners, and coaches. An interesting tidbit tweeted by an NBA communications professional can generate two or three stories written by the local beat writer in Chicago, New Orleans, or Dallas. In many cases these same stories will be posted on several different Facebook pages and also mentioned in tweets by NBA sportswriters and fans. The NBA may not have directly monetized a particular event or story, but the reader has maintained interest in the product through well-written pieces by sports writers or by members of the NBA Communications office.

This goal of creating loyal readers is why Twitter and Facebook are used by newspapers like the *Washington Post*, *New York Times*, and *USA Today*. Each one of these media companies want to try and make their readers connect over content that their writers have produced. As one example, the *Washington Post* sports department has multiple feeds, written and updated by sportswriters and editors. Soccer Insider, Wizards Insider, and Redskins Insider are all *Washington Post*-produced Twitter feeds that help inform fans and readers but also hopefully drive readers to the paper's website or to the hard copy of the newspaper. The global editor for Reuters, Dean Wright, sees new media like Twitter and Facebook as a good thing. "If great storytellers use those platforms to display their knowledge, access, expertise and abilities, I think that is a marvelous advance" (Emerick, 2009).

Twitter has also proven to be invaluable as a tool for fantasy football participants. The ability to follow tweets from players all over the league, tweets from reporters that cover each team, as well as tweets from communications professionals of each team and the NFL all permit the fantasy football aficionado to marshal plenty of information every week to establish a competitive roster (DiFino, 2009). Twitter has also made the NFL Draft interactive. Agents, players, fans, teams, and the league were all tweeting and responding to each other during the 2009 NFL Draft. College coaches on Twitter were offering tweets of congratulations to players that were just drafted (Borelli, 2009). Several teams actually announced who they had drafted via Twitter, before NFL Commissioner Roger Goodell had made the announcement on TV.

A cottage industry has developed applications (apps) to use with Twitter. Twiddeo permits updates with video. Twitrank will find the current top 150 twitterers. Twitscan can be used to troll the twittersphere for key words. Likewise, twitscoop can be used to track certain events on Twitter. Twitpic is used to share pictures, Twi8r translates shorthand and the app Strawpoll can be used to create and answer polls on Twitter. A great app for writers is bit.ly, which shortens URLs so that you can post your story on your Twitter feed. And speaking of Twitterfeed, this app can be used to post your blog! There are other lists that are compiled that are very helpful to sport communication professionals. Listorious.com has compiled an NFL Players directory for Twitter, as well as a directory for NBA Players and MLB Players that tweet. During the Vancouver Olympics you could find a list of participants with Twitter accounts.

The recent growth in Twitter use has been fueled by overseas social media adopters. It will be interesting to see if Twitter continues to grow in the United States at the pace in which it did in 2009. There have been recent indications that much of the Twitter traffic comes from a very small percentage of users (Van Grove, 2010). Active Twitter users make up for those that sign up and then either don't tweet at all or very rarely send out messages to followers (Schonfeld, 2010). User retention rates have been weak, but Twitter has started to aggressively integrate Twitter feeds with popular publishers like the *New York Times* and *Sports Illustrated*. These moves could spur future growth in the US (Van Grove, 2010).

Interactivity

Innovation in the ability of a reader to talk back to a writer or commentator will present new challenges to the sport communication professionals but can also turn casual customers into loyal fans. The ability to respond to a provocative article immediately, to engage in an online chat, or to send out an immediate tweet or email in response to a comment or event on TV can have the potential to keep the attention of an audience and build a solid base of repeat customers. Advances in the manufacture of cable modems permit opportunities for interactivity for the television viewer as well. Cameras on cell phones can prove to be an invaluable resource to the sports reporter as Dan Steinberg reports later in this chapter. Followers of your tweets become your unpaid staff, equipped with video, sound, and photography-taking ability.

The sports reporter that is responsive to his or her audience or the talk radio host that smoothly engages with listeners can rapidly build audience share and, thus, revenue for the newspaper or radio station. The number of sports talk radio stations has more than doubled since 1998; there were 251 stations nationwide in 1998. In 2007, there were 557 that talked nothing but sports (Janssen, 2009). Cell phones make it easier for sports reporters to respond not only with talk radio as a guest being interviewed, but with all of the new apps, cell phones make it easy to send an email to a player or coach, write a short message in response to a story, or send a tweet letting your followers know about an interesting or provocative story you have just read. You can post a reaction to a story on your Facebook page as well. In Chapter 2, Wright Thompson, a senior writer for ESPN.com and *ESPN The Magazine*, talks about this new world and applauds his audience. He reports that he has been able to gather new story ideas from his readers and this type of feedback enables him to relate better to his readers.

The down side to building a loyal following is the fact that you are now 'on' 24/7. Reporters with beats to cover, games to watch, or stories to write need some time to perform their major duties. This also presents problems for those communications professionals with families. Are you always working now with all of these new apps? Can you afford to get some sleep? How to compensate those in the industry that are working these hours is also an issue. A popular story written by a reporter or the website manager for a league or pro team may generate hundreds of emails. You are now available 24/7 to your boss, but also to your followers (Twitter), readers (newspaper), friends (Facebook), and your family.

TECHNOLOGY UPGRADES

Digital and 3D Television

As mentioned in the introduction to this chapter, TV viewers used to have their pick of a few over-the-air stations to watch their sports, news, and other entertainment programs. Technology has improved so much in the area of television that there is an embarrassment of riches for the TV viewer. TV has moved from fuzzy black and white pictures to color to high definition pictures that make the viewing of sporting events truly remarkable.

Camera technology has also enhanced the viewing experience. Networks place cameras below ground level on the base path at baseball games, on the top of the backboard at basketball games, and on wires and cables that enable the cameras to move electronically above the field or court during soccer, football, and basketball games. During the recent Winter Olympics in Vancouver, it seemed that a camera was placed everywhere. The ability to follow a cross country skier over the entire course or the detail you can now witness when a skier is hurtling down the ski jump is revolutionary. This type of innovation enhances the viewer's experience, which in turn should produce more viewers and, thus, more advertising.

The 2010 NCAA men's basketball Final Four was broadcast not only in high definition (HD) but also in 3D. CBS used a separate announcing team, Dave Ryan and Steve Lappas, to supplement its regular Final Four telecast. The network sent this feed to about 100 3D theatres around the country (Heistand, 2010). ESPN and Fox have already produced 3D sports content for college football. Fox will have a 3D broadcast of the 2010 Major League Baseball All-Star game (Heistand). LG Electronics is the sponsor for the CBS 3D broadcast and this TV manufacturer will also be partnering in India with a company that will do a 3D broadcast of the Cricket IPL Final Four (LG, 2010).

The movement of television signals from analog to digital has created more room for more networks to be offered by satellite, telcos, and cable operators. There are now many networks offering HD and regular signals but the additional room created by digital transmission has opened up space for more sports networks to be offered. Cable operators like Comcast also have developed their own sports networks. Comcast has the Golf Channel and Versus, and Fox Sports Network offers Fox College Sports, Fox Soccer Channel, and Fox Sports en Espanol. Both Comcast Sports Net and Fox Sports Net also have regional stations in many of the larger media markets (see Table 13.1).

All of the major professional leagues now have their own networks—NBA TV, NHL TV, NFL Network, and NHL Network. There is also the Speed Channel, Golf Channel, Horse Racing Channel, World Fishing Network, and Tennis Channel. Two major NCAA Conferences also have television networks—the Big Ten Network and the Moun-

Table 1. Regional Sports Networks	
Owner	**Regional Stations**
Comcast Sports Net	Bay Area, California, Chicago, New England, New York, Northwest, Philadelphia, Southeast, Southwest, Washington
Fox Sports Net	Arizona, Carolinas, Detroit, Florida, Houston, Indiana, Kansas City, Midwest, North, Northwest, Ohio, Oklahoma, Pittsburgh, Rock Mountain, South, Southwest, Tennessee, West, Wisconsin

tain West Network. The Big Ten Conference partnered with Fox Sports for the creation of its channel and the Mountain West Conference partnered with Comcast. This Comcast partnership may have been an indication of the direction that the cable operator was heading; in 2009 Comcast announced that they were going to buy NBC.

Streaming Video

New developments in sending "video streams" across the Internet have the potential to enlarge the viewing of live sports events around the world. ESPN360, which is available on certain Internet service providers such as Comcast, streams a large number of events live such as college sports and professional soccer games. There are many other entities that have taken advantage of this technology. Many of the Vancouver Olympic events were streamed online, even though for some fans, not enough content was offered via live streaming video (Dreier, 2010). NBC owned the video rights to these Olympics and it reserved some of the most popular live footage for TV.

The NCAA men's basketball championship has been streamed online in a partnership with CBS and the NCAA since 2003. There have been experiments with charging a subscription fee for this service but CBS has made far more money with the streaming games being free to viewers and supported with ads either built into the video player or streamed during TV timeouts during games (Stream line, 2008). The Beijing Olympics was made available online via YouTube in countries that did not have an exclusive television deal with the International Olympic Committee. Wimbledon, the PGA Tournament, and the U.S. Open have all streamed their events over the Internet. During the PGA, if you wanted to follow a particular group around the golf course, while tethered to your computer, you could do that with a click of the mouse.

YouTube and Google recently signed a deal with the India Premier League (IPL) to stream all of the IPL's cricket matches over the Internet. The IPL predicts a potential worldwide audience of 500 million fans due to the agreement (Dasgupta, 2010). The IPL has also announced that it has secured eight major advertisers for these cricket streams; among them are HSBC, Coca-Cola, Samsung, and HP. The chair of the IPL, Lalit Modi, had this to say about this landmark media deal: "This changes the world of sports broadcasting. The Internet has changed the lives of everyone and this will do the same for sport" (Andrews, 2010). YouTube plans to have 20 user-selectable camera feeds as well as highlights, interviews with players and coaches, and pitch-side reports from match analysts.

Podcasts

A podcast is defined by Gil de Zúñiga, Veenstra, Vraga, and Shah (2010) as "a digital audio or video file that is episodic, downloadable, and program-driven, mainly with a host and/or theme; and convenient, usually via an automated feed with computer software" (p. 37). Podcasts have become a popular way to share information both in audio and video formats online. A study by the Pew Internet and American Life Project found that between 2006 and 2008, the use of podcasts by Internet users increased from 12% to 19% (Luft, 2008).

Sports networks such as ESPN and CBS produce quite a number of podcasts to support their TV and radio networks. CBS Sports produces podcasts surrounding fantasy baseball, basketball, and football. There are also separate news podcasts focusing on basketball, hockey, baseball, golf, and auto racing. CBS has a large network of radio stations they can pull content from as well as their CBS Sports operation at the broadcast and cable level. ESPN has a large contingent of on-air personalities to draw from in order to produce popular podcasts surrounding programs like Pardon the Interruption, Mike and Mike in the Morning, The Herd with Colin Cowherd, and Around the Horn. ESPN also makes great use of their many ESPN owned local radio stations to provide content to their podcasts. Bill Simmons, the popular ESPN Page 2 author, has a radio show that also is an ESPN podcast. Simmons is truly a product of this new media age, delivering content via blogs, podcasts, radio, TV, and a recent book on basketball. He also has more than a million followers on Twitter.

Newspapers also produce podcasts. Later in this chapter, *Washington Post* sports reporter Dan Steinberg talks about the podcasts he has helped produce with his fellow *Washington Post* editors and writers. On the *Post* website you can find podcasts on local colleges, the Redskins, the Wizards, the Capitals, the Nationals, and content produced about the many high school teams and athletes in the DC area.

Media outlets are not the only ones utilizing podcasts. College athletic departments, in conjunction with their communications professionals, produce podcasts; many of these can be accessed via Apple's iTunes. West Virginia University is one of the schools that produce podcasts and you can find content from press conferences conducted by coaches from football, men's and women's basketball, and other sports. George Mason University's podcast is called Patriot Vision and features news and highlights surrounding their many teams and coaches.

The 2010 Vancouver Winter Olympic Games produced more than 20 podcasts that were made available on the official 2010 Vancouver Games website. The podcasts were used to highlight the Olympic athletes and also to teach fans the rules of some of the sports. Video was used to show the excitement created by some of these events and the special talents needed to compete at the Olympic level. Paralympic events were also highlighted; there were podcasts on Para Nordic skiing and wheelchair curling. Fan and coach interviews were mixed in to provide different perspectives about these winter sports and athletes.

Smart Phones

As indicated in the introduction to this chapter, the rapid improvements in smart phone technology has fueled the purchase and use of these phones in many more ways than just the old-fashioned voice conversations with friends. Companies like Apple, Motorola, and Samsung produce phones that can be used for email, text messaging, as cameras, as video cameras, and as TVs to watch sports or other entertainment. Mobile phones are now being used in India as radios. In villages where there is no FM radio service, cricket fans can listen to games live or receive regular updates via text messaging (Bellman, 2009).

CBS Mobile and MobiTV won an award for their March Madness on Demand application for the iPhone and IPod Touch (CBS Mobile, 2009). College basketball fans with iPhones could watch all 63 games that CBS televised in the 2009 men's basketball tournament on their smart phones. This app sold for $4.99 and became the most popular paid app in Apple's iTunes App Store (CBS Mobile, 2009). CBS offered this feature again for the 2010 NCAA Tournament and added some new features. The app now works over WiFi and the 3G networks along with iPhones and IPod touch; CBS also raised the price to $9.99 (Molina, 2010).

Mobile phone usage continues to grow worldwide. The International Telecommunications Union reported that there were 4.6 billion mobile phone subscriptions in 2009 and of those phones more than 600 million had broadband subscriptions (ITU, 2010). In 2000, only 12% of the world had mobile phone subscriptions (Haddad, 2008). Much of this spectacular growth can be found in China and India.

A huge market for the purchase or free use of applications has sprung up around smart phones. Major League Soccer and the Premier League have apps that provide up-to-date stats for all of their teams and players. An application called "Live Cricket Score" provides cricket scores from around the globe. The media professional that covers an NFL team or the league has available an application called NFL Stats Lite, which contains a database of stats dating back to 1985. There are applications to enable you to download the rules of the sport you are covering. The South Africa organizing committee for the 2010 FIFA World Cup has devised an app with a history of the World Cup, a schedule of all of the games, pictures of teams and athletes, and stats for teams and individual players. The downloading of apps like these for smart phones has increased 1000% over the same time frame the previous year (Brizani, 2009).

Publishers of newspapers and magazines face a dilemma with these new smart phone applications. Do they charge for their content or do they offer their content free? A great majority of these apps are free but some come with an iTunes-like cost of $.99 to $4.99 per app. The *Wall Street Journal* originally did not charge for its content but after some research, decided that they should charge a fee for this application. Unfortunately for newspaper publishers, the news category is the second-largest category now for free apps (Filoux, 2009).

An improvement in the technology needed for indoor cell phone reception will also have an effect on the continued purchase and greater use of these smart phones. Verizon, Sprint, and T-Mobile have all come out with devices that amplify cell reception indoors (Patterson, 2009). Productivity may not increase at the office, but this innovation will increase cell phone use. These new products will also permit reporters covering sports indoors greater ability to access information online, easier access to Twitter in order to post in-game updates, and also the ability to reach a source immediately if a deadline is approaching. Smart phones will also change the way reporters check into hotels and board airplanes. The communications professionals that are traveling can now download a bar code that can act as a boarding pass, track travel expenses on a new application, and also check into hotels with their phone (Yu, 2010).

ePublications

Amazon, Barnes and Noble, Apple, Sony, and several other manufacturers have dived into the online book market and the production of E-readers. Products like Nook, Kindle, iPad, BeBook, and the Daily Reader have made this new technology a hot topic in the publishing world as well as IT circles. Google has proposed to digitize a huge number of books and has entered into negotiations with several large trade groups to help deliver this content to the purchaser of these new products. This issue has already been discussed in Chapter 12 as it relates to copyrights owned by authors and publishers. Avid readers love this new technology; authors and publishers are trying to figure out how to preserve the current market for books or enlarge it without a drastic reduction of their profits. eBook developments, like all technology in today's world, change in much shorter time increments than in the 20th century.

Stephen Covey, the author of the book "The 7 Habits of Successful People" has become the first author to negotiate and sign an agreement directly with one of the eBook producers. Covey bypassed his old publisher, Simon and Schuster, and went right to Amazon (Rich & Stone, 2009). Many sports writers and their agents will certainly take note of this development. These E-readers are constantly evolving but they provide a new opportunity for sports writers as well as the publishers themselves. If you can read a book on these E-Readers, you can certainly read a magazine or a newspaper.

The *New York Times* and *Sports Illustrated* have both developed applications that work well with the new iPad eReader. Bright color pictures with an ability to also add video and links to other apps like Twitter enhance the experience for the iPad reader that chooses to read newspapers and magazines on this device. It certainly is not too much of a stretch to imagine sports information directors at colleges designing media guides that can be accessed by owners of a Nook, iPad, or Kindle. Niche sports publications have also begun offering their content in varying ePublication formats, with Deep Blue Creative one of the leading providers of this conversion service. The key for the sport communication professional with ePublications, like any new technological advancement, is to remain ahead of the proverbial curve so that when consumer demand necessitates providing content a new format, the sport communication professional will be in a position to provide it.

The Cloud

Cloud computing has become a popular topic in the area of new technology. The "cloud" provides individuals and businesses with access to shared data centers for storage, platform technologies for business use, and also many business applications. Small media companies or popular bloggers can use the cloud to back up all of their data. They don't need to continually upgrade software, which saves time and money. Their email can be managed in the "clouds" and they would have access to word processing, spreadsheets, calendars, and presentation software anywhere they are located. Google, Zoho, IBM, AOL, Microsoft, and Mozy are just a few of the companies that are competing for customers that want to take advantage of the "cloud." Reporters and sports information directors that move from hotel to hotel during their sports seasons will be able to use the cloud to access files normally stored on their computers back at the office.

Cloud computing makes the process of putting together a local news organization or a niche media company cheaper. You don't need to hire a large IT staff nor do you have to spend a large part of your budget on expensive hardware. Companies such as Microsoft and Google can provide a startup media company with the infrastructure to get up and running quickly. These companies will also provide access to software upgrades that enables smaller companies to compete with large corporations.

Google offers calendars, Picasa for pictures, YouTube for video, Gmail, Google Voice, and Google Docs for the citizen journalist or a small startup that wants to compete in the communications industry for customers or eyeballs (Boulton, 2009). Microsoft's version offers SQL Server for storage, a full suite of Office products, Exchange for hosting email, Share Point for partners or employees to share data on a secure site, and Dynamics for customer resource management (Eaton, 2010). Cloud computing could become an option for the communications department of a US sports federation or the sports information department at a university looking to cut IT expenses.

ONE REPORTER'S USE OF NEW MEDIA

Washington Post sports reporter Dan Steinberg is a big believer in Twitter. Steinberg writes a blog for the *Post* as well as a Twitter feed that he updates regularly. You can find Steinberg on Twitter @DCSportsbog, you can read his blog regularly at the *Post*'s website (http://www.thewashingtonpost.com/dcsportsblog), or you can buy a newspaper! Steinberg discusses his thoughts about new media and how he uses technology in his job.

Dan Steinberg

Q: What new media do you use as a Washington Post sports reporter?

Steinberg: I have a Blackberry that would probably qualify as a smart phone. I have a Twitter feed (@DCSportsBog) I use and check regularly and I also have a Facebook page. I do podcasts from time to time, particularly about the Washington Redskins. I blog regularly and this blog is also picked up in the daily *Washington Post*.

Q: Which of these new media has had the most impact on the sports communication business?

Steinberg: For me Twitter has revolutionized our business. I am a follower of all of the Twitter feeds of any reporter that covers my beat. I also follow all the Twitter feeds of all of the athletes within my beat. Many of the posts from the athletes serve more as entertainment but from time to time there are posts that I will include in a story. I follow someone like Bob McKenzie, who covers the NHL for *The Sporting News*. People like Adam Schefter and Chris Mortensen cover the NFL for ESPN and I also follow them. The Washington Capitals' public relations people are on Twitter and I follow them. And I followed the Twitter feeds for all *The Washington Times*, *Washington Examiner*, and Comcast SportsNet reporters.

Q: What Twitter apps do you use?

Steinberg: I have a Twitter app called "UberTwitter" that refreshes my Twitter feed every 10 minutes. I receive updates of any new Tweets from those fellow Twitterers that I follow. I also have an app that is great for posting my own blog. It is called "bit.ly" and this app compresses my blog or any other story into the necessary characters that Twitter will allow on a tweet. Bit.ly also is a great way to track how many people actually read my stories, too.

Q: What is it about Twitter that has made this form of social media so valuable to those in your business?

Steinberg: For me, it is a great way to stay on top of what is going on with all of the sports teams and leagues that I cover. Since I work for the *Washington Post*, I cover the Washington Redskins, the Caps, the Wizards, and the Nationals. Each one of these teams has their own feed that is posted by their communications department. Many of the players on these teams have Twitter feeds and so I also follow their tweets. With all of this traffic on Twitter, I can react to a particular story right away, and post my blog immediately. The blog may be posted in the afternoon, which means that the newspaper readers may not see this new information until the next day. My blog will be posted to the *Washington Post* website first and I will attach this blog to a tweet soon thereafter. If my tweet is particularly interesting to those that follow me, the blog will fly around the Twittersphere and end up in many places. Other newspapers may pick up my story, a team that I cover may post a reaction to my story on their website, or a player may react to this tweet on their Twitter feed. A follower of my feed may have more followers than I do and may refer their followers to my story. As an example, Yahoo employs many bloggers and records millions of hits on its sports blogs. If one of these bloggers picks up my story, I will attract some new fans to my blog, my Twitter feed, as well as to my newspaper.

Q: Can you provide a few examples of how a tweet by someone you follow led to a story on your blog?

Steinberg: One great example occurred during a preseason game. Ladell Betts went out on the field with a jersey that spelled his name "Bettis" like the retired running back from the Pittsburgh Steelers. I was at the game in the press box and wanted to have one of the *Washington Post* photographers take a picture of his jersey for my blog. I could not reach the photographer, so I tweeted all of my followers on Twitter and asked someone to take a picture of the jersey and send the picture to me. I received about 20 tweets and many of the pictures were surprisingly good. One of the higher quality pictures was taken by someone who was watching the game on TV.

Another example of Twitter's impact was the Redskins signing Missouri quarterback Chase Daniel. Daniel was signed as an undrafted free agent by the Redskins and Daniel had his own Twitter feed. After Daniel signed with the Redskins, he tweeted this on his Twitter feed. I posted right away that Daniel had signed. Both Daniel and I were up and out on the Internet before the Redskins had announced that he had signed with them. This is a good example of a player making news with his tweet.

Q: Of the team's that you cover regularly in the Washington area, is there one team that has been innovative in the area of new media or new technology?

Steinberg: I think the Washington Capitals have done the best job in melding new media and old media to get their message out to their fans and reporters like me that cover the Caps. Their owner, Ted Leonsis, has a background in new media and new technology, so the leadership in this area comes from the top. Ted was a longtime executive with AOL and is on the cutting edge in this area compared to other owners in the NHL and owners from other professional sports leagues.

The Washington Capitals make good use of all social media. Leonsis has his own blog, "Ted's Take," that he regularly updates. The Caps' video department regularly posts material on its website as well as on their social media pages. They will record interviews with players and post these on Twitter and Facebook. There are also frequent video posts from practice. This is one big advantage that the in-house communications people have; they have much more access to their players and coaches than the working press does. This adds value to their website.

The Caps were also trendsetters in relation to bloggers. They gave bloggers much greater access than other teams did. They were permitted in the locker room, at practice, and in all of the spaces that the working-press was allowed. This helped to enlarge the Caps' fan base. Bloggers who abused the privilege would have their credentials revoked, but many in the blogosphere are serious about their work, so this was not a regular occurrence.

The communications office for the Caps will also monitor the blogosphere or Twitter posts to make certain there are no stories out there that are simply not true. It will immediately release something on its website or tweet a response that will knock down an inaccurate story.

Q: What type of things do you do with your podcasts?

Steinberg: I use the podcast to answer questions that have been posted to the Redskins Insider Twitter feed by followers. The Redskins' editor will compile about 15 to 25 of the best questions and I will answer those questions on the podcast. *The Washington Post* will then post this on its website where it can be accessed by our audience.

Newspapers are interested in the video business because of the advertising potential. You can post a short commercial at the front of these videos that will be viewed before you can see the content.

Q: What advice would you give students that want to venture into the sport communication field?

Steinberg: I really think you need to pay attention to everything going on around you in whatever field you have entered. If you are a sports reporter, watch TV and listen to sports talk radio. Know what others that cover your beat are doing. Keep an eye on the blogosphere. There is some very good writing out there and some of these blogs may give you an idea that can help you create a new story. Don't be afraid to say that you found out something from another reporter. I picked up a very good story line from watching John Riggins's appearance on Showtime. Riggins' quote about the Washing-

MITCHELL LAYTON PHOTOGRAPHY

Coach's CORNER

by Craig Esherick

A dwindling number of coaches continue to rely on telephone calls, written letters, and in-person visits as their primary means for communicating with recruits. They also rely on press conferences and news releases to communicate with the media and/or fans. But a growing contingent of coaches are beginning to expand their methods of communication, using text messaging, Twitter, personal websites, and whatever new technology emerges to communicate either indirectly or directly with recruits, media, and fans.

One recent trend that college coaches have employed is the use of Twitter, although not all employ the same strategies when posting tweets to their followers. Some coaches use Twitter primarily as a recruiting tool. Their audience is high school or junior college athletes and these athletes' parents. Other coaches use Twitter to present their followers with a different side of their personality. They want to humanize their public image by allowing followers to receive more insight into their personal life, such as discussing the latest books they've read, movies they've watched, or activities they've done with their families. Some coaches tweet information directed toward fans, such as providing updates on how successful that day's practice was. Others like to tweet motivational thoughts they may have used in a discussion with their players.

John Calipari has the most followers (@UKCoachCalipari) of any coach in the NCAA ranks. He had close to 1 million followers in early 2010. Coach Cal readily admits that this following is directly related to the basketball fans found in the state of Kentucky.

Pete Carroll, formerly the football coach at Southern California (USC), was very involved in the creation of his online persona. He hired a former walk-on who was a journalism student to build his online presence. Ben Malcomson managed the football site, posting videos and crafting Coach Carroll's presence there and on Twitter.

Twitter can be a valuable communication tool for a coach, but this platform is not for everyone. Some coaches may resent the time commitment needed for regular postings and others may feel that Twitter takes away from their ability to have some private thoughts. Twitter can also be considered an insincere way to craft a coach's image and just another way to sidestep the traditional media.

I would advise a coach and sports information director to discuss the use of social media. Some communication professionals may think that it is vital for their coach to use these tools. If an SID is able to explain the benefits—as well as the potential pitfalls—of using social media, a coach may be more apt to embrace its use. Done with a strategic plan, such as the one employed by Coach Carroll while at USC, these communication tools can be helpful to a coach's media relations and recruiting efforts.

ton Redskins and their owner was very newsworthy; the Redskins are the team that I cover. I make regular use of my DVR on my TV at home. If I could not watch a program live and I thought it had news potential, I just record it for viewing later.

SUMMARY

With all of the talk about the death of newspapers and good sports writing, it appears that new media and the constant advances in technology may actually enhance the market for the sports story teller. With more avenues to tell stories, the opportunity for a citizen journalist to break through and become a paid blogger for an aggregator like Yahoo, Fanhouse, or the Huffington Post is much greater now than it was a few years ago. This certainly presents pressures for the media to constantly produce interesting content. The reader has a greater number of places to search to find innovative, groundbreaking stories and so does the television viewer. With all of the new sports networks being created, there is a constant need for those skilled in talking about sports on the air as well as those who are good at producing this content.

It remains to be seen if this new media can create stories with the depth that magazines and newspapers can produce; a tweet is only 140 characters. It is also a continuous concern as to the reliability and the accountability of this new generation of communication. Is the information produced accurate, well sourced, and transparent? The old media still have to stand behind their stories and be accountable for inaccuracies and bad reporting. A member of the Twittersphere that has no connection to a media company does not bear the same responsibility for mistakes.

Athletes, coaches, sports information personnel, and organizations that regularly use social media have created both opportunities and obstacles for sport journalists. News has been created by many of these tweets but there is a concern that the media has been bypassed. Athletes and coaches should be careful, however, that they take these communication devices seriously. A well thought-out plan is always the best way to proceed.

The speed with which innovation takes place in the communications industry can be dizzying. Cisco has announced that they now have a router that can download data equal in size to all of the books in print at the Library of Congress in one second. That would qualify as fast. Innovation has caused the broadcast networks and their employees many sleepless nights; the newspaper industry has had their problems, too. Who is to say that the next new media invention will not create countless new jobs in the sport communication industry?

The key for today's students will be to constantly improve their communication skills while also understanding that the ability to engage and retain their audience will be important to market survival. A strategy of making use of Twitter with your daily reporting duties may be necessary to maintain and build an audience. Learning new skills relative to video may attract another group of readers to your website or blog. Just as those in the sport communication industry had to adjust to the emergence and popularity of radio and television, they have to be ready for emerging technology and be ready and willing to adapt. Predictions that the sky is falling have been heard before, but we are still here.

DISCUSSION QUESTIONS

1. After reading this chapter, what do you think of the future of newspapers? Do you read a newspaper? Where do you regularly look for information about your favorite sports teams or athletes?
2. Do you think social media have helped or hurt the newspaper business? Is social media more valuable as a marketing tool than a communication tool?
3. Will the eBook development help the publishing industry? Do you think more young people will want to read if books and other publications are made more available in electronic formats?
4. Do you think social media have encroached on the privacy of today's athletes and coaches? How about the privacy of the communication professional? Is it a good thing that some athletes are tweeting about their personal lives?

SUGGESTED EXERCISES

1. Go to the Facebook page of the local newspaper in your area. What types of things are they posting on the site? Compare the posts to the paper's website and the newspaper.
2. Join Twitter and become a follower of a team, an athlete, and a reporter that covers that team. How regularly does each tweet? Compare and contrast their tweets for news value, fan value, and commercial value.
3. Watch an athletic event streamed to your smart phone or your computer. Compare your viewing experience with that of watching the same type of event on TV. Do you think streaming is going to replace TV or is the TV experience so much more enjoyable that this will never happen?

References

2006 FIFA World Cup broadcast wider, longer and farther than ever before. (2007, February 6). *FIFA*. Retrieved from http://www.fifa.com/about fifa/marketingtv/news/newsid=111247.html

About MaxPreps. (2009). *MaxPreps.com*. Retrieved from http://www.maxpreps.com/FanPages/about us.mxp

Access to public records. (2000). Connecticut Freedom of Information Act. Title 1–210. *Connecticut general statutes annotated*. St. Paul, MN: West Group

Alexander, D., & Alexander, K. (2003). *The law of schools, students and teachers*. St. Paul, MN: Thomson West.

Amis, J., & Cornwell, T. B. (2005). *Global sport sponsorship*. New York: Berg.

Andreff, W. & Staudohar, P. (2000). The evolving European model of professional sports finance. *Journal of Sports Economics, 1*(3), 257–276.

Andrews, R. (2010, January 20). YouTube confirms live cricket deal. *paidContent:UK*. Retrieved from http://paidcontent.co.uk/article/419-you tube-confirms-live-cricket-deal-not-in-u.s.-big-ad-push/

Angst, F. (n.d.). *Job profile: Sports information director*. About.com. Retrieved from http://sportsca reers.about.com/od/careerpaths/a/SIDprofile.htm

Artz, L., & Kamalipour, Y. R. (2007). *The media globe: Trends in international mass media*. Lanham, MD: Rowman and Littlefield Publishers.

Australia—MPAA/AJA. (n.d.). *MediaWise*. Retrieved from http://www.mediawise.org.uk/dis play_page.php?id=291

Barnes, B., & Steele, E. (2008, April 11). Lagging online, TV stations get moving. *Detroit Free Press*. Retrieved from http://www.freepress.net/news /22321

Barron, J. A., & Dienes, T. C. (2005). *Constitutional law*. St. Paul, MN: Thomson West.

BBC editorial guidelines. (n.d.). *BBC*. Retrieved from http://www.bbc.co.uk/guidelines/editorial guidelines/edguide/

Beck, H. (2008, November 19). The real O'Neal puts his cyber foot down. *New York Times*. Retrieved from http://www.nytimes.com/2008/11/ 20/sports/basketball/20shaq.html?_r=2

Beijing Olympics opening ceremony: Over 2 billion viewers tune in. (2008, August 14). *Nielsen*. Retrieved from http://en-us.nielsen.com/main/ news/news_releases/2008/august/beijing_olym pics_opening

Bellman, E. (2009, November 22). *The Wall Street Journal*. Cellphone entertainment takes off in rural India. Retrieved from http://online.wsj .com/article/SB1000142405274870453390457 4545451866310232.html

Belmas, G., & Vanacher, B. (2009). Trust and the economics of news. *Journal of Mass Media Ethics, 24*(2/3), 110–126.

Belson, K. (2009, May 4). Universities cutting teams as they trim their budgets. *The New York Times*, p. D1. Retrieved from http://www.nytimes.com /2009/05/04/sports/04colleges.html?_r=1& ref=sports

Bennett, W. J. (1993). *The book of virtues: A treasure of great moral stories*. New York: Simon & Schuster Adult Publishing Group.

Berry, R. C., & Wong, G. M. (1993). Law and business of the sports industries, Vol. II (2nd ed.). Westport, CT: Greenwood Publishing Group, Inc.

Bialik, C. (2008, September 10). Counting Olympic watchers worldwide. *The Wall Street Journal*. Retrieved from http://blogs.wsj.com/numbersguy/ counting-olympics-watchers-world-wide-410/

Biyani, G. (2009, December 28). *Apple: App stores see record-breaking Christmas*. Retrieved from http://seekingalpha.com/article/179951-apple-app-stores-see-record-breaking-christmas-?source =article_1b_author

Blitz, R. (2009, November 13). Head of World Cup bid keeps job as new board set up. *Financial Times*. Retrieved from http://www.ft.com/cms/s /0/d9af8d3a-cff4-11de-a36d-00144feabdc0.html ?nclick_check=1

Bono net policing idea draws fire. (2010, January 4). *BBC News*. Retrieved from http://news.bbc.co .uk/2/hi/technology/8439200.stm

Borges, D. (2009, February 21). Conn-frontation. *New Haven Register*. Retrieved from http://em ekanadavandcorny.blogspot.com/2009/02/cal houn-erupts.html

Bornfield, S. (2009, January 22). Mediaology: Sportscasters get sent to the penalty box. *Las Vegas Review Journal*. Retrieved from http://www .lvrj.com/neon/38130509.html

Borrelli, R. (2009, April 28). Twitter makes the 2009 NFL Draft a sports holiday to remember [Web log message]. *New Media Strategies*. Retrieved from http://nms.com/blog/post/twitter-makes-the-2009-nfl-draft-a-sports-holiday-to-remember/

Boulton, C. (2009, December 30). *Google has big plans for Google Voice, Cloud Computing in 2010.* Retrieved from http://www.eweek.com/c/a/Cloud-Competing/Google-Has-Big-Plans-for-Google-Voice-Cloud-Computing-in-2010-552678/

Bozich, R. (2007, June 11). Courier-Journal reporter ejected from U of L game. *Louisville Courier-Journal.* Retrieved from http://www.courier-journal.com/apps/pbcs.dll/article?AID=2007706110450

Braine, T. (Producer). (1985). *The not-so-great moments in sports.* [Television Program]. United States: Home Box Office.

Brandt, I. (1965). *Bill of Rights.* New York: Bobbs Merrill.

Broadcasting. (1949, November 7). Retrieved from http://jeff560.tripod.com/70.html

Brown, D., & Bryant, J. (2007). Sports content on U.S. television. In A.A Raney & J. Bryant (Eds.), *Handbook of sports and media* (pp. 77–104). Mahwah, NJ: Lawrence Erlbaum.

Brown, G., & Morrison, M. (2008). *ESPN sports almanac.* New York: Ballantine Books.

Brown, M. (2008, December 9). Inside the numbers: Avg. salary of MLB players in 2008. *The Biz of Baseball.* Retrieved from: http://www.bizofbaseball.com/index.php?option=com_content&view=article&id=2679:inside-the-numbers-avg-salary-of-mlb-players-in-2008&catid=29:articles-a-opinion&Itemid=41

Bruscas, A. (2004, February 24). Going blog wild: Anyone with a computer and an opinion can launch a media startup. *Seattle Post-Intelligencer.* Retrieved from http://seattlepi.nwsource.com/othersports/161835_blog24.htm

Bryant, J., & Holt, A. M. (2006). A historical overview of sports and media in the United States. In A. A. Raney & J. Bryant (Eds.), *Handbook of sports and media* (pp. 21–44). Mahwah, NJ: Erlbaum.

Carr, D. (2009, August 17). AOL blossoms as print retreats. *The New York Times.* Retrieved from http://www.nytimes.com/2009/08/17/business/media/17carr.html

Carter, S. L. (1996). *Integrity.* New York: Harper Collins Publishers.

Carter, T. B., Dee, J. L., & Zuckman, H. L. (2006). *Mass communication law.* St. Paul, MN: Thomson West.

Cashman, R., & Hughes, A. (1999). *Staging the Olympics.* Sydney, Australia: University of New South Wales Press.

CBS Mobile and MobiTV win global college sports award for NCAA March Madness IPhone application. (2009, June 17). Retrieved from http://www.ncaa.org/wps/portal/home?WCM_GLOBAL_CONTEXT=/wps/wcm/connect/ncaa/NCAA/Media+and+Events/Press+Room/News+Release+Archive/2009/Announcements/20090617+CBS+Mobile+Rls

Chamberlin, A. (1990). Sports information. In J. B. Parks & B. R. K. Zanger (Eds.), *Sports and fitness management: Career strategies and professional content.* Champaign: Human Kinetics.

Chamberlin, B. F. (1995). *The law of public communication.* New York: Longman Publishers.

Chao, L. (2009, December 31). Chinese author is open to settling with Google. *The Wall Street Journal,* p. 9. Retrieved from http://online.wsj.com/article/SB10001424052748704876804574628001516120702.html

Code of ethics. (n.d.). The Radio Television Digital News Association. Retrieved from http://www.rtdna.org/pages/best-practices/ethics.php?g=36

Cohen, W., & Varat, J. D. (1997). *Constitutional law* (10th ed.). New York: The Foundation Press, Inc.

College Sports Information Directors of America (n.d.). *What is CoSIDA?* Retrieved from http://www.cosida.com/About/general.aspx

Colman, P. (2009, March 4). TV groups cope with leverage troubles. *TV Newsday.* Retrieved from http://www.tvnewsday.com/articles/2009/03/04/daily.4/

Comcast, Big Ten network near deal—sources. (2008, June 16). *Reuters.* Retrieved from http://www.reuters.com/article/rbssMediaDiversified/idUSN1629760620080616

Conover, D. (2006, December 15). *Invest or fail.* Retrieved from: http://conovermedia.blogspot.com

Conrad, M. (2006). *The business of sports.* Mahwah, NJ: Lawrence Erlbaum Associates.

Consoli, J. (2005, April 19). NBC, ESPN snap up NFL packages. *AdWeek.* Retrieved from http://www.allbusiness.com/marketing-advertising/4153921-1.html

Cook, D. (2008, October 28). Monitor shifts from print to web-based strategy. *Christian Science Monitor.* Retrieved from http://www.csmonitor.com/2008/1029/p25s01-usgn.html

Cowlishaw, T. (2000, February 13). Writers remember. *Dallas Morning News.* Retrieved from http://www.dallasnews.com/sharedcontent/dws/spt/football/cowboys/classic/webspecials/landry/landrywrite.htm

CTO for fan media network in East Bay. (2007). *TechGigger.* Retrieved from http://techgigger.com

/mt/archives/2007/06/cto_for_fan_med.html

Curtis Publishing Co. v Butts. (1967). 388 US 130. U.S. Supreme Court decision.

Dasgupta, P. M. (2010, March 10). *Google catches big ticket ads on its YouTube IPL pitch.* Retrieved from http://in.news.yahoo.com/241/20100310/1268/tsp-google-catches-big-ticket-ads-on-its.html

Dealing with sources. (1993). *The Annenberg/CPB Project* [Videotape]. South Burlington, VT.

Declaration of policy. (2001). Colorado Open Meetings Law. Title 24 Article 6-401. *Colorado revised statutes annotated.* St. Paul, MN: West Group

Deggans, E. (2000, April 27). Local TV eliminating some sports reports. *St. Petersburg Times.* Retrieved from http://www.sptimes.com/News/042700/Sports/Local_TV_eliminating_shtml

Deggans, E. (2009, February 3). Super Bowl oopsie: Final Nielsen numbers show Sunday game most watched in history, after all. *St. Petersburg Times.* Retrieved from http://blogs.tampabay.com/media/2009/02/post.html

Destruction of infringing articles. (2009). Trademarks—The Lanham Act of 1946. 15 USCA 118. *United States code annotated.* St. Paul, MN: Thomson West

Dodd, M. (2004, January 5). Recognizing 'I'm 14 years late,' Rose admits he bet on baseball. *USA Today.* Retrieved from http://www.usatoday.com/sports/baseball/2004-01-05-rose_x.htm

Dreier, T. (2010, March 12). Did NBC medal at online Olympic coverage? *Streaming Media.* Retrieved from http://www.streamingmedia.com/article.asp?id=11755

Duration of copyright: Works created on or after January 1, 1978. (2005). Copyrights 17 USCA 302. *United States code annotated* St. Paul, MN: Thomson West

Eaton, N. (2010, March 6). The Microsoft blog. *Seattle Post Intelligencer.* Retrieved from http://blog.seattlepi.com/microsoft/archives/196793.asp

Ebbets Field. (2001). *Baseball-statistics.com.* Retrieved from http://www.baseball-statistics.com/Ballparks/LA/Ebbetts.htm

Edwards, B. (2008, October 17). Jamal Crawford confronts reporter who wrote a false story about him. *Fanhouse.* Retrieved from http://nba.fanhouse.com/2008/10/17/jamal-crawford-confronts-reporter-who-wrote-a-false-story-about/

Eisenstock, A. (2001). *Sports talk: A journey inside the world of sports talk radio.* New York: Simon & Schuster.

Emerick, T. (2009, July 29). Twitter leaving sports reporters out in the cold. *USA Today.* Retrieved from http://www.usatoday.com/sports/2009-07-29-twitter-sports-writers_N.htm

Enriquez, J. (2002). Coverage of sports. In W. D. Sloan & L. M. Parcell (Eds), *American journalism: History, principles, practices.* Jefferson, NC: McFarland.

ESPN 360 and Nimbus Sports enter into multi-year rights agreement for Bangladesh cricket. (2009, December 21). Retrieved from http://sportsmedianews.com/12/espn360-com-and-nimbus-sport-enter-into-multi-year-rights-agreement-for-Bangladesh-cricket/

ESPN STAR Sports renews TV Deal with Cricket Australia. (2007, June 9). *SportBusiness.* Retrieved from http://www.sportbusiness.com/news/162518/espn-star-sports-renews-tv-deal-with-cricket-australia

Evans, R. (1973). *Jean Piaget, the man and his ideas.* New York: Dutton.

Fainaru-Wada's statement to the court. (2006, September 22). *San Francisco Chronicle,* A14.

Family educational and privacy rights. (2010). Family Educational Rights and Privacy Act of 1974. 20 USCA 1232g. *United States code annotated.* St. Paul, MN: Thomson West.

Farmer, S., & Johnson, G. (2008, August 22). Gene Upshaw, NFL players union leader, dead at 63. *Los Angeles Times.* Retrieved from http://articles.latimes.com/2008/aug/22/local/me-upshaw22

Fawcett Publications, Inc. v Morris. (1962). 377 P. 2d 42. Oklahoma state court decision.

FCC Freedom of Information Act. (n.d.). *Federal Communications Commission.* Retrieved from http://www.fcc.gov/foia

Feb. 19, 2009: A horrible day in Indiana sports. (2009, February 20). Retrieved from http://bleacherreport.com/articles/127138-a-horrible-day-to-be-an-indiana-fan

Feinman, J. M. (2006). *Law 101.* New York: Oxford University Press.

Fenton, B., & Blitz, R. (2009, November 13). Premier League papers over splits. *Financial Times.* Retrieved from http://www.ft.com/cms/s/0/4cdd8a42-cff4-11de-a36d-00144feabdc0.html

Ferguson, D. (2010, March 24). Arnold Palmer: Tiger Woods should 'open up'. *The Huffington Post.* Retrieved from http://www.huffingtonpost.com/2010/03/24/arnold-palmer-tiger-woods_n_511935.html

Feschuk, D. (2009, February 17). Bosh, NBA all a-Twitter over latest blogging fad. *Toronto Star.* Retrieved from http://www.thestar.com/Sports/NBA/article/588483

Filoux, F. (2009, November 9). *The IPhone is no media savior.* Retrieved from http://www.thebig

money.com/articles/0s-1s-and-s/2009/11/09/iphone-no-media-savior

Finder, C. (2002, July 18). The big picture: KDKA-TV alters sports approach. *Pittsburgh Post-Gazette*. Retrieved from http://www.post-gazette.com/sports/columnists/20020718thebig5.asp

Fixmer, A. (2008, September 5). Beijing attracted most viewers, Nielsen says. *Bloomberg News*. Retrieved from http://www.bloomberg.com/apps/news?pid=conewsstory&refer=conewstkr=62553Q%3AUS&sid=aBQhOOTmtmQ

Freedman, J. (2007). The fortunate 50. *Sports Illustrated*. Retrieved from http://sportsillustrated.cnn.com/more/specials/fortunate50/2007/

Friedman, T. (2005). *The world is flat*. New York: Farrar, Strous and Giroux.

Gantz, W., & Wenner, L. A. (1991). Men, women and sports: audience experiences and effects. *Journal of Broadcasting and Electronic Media*, *35*(2), 233–243.

Garner, B. (2009). *Black's law dictionary* St. Paul, MN: Thomson West.

George, B. (2008, July 23). Oklahoma State quarterback often passed over. *Dallas Morning News*. Retrieved from http://www.dallasnews.com/sharedcontent/dws/spt/colleges/osu/stories/072308 dnspobig12sider.42f1958.html

Germany 2006 in numbers. (2006, July 12). Retrieved from http://www.fifa.com/worldcup/archive/germany2006/news/newsid=29594.html

Gertz v Robert Welch. (1974) 418 US 323. U.S. Supreme Court decision.

Gibson, P. (2009). Examining the moral reasoning of the ethics of the advisor and the counselor. *Public Integrity*, *11*(2), 105–120.

Giersch, J. (2009). Lessons in ethics in American high schools. *Public Integrity*, *11*(3), 251–260.

Gietschier, S. (1994, April 11). Covering the bases. *The Sporting News*.

Gil de Zúñiga, H., Veenstra, A., Vraga, E., & Shah, D. (2010). Digital democracy: Reimagining pathways to political participation. *Journal of Information Technology & Politics*, *7*(1), 36–51.

Gitlow v NY. (1925) 268 US 652. U.S. Supreme Court decision.

Golden, C. (2008, May 6). Benson's production sunk long before his boat trip. *Austin* (TX) *American-Statesman*. Retrieved from http://www.statesman.com/opinion/content/sports/stories/other/05/06/0506golden.html

Goldfarb, Z. (2007, December 3). Can youth sports coverage pay off online? *Washington Post*, D1.

Golenbock, P. (1984). *Bums: An oral history of the Brooklyn Dodgers*. New York: Pocket Books.

Googlemania splits US and EU. (2009, September). *Inter-Media*, *37*(3).

Gorman, B. (2009, February 24). ESPN spending $1.1 billion for NFL rights, $300 million for MLB, $270 million for NASCAR. *Wall Street Journal*. Retrieved from http://tvbythenumbers.com/2009/02/24/espn-spending-11-billion-for-nfl-rights-300-million-for-mlb-270-million-for-nascar/13350

Green, D. (1991, October). Getting in on tape: What if you don't tell them? *FineLine: The Newsletter on Journalism Ethics*, *3*(9), pp. 1, 8.

Greppi, M. (2002, August 19). Time out for sports? Local stations debate how much coverage viewers really want. *New Orleans Times-Picayune*, p. 9.

Griffin, E. (1997). *A first look at communication theory*. New York: McGraw-Hill.

Haag, P. (1996). The 50,000-watt sports bar: Talk radio and the ethic of the fan. *The South Atlantic Quarterly*, *9*(2), 453–470.

Haddad, A. (2008, September 27). Increasing mobile cellular subscriptions throughout the developing world. *Media Global*. Retrieved from http://www.mediaglobal.org/article/2008-9-27/increasing-mobile-cellular-subscriptions-through out-the-developing-world

Halberstam, D. (1989). *The summer of '49*. New York: Avon.

Hamilton, A., Jay, J., & Madison, J. (1961). *The Federalist papers*. New York: The New American Library of World Literature. (This text taken from the originally published McLean edition of 1788).

Health information privacy. (n.d.). U.S. Department of Health & Human Services. Retrieved from http://www.hhs.gov/ocr/privacy/hipaa/faq/ferpa_and_hipaa/index.html

Heard, R. (1980). *Oklahoma vs. Texas: When football becomes war*. Austin, TX: Honey Hill Publishing.

Herberg, W. (1956). *The writings of Martin Buber*. New York: Meridian Books.

Herring, C. (2009, July 16). A privacy law that protects students, and colleges, too. *The Wall Street Journal*. Retrieved from http://online.wsj.com/article/SB124770187218048509.html

Hiestand, M. (2004a, January 30). Super Bowl hype: Part of the game. *USA Today*. Retrieved from http://www.med.sc.edu:1081/superbowl2004.htm

Hiestand, M. (2004b, August 19). 1984 TV ruling led to widening sweep of the college game. *USA Today*. Retrieved from http://www.usatoday.com/sports/columnist/hiestand-tv/2004-08-19-hiestand-college-football_x.htm

Hilmes, M. (1997). *Radio voices*. Minneapolis, MN: University of Minnesota Press.

Hirschorn, M. (2009, January-February). End times. *The Atlantic*. Retrieved from http://www.theatlantic.com/doc/200901/new-york-times

History of the *Sporting News*. (2009). *The Sporting News*. Retrieved from http://www.sportingnews.com/archives/history/1886a.html

Holtzclaw, M. (2007, August 29). Channel 3 dropping nightly sports news. *Hampton Roads Daily Press*. Retrieved from http://www.dailypress.com/news/dp-13341sy0aug29,0,5677004.story?coll=hr_tab01_layout

Hruby, P. (2005, January 19). All kidding a sideline. *Washington Times*. Retrieved from http://www.bonniebernstein.com/press/articles/washington times/washtimes_01_19_05_top.html

Hubbuch, B. (2009, March 10). Manuel talks Sanchez release. *New York Post*. Retrieved from http://blogs.nypost.com/sports/mets/

Hudson, D. L, Schultz, D., & Vile, J. R. (2009). *Encyclopedia of the First Amendment*. Washington, DC: CQ Press.

Humphrey, M. (2009, March 15). NASCAR hasn't 'jumped the shark,' but Jaws and friends better watch out. *Orlando Sentinel*. Retrieved from http://blogs.orlandosentinel.com/sports_nascar/2009/03/nascar-hasnt-jumped-the-shark-but-jaws-and-friends-better-watch-out.html

ICE's operation faux bowl results in seizure of more than $430,000 in counterfeit items. (2010, February 18). Retrieved from http://www.ice.gov/pi/nr/1002/100218miami.htm

ICE seizes $197,000 worth of counterfeit items during NBA All-Star 2010. (2010, February 15). Retrieved from http://www.ice.gov/pi/nr/1002/100215dallas.htm

Inside USA Basketball. (n.d.). Retrieved from http://usabasketball.com/inside.php?page=inside

James, M. (2008, July 26). NFL to stream Sunday-night football games online. *Los Angeles Times*. Retrieved from http://blog.modernfeed.com/?p=590

Janssen, S. (Ed.). (2008). *The world almanac 2008*. New York: Reader's Digest.

Johnson, S. (2009, June 5). How Twitter will change the way we live. *Time Magazine*. Retrieved from http://www.time.com/time/business/article/0,8599,1902604,00.html

Johnston, B. D. (2008). Rethinking copyright's treatment of new technology strategic obsolescence as a catalyst for interest groups. *NYU Annual Survey of American Law*, *64*(1).

Jones, A. (1991, June 13). The media business: The National Sports Daily closes with today's issue. *New York Times*. Retrieved from http://query.nytimes.com/gst/fullpage.html?res=9D0CE3DB1738F930A25755C0A967958260

Journalism and ethics integrity project. (1998). *Radio and Television News Directors Foundation*. Retrieved from http://www.rtnda.org/research/judg.shtml

Kaczor, B. (2009, August 21). Florida State NCAA appeal FOIA request. *The Miami Herald*. Retrieved from http://www.miamiherald.com/news/florida/AP/story/1196087.html

Kaczor, B. (2009, October 14). Court ruling-public records. *The Associated Press*. Retrieved from http://associatedpress.com/FOI/foi_101509a.htm

Kang, C. (2009, November 14). Google narrows book rights in revised settlement. *The Washington Post*. Retrieved from http://voices.washingtonpost.compostech2009/11googles_curbed

Keith, J. (1985). Tough public relations problems. In *NCAA public relations and promotional manual* (NCAA, Ed., p. 69). Mission, KS: The National Collegiate Athletic Association.

King, P. (2009, March 24). DirecTV deal is lockout insurance. *Sports Illustrated*. Retrieved from http://sportsillustrated.cnn.com/2009/writers/peter_king/03/24/meetings/index.html

King, P. (2008, May 2). Monday morning quarterback. *cnnsi.com*. Retrieved from http://www.cnnsi.com/2008/writers/peter_king/05/02/rankings/4.html

Kramer, S. (2008, July 28). 'Sporting News Today' publisher: New digital daily has 75,000 subs, aims for 250,000 before ad push. *paidContent.org*. Retrieved from http://paidcontent.org/entry/419-first-look-sporting-news-today/

LaRosa, J. (2009, February 16). No turning back: An interview with Billie Jean King. *tennis.com*. Retrieved from http://www.tennis.com/features/general/features.aspx?id=164732

Lee, J. (2009, October 2). Rio de Janeiro wins bid for 2016 Summer Olympics. *Vancouver Sun*. Retrieved from http://www.vancouversun.com/sports/2010wintergames/Olympics+Janeiro+wins+2016+Summer+Games/2059424/story.html

Legislative declaration. (2001). Colorado Open Records Act. Title 24 Article 72–201. *Colorado's revised statutes annotated*. St. Paul, MN: West Group

Lemire, J. (2009, March 2). Hoops on the sly. *Sports Illustrated*. Retrieved from http://vault.sportsillustrated.cnn.com/vault/article/magazine/MAG1152470/index.htm

LG Electronics 3D TV enters India market. (2010,

March 9). Retrieved from http://www.trading markets.com/news/stock-alert/lgepf_lg-electron ics-3d-tv-enters-india-market-832916.html

Lights out for GE's NBC, as ESPN/ABC take over NBA rights. (2001, December 17). *Sports Business Daily*. Retrieved from https://www.sportsbusi nessdaily.com/article/61784

Limitations on exclusive rights; fair use. (2005). Copyrights 17 USCA 107. *United States code annotated*. St. Paul, MN: Thomson West

Lincoff, B. (2009). Common sense, accommodation and sound policy for the digital music marketplace. *Journal of International Media and Entertainment Law, 2*(1), 1–64.

Lowry, T. (2008, November 7). University of Texas plans sports TV channel. *Business Week*. Retrieved from http://www.businessweek.com/bw daily/dnflash/content/nov2008/db2008117_998 978.htm

Luft, O. (2008, August 29). Podcasts' popularity surgest in US. *The Guardian*. Retrieved from http://www.guardian.co.uk/media/2008/aug/29 /podcasting.digitalmedia

Mabunda, L. M., & Mikula, M. (Eds.). (1999). *Great American court cases* Boston: The Gale Group.

Machiavelli, N. (2003). *The prince*. G. Bull, Trans. New York: Penguin Books.

Mack, C. (1950). *My 66 years in the big leagues*. Philadelphia: John C. Winston.

Maddex, R. (2006). *State Constitutions of the US*. Washington, DC: CQ Press.

Maneker, M. (2009, December 27). E-books spark battle inside the publishing industry. *The Washington Post*. Retrieved from http://www.washing ton.com/wp-dyn/content/article/2009/12/24 /AR2009122403326.html

Manion, J., Meringolo, J., & Oaks, R. (1991). *A research guide to Congress* (2nd ed.). Washington, DC: Legi-Slate, Inc.

Marbury v Madison. (1803). 5 US 137. U.S. Supreme Court decision.

Martzke, R. (2003, June 6). NBC keeps rights for Olympic broadcasts through 2012. *USA Today*. Retrieved from http://www.usatoday.com/sports /olympics2003-06-06-nbc_x.htm

Martzke, R. (2004, January 7). Rose's admission puts Gray's interview in different light. *USA Today*. Retrieved from http://www.usatoday.com /sports/columnist/martzke/2004-01-07-martzke _x.htm

McCartney, C. (2009, April 29). Spring's biggest winners and losers. *Sports Illustrated*. Retrieved from http://sportsillustrated.cnn.com/2009/writ ers/cory_mccartney/04/28/spring-winners-losers /index.html?eref=T1

McCombs, M. E., & Shaw, D. L. (1972, Summer). The agenda-setting function of mass media. *Public Opinion Quarterly, 36*, 176–187.

McKindra, L. (2009, August 28). Media-guide proposals affect more than bottom line. *NCAA News*. Retrieved from http://www.ncaa.org/wps/ ncaa?key=/ncaa/ncaa/ncaa+news/ncaa+news+on line/2009/association-wide/media-guide+propos als+affect+more+than+bottom+line_08_28_09_ ncaa_news

McManis, C. R. (2009). *Intellectual property and unfair competition* (6th ed.). St. Paul, MN: Thomson West.

McMasters, P. (2009). FOIA: It's always there. *Society of Professional Journalists*. Retrieved from http://www.spj.org/foiaabout.asp

Meet Rodney. (2008). *Tider Insider*. Retrieved from http://www.tiderinsider.com/rodney.html

Merrill, J. C. (1997). *Journalism ethics*. New York: St. Martin's Press.

Meyer, P. (2009, August 19). Lines are blurring in strange new world of journalism. *USA Today*. Retrieved from http://blogs.usatoday.com/oped /2009/08/letters-lines-are-blurring-in-strange-new -world-of-journalism-.html

Milian, J. (2009, June 4). Dollars and sense: College sports media guides starting to vanish. *Palm Beach Post*. Retrieved from http://www.palm beachpost.com/sports/content/sports/epaper/2009 /06/04/0604mediaguides.html

Miller, S. (2008, November 24). Playing the online field. *Multichannel*. Retrieved from http://www .multichannel.com/article/CA6617210.html

Mills, E. (2010, January 5). *Study: Three-quarters of U.S. adults use Internet*. Retrieved from http:// news.cnet.com/8301-1023_3-10425965-93.html

Moore, R. J. (2010, January 26). New data on Twitter's users and engagement [web log message]. Retrieved from http://themetricsystem.rjmet rics.com/2010/01/26/new-data-on-twitters-users -and -engagement/

Murdoch and Microsoft on brink of major news deal. (2009, November 23). *Silicon Republic*. Retrieved from http://www.siliconrepublic.com /news/article/14496/business/murdoch-and-micro soft-on-brink-of-major-news-deal

Murdoch, R. (2009, December 8). Journalism and freedom. *The Wall Street Journal*. Retrieved from http://online.wsj.com/article/SB100014240527 48704107104574570191223415268.html

Murschel, M. (2009, May, 11). College media guides going the way of the CB radio [Web log post]. *Orlando Sentinel*. Retrieved from http://blogs.orlandosentinel.com/sports_college/2009/05 /college-media-guides-going-the-way-of-the-cb-radio.html

Naisbitt, J. (1982). *Megatrends*. New York: Warner Books.

Nakashima, R. (2008, April 16). New data reveal online video views are soaring. *Associated Press*. Retrieved from http://ap.google.com/article /ALeqM5hWmYHx6DsrueS3AELpAAcaH0cv FQD903O1EO0>

Nardi, B., Schiano, D., Gumbrecht, M., & Swartz, L. (2004, December). Why we blog. *Communications of the Association for Computing Machinery*, 41–46.

National Intellectual Property Rights Coordination Center. (2010, February 3). Retrieved from http://www.ice.gov/pi/iprctr/index.htm

NCAA academic reform. (n.d.). National Collegiate Athletic Association. Retrieved from http:www.ncaa.org/wps/portal/ncaahome?WCM_GLOBAL_CONTEXT=/ncaa/NCAA/Academics%20and%20Athletes/Education%20and%20Research/Academic%20Reform/

Neff, C. (1987). Portrait of the sportswriter as a young man. *Gannett Center Journal*, 1(2), 47–55.

NFL, Comcast settle dispute. (2009, May 19). *Associated Press*. Retrieved from http://sportsillustrated.cnn.com/2009/football/nfl/05/19/network -comcast.ap/index.html

Nicholas, P. (2009, October 4). President Obama behind the scenes lobbying for Chicago Olympics. *Chicago Tribune*. Retrieved from http://www .chicagotribune.com/news/chi-oly-obama-lobby ingoct04,062892.story

Nielsen television ratings for network primetime series. (2009, March 15). *Nielsen Media Research*. Retrieved from http://tvlistings.zap2it.com/rat ings/weekly.html

NY Times v Sullivan. (1964). 376 US 254. U.S. Supreme Court decision.

O'Keefe, E. (2009, December 9). Federal agencies must post public data online. *The Washington Post*. Retrieved from http://www.washingtonpost .com/wp-dyn/content/article/2009/12/08/AR20 09120804121.html

Palmer, K. E. (2000). *Constitutional amendments*. Farmington Hills, MI:Gale Group.

Papper, B. (2006). Future of news survey. *Radio and Television News Directors Association*. Retrieved from http://www.rtnda.org/pages/media_items /future-of-news-survey-2006493.php?id=493

Pardon the interruption. (2009, February 17). *ESPN*.

Parr, B. (2010, March 4). Twitter hits 10 billion tweets. Retrieved from http://www.mashable .com/2010/03/04/twitter-10-billion-tweets-2/

Parsons, B. (2009, May 12). Live from ACC meetings: Some quick hits [Web log post]. *Orlando Sentinel*. Retrieved from http://blogs.orlandosen tinel.com/sports_college/2009/05/live-from-acc-meetings-some-quick-hits.html

Patterson, B. (2009, January 30). *Femtocells aim to boost indoor cell reception*. Retrieved from http://tech.yahoo.com/blogs/patterson/35428j_ylt=Ar Jemb4LUDHQp610GjhOZqDAFLZA5

Patton, P. (1984). *Razzle-dazzle*. New York: Dial Press.

Perse, E. (1992). Predicting attention to local television news: Needs and cognition and motives for viewing. *Communication Reports*, 5(1), 40–49.

Plaschke, B. (2000, January-February). The reporter: 'That's twice you get me. I'm gonna hit you right now, right now!' *Columbia Journalism Review*, pp. 42–44.

Potter, M. (2004, October 6). Atmosphere: Scooping up after the Buffs. *Associated Press Sports Editors*. Retrieved from http://apse.dallasnews.com /news/2004/100604colorado.html

Powe, Jr., L., A. (1991). *The fourth estate and the Constitution*. Berkley, CA: University of California Press.

PSO schools by state. (2007). *Prep Sports Online*. Retrieved from http://www.pso.com/s-pso.php

Public information; this section does not apply. (2007) The Freedom of Information Act of 1966 5 USCA 552b. *United States code annotated*. St. Paul, MN: Thomson West.

Public policy. (2006). The Indiana Open Door Law of 1977. Title 5-14-3-1. *Burns Indiana statutes annotated*. Charlottesville, VA: Matthew Bender and Co.

Pucin, D. (2009, June 18). Athletes turn to Twitter to get their message out. *Los Angeles Times*. Retrieved from http://article.latime.com/2009/jun /18/sports/sp-kevin-mchale-twitter18?pg=2

Pursell, C. (2008, August 24). Sports: TV's power play. *TV Week*. Retrieved from http://www.tvweek .com/news/2008/08/sports_tvs_power_play.php

Raissman, B. (2002, December 20). With Burk, Gumbel didn't get 'real.' *New York Daily News*. Retrieved from http://www.nydailynews.com /archives/sports/2002/12/20/2002-12-20_with _burk__gumbel_didn_t_get.html

Rao, L. (2009, December 28). *November search term biggest movers*. Retrieved from http://seek ingalpha.com/article/180037-novmeber-search-term-biggest-movers?source=article_1b_articles

Recovery for violation of rights. (2009). Trademarks—The Lanham Act 15 USCA 117. *United States code annotated*. St. Paul, MN: Thomson West.

Reisinger, D. (2009, September 1). NFL bans tweeting before, during, after games. *CNet News*. Retrieved from: http://news.cnet.com/digital-media/?categoryId=9823097

Report: Hockey star Jeremy Roenick text messages a reporter that he's retiring. (2007, July 4). *Associated Press*. Retrieved from http://www.foxnews.com/story/0,2933,288093,00.html

Rich, M., & Stone, B. (2009, December 14). Top author shifts e-book rights to Amazon.com. *New York Times* Retrieved from http://www.nytimes.com/2009/12/15/technology/companies/15amazon.html

Roy Williams goes off on Bonnie Bernstein [Video file]. Retrieved from http://www.youtube.com/watch?v=WqOlwEYrT0I

Sabine, G. H. (1960). *A history of political theory*. New York: Holt, Rinehart and Winston, Inc.

Sandomir, R. (2003, September 10). The decline and fall of sports ratings. *The New York Times*. Retrieved from http://www.nytimes.com/2003/09/10/sports/10ratings.html

Sandomir, R. (1997, January 17). As FOX prepares bash, CBS yearns to return to the NFL's fold. *New York Times*. Retrieved from http://query.nytimes.com/gst/fullpage.html?res=9D05E1DD173BF934A25752C0A961958260&sec=&spon=&pagewanted=all

Sartre, J. P. (1957). *Existentialism and human emotions*. New York: Philsophical Library, Inc.

Sayre, A. (2010, January 29). NFL: 'Who Dat' gear violates Saints trademark. *The Huffington Post*. Retrieved from http://www.thehuffingtonpost.com/2010/01/28/nfl-who-dat-gear-violates_n_440708.html

Schexnaydre, D. (2008, February 26). Asante Samuel . . . holy crap. *NOLA sports report*. Retrieved from http://blog.nola.com/nolasports/2008/02/asante_samuelholy_crap.html

Schonfeld, E. (2010, March 29). Twitter and the nine-month bounce. Retrieved from http://techcrunch.com/2010/03/29/twitter-nine-month-bounce/

Schroeder, G. (2009, July). President's column: To print (media guides) or not to print? *The Fifth Quarter, 47*. Retrieved from http://www.sportswriters.net/fwaa/fifthdown/july09/index.html

Schultz, B. (2005). *Sports media: Planning, producing and reporting*. Boston: Focal Press.

Schultz, B. & Sheffer, M.L. (2009, August 8). The future of news? A study of citizen journalism and journalists. Paper presented to AEJMC national convention, Boston, MA.

Schultz, B. & Sheffer, M.L. (2008). Blogging from the labor perspective: Lessons for media managers. *The International Journal on Media Management, 10*(1), 1–9.

Schultz, B., & Sheffer, M. L. (2007). Sports journalists who blog cling to traditional values. *Newspaper Research Journal, 28*(4), 62–76.

Scorecard. (2000, July 10). *Sports Illustrated*. Retrieved from http://vault.sportsillustrated.cnn.com/vault/article/magazine/MAG1019642/index.htm

Shapiro, M. (2000, January-February). The fan: 'Sports journalism is about myths and transcendent moments.' *Columbia Journalism Review*.

Shapiro, M. (2000, January-February). The fan. *Columbia Journalism Review*, pp. 39, 50–51.

Shipley, A. (2009, December 22). Deteriorating USOC-IOC relations threaten both organizations. *The Washington Post*. Retrieved from http://www.washingtonpost.com/wp-dyn/content/article/2009/12/21/AR2009122101900.html

Shorupski, J. (1989). *John Stuart Mill*. New York: Routledge.

Shutt, S. (1998, June). *How 2BN SID*. Author.

Shutt, S. (1998, June). *How 2BN SID*, p. 16.

Site, stations showcase local H.S. sports. (2009, September 28). TVNewsCheck. Retrieved from http://www.tvnewscheck.com/articles/2009/09/28/daily.9/?promo

Skiles to Villanueva: No halftime tweets. (2009, March 18). *ESPN*. Retrieved from http://sports.espn.go.com/nba/news/story?id=3990853

Smillie, D. (2009, February 12). Ken Paulson's paper passion. *Forbes.com*. Retrieved from http://www.forbes.com/2009/02/12/newspapers-usa-to-day-ken-paulson-business-media_0212_paulson.html

Smith, C. (1987). *Voices of the game*. South Bend, IN: Diamond.

Smith, R. A. (2008). *Becoming a public relations writer: A writing process workbook for the profession* (3rd ed.). New York: Routledge.

Sodhi, D. S. (1981). *The attorney's pocket dictionary*. West Hartford, CT: Law and Business Publications, Inc.

Sowell, M. (2008). The birth of national sports coverage: An examination of the New York Herald's use of the telegraph to report America's first "championship" boxing match in 1849. *Journal of Sports Media, 3*(1), 51–75.

Spoiled sports: Will the digital media finish off sports reporting as a credible form of journalism? (2008, January 29). 8th Journalism Leaders Forum, University of Central Lancashire.

Sport. (n.d.). *Al Jazeera*. Retrieved from http://english.aljazeera.net/sport/

Sporting News radio network. (2009). *RadioTime*. Retrieved from http://radiotime.com/program/p_20650/Sporting_News_Radio_Network.aspx

SportsCenter of the decade, the 90s. (1999, December 14). *ESPN*. [Television program].

Sports Illustrated facts. (2009). *Sports Illustrated*. Retrieved from http://sportsillustrated.cnn.com/thenetwork/tour/sifacts/

Sports reporters wanted. (2008). *The Fan Media Network*. Retrieved from http://www.fanmedianetwork.com/index.php?option=home&task=learnmore

Sports-talk radio host. (1999, September 7). *ESPN*. Retrieved from http://espn.go.com/special/s/

Staff bios. (n.d.). Retrieved from http://www.usabasketball.com/inside.php?page=staff

State of the blogosphere, 2008. (2008). *Technorati*. Retrieved from http://technorati.com/blogging/state-of-the-blogosphere/

Sterling, C. H. (1984). *Electronic media, a guide to trends in broadcasting and newer technologies, 1920–1983*. New York: Praeger.

Stevens, P. (2009, August 20). Schools ponder turning the page: Future of traditional paper media guides is in doubt. *The Washington Times*. Retrieved from http://www.washingtontimes.com/news/2009/aug/20/schools-ponder-turning-the-page/

Stewart, L. (2004, November 9). New TV deal gives NFL the night shift. *Los Angeles Times*. Retrieved from http://articles.latimes.com/2004/nov/09/sports/sp-nfltv9

Stewart, L. (1998, January 13). CBS gets the NFL back. *Los Angeles Times*. Retrieved from http://articles.latimes.com/1998/jan/13/sports/sp-7916

Stovall, J. G. (2009). *Writing for the mass media* (7th ed.). Boston: Allyn & Bacon.

Stream line: CBS to provide live online broadcast of Final Four (2008, April 8). *SportsBusiness Daily*. Retrieved from http://www.sportsbusinessdaily.com/article/119776

Subject matter of copyright. (2005). Copyrights 17 USCA 102 (a) *United States code annotated*. St. Paul, MN: Thomson West.

Suns deny report they will fire head coach Terry Porter. (2009, February 13). *KTAR.com*. Retrieved from http://www.ktar.com/sports/?nid=21&sid=1084503

Sunshine week survey. (2009). *The Associated Press*. Retrieved from http://associatedpress.ocm/FOI/public.html

Super Bowl media credential requests dip. (2009, January 29). *Richmond Times-Dispatch*. Retrieved from http://www2.timesdispatch.com/rtd/sports/professional/professional_football/article/MEDIGAT_20090128-210203/191635/

Taciturn Armstrong sparks Twitter media boycott. (2009, May 22). Retrieved from http://www.sbs.com.au/cyclingcentral/news/1057/Taciturn-Armstrong-sparks-Twitter-media-boycott

Texas Tech v Spiegelberg. (2006). ND Texas 461 F. Supp. 2d 510.

The history of WKMG-TV. (2003). *WKMG Television*. Retrieved from http://www.local6.com/orlpn/insidewkmg/stories/insidewkmg-20000911-122225.html

The New York Times Company policy on ethics in journalism. (2005, October). Retrieved from http://www.nytco.com/press/ethics.html

The Vancouver 2010 Olympic Winter Games: By the numbers. (2010, February 28). Retrieved from http://www.vancouver2010.com/paralympic-games/news/the-vancouver-2010-olympic-winter-games-by-the-numbers_301160ld.html

The world in 2009: ICT facts and figures. (n.d.). Retrieved from http://www.itu.int/net/pressoffice/backgrounders/general/pdf/3.pdf

This history of X games. (2007, July 30). *ESPN*. Retrieved from http://skateboard.about.com/cs/events/a/XGamesHistory.htm

Thomsen, I. (2008, February 13). Have game, will travel. *Sports Illustrated*. Retrieved from http://sportsillustrated.cnn.com/2008/writers/ian_thomsen/02/13/international.expansion/index.html

Tint of brown. (1994). *75 seasons: The complete story of the National Football League, 1920–1995*. Atlanta: Turner Publishing.

Time, Inc. v Firestone. (1976). 424 US 448. U.S. Supreme Court decision.

Tint of brown. (1994). *75 seasons: The complete story of the National Football League, 1920–1995*. Atlanta, GA: Turner Publishing.

T.J. Houshmandzadeh expresses Eagle love through text message. (2009, February 27). *Yahoo!Sports*. Retrieved from http://sports.yahoo.com/nfl/blog/shutdown_corner/post/T-J-Houshmandzadeh-expresses-Eagle-love-through?urn=nfl,144668

Top 10 most embarrassing TV/radio interview moments. (2004, August 6). *Sports Illustrated*. Retrieved from http://sportsillustrated.cnn.com/2004/scorecard/08/05/interviews/

Transcript of 'NYT' speech announcing 100 layoffs; Keller: 'We intend to move quickly.' (2008, February 15). Retrieved from http://gawker.com/5003137/transcript-of-nyt-speech-announcing-100-layoffs-keller-we-intend-to-move-quickly

Tremblay, S., & Tremblay, W. (2001). Mediated masculinity as the millennium: The Jim Rome show as a male bonding speech community. *Journal of Radio Studies, 8*(2), 271–291.

Trubow, A. (2009, February 23). Texas picks up 12th commit. *Austin American-Statesman.* Retrieved from http://www.statesman.com/blogs/content /sharedgen/blogs/austin/longhorns/index.html

TV data. (n.d.). Retrieved from http://www.fifa.com /aboutfifa/marketing/factsfigures/tvdata.html

TV news: It doesn't play in Peoria. (2009, March 6). *TV Newsday.* Retrieved from http://www.tv newsday.com/articles/2009/03/06/daily.7/

TV newsrooms lose 360 positions. (2008, October 8). *Broadcast Engineering.* Retrieved from http:// broadcastengineering.com/news/newsrooms-lose -positions-1008/

Twitter changing the way sports news is disseminated. (2009, July 30). *SportsBusinessDaily.* Retrieved from http://www.sportsbusinessdaily .com/index.cfm?fuseaction=sbd.preview&article Id=132143

Umstead, R. T. (2008, September 6). DirecTV: HD is Sunday's new 'ticket.' *Multichannel News.* Retrieved from http://www.multichannel.com /article/134613-DirecTV_HD_Is_Sunday_s_ New_Ticket_.php

Van Grove, J. (2010, March 3). *Twitter trends to follow.* Retrieved from http://mashable.com/2010 /03/29/twitter-trends-follow/

Wamsley, K., & Young, K. (Eds.). (2005). *Global Olympics: Historical and sociological studies of the modern games.* Oxford: Elsevier.

Wann, D. L. (2006). The causes and consequences of sport team identification. From A. A. Raney & J. Bryant (Eds.), *Handbook of sports and media* (pp. 331–352). Mahwah, NJ: Lawrence Erlbaum.

Wanta, W. (2006). Sports coverage in print. From A. A. Raney & J. Bryant (Eds.), *Handbook of sports and media* (pp. 105–116). Mahwah, NJ: Lawrence Erlbaum.

Wicker, T. (1978). *On press.* New York: Berkley Publishing Corporation.

Wilcox, D. L., Ault, P. H., & Agee, W. K. (1992). *Public relations: Strategies and tactics.* (3rd ed.). New York: Harper Collins.

Wilcox, D. L., & Cameron, G. T. (2009). Public relations: Strategies and tactics (9th ed.). Boston: Allyn & Bacon.

Wilcox, J. (2009, December 9). *Mobile Internet is 450 million users strong and doubling in four years.* Retrieved from http://www.betanews.com/joe wilcox/article/Mobile-Internet-is-450-million-users -strong-and-doubling-in-four-years/1260413839

Wilner, B. (2009, August 31). *NFL: Social media OK before, after games.* Retrieved from http:// www.abcnews.go.com/print?id=8456802

Wired, zapped and beamed; 1960s through 1980s. (2009). *Federal Communications Commission.* Retrieved from http://www.fcc.gov/omd/history /tv/1960-1989.html

Woodson, A. (2007, October 6). Net effect: Yahoo!Sports scores the upset. *Hollywood Reporter.* Retrieved from http://www.hollywoodreporter .com/hr/content_display/business/news/e3ia9f1b 97c9ccc511dcbd80ec6a0d78dbd

Woolley, J. T., & Peters, G. (1996, October 2). Statement on signing the Electronic Freedom of Information Act Amendments of 1996. *The American Presidency Project.* Retrieved from http://www.presidency.ucsb.edu/ws/index.php? pid=52035

Wong, G. (2002). *Essentials of sports law* (3rd ed.). Westport, CT: Praeger.

World Series ratings. (2008). *Baseball almanac.* Retrieved from http://www.baseball-almanac.com /ws/wstv.shtml

Yannity, M. (2009, February 11). Huskies football. *Seattle Post-Intelligencer.* Retrieved from http:// blog.seattlepi.nwsource.com/huskiesfb/archives/ 161784.asp

Yu, P. K. (2007). *Intellectual property and information wealth*, Volume I. Hartford, CT: Praeger.

Yu, R. (2010, March 5). Smart phones have changed the way we travel. *USA Today.* Retrieved from http://www.usatoday.com/tech/news/2010-03-05 -airphones05_CV_N.htm

Yutang, L. (Ed.). (1966). *The wisdom of Confucius.* New York: Random House.

Index

About the Authors

Brad Schultz, PhD, is an associate professor in the School of Journalism and New Media at the University of Mississippi. His academic credentials include a bachelor's degree in journalism from the University of Missouri (1984), a master's in telecommunications from Southern Illinois (1999), and a doctorate from Texas Tech in 2002.

Schultz's area of research interest is the effect of new technology on sports journalism. He has published nearly two dozen research articles in scholarly journals, including the *International Journal on Media Management*, the *Newspaper Research Journal*, the *Journal of Communication Studies*, the *International Journal of the History of Sport*, and the *International Journal of Sport Communication*. He has also presented two dozen papers at scholarly research conferences in the US and Canada. In 2006, Schultz launched the *Journal of Sports Media*, a scholarly journal that publishes twice a year. He continues to serve the journal as editor-in-chief.

This is Schultz's fourth book. His previous works include *Sports Media: Planning, Production and Reporting* (2005, Focal Press), *Broadcast News Producing* (2004, Sage) and *Sports Broadcasting* (2001, Focal Press). This year, his chapter on Sport Communication will appear in *Introduction to Sport Management* to be published by Kendall-Hunt.

Prior to entering academia, Schultz spent 15 years in local television sports and news as an anchor, reporter, news director, producer, editor, videographer, and writer.

Philip H. Caskey, MA, is in his 11th season with the West Virginia University (WVU) Athletic Department and was promoted to Associate Sports Information Director in December 2008, after serving his previous tenure as the office's assistant.

A native of Martinsburg, West Virginia, Caskey is the primary media relations contact for Mountaineer women's basketball and serves as the secondary contact for WVU football. He also assists with the overall operation of WVU's 15 other varsity sports and supervises a student staff that consists of three graduate assistants and two student assistants.

Prior to his full-time tenure in the Sports Communications office, Caskey served two years as a graduate assistant in the office from 1999–2001 as the primary media relations liaison for Mountaineer baseball, wrestling, and men's soccer.

A seven-time award-winning College Sports Information Director's of America national and district feature writer, Caskey is also an adjunct instructor in WVU's College of Physical Activity and Sport Sciences graduate sport management program and

WVU's Perley Isaac Reed School of Journalism online curriculum classes. He has also served as media coordinator for numerous WVU and NCAA hosted sporting events.

Caskey earned his BS in journalism, with a specialization in public relations, from WVU in 1999. He earned his master's degree, also from WVU, in sport management in 2001.

Craig Esherick, JD, is an assistant professor in the School of Recreation, Health and Tourism at George Mason University. He teaches courses in sport management, sport governance and policy, and sport law. Prior to joining the faculty full time he was an adjunct professor at George Mason and an instructor at New York University.

Esherick was formerly the head men's basketball coach at Georgetown University from 1999–2004, taking over for Hall of Fame coach John Thompson, for whom he served as an assistant coach since 1982. Esherick compiled a record of 103-74 during his tenure as head coach at Georgetown, where he played from 1974–78. He led the Hoyas to the 2001 NCAA Tournament Sweet 16 and the 2003 National Invitational Tournament championship game. As an assistant, Esherick was part of three Elite Eight teams and two Final Four squads, including the 1984 team that won the national championship. He also served as an assistant coach on the 1988 U.S. Olympic team that earned a bronze medal at the Seoul Games.

Following his coaching career, Esherick was a writer and hosted an online radio show with AOL Sports. He then served as the vice president of athletic relations for CSTV while also providing content for the cable sports network. Esherick has also served as a television color commentator for college basketball games produced by the MidAtlantic Sports Network, ESPNU, Verizon FIOS, Comast, and Cox. He is also a member of the Arlington County (VA) Sports Commission.